The Cambridge Companion to Handel

WITHDRAWN

Cambridge Companions to Music

The Cambridge Companion to the Clarinet
Edited by Colin Lawson

The Cambridge Companion to the Recorder
Edited by John Mansfield Thomson

The Cambridge Companion to the Violin
Edited by Robin Stowell

The Cambridge Companion to Brass Instruments
Edited by Trevor Herbert and John Wallace

The Cambridge Companion to Bach
Edited by John Butt

The Cambridge Companion to Chopin
Edited by Jim Samson

The Cambridge Companion to Handel
Edited by Donald Burrows

The Cambridge Companion to Schubert
Edited by Christopher H. Gibbs

The Cambridge Companion to

HANDEL

Edited by DONALD BURROWS

Professor of Music, The Open University, Milton Keynes

CAMBRIDGE
UNIVERSITY PRESS

PUBLISHED BY THE PRESS SYNDICATE OF THE UNIVERSITY OF CAMBRIDGE
The Pitt Building, Trumpington Street, Cambridge, United Kingdom

CAMBRIDGE UNIVERSITY PRESS
The Edinburgh Building, Cambridge CB2 2RU, UK
40 West 20th Street, New York, NY 10011–4211, USA
477 Williamstown Road, Port Melbourne, VIC 3207, Australia
Ruiz de Alarcón 13, 28014 Madrid, Spain
Dock House, The Waterfront, Cape Town 8001, South Africa

http://www.cambridge.org

First published 1997
Reprinted 2002

Printed in the United Kingdom at the University Press, Cambridge

Typeset in Adobe Minion 10.75/14 pt, in QuarkXpress™ [SE]

A catalogue record for this book is available from the British Library

Library of Congress Cataloguing in Publication data
The Cambridge Companion to Handel / edited by Donald Burrows.
      p.   cm. – (Cambridge companions to music)
   Includes bibliographical references, work list, and index.
   Contents: Background – The music – The music in performance.
   ISBN 0 521 45425 5 (hardback) – ISBN 0 521 45613 4 (paperback)
   1. Handel, George Frideric, 1685–1759 – Criticism and
   interpretation.   I. Burrows, Donald.   II. Series.
   ML410.H13C2   1997
   780′.92–dc21   96–50935 CIP

ISBN 0 521 45425 5 hardback
ISBN 0 521 45613 4 paperback

Contents

Plates

Contributors

Graydon Beeks is Director of Music Programming and Facilities, and Associate Professor of Music, at Pomona College, Claremont, California, and a member of the Editorial Board of the Hallische Händel-Ausgabe. Since 1991 he has served successively as President and Vice-President of The American Handel Society.

Terence Best is a member of the Editorial Board of the Hallische Händel-Ausgabe, and a founding Council Member of the Handel Institute. His editions of Handel's music for HHA include five volumes of instrumental music and the opera *Tamerlano*.

Malcolm Boyd's writings include books on Palestrina, Bach, Domenico Scarlatti and the Welsh composers Grace Williams and William Mathias. He was, on his retirement in 1992, Reader in Music at the University of Wales, Cardiff.

Donald Burrows is Professor of Music at the Open University, Milton Keynes, a founding Council Member of the Handel Institute, a member of the Editorial Board of the Hallische Händel-Ausgabe and General Editor of the Novello Handel Edition. His publications include the 'Master Musicians' biography of Handel and music editions of several major works by Handel, including *Messiah*, *Belshazzar*, *Alexander's Feast* and the complete Violin Sonatas.

John Butt is Lecturer in Music at Cambridge University and Director of Studies in Music at King's College; from 1989 to 1997 he was University Organist and Professor in Music at the University of California, Berkeley. The author of several books on Bach and the German Baroque, he is also active as a performer on the organ and harpsichord.

Winton Dean is the author of major reference works concerning Handel's principal compositional genres, *Handel's Dramatic Oratorios and Masques* and (with John Merrill Knapp) *Handel's Operas, 1704–26*. He has been a visiting professor at the University of California, Berkeley, and at Vassar College.

Anthony Hicks is a freelance writer on music, and in particular that of Handel. His publications include the work-list for the Handel article in *The New Grove Dictionary of Music and Musicians*.

Robert Hume is Edwin Erle Sparks Professor of English Literature at the Pennsylvania State University. His publications as author, co-author and editor include *Henry Fielding and the London Theatre*, *A Register of English Theatrical Documents, 1660–1737*, and *Italian Opera in Late Eighteenth-Century London*.

David Ross Hurley is Assistant Professor of Music at Pittsburg State University, Kansas. He is the author of *Handel's Compositional Choices: the Genesis of the Oratorios, 1734–1748*.

H. Diack Johnstone is Tutorial Fellow in Music at St Anne's College, Oxford and Lecturer at St John's College. A member of the Editorial Committee of *Musica Britannica*, he has edited two large-scale works by Maurice Greene for that series, and also (with Roger Fiske) the eighteenth-century volume in the *Blackwell History of Music in Britain*.

C. Steven LaRue edited the *International Dictionary of Opera* (1993), and is author of *Handel and His Singers* (1995).

Lowell Lindgren, Professor of Music at the Massachusetts Institute of Technology, is the author of *Musicians and Librettists in the Correspondence of Gio. Giacomo Zamboni* (1991), and editor of Antonio Bononcini, *Fifteen Sonatas for Violoncello and Continuo*.

Judith Milhous is Distinguished Professor of Theatre History in the Ph.D. Program in Theatre, City University of New York, Graduate Center. Her publications as author, co-author and editor include *Thomas Betterton and the Management of Lincoln's Inn Fields, Vice Chamberlain Coke's Theatrical Papers, 1706–1715*, and *Italian Opera in Late Eighteenth-Century London*.

Ruth Smith is the author of articles on the intellectual contexts to Handel's English oratorios and the achievements of Charles Jennens, and the book *Handel's Oratorios and Eighteenth-Century Thought* (1995).

Mark Stahura completed his doctoral studies on the subject of Handel's orchestrational techniques at the University of Chicago.

Carlo Vitali is a librarian in Bologna and a freelance author and translator for several publishing houses and broadcasting stations in Italy, Switzerland, Germany, France, the Netherlands, Great Britain and the United States.

William Weber, a historian at California State University, Long Beach, has written *Music and the Middle Class* (1976) and *The Rise of Musical Classics in Eighteenth-Century England* (1992), and co-edited *Wagnerism in European Culture and Politics* (1984).

Preface

The aim of this Cambridge Companion is to present you with a rounded view of Handel and his music. While it is neither a biography nor a blow-by-blow survey of each of Handel's works, it is intended to cover the main influences on Handel's life and career, and to give a balanced treatment to his music: approximately equal space has been devoted to opera and oratorio, the two principal genres in which he worked, and some attention has been given to the other genres in which he composed. If a volume of this size cannot be comprehensive, I hope that it will at least be companionable. The chapters introduce the interested musician – whether listener, performer, historian or student – to some of the most important topics and issues which bear on Handel the composer. One topic that the book does not attempt to cover is that of reception history. Given the fact that choices had to be made about content, it seemed more appropriate to approach the subject of Handel through the positive route of presenting and surveying the materials that might lead us to an imaginative recreation of the circumstances of Handel's life and music, rather than exposing the various ways in which subsequent ages 'got it wrong' – more spectacularly with Handel than with many other composers, as it happens.[1] However, a partial exception to this principle has been made in the case of Handel's operas (Chapter 17), since there has been no continuous performing tradition in this genre and our practical experience of it has been gained through modern performances: while, to some extent, imaginative contact can be made with the other genres of Handel's music through recordings and concert performances, the understanding of opera requires the experience of stage presentation.

When I invited authors to contribute to the *Companion*, I on one hand approached established specialists, asking them to provide accessible introductions to topics in which they have developed experience and expertise, and on the other hand involved some younger scholars who are active with new topics and approaches. If in the course of time the result may be seen as the product of the present generations, I take courage from the fact that the second half of the twentieth century has been a particu-

---

[1] The latter approach might also imply a negative view of the pursuit of reception history itself, which would be unjustified. It would also be simplistic to see 'Handel reception' as a single unitary topic: the reasons for reviving or maintaining Handel's music have varied according to time and place, as have the treatments of his music.

larly fruitful time for Handel scholarship and performance: the contents of the book reflect only part of the bubbling activity. Furthermore, the subject has not been approached from a narrow perspective: several of the authors for Part I of the book would not consider themselves primarily to be 'Handel specialists', but have expertise in areas that contribute essential background to his career.

I take this opportunity to thank those who have brought this book into being: to the contributors, for surviving with a good grace successively (and metaphorically) the heavy hand and heavy foot of the editor; to the owners of material used in the illustrations; to Victoria Cooper, who encouraged the book at Cambridge University Press; to Michael Talbot, who translated Chapter 2 and commented on Chapter 13 when it was in draft; to Jacob Simon and Lowell Lindgren for assistance over illustrations; to Anthony Coulson for library assistance; and to Rosemary Kingdon for bearing a substantial brunt of the word processing.

The following conventions are used in the book:

British Currency: Values have not been converted to decimal currency. There were 20 shillings (s) to a pound (£), twelve pence (d) to a shilling: the columns in Plate 12 show pounds/shillings/pence. Fees were commonly paid in guineas and half-guineas (£1. 1s. 0d and 10s. 6d respectively).

Dates: Years are given in 'New Style', with the year beginning on 1 January.

Handel's works: These are referred to by the 'HWV' numbers from Bernd Baselt's catalogue in vols. I–III of the *Händel-Handbuch*. 'HWV 70/32' refers to movement 32 ('Waft her, angels') from HWV 70 (*Jephtha*).

Libraries: *RISM* sigla, omitting GB for British locations, are used for references to the libraries with the major collections of Handel's autographs and performing scores.

Britain: Cfm – Fitzwilliam Museum, Cambridge

              Lbl – The British Library, London

Germany: D-Hs – Staats- und Universitätsbibliothek Carl von Ossietsky, Hamburg

              D-MÜs – Santini Collection, Diözesan-Bibliothek, Münster (Westfalen)

Donald Burrows

Chronology

Year	Biography	Music and musicians
1685	Handel born, 23 February, at Halle, son of Georg Händel and his second wife Dorothea (née Taust)	J. S. Bach born at Eisenach, 21 March John Gay born, 30 June Domenico Scarlatti born, 26 October
1686		
1687		Lully dies Geminiani and Galliard born
1688		
1689		
1690		Gottlieb Muffat born
1691		Purcell, *King Arthur*
1692	Begins to study under Zachow in Halle, following a visit to Weissenfels	Purcell, *The Fairy Queen*
1693		
1694		Purcell, D major Te Deum and Jubilate
1695		Giuseppe Sammartini born Purcell dies
1696	?Visit to Prussian court at Berlin	Greene born
1697	Handel's father dies	
1698		
1699		Hasse born
1700		G. B. Sammartini born N. A. Strungk dies
1701	Takes first communion at Marktkirche, Halle ?First contact with Telemann in Leipzig	
1702	Registers as a student at Halle University; appointed organist at Domkirche in Halle	
1703	Moves to Hamburg, where he is befriended by Mattheson Begins career at Hamburg opera house as a back-desk violinist	
1704	Composes first opera, *Almira* (German/Italian)	
1705	*Almira* and *Nero* produced in Hamburg	Clayton's English opera *Arsinoe* Italian opera *Gli amori d'Ergasto* inaugurates Queen's Theatre, London
1706	Composes operas *Florindo* and *Daphne* Leaves Hamburg for Italy, probably going first to Florence	Bononcini's *Camilla* performed in London
1707	In Rome, composes Latin church music, Italian cantatas and *Il trionfo del Tempo* Composes *Rodrigo* for Florence Possibly goes to Venice for Carnival season and meets Alessandro Scarlatti	Buxtehude and Jeremiah Clarke die

Year	Biography	Music and Musicians
1708	*La Resurrezione* performed in Rome, with orchestra led by Corelli At Naples, Handel completes *Aci, Galatea e Polifemo* for the wedding of the Duke of Alvito Possibly goes to Florence and Venice at the end of year	*Florindo* and *Daphne* produced at Hamburg, in Handel's absence J. S. Bach appointed organist and chamber-musician to Duke Wilhelm Ernst at Weimar John Blow dies The castrato Nicolini comes to London to join opera company
1709	Goes to Venice, where *Agrippina* is performed, and he probably receives encouragement from Hanoverian and English visitors	
1710	Leaves Italy and is appointed Kapellmeister to Elector of Hanover Visits court of Elector Palatine at Düsseldorf, and travels to London	Pergolesi, T. A. Arne and W. F. Bach born
1711	Performs before Queen Anne at St James's Palace, and his first London opera *Rinaldo* performed at the Queen's Theatre, Haymarket Returns via Düsseldorf to Hanover	Boyce born Publication of Vivaldi's Op. 3 concertos (*L'estro armonico*) in Amsterdam
1712	Returns to London and composes *Il Pastor Fido* and *Teseo* During this and following year stays for various periods with the Earl of Burlington and 'Mr Andrews of Barn-Elms'	Zachow dies J. C. Smith jun. born
1713	'Utrecht' Te Deum and Jubilate performed at Thanksgiving Service at St Paul's Cathedral Granted annual pension by Queen Anne	Corelli dies François Couperin, *Pieces de clavecin*, Premier Livre, published in Paris
1714	Te Deums by Handel performed in Chapel Royal at services marking arrival in London of the Hanoverian family	C. P. E. Bach and Gluck born Publication of Corelli's Op. 6 Concerti Grossi in Amsterdam
1715	Composes *Amadigi*	
1716	? Composes *Brockes Passion* Perhaps travels to Germany in second half of year, persuading Johann Christoph Schmidt to come to London from Ansbach	William Croft's music performed at Royal Thanksgiving Service, St Paul's Cathedral
1717	Opera company at King's Theatre, Haymarket, closes *Water Music* played on the River Thames Begins association with James Brydges at Cannons, for whom he writes anthems and Te Deum	J. S. Bach appointed Kapellmeister to Prince Leopold at Cöthen
1718	Composes *Acis and Galatea* and *Esther*, both probably performed at Cannons	
1719	Formation of the Royal Academy of Music for the production of opera: Handel visits the continent to engage singers	Leopold Mozart born
1720	Royal Academy of Music opens, with Porta's *Numitore* and then Handel's *Radamisto* 'Premier Volume' of Keyboard Suites published Senesino joins Royal Academy company	

Year	Biography	Music and Musicians
1721	Composes *Muzio Scevola* (Act III) and *Floridante*.	J. S. Bach dedicates concertos to Margrave of Brandenburg
1722	Composes *Ottone* Cuzzoni comes to London to join Royal Academy company	J. A. Reinken dies
1723	Granted annual pension as 'Composer of Musick' for the Chapel Royal Composes *Flavio* Established as music master to Royal Princesses by 9 June, and moves into London house at Brook Street	J. S. Bach takes up posts in Leipzig
1724	*Giulio Cesare* and *Tamerlano* performed, the cast of *Tamerlano* including the tenor Borosini Composes 'Solo Sonatas' at this period	First performance of J. S. Bach's *St John Passion* in Leipzig
1725	Composes *Rodelinda*	J. P. Krieger and Alessandro Scarlatti die. Publication of Telemann's *Harmonischer Gottes-Dienst* in Hamburg
1726	Composes *Scipione*, *Alessandro* and *Admeto* London debut of Faustina in *Alessandro*	First meeting of the 'Academy of Vocal Musick' (later, Academy of Ancient Musick)
1727	Composes *Riccardo Primo*, also Coronation Anthems for King George II and Queen Caroline Walsh publishes 'Second Volume' of Keyboard Suites	First performance of J. S. Bach's *St Matthew Passion* in Leipzig Croft dies
1728	Composes *Siroe* and *Tolomeo* Last Royal Academy season	Gay/Pepusch, *The Beggar's Opera* Steffani dies
1729	Handel (with Heidegger) establishes new opera company in London. Travels to Italy to engage singers Completes *Lotario* as first opera for new London company, with Strada as the leading soprano	Nicola Haym dies
1730	Composes *Partenope* Senesino returns to London as leading man for Handel's operas Handel's mother dies in Halle	J. B. Loeillet dies (in London)
1731	Composes *Poro* and *Ezio* Bass soloist Montagnana joins opera company	Publication of J. S. Bach's *Clavier-Übung* (Part I) in Leipzig
1732	Composes *Sosarme* and *Orlando* Following a performance of *Esther* by Chapel Royal choristers at Crown and Anchor Tavern, Handel introduces *Esther* and *Acis and Galatea* into his theatre season	Arne/Lampe productions of 'English operas' (including *Acis and Galatea*) at Little Theatre, Haymarket Haydn born *Teraminta* (Carey and J. C. Smith jun.) produced Opening of Rich's Covent Garden Theatre Walther's *Musicalisches Lexicon* published in Leipzig
1733	Composes *Deborah* and *Athalia*. Visits Oxford and performs oratorios at Sheldonian Theatre and Christ Church Hall Composes *Arianna*. Loses opera singers (except Strada) to Opera of the Nobility and engages a new castrato, Carestini	J. S. Bach visits Dresden, and presents MS of B minor Mass to Elector of Saxony Couperin dies Opera of the Nobility opens at Lincoln's Inn Fields Theatre, with Porpora as principal composer

Year	Biography	Music and Musicians
	Walsh publishes editions of Handel's 'solo' sonatas ('Op. 1') and trio sonatas (Op. 2) with spurious 'Roger' title pages	
1734	Composes *Parnasso in Festa*, and anthem HWV 262 for wedding of Princess Anne and Prince Willem in French Chapel, St James's Palace Composes *Ariodante* Opera of the Nobility occupy King's Theatre and Handel takes his opera company to Covent Garden theatre, opening with revival of *Il Pastor Fido* featuring Madame Sallé's dancers. Walsh publishes 6 Concerti Grossi Op. 3, all based on earlier compositions, and revised edition of 'Second Volume' of Suites	Opera of the Nobility perform Handel's *Ottone* J. S. Bach's *Christmas Oratorio* performed
1735	Includes oratorio performances in his opera season, and introduces organ concertos Composes *Alcina* Walsh publishes 6 keyboard fugues, composed 15–20 years previously	J. Krieger dies J. C. Bach born
1736	Completes *Alexander's Feast* and concerto HWV 318, also *Atalanta*, *Giustino*, *Arminio* and *Berenice*, for Covent Garden season Anthem HWV 263 performed at wedding of Prince of Wales in Chapel Royal Arrival of Annibali, second castrato, to join Conti in Handel's Covent Garden company	John Walsh, sen., music publisher, dies and is succeeded in business by his son Pergolesi, Weldon and Caldara die
1737	Composes new version of *Il Trionfo del Tempo* Last seasons of Handel's Covent Garden opera company, and of Opera of the Nobility at the King's Theatre Indisposed during last weeks of Covent Garden season: reports of 'paraletick disorder' Visits Aix-la-Chapelle for health-cure. Joins new company, probably managed by Heidegger, at King's Theatre. Composes *Faramondo*, Funeral Anthem following the death of Queen Caroline, and *Serse*	Carey and Lampe produce *The Dragon of Wantley*, partly a parody of Handel's *Giustino*, at Little Theatre, Haymarket
1738	Publication of full score of *Alexander's Feast* Receives benefit night at Opera House Roubiliac statue of Handel erected in Vauxhall Gardens Composes *Saul*, *Imeneo* and *Israel in Egypt* Jennens reports that Handel has acquired novel new instruments (carillon, organ) for the next season First set of organ concertos (Op. 4) published by Walsh	C. P. E. Bach appointed harpsichordist to Crown Prince Friedrich of Prussia Two editions of D. Scarlatti's *Essercizi per Gravicembalo* published in London First meeting of Fund for the Support of Decay'd Musicians (Handel a founder member) Heidegger advertises for a subscription for 1738–9 opera season, but abandons the plan after insufficient response
1739	Gives mixed season of English and Italian works at King's Theatre Trio Sonatas Op. 5 published by Walsh Composes *Song (Ode) for St. Cecilia's Day* and Concerti Grossi Op. 6 Begins season of performances of English works at Lincoln's Inn Fields Theatre	Hickford's Concert Room 'removes' from Poulton St to Brewer St: raffle of Clay (musical) clock, and picture of Handel set up in the new room

Year	Biography	Music and Musicians
1740	Composes *L'Allegro, Il Penseroso ed il Moderato* and Organ Concerto HWV 306 (with obbligato pedal part) Op. 6 Concerti published Travels to continent in summer: on return to London, revises *Imeneo* and composes *Deidamia*, for new season at Lincoln's Inn Fields 'Second Set' of organ concertos published	Lotti dies J. S. Bach visits Halle Samuel Arnold born Mattheson's *Grundlage einer Ehren-Pforte* published in Hamburg
1741	Gives last performance of Italian opera in London Composes *Messiah, Samson* and Italian duets Attends first performance of the new 'Middlesex' opera company Leaves London for Dublin, travelling via Chester and Holyhead. Begins first subscription concert series at Dublin with *L'Allegro*	Fux and Vivaldi die
1742	Completes two six-concert subscription series in Dublin, followed by first performances of *Messiah* Returns to London and completes score of *Samson*	
1743	Presents oratorio season at Covent Garden Composes *Semele*, 'Dettingen' Te Deum and Anthem, and *Joseph and his Brethren*	'Middlesex' Italian opera company opens at King's Theatre, with *Rossane*, a version of Handel's *Alessandro*. Boccherini born
1744	Presents second oratorio season at Covent Garden Composes *Hercules* and *Belshazzar* Begins ambitious oratorio subscription season at King's Theatre for 1744–5	'Middlesex' opera company collapses
1745	Oratorio season meets difficulties, but continues Visits 'the country' in the summer	
1746	Composes *Occasional Oratorio* and *Judas Maccabaeus*	Re-formed 'Middlesex' company opens with Gluck's opera *La Caduta de' Giganti*: Gluck in London W. F. Bach appointed organist at Liebfrauenkirche, Halle
1747	Presents first non-subscription oratorio season at Covent Garden Contralto Galli joins Handel's company Composes *Alexander Balus* and *Joshua*	J. S. Bach visits Friedrich II at Potsdam Bononcini dies
1748	Composes *Solomon* and *Susanna*	J. G. Walther dies
1749	New leading soprano, Frasi, joins Handel's company Composes *Fireworks Music* Gives first charity performance for Foundling Hospital Composes *Theodora* Visits Bath Writes incidental music for projected production of Smollett's play *Alceste*	Galliard and Heidegger die
1750	Covent Garden cast includes new castrato, Guadagni	J. S. Bach dies Giuseppe Sammartini dies (in London)

Year	Biography	Music and Musicians
	Handel's first *Messiah* performances at Foundling Hospital	
	Makes his will	
	Re-uses much of the music from *Alceste* in *The Choice of Hercules*	
	Visits continent: plays organs in Holland	
1751	Composes last instrumental work, Organ Concerto HWV 308	Albinoni dies
	Composition of *Jephtha* interrupted by problems with eyesight	
	Travels to Bath and Cheltenham	
	Handel's pupil J. C. Smith junior returns to London to assist with management of oratorio seasons	
1752	Remaining eyesight deteriorates	Pepusch dies
		J. F. Reichardt born
1753	At Foundling Hospital *Messiah* performance plays 'voluntary' on organ – the last newspaper report of him playing in public.	
1754	First surviving account list for Foundling Hospital performances	
	Dictates and signs letter to Telemann	
1755	Attains seventieth birthday	*The Fairies* (J. C. Smith, jun.) produced at Drury Lane
		Greene dies
1756	Adds first codicil to will, with bequests to Morell and Hamilton	Mozart born
1757	Handel possibly more active, and collaborates with Morell over adaptation of *Il Trionfo del Tempo* into *The Triumph of Time and Truth*	J. Stamitz and D. Scarlatti die
	Adds further codicil to will: bequests to John Rich and Jennens, and copies of *Messiah* (score and parts) to Foundling Hospital	
1758	Visits Tunbridge Wells, possibly with Morell	
1759	Attends *Messiah* performance on 6 April and intends to travel to Bath, but is too ill to do so	
	Adds 4th (final) codicil to will: bequests include £1000 to Decay'd Musicians Fund and £600 provision for a monument at Westminster Abbey	
	Dies at his home in Brook Street at about 8 a.m. on 14 April (Easter Saturday); funeral at Westminster Abbey, 20 April	

Introduction

Donald Burrows

Handel is at the same time one of the most accessible and one of the most elusive of the major creative figures in Western music. The 'Hallelujah Chorus', 'Handel's Largo', the Hornpipe from the *Water Music* and the opening of 'Zadok the Priest' are examples of pieces of his music that have had sufficient appeal to find their way into 'popular' consciousness at various times during the twentieth century. Moreover, Handel's broad, attractive musical style seems to present few problems for the listener: it is to be heard in the background in restaurants and aircraft cabins, the choice of company managements that wish at the same time to find a pleasingly neutral aural background and to flatter their clientele with allusions to 'high' culture. No one would begrudge Handel this place in the sun: indeed, most of us would prefer that, if the aural wallpaper is to be inevitable, it should be worth listening to. But of course there is a danger that the music will be taken for granted: it is heard so often that everyone 'knows' it: it is assumed that there is no more to be said, and even repeat performance borders on the superfluous for real musicians. Mozart's 40th symphony and Beethoven's Fifth suffer this same hazard, but perhaps the danger to Handel is more subtle: his style is in itself some-times apparently so effortless as to discourage further investigation. Yet there is indeed more to be said, and more questions to be asked, about the context in which Handel's style developed, about the novelty of his own mature style, about the compositional skill that lies behind the apparently effortless fluency, and behind his knack of setting up a mood or an emo-tional intensity with the simplest musical means.

His biography presents a similar challenge, not only in the ever-contentious area of the relationship between a creative artist's 'life' and 'works', but also in the relationship between the man and his environ-ment. We can locate Handel as to time and place in various successive environments; thus we can see ways in which he was affected by current circumstances, and ways in which he seems to have moulded the lives of those around (and after) him. But in many areas the relationship is not clear: so unclear, in fact, that it seems probable that Handel, if not actually rejecting some features of his surroundings, at least opted out of involve-ment. How we relate Handel to (for example) contemporary London depends on our image of what London was like. A sentimental view might have Handel taking lunch with Pope and dinner with Hogarth. Not only is there no biographical justification for this, but the association is misleading, for these personalities interpreted the London around them in terms of their own individual perceptions. The images that make up *The Rake's Progress* form a cleverly constructed narrative, and it would be naive to accept them as realistic everyday scenes from contemporary London life. More significantly, Handel did not seem to share the rather puritan and pessimistic view of humanity that gives such force to Hogarth's pictures. Handel, with his Lutheran upbringing, might well have been shocked to know that a century after his death Edward Fitzgerald would describe him as 'a good old Pagan at heart', but there is certainly something positive and life-affirming about his music. This is not to say that Handel shirks or down-plays serious situations in his music: if anything, the endings to *Tamerlano* and *Theodora* received more severe musical settings than the words absolutely required. But overall, tragedy is matched by comedy: sometimes things turn out well, sometimes badly; and sometimes humans act from generous rather than mean motives. Such, as far as we can gather anything at all on the matter from his music, seems to have been Handel's world-view, and the sheer exuberance of his melodies and harmonies suggests that he found life a positive experience. Working in the theatre might have involved arguments with leading singers as an occupational hazard, but these paled into insignificance on a night when an opera or oratorio went well in performance.

Part I of the *Companion* deals with the background to Handel's career, and the relevant topics alter as we move through his life. In his early years, interest centres on the composer's early experiences, on his upbringing in Halle and the type of education (general and specifically musical) that he received (Chapter 1). The political background to his early years is also important: we need to remember that neither 'Germany' nor 'Italy' were single unitary states. Handel seems to have identified himself as a 'Saxon', but he was born a Prussian citizen: seventeenth-century Halle had been a victim of occupation in the Thirty Years War. While war had been a recent memory in the city of Handel's childhood, it was also a current fact of life in Italy, whose states were at the centre of the conflict between Habsburg and Bourbon interests in the first decade of the eighteenth century (Chapter 2). Handel's travels to Florence, Rome, Naples and Venice in the early years of the eighteenth century involved finding a way through the current political turmoil and making the best of the various musical opportunities that each place had to offer. By the time Handel came to London in 1710 a European peace was in prospect, though Britain's part in it was controversial, and was especially viewed as such in Hanover, whose princely house was anticipating its succession to the British throne (recently secured as an entity by the Act of Union) on the death of the ailing Queen Anne. The political, social and religious context that Handel found in London was very different from those of Germany and Italy, but it provided a setting in which he could develop his mature career (Chapter 3). Nevertheless, the most directly influential circumstances in London were the places in which Handel worked and the people who were his professional colleagues. His career developed primarily in the London theatres: we need to know not only about the buildings themselves, but also about the institutional arrangements for the management of the theatre companies, and about London's professional theatrical ambience into which Italian opera, and eventually Handel's oratorio-type works, were gradually absorbed (Chapter 4). Eighteenth-century London had its own flourishing concert scene, and indeed its own tradition of English dramas-with-music: Handel's professional activities can, in one aspect, be seen as just one element in the entertainments available to Londoners (Chapter 5). But London was also a cosmopolitan place: Handel was, especially in his first years in London, identifiable as yet another immigrant, working in the foreign medium of Italian opera. Handel's professional colleagues (and sometimes rivals) included a surprisingly large number of Italians who had ended up in London: some of them stayed for only a short time, while others were active for several seasons or even became permanent residents (Chapter 6). His day-to-day associates, whether musicians or those working in necessary ancillary activities such as libretto-writing or set-designing, were indeed a cosmopolitan social group within London society. Not so the librettists for Handel's oratorio-style works, who came from the ranks of cultured English gentlemen: these were not necessarily professional theatre-folk but they had an interest in English literature and, often, in theology and biblical scholarship (Chapter 7). Their importance to Handel's later career as providers of texts for musical setting is obvious, but they form the 'background' in a subtler way as well.

Recent experience in preparing a biography of Handel,[1] in which I have to some extent re-lived the events of his life, has persuaded me that Handel probably showed a strong interest in current developments in English literary culture only during his first decade in London. The primary evidence for his association with Hughes and Arbuthnot comes from his first years in London: his closest contact with 'literary' circles (including perhaps Pope and Gay) came at Burlington House and Cannons, all before 1720. In the 1720s the literary focus of his life was, if anything, Italian. In the 1730s, when he introduced English-language works into his theatre programmes, he was apparently entirely unresponsive to Aaron Hill's plea that he should take a lead in the development of a new school of English musical drama: my strong impression is that, although he no doubt took an intelligent interest in what was going on around him – in the ideas of *literati*, theologians, philosophers or painters – these were not central passions, nor did they exercise a direct influence on his creative activities. Handel was probably rather conservative in outlook, preferring stability to the injection of revolutionary new ideas: it is arguable, therefore, that the ferment of literary, critical and theological activity which had a stronger effect on some of his London contemporaries was mediated to Handel principally through the attitudes implicit in the texts that he set to music. Only very rarely does it seem that Handel objected strongly to what his librettists served up for him, and then his objections were as likely to be on practical, dramatic or musical grounds. Admittedly we do not know much about the librettos that Handel was offered but never set, or his reasons for such rejections. But we can pay attention to the content of the texts that he did set, which he must have found at least acceptable, and to the characters of the people who created them.

Part II of the *Companion* deals with Handel's music itself. The musical form in which Handel composed most is the aria for solo voice, variously accompanied by orchestra, instrumental ensemble or basso continuo alone: in all he composed more than 2,000 arias in his operas, oratorios and cantatas. Handel's approach to the aria therefore makes a natural starting-point (Chapter 8). It seems very likely that the two things which Handel found most stimulating, apart from the practical excitement of bringing works to performance, were a good libretto (which need only be 'good' in that it fired his imagination with dramatic situations and literary images that could be conveyed effectively through musical setting) and the craft of composition itself. The latter had two major aspects: what we may call the short-term effect of setting up a particular mood or a particular level of emotional intensity, and the more long-term constructional skill of keeping a movement alive once it was under way. In both of these (which one may, by analogy, think of as 'rhetorical' skills, as means of keeping the musical argument alive) Handel was a master. His mastery was so highly developed technically that it must have become largely instinctive – hence the speed with which, in bursts of intense creative effort, he could complete a major score. But the musical thinking that went into his compositional processes is to some extent accessible. One very valuable source of evidence is the large quantity of Handel's autograph music that survives. It gives almost complete coverage of Handel's mature compositions, though it consists mainly of final composition drafts rather than sketches from the earlier stages of creative evolution. Nevertheless, Handel's autographs reveal how he went about the business of composition, both in matters of detail and in larger issues of formal construction (Chapter 9). His working methods included the 'borrowing' of musical material, from himself and from other composers. This practice has been a source of controversy since the composer's own lifetime, and has tended to divert attention away from the creative skills that constituted 'composition' for Handel: but, properly regarded, the use that he made of pre-existing music gives us one way of approaching his particular genius.

If we take a broad view of Handel's works, he can be credited with two innovations: the invention of large-scale English theatre oratorio and of its accidental adjunct, the organ concerto. In his London theatre oratorio-type works Handel to some extent brought together Italian and English musical traditions. The result is a genre which is undeniably effective in performance but which defies simple comprehensive description: this is partly because of the richness and diversity of the contributing elements and partly because the genre continued to develop with each new work (Chapter 10). In his preface to *Samson*, Handel's librettist Newburgh Hamilton described Handel's oratorios as a 'musical Drama . . . in which the Solemnity of Church-Musick is agreeably united with the most pleasing Airs of the Stage'. Hamilton's perception of 'the Solemnity of Church-Musick' was the result of another of Handel's creative innovations, though this time in terms of style rather than genre: his 'Utrecht' Te Deum and Jubilate, and Coronation Anthems, set new standards of solidity and scale for English church music, as his *Dixit Dominus* may have done earlier for Latin settings in Rome. But there is more to Handel's church music than these grand-scale works: the repertory, although not as extensive as that for the operas and oratorios, covers pieces written for differing circumstances, liturgical contexts and performing conditions (Chapter 11). Related performing conditions link together Handel's 'solo' sonatas, trio sonatas and cantatas which, although usually regarded separately through a rather artificial division between vocal and instrumental genres, are treated here in terms of the 'chamber music' context for which they were mainly conceived (Chapter 12). By contrast, although parallels may be drawn between the solo aria and a movement from a concerto featuring a solo instrument, Handel's orchestral music really forms a separate entity, related to the development of orchestral music in France and Italy in the period of Handel's youth (Chapter 13). Consideration of Handel's keyboard music brings us back full circle to the earliest period of his biography and his musical career, for many of his formative musical influences are attributable to the keyboard training he received under Zachow in Halle, and his initial reputation was made as a keyboard virtuoso, a role that combined composition, improvisation and performance (Chapter 14).

Since music is ultimately a performing art, our stimulus to the study of Handel's music, as for that of any other significant composer, is that his pieces 'work' – that is, that they affect the listener (and performer) – in practice. Part III therefore deals with some issues that arise when the music, as received in Handel's score, is converted into the musical experience. For Handel's Italian contemporaries, opera was a literary as much as a musical medium: Metastasio was highly regarded for his poetic diction as well as for his ingenuity in plot-construction, and it is arguable that, for Italians, drama remained effectively synonymous with opera until well into the twentieth century. Handel seems to have become fully at home in, and fully committed to, contemporary Italian culture during his years in Italy, which were what we might describe as the 'probationary' period of his career, following his apprenticeship in Germany. A good colloquial command of foreign languages seems to have been among the skills that came to Handel fairly easily: Charles Burney never forgot the impression made on him by his youthful contact with the composer 'swearing in four or five languages'.[2] But patience with the niceties and refinements of languages was probably not one of the features of Handel's personality: of the Italian librettists with whom he worked in London, it seems likely that he formed a much closer relationship with the practical, musicianly, Nicola Haym than with the more 'literary' Paolo Rolli who, for his part, probably resented the fact that a German composer was beating Italians at their own game. The extent of Handel's practical competence in Italian, as well as being an interesting topic in itself, has practical consequences. Under what circumstances should we correct Handel's linguistic 'mistakes' when it comes to performance, and where (as with some parallel examples of Handel's individual treatment of the English language) should we preserve the character of the sounds he intended (Chapter 15)?

Perhaps no area of Handel performance has been more affected in the years between 1900 and 2000 than the sound of the orchestra. The 'early music' revival of the twentieth century is a complex subject, but the movement's origin was stimulated partly by simple musical curiosity – a curiosity that challenged the proposition that old instruments and techniques had become obsolete because they 'didn't work', and that was disturbed by the mis-match between an imaginative aural reading of the score and the timbres that were available in current conditions. Complete 'authenticity' may be a chimera, but that does not diminish the value, indeed the necessity, of pursuing the appropriate sounds and styles for Handel's music. Such a pursuit must take as its starting-point what is known about Handel's use of the orchestra, including those features in his scores which were not fully notated in the form expected by modern conventions (Chapter 16).

Finally, we take a last look at the major genres of opera and oratorio. *Opera seria* as a genre did not enjoy a good press for a couple of centuries after Handel's death. The criticisms of the genre, as embodied in the 'classic' statement contained in the dedication to the printed score of the Calzabigi/Gluck *Alceste* (1769), concerning its reliance on vocal ornamentation and the drama-impeding form of the *da capo* aria, have remained influential, and indeed relevant in terms of the very different operatic genres that have developed in succession since 1750. It is perhaps less fruitful to expend the energy on vigorous denials that *opera seria* is a 'concert in costume' than to record that, on some nights at least, the genre has provided powerful theatrical experiences, in which conflicts and interactions of characters, and those wider resonances about the human condition that arise from the audience's emotional participation with events on stage, have been stirred rather than hindered by a medium that allows the time-stopping quality of powerful emotion sufficient room for its musical expression, and in which ornamentation becomes a natural means of emotional discharge. But even Handel's music cannot guarantee this experience every night, and authenticity has been slower to reach the stage – in styles of movement, costume and stage design – than the orchestra pit. A good preparation for attendance at a performance of one of Handel's operas written for London is to read through the dual-language libretto that was printed for the work's first performance:[3] this, combined with a knowledge of what, in general terms, Handel could do with the operatic aria, is usually sufficient to set aside any lingering doubts about the effectiveness of the medium. It is sadly a matter of record that what is seen in the theatre has often fallen short of the imaginary – and to a large extent realisable – ideal: when gesture and the stage picture are at odds with the style of the music, Handel would usually have been better served with a concert performance. Nevertheless, the gradual re-establishment of Handel's operas on the stage has been an important development of modern times, and there is a growing realisation that the operas are practical musical-dramatic entities: furthermore, recordings of complete (or near-complete) opera scores have brought the music into public access in a way that would have been unimaginable even in 1950. But it still remains true that the public with experience of Handel's operas in performance, whether in the theatre or on record, remains substantially smaller than that for his oratorios, so there is accordingly more explaining to do (Chapter 17).

If the revival of *opera seria* involves the re-creation of circumstances in which the genre makes dramatic and musical sense, it might be argued that such efforts are not necessary for oratorio, which has enjoyed something of a continuous performance tradition since Handel's lifetime and, as a 'concert' genre, has fewer complications for modern performance. Furthermore, we have a century's experience of attempts at 'authentic' performance of the oratorios behind us, since A. H. Mann's pioneering performances of *Messiah* in the 1890s. Nevertheless, while certain aspects of modern oratorio performances have undoubtedly returned to the spirit of the originals and, as with the operas, the lesser-known works are now becoming well represented in recording catalogues, it is still difficult to recover the ambience for which they were created. Perhaps it is too much to expect that we shall ever experience Lenten theatre seasons in which some Handel oratorios are appreciated as 'new' works, in which the performers are working in a musical style which commands their undivided attention for a few weeks, and in which no one expects to be out of the doors within three hours of the start of the performance. But that is no reason for ignoring what can be known of the musical arrangements of Handel's own performances, even though the evidence does not give us complete information on a few fundamental matters, such as the way that Handel arranged his performers in the theatre (Chapter 18). However imperfect the execution, oratorios (or any other works of Handel's) make most sense when performers and audiences share some understanding of the work itself, as conceived by the composer and (where relevant) the librettist. It is for this reason that matters of performance practice are not the exclusive prerogative of performers, but are part of the legitimate interest of the listener as well. It will be interesting to see how Handel's works fare as the three-hundredth anniversaries of their first performances come round.

PART I

Background

1 Germany – education and apprenticeship

John Butt

Scholars outside Germany have, with good reason, tended to avoid a direct confrontation with the first twenty-one years of Handel's life. First, there are few primary sources relating to his upbringing and education, and the secondary material from the eighteenth century is fraught with obvious inaccuracies and misunderstandings. Furthermore, whatever can be gleaned from the most influential accounts – most notably Mainwaring's of 1760[1] – might seem, on first sight, irrelevant to a composer whose talents and international exposure seem to stretch well beyond the confines of Halle and Hamburg.

Two of Handel's earliest English biographers, Mainwaring and Hawkins,[2] both try to portray the composer as an isolated genius, who – in Hawkins's view – learned to play the clavichord with virtually no previous experience of music. Even the most significant German biographer, Chrysander (who otherwise fills in many of the spaces in previous accounts of the German years), tends to underplay the achievement of Handel's teacher, Zachow, in order to emphasise the composer's innate talent.[3] More recent writers have, fortunately, redressed the balance, showing quite clearly that Handel did not miraculously spring fully formed into cosmopolitan musical life.[4] Nevertheless, surprisingly few have observed the sheer variety of musical institutions and patronage that Handel experienced before he left Germany, something which undoubtedly contributed to his uncanny ability to handle both court support and public financing during his active career in England.

Naturally, a study of the political, educational and musical environment of Handel's early years is not likely to provide a complete explanation for all his later achievement. However, it can at least give us some sense of how a figure such as Handel emerged, how the particular talents he possessed could have been developed to such an extraordinary degree, even before his Italian sojourn.

Halle, Weissenfels and their musical environments

A brief outline of Halle's fortunes in the late seventeenth century is appropriate here.[5] Although Handel was born nearly forty years after the end of the Thirty Years War, its outcome would still have conditioned much of his childhood environment. Most significant in this respect was one of the provisions of the Treaty of Westphalia from 1648, in which Halle, along with the rest of the Archbishopric of Magdeburg, was promised to the 'Great Elector', Friedrich Wilhelm of Brandenburg, on the death of the then administrator, Duke August of Saxony. The latter did not die until 1680, so the change in administration would have been fresh in the minds of the Handel household; indeed Handel's father, Georg Händel, had held a major position as court surgeon. In 1680 the court (now headed by August's son, Johann Adolph), retreated to the new sumptuous palace at Weissenfels, some twenty miles from Halle.

The late administrator had actually resided at the Moritzburg palace in Halle, so the city lost something of its autonomy when power moved to Berlin. Any sense of unease in 1680 would have been exacerbated by the horrendous plague that soon broke out, killing over half the inhabitants, followed by a devastating fire. Elector Friedrich Wilhelm was of the reformed confession and demanded tolerance of Calvinists throughout the Duchy of Brandenburg, despite the predominance of Lutheranism. In 1685 he passed an edict to allow French Huguenots to settle in Halle and, a few years later, Calvinist refugees from the Palatinate and a number of Jews also arrived. While the Elector's own religious outlook obviously lay behind these measures, the repopulation of the city was also of prime concern. In the event, the immigrants were extremely successful in revitalising the economy and developing Halle into a major manufacturing centre.

The worship and musical establishment of the principal church, the Marktkirche (or Marienkirche), was largely unaffected by these changes. Friedrich Wilhelm Zachow became organist in 1684, and every three weeks he presented concerted church music with the town musicians and choice singers from the Lutheran school (Gymnasium). Like several of his predecessors, Zachow was overall director of music, although it was more usual elsewhere for a cantor (a staff member from the local Lutheran 'Latin' school or Gymnasium who had particular responsibility for music) to hold this position. In Halle, the cantors still directed the music in the other churches and gave the boys who worked under Zachow's direction their preliminary training.

The Lutheran Gymnasium in Halle maintained most of its activities during the period of transition. The talented Rector (head teacher), Johann Praetorius, provided some degree of stability. Not only was he extremely musical and an accomplished composer,[6] he also promoted theatrical presentations, particularly 'Comedies', serenades and Singspiele during the 1680s and 1690s.[7] While none of these was likely to have been a fully-fledged opera, they must have been a significant avenue for the performance of dramatic music in Halle. Indeed, the previous regime of Duke August of Saxony had been noted for its operatic endeavours, so the school presentations would have appealed to those hankering for a lost era. Furthermore, one of Praetorius's deputy rectors, Albrecht Christian Rotth, wrote one of the most significant studies of German poetry and dramaturgy in the High Baroque, his *Vollständige deutsche Poesie* of 1688.[8]

Unfortunately, the school records are somewhat incomplete during the 1690s, so we have no direct record that Handel attended the Gymnasium. However, both Mattheson and the Halle chronicler Dreyhaupt (writing in 1749–50) affirm that he was educated there.[9] Handel's father had himself attended the Gymnasium and was a close associate of the current school rector, Praetorius; both were members of a small committee formed in 1682 to provide relief for victims of the plague.[10] Moreover, it would hardly have been likely that Handel could have matriculated at the University of Halle in 1702 without having experienced a thorough school education.

The curriculum of the Gymnasium was indeed impressive, the youngest pupils in the tenth class (Decima) beginning with the Lutheran Catechism, German and Latin reading, writing, counting and biblical stories. In subsequent classes the pupils would have worked through grammar and syntax, Latin composition, geography and letter-writing. From the sixth class Greek was introduced, followed by study of Tacitus and Ovid, the Greek New Testament, and the composition of German and Latin poetry. The uppermost classes (Secunda and Prima) covered Cicero and Horace, Socrates and Plutarch, Hebrew writing, 'elegant style', logic, ethics and physics and the arts of oratory and disputation.[11] Significantly, music seems not to have been studied as an academic subject, but practical instruction took place at noon each day.

While the Gymnasium seems to have preserved traditional Lutheran education at a high level, the new regime encouraged several new educational establishments and this led to an intellectual intensification that was without rival in the area of Brandenburg-Prussia. Given the Calvinist affiliations of the House of Brandenburg, dissidents from within the Lutheran church itself were tolerated, most notably the Pietists, who shared many articles of faith with the Calvinists. These Lutherans promoted an archetypally personal and emotionally involved religious life, and were as devoted to good works as they were opposed to elaborate liturgy, complex music and most forms of drama.

Together, the Calvinist and Pietist influences had a marked effect on the musical life of Halle. The town council complained in 1695 that 'there is too much figural church music [i.e. polyphonic and concerted pieces], it is too long and unedifying, pleasing only to the cantors and organists, and should be modified with songs of penitence and thanks that can be sung by the entire congregation'. Furthermore, a church ordinance of 1702 forbade the use of Latin in the liturgy: even the Ordinary of the Mass was to be sung in German.[12]

The influx of such figures as the Pietist August Hermann Francke and the jurist Christian Thomasius was instrumental in the founding of the Friedrich-University of Halle in 1694. Not surprisingly, the ancient science of music was not to be found on the curriculum of a university devoted to Pietist (and, increasingly, Enlightenment) causes. Nevertheless music played an important part as a peripheral activity: town musicians were frequently employed for university ceremonies and a variety of city ordinances against unsociable student music-making, from 1698 onwards, point towards a rich amateur culture.[13]

One new German musical institution that had been developing during the closing decades of the seventeenth century was the *Collegium musicum*, a student-based concert organisation that often achieved professional standards; this is the single most important precursor of the modern concert tradition in Germany. It is highly significant that the first reports of such groups in Halle were made in 1700–2 by the young student Heinrich Brockes, who was subsequently author of the most significant Passion libretto of the early eighteenth century, set by Handel, among others.[14] Brockes held concerts in his own rooms every week, so he was probably a focal point for student music-making.

Another centre for music was the so-called Cathedral (Dom), where Handel served as organist during 1702–3. This had traditionally been the chapel for the administrator of the Archbishopric of Magdeburg, so the Elector maintained his claim to the building, and in 1688 gave over the Cathedral to the Calvinist congregation from the Palatinate. Not only did this cause much strife for the existing Lutheran congregation, it also meant a radical reduction in liturgical music. Handel's musical duties amounted to little more than psalm introduction and accompaniment.[15] Furthermore, most of the other weekly teaching duties traditionally connected with the post were waived, because he was a Lutheran and not a Calvinist.[16] However, according to the document relating to his successor as organist, he was also expected to direct capable performers of vocal and instrumental music in his own house. It may be that the loss of liturgical music led to an association of the post with private music-making, by way of compensation. This might explain why Handel was particularly interested in this post, which probably allowed an even wider field of music-making than Zachow would have maintained at the Marktkirche.

Furthermore, a royal privilege was given for an oboe band to perform in the cathedral on Sundays and feast days, together with the organist, as accompaniment to the psalms and songs of the reformed liturgy.[17] According to one – albeit barely authenticated – anecdote, Handel was infatuated with the oboe during the early years of his career.[18]

The musical attitude of Handel's family has been subject to much conjecture and, since Mainwaring's time, Handel's father has been branded an enemy of music against whom the son's talents miraculously won out. Given the apparent association between Mainwaring and close friends of the composer, we should probably accept that there is an element of truth in his account.[19] In fact, antipathy towards music *as a profession* was not unusual in the culture of the time. Telemann's experiences were almost directly analogous to Handel's: according to his autobiography, he set off to Leipzig to study law, following his mother's wishes, but was 'sidetracked' back into music partly as a result of his visit to Handel in Halle en route.[20] As the pastor Sebastian Kirchmaier wrote in the foreword to Georg Falck's *Idea boni cantoris*, a Lutheran singing treatise of 1688, 'Most people love and learn gladly only those arts which adorn and fill the purse, or which otherwise bear profit or adornment.'

This is not to say that musicians could not earn high salaries; indeed Zachow seems to have been well rewarded and to have belonged to the upper ranks of the city hierarchy.[21] But the parents of both Telemann and Handel doubtlessly preferred the profession of law as being both highly respectable and also very desirable in an environment of increasingly centralised absolutism.[22] It should be remembered, though, that Georg Händel was soon persuaded by his royal master that there was nothing unrespectable about the profession of music and that the world deserved a talent such as Handel's.[23] Indeed, some sources imply that Georg sent his son to study with Zachow on his own initiative.[24] Moreover, the evidence suggests that the father was familiar with – if not well disposed towards – music as an entertainment: the wife of the surgeon to whom he was apprenticed in 1637 was the daughter of the influential English violinist William Brade;[25] in the 1670s Georg Händel was very close friends with the royal Kapellmeister David Pohle, one of the founders of the Halle opera, and the organist Christian Ritter.[26] Furthermore, the famed Kapellmeister at the Weissenfels court, Johann Philipp Krieger, was a distant relation of the Händel family and, given Georg's bi-monthly visits to the court from 1688, the two were doubtless well acquainted. Indeed, the Weissenfels opera was the direct successor of the Halle court opera, so it was probably closely and enthusiastically followed by the ageing surgeon.

Georg Händel was first appointed private valet and surgeon to Duke

August (of Halle) in 1660; he earned a high reputation as a doctor and the Duke also granted him the privilege to sell wine in 1668.[27] Naturally he lost all these privileges on August's death in 1680, although he was soon able to secure an honorary title at the Brandenburg court. Not until 1688 was he able to reclaim his former post in the Saxon court, now at Weissenfels.[28] Given that his duties involved visiting the court every eight weeks, it is likely that the young Handel accompanied his father there on a number of occasions, and not merely on a single trip at the age of seven, as stated by Mainwaring.[29] After all, the journey was barely more than twenty miles.

While the early German opera of Halle would have been of the Singballett/Schauspiel genre, with intermittent music, the newer establishment at Weisenfels was able to mount full-length operas from 1685.[30] The operas of Kapellmeister Krieger were obviously the most significant productions, but there were also guest performances from the 'public' opera houses at Leipzig and Hamburg. The church and instrumental music at the court was no less impressive, with a repertory of many Italian works and Krieger's own cantatas and sonatas.[31] Given that Duke Johann Adolph spared no expense in establishing his court music, Weissenfels was, for a time, unequalled among the Saxon courts, drawing its musicians from a wide range of local and more distant institutions.[32] It is difficult to avoid the conclusion that the much-travelled Krieger, who knew so many internationally prominent musical figures, must have been a major influence on his distant relative, the young Georg Friedrich Handel.[33]

Music education in school and study with Zachow

On the assumption that Handel attended the Gymnasium in Halle, it seems likely that his education there began in August 1692 (when there happens to be a gap in the records) at the age of seven.[34] Mainwaring claimed that Handel made his eventful visit to Weissenfels and subsequently began his study with Zachow at around that age.[35] On the other hand J. G. Walther, in the earliest biography of Handel, states that he went to Zachow in 1694, a date we should take seriously since Walther is virtually the only eighteenth-century commentator to give the correct year for Handel's birth.[36] Furthermore Dreyhaupt, the informative chronicler of Halle writing *c.* 1749, also gives 1694 as the outset of Handel's study with Zachow.[37]

If Handel went to school at seven and began his specialist training at nine or ten, this would still allow much of Mainwaring's story to stand.

Handel would have received his elementary training in school, discovered his talent for keyboard playing and perhaps acquired from school the clavichord for his secret practice in the family house.[38] Within two years he could have advanced enough to impress the prince at Weissenfels and he might also have encountered Zachow, as a member of the school choir which sang in the Marktkirche. Handel's musical education at the Gymnasium, under the two cantors and rector, presumably continued after he began his studies with Zachow; the two forms of tuition would have complemented one another in a variety of ways. However, given that the school education would have begun first and would have been the less specialized pursuit, it makes sense to examine that first.

The School Ordinance of 1661 was still valid in Handel's time, although it must have been updated in a number of matters, particularly regarding the repertory to be performed in church.[39] As is typical in Lutheran schools of the time, the entire school body is divided into classes of different levels of musical training, and from this body are formed the choirs that perform in the various churches of the locality. Instruction begins at noon every day and the cantor is to open each lesson with songs in two to four parts, even if all the boys are not yet present. The actual course of instruction begins in the lowest classes (Decima and Nona) with study of the chorales and psalms for the next Sunday's worship. After this, the boys learn musical notation and begin to sing the same chorales in parts, followed by pieces in progressively complex polyphony. The pre-scribed authors for instruction books are noticeably conservative, dating from the previous century (Faber, for basic notation; Dressler and Glarean, for the study of modes). Likewise, the music for high feasts is to be taken from the era stretching from Josquin to Lassus; indeed, there is a certain resistance to music in newer styles.

The arrival of Zachow at the main church had evidently changed matters somewhat, and by Handel's time the 'new Italian style' must have been more or less accepted, at least for certain occasions. Study of modes was rapidly dropping from German instruction during the latter half of the century, and indeed Handel once stated that he saw little need for the modes in modern composition; nevertheless there is evidence that Handel had acquired a certain degree of knowledge.[40] None of the instruction books prescribed by the 1661 ordinance would have prepared the pupil sufficiently for the sort of music that Zachow was writing, so it is likely that the cantors updated the material, and it is possible that they used some of the more recent pedagogic publications.

One published instruction book that may have been used by the more advanced students at the Gymnasium was the *Rudimenta Musices* (Mühlhausen 1685) by Wolfgang Mylius, a former pupil of Christoph

Bernhard at the Dresden court, who had also studied in Vienna and who was now Kapellmeister at the court of Gotha.[41] This comprehensive tutor takes the pupil through all the fundamentals of notation, and gives advice on good vocal style, good diction and an expressive presentation of the text. Most interesting of all are the chapters on the correct vocal *Manier* – in other words, the Italian style of ornamented singing that is so comprehensively codified in German school books of the seventeenth century.[42] The repertory of ornaments is astonishingly detailed, ranging from basic dynamic shading and simple appoggiaturas, through rhythmic alteration and trills to the most complicated passage-work. Particularly useful are Mylius's monodic musical examples in which the remarkable profusion of ornaments to be added is actually specified with abbreviations.[43] It is quite clear that Mylius is not merely preparing boys for church music (indeed, he recommends particular care and discretion in polyphonic pieces); he remarks that he cannot possibly give all the information required to perform recitative in 'comedies, tragedies and such sung operas', thus implying that the book provides the fundamentals for such arts without outlining all the applications. One may well imagine Johann Praetorius using a book of this kind to prepare the boys for his school comedies in the 1680s and 90s.

Mylius is by no means alone in outlining some of the details of Italianate singing. Advice of this kind had begun to appear in German sources during the last decade of the sixteenth century, and many new treatises appeared during the two decades after 1685.[44] Some of these provide advice on instrumental performance: G. Falck (1688), for instance, includes instruction on the violin and viol with detailed advice on posture, bow-grip and bowing rules; J. C. Stierlein introduces the student to figured bass. D. Merck's *Compendium* (1695) is the first German treatise devoted entirely to instructing the youth in string instruments. It thus does not seem surprising that Handel was able to play ripieno violin parts when he first arrived in Hamburg in 1703; quite possibly he was familiar with several other instruments by the time he had finished school and participated in some of Halle's *Collegia*.

The most impressive, or at least the most comprehensive, of all the treatises addressed to schools and the education of youth is D. Speer's *Grundrichtiger Unterricht der musikalischen Kunst* (1697). This 'four-leafed clover' (as it is subtitled) covers the standard rules of notation and singing, figured bass, instruments (the fundamentals of strings, brass and flutes) and, finally, the rules of composition. Speer evidently drew on his wide experience – especially apparent in his extensive knowledge of wind instruments – both as a school teacher and as a town musician. He was also clearly adept at keyboard instruments, since the chapter devoted to

them is the most extensive. While all matters of a theoretical or specula-
tive nature are omitted, the student is given a grounding in composition,
working first from figured bass (as part of the keyboard practice) through
to the rules of counterpoint. The latter are taught using figured-bass
numerals, so it is clear that counterpoint is basically to be seen as a two-
part texture, firmly grounded in the movement of the bass.

Speer's treatise provides a useful transition to the other side of
Handel's musical education, his study with Friedrich Wilhelm Zachow.
Like Speer, Zachow began his career as a *Stadtpfeifer*, but advanced to the
socially higher station of town organist.[45] He would have taught
composition as a very practical matter, although the wide range of styles
and expression in his oeuvre suggests that he relished the many possibilities of the art. Mainwaring's account of Handel's study with Zachow
seems plausible in the light of this and other evidence, so it is worth
recounting it here:[46]

> The first object of his attention was to ground him thoroughly in the
> principles of harmony. His next care was to cultivate his imagination, and
> form his taste. He had a large collection of Italian as well as German music:
> he shewed him the different styles of different nations; the excellences and
> defects of each particular author; and, that he might equally advance in the
> practical part, he frequently gave him subjects to work, and made him copy,
> and play, and compose in his stead. Thus he had more exercise, and more
> experience than usually falls to the share of any learner at his years.

This implies a two-part programme: first a study of the ground-rules of
the art and then a massive study of existing examples. Mainwaring is most
vague in respect to the first part; what were 'the principles of harmony'?
Most probably Zachow did not follow a specific treatise, but we might
situate his method somewhere between the older compositional theory of
Printz (reprinted in 1696) and the newer method of Niedt (1700–17).[47]
Printz begins his theory of 'musical poetics' with a study of intervals,
together with syllabic stress and metres. Thus the principles of harmony
are intimately connected with the rhythm and metre of text, and the art of
text-setting. After an extensive study of intervallic progressions in a
variety of note values, modes and cadences, Printz proceeds with a
method of stimulating the invention. This is grounded in the concept of
variation, achieved through knowledge of an enormous repertory of
ornamental figures, methodically classified by Printz. The incipient composer thus learns to vary and expand a given idea through the judicious
use of ornamental figures and their permutations; furthermore, this
experience encourages him to invent further themes. The last section of
Printz's composition theory is an introduction to figured bass, an art

which – like variation – bridges the fields of composition and performance.

The first immediate difference in Niedt's theory is the fact that he deals with figured bass first (something also to be observed in Speer's treatise). Niedt's affirmation that 'the thorough-bass is the most complete foundation of music' suggests that the traditional intervallic rules of counterpoint were now generally seen through and within the concept of figured bass. All notes, in an implied four-part texture, are related to the bass line. Even at this elementary stage Niedt introduces variation of the texture, a simple two-part fugue and the rules of modulation. Book II deals with variation, providing a glossary of ornamental figures not unlike that of Printz. In all, this approach tends to meld together the complementary concepts of structure and ornament: the ornamental variation of one piece can be the thematic material of another; a single bass progression can work as the basis of a plethora of otherwise distinct pieces. There is never any sense that the composer must create anything entirely new; he should rather become skilful in the manipulation, extension and variation of existing material:[48]

> The eager learner can imitate these and similar skilful *Manieren* [patterns] taken from compositions of good Masters, or, after hearing such skilful passages and patterns, he can commit them forthwith to paper and see what they consist in. Let me assure him that he will suffer no harm from this practice, but will discover that, in time, he himself will think of many *Inventiones.*

It is only in the last (unfinished) part of Niedt's course that he deals with counterpoint proper, but it is quite clear that he sees this as a refinement and reiteration of the previous thorough-bass theory, not as a completely new subject, requiring 'large Spanish spectacles'.[49] Indeed much is repeated from the first part, and Niedt frequently uses figured-bass numerals in his instructions about counterpoint (just as Speer did). The remaining chapters of this unfinished book include an irreverent and inadequate study of canon, and a survey of motets, chorales and short arias.

To return to Handel's study with Zachow, we might then surmise that his first study was figured bass, followed by the art of variation and elaboration, and ending with an examination of more complex contrapuntal devices. In no sense would he have studied counterpoint as a purely abstract, timeless art; everything would have been directed towards practical needs and the cultivation of a wide stylistic and affective repertory. This leads into the second and most essential part of Zachow's curriculum: the copying, performing and critical study of exist-

ing music. The only clue we have to the repertory concerned is the celebrated (but unfortunately lost) notebook, dated 1698, and first described
by William Coxe in 1799:[50]

> It contains various airs, choruses, capricios, fugues, and other pieces of
> music, with the names of contemporary musicians, such as Zackau, Alberti,
> Frobergher, Krieger, Kerl, Ebner, Strunch. They were probably exercises
> adopted at pleasure, or dictated for him to work upon, by his master. The
> composition is uncommonly scientific, and contains the seeds of many
> of his subsequent performances.

In other words, this was a fairly comprehensive miscellany of vocal and
keyboard pieces from German lands of the late seventeenth century. It
was through imitation of south German models, such as Froberger and
Kerll, that Handel would have become adept at 'strict counterpoint', and
we may assume that he amassed works of as many different styles as he
could in other notebooks.

Opera centres outside Halle and Weissenfels: Berlin, Leipzig and Hamburg

Handel's visit to Berlin was first recounted by Mainwaring, but his
version of the story has to be emended to take into account various
chronological factors.[51] Mainwaring's date of 1698 does not accord with
his report of the ill health of Handel's father at the same time (since he
had died the year before) or his reference to the King of Prussia (whose
coronation did not take place until 1701).[52] Then there is the issue of
Handel's encounter with the Italian composers Ariosti and Bononcini at
the Berlin court: Ariosti worked there from 1697 to 1703 but Bononcini
did not arrive until 1702. Given that Händel senior had an honorary post
at the Berlin court,[53] it is certainly possible that the young composer was
introduced to the Elector before his father's death, and that the prince –
like Johann Adolph of Weissenfels – took an interest in the boy's musical
development. It is thus possible to infer at least two visits to Berlin, one in
1697, before the death of Georg Händel, and another in 1702.[54] In any
event, Berlin would have offered Handel his first direct encounter with
Italian musicians and composers, and a chance to see them working
within a sumptuous court opera.

Mainwaring did not mention Handel's visits to Leipzig, a major
trading city quite close to Halle. Information about these visits surfaces in
Mattheson's publication of Telemann's autobiography, where Telemann
refers to their regular communication and 'the frequent visits we made to

each other'.[55] This would suggest that the two composers met one another regularly in the period *c.* 1701–3, after Telemann's arrival in Leipzig and before Handel's departure for Hamburg.

Leipzig would have introduced Handel to an entirely new concept of operatic production: the public opera established by Nicolaus Adam Strungk. Handel's borrowings from the latter's keyboard works might imply that he encountered Strungk in Leipzig, and he must have known at least some of the twenty operas that Telemann composed during this period.[56] Baselt suggests that the cantor of the Thomaskirche, Johann Schelle, would also have been an important figure to Handel, on account of his biblical oratorios.[57] We must furthermore consider the influence of the organist Johann Kuhnau, who succeeded to Schelle's post in 1701. Mattheson generally speaks very highly of Kuhnau – who had published four sets of keyboard pieces by 1700 – particularly as a contrapuntist, and as one of the few composers of his age to consider melody, rather than directing everything towards harmony. He states that Handel at this time was even stronger than Kuhnau in improvised fugue and counterpoint, but that Kuhnau's pieces (in contrast to Handel's?) were all melodic and readily singable.[58] Telemann too acknowledges the influence of Kuhnau as a model for fugue and counterpoint, although he – in interesting contradiction to Mattheson – states that he and Handel had to turn to each other for the study of melodic style.[59]

It is in Hamburg that the facts of Handel's early career become more certain, owing to the direct account of his friend Johann Mattheson.[60] We do not know exactly how Handel came to move to Hamburg. Certainly, as one of the most prosperous cities in Europe, which had managed to survive the Thirty Years War virtually unscathed, it would have been an attractive centre. As a free city, it was not beholden to any particular ruling family and was, throughout the seventeenth century, the trading capital of northern Germany. It was already well known in musical circles as the home of the first public opera in Germany, founded in 1678 and largely supported by the business community; indeed, a specially designed opera house had been erected in the centre of town. Furthermore, Matthias Weckmann's *Collegium musicum*, founded in 1660, was perhaps the most significant public concert organisation before the eighteenth century. Handel had many acquaintances in Halle who could have introduced him to the city: the most obvious was the enthusiastic music-lover Heinrich Brockes; another of Handel's Halle contemporaries, Barthold Feind, also comes to mind.[61] Johann Theile, a former resident of Hamburg and one of the founders of the opera, was a close friend of Zachow, so he too might have played a part.[62] There may even have been connections through the Weissenfels court; after all, guest appearances from the Hamburg opera at Weissenfels were not uncommon. Reinhard Keiser himself – arguably the strongest musical influence on Handel during his Hamburg years – spent some time in Weissenfels during this period.[63]

Mattheson claimed to have introduced Handel to a wide range of musical activities throughout the city. Handel's operatic career began modestly as a second violinist in the opera orchestra, but he was soon working as a harpsichordist and writing his own operas, with or without the support of Keiser.[64] Mattheson complains of the extraordinary length of Handel's early arias and his almost unending cantatas,[65] and states that he could only write full and well-developed harmony, without any true sense of taste or melody.

Here we may perhaps sense the conflict between the old order of Lutheran composers and the influence of early-Enlightenment thinking, where the emphasis was placed upon simplicity, 'natural' melody and the appropriateness of music for any particular text or dramatic situation. Handel had learned much about the 'stuff' of music from his studies with Zachow and his intense engagement with manuscript anthologies of music; now he was finishing his education with what Mattheson termed the 'high school of opera', learning how to apply his craft. On the other hand, Handel had much to teach the 'modern' Mattheson; according to the latter, Handel enjoyed many meals at the table of Mattheson's father, and there Mattheson learned as much about counterpoint from Handel as he taught Handel about musical drama. Handel apparently had many pupils at this time,[66] which suggests that his skills as a composer were well recognised.

When Handel expressed indifference to the collection of Italian music shown to him by the Prince of Tuscany in Hamburg,[67] he might well have been viewing it with the critical eye of a Kuhnau or Zachow. The Germanic music education he had received stressed not only deeply wrought musical textures but also an intense awareness of the potential of any particular piece or theme. In this sense, he already had more than enough tools for fluent and efficient compositional practice. Moreover, the musical establishments in Halle, Weissenfels, Berlin, Leipzig and Hamburg had provided him with a remarkable breadth of experience, covering virtually every musical genre of the age.

2 Italy – political, religious and musical contexts

Carlo Vitali

Demography, economy and social class

It is estimated that, at the end of the seventeenth century and the beginning of the eighteenth, Italy, inhabited by about 12 million people, had an urban population fluctuating between 14 and 19 per cent of the total. This was a higher percentage than in Germany (8–11 per cent) and compared well with the English figure (13–16 per cent). Nevertheless, the future Anglican bishop and parliamentarian Gilbert Burnet, who in 1685 traversed a large part of the Italian peninsula from Milan to Naples, was astonished 'how there should be so much poverty in so rich a country, which is all over full of beggars'.[1] The most populous Italian city was Naples, with about 250,000 inhabitants (half as many as London but equal to Amsterdam, Frankfurt and Leipzig put together); some distance behind came Milan, Venice, Rome and Palermo, with populations of between 100,000 and 140,000 (thus of the same order of magnitude as Vienna, with just over 100,000 people), while Genoa, Bologna and Florence, each mustering between 60,000 and 80,000 inhabitants, had stagnant population figures or had even slightly regressed in the previous hundred years.

Italy suffered a dramatic social and economic decline in the seventeenth century, as a result of the reduction in importance of the Mediterranean area following the rise of the great maritime empires and the powerful centralised monarchies north of the Alps. The production of woollen cloth fell in Milan from 15,000 pieces per annum to little more than 3,000 – a tendency followed by other centres in Lombardy such as Como, Monza and Cremona, as well as by Florence. The decline can be traced across several established industries in Venice, such as ship-building and the manufacture of silk fabric and soap,[2] while new technologies did not take their place.[3] Meanwhile, the long-term public debt of the Republic grew inexorably, from 8 million ducats in 1641 to 50 million in 1714.[4]

In the countryside the process of depopulation became more marked, especially in central and southern Italy. Whole villages were abandoned, and intensive farming was replaced by large estates and cattle-raising. In the Sienese *Maremma* the sown acreage was reduced by a third between 1630 and 1692; in the Roman *Agro* it even declined to a tenth of the land area. During the last twenty years of the seventeenth century, exports of cereals and wine from Campania and Puglia fell to virtually nothing. The balance of trade worsened and inflation set in: for instance, Naples devalued its ducat by 10 per cent in 1689. Significantly, all these tendencies ran in parallel with the multiplication of noble titles; the feudal yoke came to weigh more heavily both on individuals and on whole rural communities, whom the central power delivered over to the rapacious overlordship of old and new barons in return for replenishing its ever-exhausted exchequer. This process reached its peak in the territories subject to the Spanish crown: in the Kingdom of Naples the number of princes, dukes and marquises almost quintupled during the seventeenth century, while in the Duchy of Milan feudal titles mushroomed from 183 to 433. Even the Venetian patriciate, in partial repudiation of its mercantile and republican origins, acquired extensive landholdings on the mainland, where it built magnificent villas that testify to the increasing diversion of its resources from productive investment into conspicuous consumption. In Tuscany the absolutism of the Medici family was consolidated: a network of feudal ownership, both lay and clerical, was re-created over the whole territory, to such an extent that only a quarter of the arable land could be bought and sold on the open market.

The same vicious circle of re-feudalisation, concentration of land-ownership and urban pauperism occurred in the Papal States. When Benedetto Odescalchi became pope, as Innocent XI, in 1676, the deficit of the papal Curia mounted each year by 170,000 scudi.[5] But Rome was a city of princes, where each cardinal maintained his own court and about ninety families belonging to the old or the new nobility monopolised the bulk of the income derived from the Roman *Agro* and *Maremma*, as well as from the interest on the public debt. The rest was divided mainly among the secular and regular clergy and that part of the citizenry active in the professions (in 1705 Arcangelo Corelli owned fifty-seven 'lochi di monte', or public debt certificates), the Curia or the administrative bureaucracy. The remaining inhabitants of the Eternal City had to make do with petty commerce or manual trades, if they did not choose to seek refuge under the umbrella of a *padrone* as domestic servants or 'clients' and thereby expose themselves to the ever-present risk that a bad harvest or a political upheaval following the election of a new pope would drive them back into beggary.

The situation was less wretched in those other provinces of the Papal States that enjoyed some degree of local autonomy: for instance, the

Marches, which included the Adriatic ports of Ancona and Pesaro, or the *Legazioni* of Bologna and Ferrara. Here the great landowners were not content to extract income from their tenants in the shape of ground-rents and tithes, but actively promoted the grain trade and land-improvement projects in the low-lying parts of the Po valley, always threatened by floods. Thus in 1682 the young Bolognese count Ercole Pepoli inherited from his grandfather Odoardo – besides the title of Senator and three town-palaces in Bologna, Ferrara and Venice – a fortune comprising landed estates, intensively worked small-holdings and prize herds of thoroughbred horses and cattle. At the opposite end of the social scale, a fully qualified master mason could earn, according to circumstances, the equivalent of 7–10 kilograms of bread per working day (because of church holidays, only 180–200 days in the year counted as such). Below this modest enough living standard seethed the masses of the 'poor', in their varying number and degree of poverty. In a relatively little urbanised area such as the Duchy of Savoy only 35,492 out of 1,500,000 inhabitants (2.5 per cent) were classified as beggars in a census carried out in the first years of the eighteenth century, but this was a happy exception. In the larger cities this percentage probably needs to be multiplied by ten to fifteen.

Culture and politics: Italy and its statelets

It is hard to say whether there existed an Italian national character beyond the facile stereotypes, mostly unflattering, that Italians from different regions ascribed to one another and which foreigners tended to take over. According to the Sieur de Rogissart, the author of a tourist guide published in 1706 and reprinted up to 1743,[6] 'tous les peuples d'Italie, & particuliérement celui de Naples, sont très-mous & très paresseux' ('all the peoples of Italy, and especially the Neapolitans, are very languid and lazy'); Rogissart also remarked on the tendency of the latter to extravagant and exaggerated language. He then considered the Venetians, whose fondness for vacuous ceremonies he deplored. The Bolognese he found odd and politically muddled, but with a love of culture and good food. The Florentines were hard-working, sober, lively-spirited and hospitable to strangers, but madly jealous when it came to their own women. The Milanese were pacific, submissive towards authority and commercially minded, and so on.

Regional differences existed even among the well-educated, who nevertheless manifested a certain degree of common consciousness based, first, on the myth of the Roman past and, secondly, on the reality of a shared language. In 1691 the Accademia della Crusca brought out the third edition of its dictionary (*vocabolario*), which reaffirmed the primacy of the Florentine standard of the fourteenth and fifteenth centuries; however, this primacy was not accepted by other Tuscans, such as the Sienese writer Girolamo Gigli, or by Lombard (Maggi, Lemene), Emilian (Muratori), Venetian (Zeno) or southern (Gravina) authors. But when the French Jesuit Bouhours attacked *en bloc* all Italian culture of the previous (seventeenth) century, accusing it of sterility and over-elaboration, Marquis Orsi led the defence from Bologna.[7] It is often claimed that papal condemnation of Galileo caused the Italian intelligentsia to abandon the experimental sciences and, fearful of censure from the Church, to seek refuge in less risky erudite pursuits. Yet, of the sixty-nine foreigners elected Fellows of the Royal Society of London between 1667 and 1709, no fewer than twenty-three were Italians.[8] Moreover, even the poetic academies – notably the Arcadian Academy, which was founded in Rome in 1690 by former attenders at the salon of ex-Queen Christina of Sweden and soon branched out into innumerable local 'colonies' – were significant for other achievements than the production of mediocre pastoral-erotic verse. It is they, rather than the dreary lexicographers of the Crusca, who are entitled to take the credit for the creation of that Italian *koiné* (common language) which, moving along the channels opened by opera librettos, quickly fanned out all over the world, reaching the educated elites of Vienna and St Petersburg, Lisbon and Boston. In the face of this upper-class, cosmopolitan culture, the Italian masses remained, however, virtual foreigners in their own country. True, the fathers of the Scolopian order combated illiteracy; missionary preachers reached the most isolated rural areas; a network of parishes, welfare organisations and confraternities despatched their task of elementary acculturation (and, naturally, of social control in accordance with the strategy of the Counter-Reformation). But foreign observers remarked how the outward conformity of the people was undermined, especially in the south, by pagan survivals, superstition and criminal deviance. The prisons of Naples, Rogissart noted, were always full, thus justifying the conventional description of the city as 'a paradise inhabited by devils'.

With regard to territorial divisions, at the dawn of the eighteenth century Italy found itself carved up into a jigsaw puzzle of small states, in accordance with the prescriptions of the Peace of Westphalia (1648), which, except for a few details, went back to the Treaty of Cateau-Cambrésis (1559) between France and Spain. The latter power held sway over an area of 140,000 square kilometres, or a good half of the present territory of the Italian Republic. It controlled the Duchy of Milan (ruled by a governor), the kingdoms of Naples, Sicily and Sardinia (each of which was entrusted to a viceroy with wide powers) and a chain of strategic fortresses along the Tuscan coast, which were termed the 'Presidii'.

Such a massive presence on the peninsula could not but influence the policy of other, nominally independent states. This was especially true of the warlike Duchy of Savoy, which identified itself as half-French in outlook,[9] and the aristocratic republic of Genoa (with its Corsican appendage). Elsewhere, Spanish influence was counter-balanced not only by that of France, initially under Richelieu and later under Mazarin and the Sun King, but also by that of the Austrian Habsburgs. For the Venetian Republic the Austrians were an ally in the centuries-old struggle against the Turks; but the Austrians were also, no less than the Ottomans, rivals of the Venetians for domination of the Balkans and the Adriatic, as well as an ever-present strategic threat by virtue of their control of the Alpine passes through which the Republic conducted trade with central and northern Europe. The Papal States suffered from the contradiction between the 'universal' role of the papacy and its strange constitutional form as an absolute, but elective, 'monarchy', which made it liable to instability in foreign policy, factionalism and nepotism. Despite the reforming zeal displayed by two of the popes who reigned between 1676 and 1700 (Innocent XI Odescalchi and Innocent XII Pignatelli, separated by the brief but unhappy episode of the pontificate of Alexander VIII Ottoboni), the international image of the Papal States continued to deteriorate: Bishop Burnet (naturally not immune to Anglican prejudice) described papal rule as 'worse than the government of Turkey'. In the Grand Duchy of Tuscany, formerly an oasis of good administration and religious tolerance, the degenerate Medici dynasty finally faced extinction, even if accompanied to the end by vestiges of its magnificent patronage. The symbolic figure here is Grand Prince Ferdinando, the chronically unwell son of an ill-starred union between the bigoted Cosimo III and Princess Marguerite-Louise of France. He himself contracted a childless marriage with Violante of Bavaria, though he preferred the attractions of the singer Vittoria Tarquini and, more dubiously, those of the castrato Checchino de Castris. Devoted to the arts and humanities as a whole (he corresponded with Leibniz, with the Venetian painter Sebastiano Ricci, with Zeno and Vallisnieri), Ferdinando was also a musician of more than amateur accomplishment. He organized operatic seasons in Florence, Leghorn and his summer residence at Pratolino, supported Cristofori's experiments leading to the invention of the fortepiano, and acted as a patron towards Pasquini, Steffani and Alessandro Scarlatti: being as fickle in aesthetic as in amorous matters, he soon abandoned Scarlatti for the Bolognese composer Perti.

No effective political role was played by the duchies of Parma, Modena and Mantua, seats of ancient Renaissance dynasties refined in the gentle arts but weak on the battlefield, or by a handful of feudal statelets (Piombino, Massa and Carrara, Guastalla and Mirandola) and the city-states of Lucca and San Marino, both republics. This archaic mosaic of political fragments, incomprehensible to a Frenchman, Spaniard or Englishman, perhaps reminded Handel of his German homeland, divided into dozens of principalities, margravates and ecclesiastical or secular baronies, whose rulers clothed themselves in high-sounding titles that a good diplomat had to study very carefully in order not to commit a *faux pas*. For the sake of his own survival, Handel had to make similar use of his diplomatic skills when he wandered through the Italian labyrinth – especially since the peninsula had for the past five years been the theatre of a major military conflict that would ultimately transform its aspect profoundly.

The war of the Spanish Succession and its impact on Italy

Charles II of Spain died without a direct successor on 1 November 1700, whereupon the long-awaited struggle for his heritage broke out between Louis XIV and Emperor Leopold I. The conflict between France and Austria, each backed by an international coalition, forced even the smaller Italian states to take sides. This they did without much enthusiasm, knowing that whatever possible advantages might accrue to them were outweighed by the certain risks. Initially, the only Italian state to come out openly on the side of the Bourbons was Piedmont, whose duke, Vittorio Amedeo II, gave his daughter Maria Luisa in marriage to Philip V, pretender to the Spanish throne. Ferdinando Carlo Gonzaga, the Duke of Mantua, pretending to give in to threats but in reality bribed into compliance by Louis XIV, precipitately opened his borders to a French expeditionary force of 15,000 men, even though his territory was a fief of the Emperor. The Republic of Genoa and Grand Duke Cosimo of Tuscany did not dare to give expression to their theoretically pro-French stance but instead pursued their own commercial and maritime interests. Venice declared its strict neutrality, as did the new pope Clement XI, notwithstanding strong pressures on him from both sides that he resisted only at the cost of displeasing both equally.

One of the main theatres of action in the war was the fertile valley of the river Po. Two cousins from the house of Savoy faced one another on opposing sides: Prince Eugene, the Austrian field-marshal, and Duke Vittorio Amedeo, generalissimo of the Franco-Spanish forces in Italy. The opening offensive of the Imperial armies (1701–2), who overran Ferrara and Parma and besieged Mantua and Cremona, was halted by the French under the Duke of Vendôme. Moreover, the conspiracy of the Prince of Macchia (1701), an attempt at a pro-Austrian uprising in Naples led by a section of the nobility and of the professional-intellectual class, failed for lack of popular support. In the next two years the French armies went on a counter-offensive in Lombardy, but the defection to the opposing camp of the Duke of Savoy forced Marshal Catinat to concentrate his efforts on Piedmont and to besiege Turin. In September 1706 the decisive battle was fought just outside the walls of Turin, one of the most heavily fortified cities in Europe. The Bourbon forces suffered a bloody defeat; in the brief period of twelve months the principal Spanish territories changed hands, and in Italy Viennese hegemony replaced that of Madrid. On 24 September 1706 the Imperial forces entered Milan. In the summer of 1707 a corps of just 8,000 soldiers under the command of Count von Daun, crossing the Papal States and passing close to a terrified Rome, overcame the enemy defences on the river Garigliano and so opened the way to Naples, which was occupied on 7 July by the first Austrian viceroy, Count von Martinitz; he was followed in the course of the next three years by Daun and then by Cardinal Vincenzo Grimani. In 1708 the Gonzaga Duke of Mantua, who had been declared a felon and deposed, was replaced by an Imperial governor, Prince Philip of Hesse-Darmstadt, a veteran of the Neapolitan campaign. Both he and Grimani have earned a place in musical history, as patrons of Vivaldi and Handel respectively. In September 1708, thanks to the support of the English fleet, the Habsburgs finally occupied Sardinia, previously controlled by Philip V. Also in 1708, Emperor Joseph I (a Catholic, but a less observant one than his father whom he had succeeded in 1705) ordered Daun to invade the Papal States from the north in order to punish Clement XI for his slowness in joining the winning side. Paying no heed to his excommunication, Daun defeated the pontifical army commanded by General Luigi Ferdinando Marsigli and forced the Pope to sign a dishonourable peace (15 January 1709). From that moment onwards, with the establishment of a *pax austriaca* that was eventually confirmed by the treaties of Utrecht (1713) and Rastatt (1714), the Italian peninsula was spared further warfare, though this continued unabated, with varying fortunes, in Spain, France and the Low Countries.

However, the barbarisation and pauperisation that were the tragic consequences of the events of the previous decade took a long time to recede. The neutrality of Venetian, Modenese and Papal territory had been violated by both sides, who torched and pillaged freely. In 1705 the military governor of Turin offered a reward of half a louis d'or for every French head delivered to him, and in retaliation the Duke of Vendôme proclaimed that for every soldier of his killed he would hang ten Piedmontese. A large part of Turin having been destroyed by the French artillery, the Austro-Piedmontese, on their capture of Tortona, massacred the garrison and the civilian population indiscriminately. The shortage of food, which had already become serious in the 1690s after a series of bad harvests, worsened after the outbreak of hostilities. A dramatic index of this situation is provided by the number of children found abandoned in the city of Milan. Rising from 3,590 in the period 1680–9, it stabilised at over 5,300 in each of the next two decades. Only in the decade 1710–19 did it come down (very slightly) – to 5,104. Of these foundlings, a mere 10–12 per cent survived into their third year. The depths of the crisis were reached in the terrible winter of 1709, illustrated in an etching by the popular Bolognese engraver Giuseppe Maria Mitelli which was captioned: 'Hunger and poverty. Great cold and bareness. War everywhere. Disease and death'. Only the good harvests of 1709 and 1710 brought some relief to the exhausted populations. The Bolognese celebrated the event with public masked balls and an unusually high number of operatic performances; they even opened a new theatre, the Marsigli-Rossi.

The phases of the war, as briefly described above, could not fail to exert a double influence on Handel's period in Italy: first, in his travels from one centre to another; secondly, in the texts that his patrons gave him to set to music. Modern scholarly studies have engaged in much speculation about the second aspect.[10] However, it is probably misleading to interpret the taking of sides by the Italian nobility in terms of membership of this or that party. Certainly one may speak, as many do, of the 'Imperial party' or the 'Bourbon party', but only with the proviso that in most cases it was not a matter of ideologically motivated loyalty but rather one of steering a sometimes erratic course between complicated dynastic or family interests. 'Franza o Spagna pur che se magna' ('France or Spain, the thing is to eat') was the watchword of the Neapolitan *lazzaroni* (the city's sub-proletariat) in the sixteenth century, but even the nobility subscribed to this ethos in the early eighteenth century, as demonstrated by the actions of the Duke of Savoy.

Music in Italy at the dawn of the new century

Seeking to account for Handel's decision to visit Italy, his biographer Mainwaring observed:[11]

> The number of schools and academies for Music subsisting in the different
> quarters of this country, and the vast encouragements afforded to those
> who excel in the Art, have long conspired . . . to render it the most eminent
> part of the world for its Composers, Singers and Performers.

The word 'academy' (*accademia* in Italian) had at this time many different meanings. These covered not only literary salons, where music often had a substantial role (especially in the guise of chamber cantatas), but also organisations of musicians, in which religious devotions, welfare, maintenance of professional standards and 'trade union' matters combined in varied proportions. Notable academies of the second kind were the Accademia Filarmonica of Verona, founded in 1543, the Accademia della Morte and the Accademia dello Spirito Santo of Ferrara (respectively 1592 and 1597), the Accademia Filarmonica of Bologna (1666) and the numerous professional bodies invoking the name of St Cecilia that existed in Venice, Rome, Palermo and elsewhere. Some of these organisations aspired also to act as 'schools', in the sense of centres of advanced musical instruction; basic instruction was left, however, to private teachers or to an assortment of welfare institutions (*scuole pie, conservatori, ospedali*) populated in the main by foundlings, orphans and the offspring of the poor. Among such institutions were the four famous *ospedali* of Venice, where only female residents received musical training, and the four conservatories of Naples, attended exclusively by male students. However, similar (albeit less well-known) 'conservatories' existed in Bologna, Rome, Milan, Palermo and many other cities. The great cathedrals and collegiate churches maintained their choir schools, of which those of San Petronio (Bologna), Sant'Antonio (Padua) and San Pietro in Vaticano (Rome) are some of the best documented.

The professional outlets for trained musicians were no less varied. In terms of prestige and remuneration there was a wide gulf between the rank-and-file violinist or choir-member, who often had to hold posts in several minor establishments concurrently merely in order to survive, and the celebrated instrumentalist-composer in the service of a princely court or of a great basilica, who could count on 'vast encouragements', to borrow Mainwaring's phrase. At the end of the seventeenth century Duke Francesco II of Modena used to give presents of diamonds to his musical staff, including the 'cellist Domenico Gabrielli, and even allowed his own physician to treat them. Around the same time Grand Prince Ferdinando de' Medici, Prince Marcantonio Colonna and Cardinal Pietro Ottoboni engaged in a long diplomatic tussle for the privilege of taking the famous harpsichordist Bernardo Pasquini into their service. It was the same Ottoboni who, between 1690 and 1713, treated his employee Arcangelo Corelli almost as a member of his family. Even higher on the social scale stood the *maestro di cappella*, or choirmaster, who was, as a rule, also a composer of vocal music. The peak of the profession was reached, however, by solo singers, especially castratos. Some of the latter enjoyed unparalleled upward social mobility, crowning their careers with the acquisition of large land-holdings and even noble titles. This state of affairs can be illustrated by a few examples.

In the most famous and wealthy of all Italian *cappelle* (a term denoting the complete musical establishment of a church, instrumentalists as well as singers), which was that of San Marco in Venice, *primo maestro* Giovanni Legrenzi (1626–90) and his immediate successors Volpe, Partenio and Biffi drew the same salary, 400 ducats annually, that Monteverdi had once enjoyed. The *vicemaestro* and the two principal organists each earned 200 ducats. All of them were totally at liberty, provided that the performance of their duties in the ducal church did not suffer, to supplement their pay by directing music at one of the *ospedali* or by accepting occasional commissions from theatres, other churches or private patrons. At the time of Handel's sojourn in Venice (1709–10, with possible visits in the preceding two years) deputy *maestro* Carlo Francesco Pollarolo was a successful composer of operas, of which he had written well over sixty and of which many had seen revivals; the first organist, Antonio Lotti, was fast following along the same path, while the second organist, Benedetto Vinaccesi, had produced a considerable amount of secular chamber music (sonatas and cantatas) that was highly regarded by connoisseurs. The basilica of San Petronio in Bologna, in the late seventeenth century a rival to San Marco in the quality and magnificence of its musical performances, had been reorganised in 1701, with a drastic cut in the salary bill, after five years of inactivity. True, the *maestro di cappella*, Giacomo Antonio Perti, earned a respectable annual salary of 600 Bolognese lire, about half as much as his Venetian counterpart Biffi earned, but the leader of his orchestra (Leonardo Brugnoli, one of Corelli's teachers) was now paid only 72 lire, as compared with almost 250 lire in 1695. The Bolognese singers received between 48 and 126 lire according to their ability and length of service. Alessandro Scarlatti's ephemeral appointment (1707) as *maestro* to the Roman basilica of Santa Maria Maggiore brought him the annual salary of 144 scudi, about the same as Perti's post. Like his colleagues elsewhere, he had a right to various additional perquisites, which included free lodging. Even so, Scarlatti must have considered the position insufficiently remunerative for the maintenance of his large family, because in 1709 he resigned it and returned to Naples. Allowing for the difficulty of comparing salaries whose real value was affected by variations in both the cost of living and rates of exchange between different currencies, one thing nevertheless appears certain and constant: a composer, even if he had attained the most coveted position in a 'public' institution, had no choice but to take on extra work for private patrons or opera houses if he wished to live in moderate comfort.

Perti provides us with an example of a financially successful opera composer. In 1696 the Tordinona theatre in Rome offered him 400 ducatoons, equivalent to 4,200 Bolognese lire, to compose and direct his opera *Penelope la casta*, throwing in an additional 40 scudi for his travel expenses and 20 scudi a month for subsistence. For operas produced in his private theatre at Pratolino, Ferdinando de' Medici paid Perti the following fees: in 1700, for the second and third acts of *Lucio Vero*, 60 doppie (just under 1,000 Bolognese lire); in 1708, for *Ginevra, principessa di Scozia*, 300 scudi (more than 1,200 lire); in 1709, for *Berenice, regina d'Egitto*, 100 doppie (about 1,600 lire, the equivalent of thirty-two months' pay in his post at San Petronio) plus a silver dish. Certainly, Perti had a privileged status: in 1711 a middle-ranking theatre in Bologna, the Teatro Marsigli-Rossi, paid his young pupil Luca Antonio Predieri a mere 300 lire for the score of *La costanza al cimento*, without reimbursing his copying costs.

But even the large sums earned by fashionable composers pale into insignificance before the amounts paid to the leading operatic singers for a single season. A surviving 'price-list' of female singers dated 1700 puts at the top, with 500 doppie, Maria Maddalena Musi, nicknamed 'La Mignatta': retiring from the stage in 1703, she married a noted Bolognese lawyer, to whom she brought a dowry of 75,000 lire. Next on the list, with 260 doppie, is Diamante Scarabelli, who was to sing the title-role in Handel's *Agrippina* nine years later. Then come Vittoria Rizzi, with 200 doppie, and Francesca Vannini (future wife of the great bass Giuseppe Maria Boschi, whom she partnered in London during Handel's first season in 1711), with 100 doppie, equivalent to 160 sequins or nearly 570 ducats. Castratos were paid as much or even more. At the beginning of the century the minimum payment for a season at one of the principal Venetian or Neapolitan theatres was 150–200 sequins for a 'second' or 'third' man;[12] this figure needs to be multiplied at least three or four times to arrive at the fee commanded by the best 'leading men' (*primi uomini*), such as Nicola Grimaldi (popularly known as 'Nicolino di Brunswick'), who was made a *cavaliere* by the Republic of Venice in 1705 and dominated the seasons at the Haymarket Theatre in London between 1708 and 1717, or Francesco Bernardi, 'Il Senesino', who between 1707 and 1709 was just rising to fame on the stages of Vicenza, Venice, Bologna and Genoa. The musical strengths of these two singers, both altos with an extraordinary low register and a preference for noble, 'pathetic' utterance over vocal pyrotechnics, seem to coincide with the personal preference of the young Handel with regard to leading male voices, as the parts that he wrote for them in London (in *Rinaldo* and *Giulio Cesare*, for example) show.

Opera

In *Settecento* Italy an evening at the opera was not an exotic entertainment enjoyed exclusively by closed court circles. The very design of
Italian-style theatres, which spread only gradually north of the Alps, is
recognisable as an embodiment of the social system of the *ancien régime*,
where the public becomes an active and passive participant in a process of
social communication going far beyond the potential (and often none too
clear) political implications of the opera's subject: the boxes are for the
rentier class and the wielders of state power; the stalls are for the Third
Estate; the upper circle is for the Plebs. In 1706, discussing with some
anxiety the corrupting influence that their love of opera had on the
morals of the common people, the critic Ludovico Antonio Muratori
blamed the bad example set by the leaders of society – even if that did not
stop him congratulating his friend Apostolo Zeno on the success of his
librettos.[13] In fact, all social classes willingly did their bit to make this
entertainment possible: the nobility with its capital and organisational
ability; the bourgeoisie with its technical and artistic talents; the artisan
class with its manual skills. The government kept a careful eye on everything with the help of its constables and censors, not infrequently intervening with bans and suspensions. In Venice, as elsewhere, an opera
libretto – hence the opera itself – had to be licensed by both a civil and an
ecclesiastical censor. An opera was an affair of state.

In keeping with the prevailing political polycentrism, opera percolated
through Italian society in a manner unparalleled elsewhere. In countless
small cities of the Marches, the *Romagne*, Tuscany, Lombardy and the
Veneto not only Carnival (the period from 26 December to Shrove
Tuesday, which was the regular season for operas, banquets, balls and
revels of every kind) but also a fair, a religious festival or a change of governor could be enough to bring into being a short operatic season, even if
this was limited to a few performances of a single work. Metropolitan
centres such as Bologna, Milan, Florence and Naples could afford the
luxury of several opera houses, sometimes distinguished from each other
by the price of their tickets and hence the social standing of their audiences. The foremost centre for opera was without question Venice,
already the European capital of tourism and pleasure. It was not by
chance that Venice became, in 1637, the first city to boast public opera-
houses to which anyone could gain admittance simply by purchasing a
ticket. Easy-going as ever, the Venetians named their opera houses
indifferently after their proprietors or after the nearest church. Some of
these theatres failed to survive into the new century – the most illustrious
casualty was SS. Giovanni e Paolo, belonging to the Grimani family,

which closed its doors in 1699 after about forty years of activity, while San Luca (also known as San Salvatore), owned by the Vendramin family, went over to spoken drama. In the first decade of the eighteenth century the San Cassiano (Tron), San Moisè (Zane), San Fantino (Michiel), Sant'Angelo (Marcello and others) and above all the prestigious San Giovanni Gristostomo (Grimani) houses remained in operation. In 1710 the Grimani family reasserted its traditional supremacy in Venetian operatic life by turning a second theatre over to opera – the San Samuele, which it had owned for many years. Although our information is a little incomplete, it is possible to calculate that during the first decade of the new century – a time of war, one must remember – Venice was treated, in round figures, to 100 operatic productions, as against 40 in Naples, 50 in Florence (including Pratolino) and 25 in Bologna, where the closure of public theatres was decreed from 1701 to 1705. In prohibiting opera, the government of Bologna was following the example of the mother city Rome, where a papal ban on opera, enacted in 1698 and renewed after the earthquake of 1703, lasted until 1709.

Success in opera, always a precarious achievement, relied in the first place on the singers and the composer, but an equal contribution was made by the set-designer and the costumier, even though these were regarded as mere artisans. When, in 1699, Ferdinando Bibiena, the greatest theatrical 'architect' of the Baroque period and the head of a dynasty destined to colonise all Europe from Lisbon to Stockholm, underwent the humiliation of a public beating by the Duke of San Pietro, he was unable to protest against the affront to his own personal dignity, having instead to invoke the injured honour of his patron Francesco Maria Farnese, Duke of Parma. Very different was the case of the librettist, who was in theory the brains behind the whole operation and thus the most common butt of an audience's ill humour. Zeno, a scholar and a Venetian patrician, would have considered it dishonourable to write librettos for money: for this reason, Ferdinando de' Medici responded to Zeno's dedication to him of *Faramondo* (1699) with the present of five kilograms of silverware. Similarly, when he came to claim from the Milanese impresario Piantanida a 'just recognition' for the libretto of *Engelberta* (1708), Zeno took refuge behind the shoulders of his co-writer Pietro Pariati, whom he described as 'a poor man and a foreigner'. Professional – that is, mercenary – librettists, such as Matteo Noris from Treviso and Silvio Stampiglia from Rome, were in a small minority; the rest were, or at least claimed to be, *dilettanti* – a term that then lacked its pejorative modern associations. Antonio Salvi (1664–1724), several of whose librettos were later adapted for Handel's London operas, was the personal physician to Prince Ferdinando. Nicola Giuvo, the author of Handel's *Aci, Galatea e Polifemo*

(HWV 72, Naples 1708), earned his living as a secretary and librarian to prominent Neapolitan families.

In the final analysis the nature of opera, as a complex 'total work of art', ensured that deficit and bankruptcy were endemic. From an examination of the many operatic balance-sheets that have come down to us, we may estimate that in any opera-house, whatever its degree of prestige, the fees paid to the singers constituted 40–50 per cent of the expenditure, and that the income from the sale of tickets and lease of boxes seldom amounted to more than 75 per cent of the outgoings. The deficit was covered by patrons; the profit, if any, earned by the impresario was derived mainly from his customary collateral activities: selling refreshments and running a casino. In Venice, members of the Grimani family took personal charge of the seasons at San Giovanni Grisostomo, patiently negotiating by letter with the Dukes of Mantua and Modena, the Grand Prince of Tuscany and other rulers for the release of the singers in their service. Love of art for its own sake was certainly an element in these dealings, but one senses as well the operation of a quasi-political diplomacy aimed at improving the connections and reputation of the Grimani family itself. In a typical court theatre such as the Teatro Regio of Turin the sovereign would contribute from his own purse towards the costs incurred by the consortium of nobles (commonly referred to in contemporary sources as *cavalieri*), presided over by one of their number who acted as artistic director; here, the impresario was little more than the franchise-holder of a public service. Though the involvement of a sovereign was exceptional, this was otherwise the most widely practised method of operatic organisation: it was adopted, for example, by the elegant Malvezzi theatre in Bologna.

Naples was different: during the whole of the seventeenth century touring companies, supported by a so-called *ayuda da costa* provided by the Spanish viceroy, were the suppliers of opera, until the Duke of Medinaceli (active between 1696 and 1702) took the initiative of making San Bartolomeo a court theatre in the strict sense of the term, for which he paid heavily out of his own pocket. In the first years of Austrian rule Cardinal Vincenzo Grimani and his successors entrusted the organisation of opera in Naples to agents such as the Bolognese Count Francesco Maria Zambeccari and the impresarios Nicola Serini and Andrea del Po. (The last-named, by profession a stage 'engineer' and set-designer, distinguished himself by the grandiosity and ambitiousness of his activities during the period 1689–1713.) In 1708–10 Zambeccari estimated that managing the San Bartolomeo theatre could make an annual profit of 1,000 ducats; he lamented, however, the 'execrable taste' of the Neapolitans, who preferred to flock to the Teatro dei Fiorentini, where operas in local dialect were given (these works, almost incomprehensible to north Italians, were in fact the ancestors of Neapolitan *opera buffa*). On the other hand, San Bartolomeo and the Teatro dei Fiorentini itself did not spurn composers from north and central Italy during the first decade of the eighteenth century: they performed works by Aldrovandini, Giovanni Bononcini, Albinoni, Carlo Francesco Pollarolo, Lotti and the adoptive Venetian Francesco Gasparini. But these operas were systematically adapted to conform to conservative Neapolitan taste, which still demanded comic roles even in serious (heroic) opera, liked recitatives to be short and required a greater number of arias than were employed elsewhere (including a good number of barcarolles, sicilianas and other genre-pieces of popular inspiration). Masters of this kind of 'customisation' were Giuseppe Vignola, the organist of the viceregal chapel and a composer of operas in his own right, Domenico Sarri and the elder Scarlatti.

A composer needed to take cognisance of the expectations of his audience and his patrons if he was to achieve success in opera. Perti, about to begin a collaboration with the theatre of Pratolino (which eventually lasted ten years) with the composition of *Lucio Vero* in 1700, found himself instructed by Grand Prince Ferdinando to be concise, avoiding over-long repeats and instrumental ritornellos, and to write arias that were 'as little pathetic as possible'. Only a few months later, however, his Neapolitan patroness Aurora Sanseverino, Duchess of Laurenzano (who from 1698 onwards had commissioned from him cantatas, duets and other pieces expressly 'in the pathetic style, as your nature inclines'), reproached him for writing too few arias in his opera for Florence. If we now consider that this same Duchess was the mysterious 'Donna Laura' hinted at by Mainwaring as the lady who commissioned *Aci, Galatea e Polifemo*,[14] we gain an idea of the different, sometimes contradictory pressures under which Handel worked as a visiting composer of opera in Italy.

Geographical variations and personal idiosyncrasies apart, one cannot deny that a tendency towards a common operatic language – rather simplified in comparison with other vocal music – was developing. In 1706 Alessandro Scarlatti, who in twenty-seven years had already written about fifty operas, was told by Grand Prince Ferdinando to write 'music that is rather undemanding and noble, and also rather cheerful when the situation warrants it'.[15] In 1709 Zambeccari explained Scarlatti's lack of success in Naples – in the wake of his reverses in Venice during Carnival 1707 and his abandonment by Ferdinando one year later – by reference to his surfeit of learning and contrapuntal elaboration: 'he is so good that he turns out bad, since his works are very demanding, resembling chamber music . . . his style in opera does not please, for there one needs cheerful stuff and saltarellos, as they have at Venice'.[16]

Other genres and styles; music publishing and marketing

We must turn from opera and look to the chamber duet and the cantata, as well as to instrumental music, to find more refined examples of the contemporary composer's art – refined, that is, in relation both to expressive aims and to harmonic and contrapuntal resource. In these more intimate genres the mastery of Scarlatti, Gasparini and the younger Carlo Maria Clari was widely recognised, but connoisseurs still remembered and valued the marvellous chamber compositions of Stradella, assassinated in 1682. All these musicians provided Handel with ideas, not only of a general kind but also, concretely, in the shape of musical themes. A similar situation obtained in sacred music. Handel showed less interest in the late fruits of Roman polyphony (in the tradition of Palestrina) than in the opulence and many-sidedness of the north Italian *concertato* style characterised by dramatic opposition of two or more *cori*, frequent opportunities for florid solo singing, and elaborate orchestration that was often lent extra splendour by the sound of trumpets and timpani. In this kind of music the leading masters included Perti, already discussed, and more especially his predecessor at San Petronio, Giovanni Paolo Colonna, who was Clari's teacher. But to judge from the borrowings found in the church music of his Italian period, such as *Dixit Dominus* HWV 232 and *Laudate pueri* HWV 237 (to say nothing of those in the later English works *Israel in Egypt*, the 'Utrecht' Jubilate and the 'Dettingen' Te Deum), Handel had regard also for certain minor composers of sacred music, among them Dionigi Erba and Francesco Antonio Urio, a protégé of Ferdinando de' Medici.

In instrumental music, which, alongside the cantata, was the type that enjoyed most favour among amateur musicians, the past, the present and the future coexisted in the form of three major genres cultivated throughout the peninsula: the trio sonata, the concerto with multiple soloists (*concerto grosso*, in the modern sense of that term) and the solo concerto. The three most representative composers, whose printed works were rapidly disseminated north of the Alps, being eagerly 'pirated' by Dutch and English publishers, were Corelli, Torelli and Albinoni. It was mainly through their example that Italian composers of instrumental music began *en masse* to desert their native publishers, who were still mostly wedded to the antiquated technique of printing music from movable type, and instead to place their works with northern firms, which employed the more flexible and elegant method of engraving on copper plates. Torelli led the way with his Op. 6 (Augsburg, 1698); he was followed by Albinoni with his Op. 6 (Amsterdam, *c.* 1711), Vivaldi with his

Op. 3 (Amsterdam, 1711) and Corelli with his Op. 6 (published in 1714, the year after his death).

The final result of this process was evident, half a century later, to Burney, whose graphic description conveys the extent of Italy's socio-economic backwardness in this respect as in so many others:[17]

> The art of engraving music there [Venice] seems to be utterly lost, as I was not able to find a single work printed in the manner we print music in England. In the first place, there is no such thing as a music *shop* throughout Italy . . . Musical compositions are so short-lived in Italy, such is the rage for novelty, that for the few copies wanted it is not worthwhile to be at the expense of engraving and of the rolling-press. Indeed, there, as in Turkey, the business of a transcriber [music copyist] furnishes employment for so many people that it is cruel to wish to rob them of it, especially as that trade seems more profitable than any other.

Handel's career in Italy

An accurate reconstruction of Handel's movements in Italy remains a distant goal. There are still lacunae and questions that only new discoveries in archives may resolve. The traditional account deriving from Mainwaring's biography of Handel[18] is clearly rather confused in its chronology, but some of its details have received surprising confirmation from recent researches: these details include Handel's love affair with the singer Vittoria Tarquini, which seems to have dampened somewhat his relationship with Grand Prince Ferdinando, and also the role played by the mysterious 'Donna Laura' – now identifiable as the Duchess Aurora Gaetani d'Aragona, *née* Princess Sanseverino, who was in many respects a central figure in Neapolitan cultural life at the time.[19] Here is a summary of what is known so far about Handel's time in Italy:

1706

Mainwaring relates that Handel arrived in Italy a short time after Grand Prince Ferdinando, who had visited Hamburg in the winter of 1705–6.[20] We do not know whether Handel took the overland route, proceeding via Hanover, Nuremberg, Munich, Innsbruck and the Brenner Pass – which would have brought him close to his native Halle – or whether he opted instead for another traditional commercial route, which was longer but more comfortable and, above all, allowed him to avoid the Po valley, just then the scene of armies in conflict: this second itinerary would have taken him up the Rhine valley as far as Basel, from where he would have descended the Rhône valley, passing via Lyons to Marseilles, where he could set sail for Genoa and then Leghorn (Livorno), in the heart of Medici territory. It seems very likely that Handel stayed in Florence for the first time in the autumn of 1706, and probably reached Rome before the end of that year.

1707

14 January: The Roman diarist Valesio noted: 'In this city there has arrived a Saxon, who is an excellent harpsichordist and composer and today displayed his skill on the organ at the church of San Giovanni.'[21] Handel probably remained in or near Rome for most of the year: between mid-February and mid-October Cardinal Pamphili and Marquis Ruspoli made payments for his compositions (various cantatas and the oratorio *Il trionfo del Tempo* HWV 46a).
22 February to 19 March: Handel joins the retinue of Marquis Ruspoli. He participates in a stag-hunt at Cerveteri and a visit to the port of Civitavecchia.[22]
April: Handel, in Rome, signs the autograph of *Dixit Dominus* HWV 232.
18 May to 22 June: Handel is a guest of the Ruspoli family at the Palazzo Bonelli in the Piazza Santi Apostoli (Rome) and at their country seat of Vignanello.
8, 13 July: Handel, in Rome, signs the autographs of *Laudate pueri* (HWV 237) and *Nisi Dominus* (HWV 238).
24 September: Annibale Merlini writes to Grand Prince Ferdinando, mentioning the 'famous Saxon' who 'constantly plays' for the Ottoboni and Colonna households.
19 October: Leaving Rome, Handel passes Selva di Grosseto on his way to Florence.
End of year (November or December): *Rodrigo*, Handel's first opera in Italy (HWV 5), is staged at the Teatro del Cocomero, Florence.
December: In Venice?

1708

January–February: Handel is in Venice (the Carnival season ends on 21 February), where he meets the Duke of Manchester and makes friends with Domenico Scarlatti.
26 February: Handel is again in Rome, staying with the Ruspoli household; the copyist Angelini is paid for a cantata by him.
3 March: Handel, in Rome, signs the autograph of his cantata *Lungi dal mio bel nume* (HWV 127a).

Early April: Still in Rome, Handel finishes *La Resurrezione* HWV 47, which is performed during Easter week at the Palazzo Bonelli.

8 May: Ruspoli's accountant settles Handel's subsistence expenses.

16 June: Handel, in Naples, signs the autograph of his serenata *Aci, Galatea e Polifemo* (HWV 72).

12 July: Still in Naples, Handel signs the autograph of his trio *Se tu non lasci amore* (HWV 201a).

July (second half) to September (beginning): Handel is again in Rome, staying with the Ruspoli household.

July or early August: Handel sets to music the cantata *Hendel, non può mia musa* (HWV 117), on a text by Cardinal Benedetto Pamphili.

11–12 September: Handel leaves Rome and the Ruspoli family.

Mid-September (?): Handel is possibly present at the performance of Perti's *Ginevra* at Pratolino, near Florence. It is uncertain whether, at this point, he returned to Rome for a while or stayed in Florence, while continuing to fulfil commissions coming from Rome and, in particular, its Senate (the sacred cantatas *Ah! che troppo ineguali* HWV 230 and *Donna, che in ciel* HWV 233 point to such a connection, despite the absence of documentary evidence or precise chronological indications). Between October 1708 and February 1709 the Ruspoli and Pamphili accounts list payments for 'alterations and patching' to earlier works by Handel, though without confirming his presence in Rome: in fact, the participation of such other composers as Carlo Cesarini (Pamphili's *maestro di cappella*) in these revisions suggests that Handel was absent. On the other hand, the meeting with Agostino Steffani reported by Mainwaring, which for various reasons can have taken place only at this time, argues for his presence.

1709–10

There is no reliable information on Handel's movements until autumn 1709. It has been suggested that he attended the performance of Perti's *Berenice* at Pratolino on 30 September 1709.[23] Handel's presence in Siena in March 1709 for the performance of the sacred cantata *Il pianto di Maria* (HWV 234), which Fabbri believed to have taken place on Good Friday by command of Ferdinando de' Medici, is a complete myth: this cantata is actually a composition by Giovanni Ferrandini (1709–1791), and the document reporting the event is inauthentic.[24] So 1709 is mostly a 'blank' year for information about Handel's activities.

9 November 1709: Handel prepares to return from Florence to Germany via Venice. He obtains letters of recommendation from Ferdinando de' Medici addressed to Prince Carl Philipp of Neuburg, Governor of the Tyrol, and to Johann Wilhelm, Elector Palatine of the Rhine.

November 1709 to February 1710: *Agrippina* (HWV 6) is staged in Venice as the first Carnival opera at San Giovanni Grisostomo theatre. Carnival ends on 4 March 1710: by 9 March Handel has already left Innsbruck on his journey away from Italy.[25]

It is not easy to state unequivocally what hopes and goals Handel had when he travelled to Italy and to what extent he realised them. He arrived there at the age of twenty-one and stayed for about three and a half years – far too long for a simple visitor with an interest in Italian culture or monuments. It is clear, however, that the image of himself that Handel wished to project was that of a gentleman, not a professional musician seeking employment. He was accompanied by some kind of servant, perhaps a secretary. If Mainwaring is to be believed, he preferred, true to his spirit of independence, to turn down an allowance offered to him by the Grand Prince of Tuscany, instead drawing on his own capital for his initial expenses (200 ducats). Nevertheless, at Rome, Naples and 'most other places' he reportedly 'had a palazzo at command, and was provided with table, coach, and all other accommodations'.[26] The accounts of the Ruspoli family, his principal hosts in Rome, show that he consumed – presumably not by himself – a truly enormous quantity of victuals. This suggests that he was entertained on a lavish scale. Cardinal Pamphili paid public tribute to him, penning (and giving to Handel himself to set to music) the text of a fulsome cantata in his praise (*Hendel non può mia musa*). The testimonial on Handel's behalf written by Grand Prince Ferdinando to his brother-in-law, the Elector Johann Wilhelm, speaks of his 'civility of manners, wealth of honest feelings and a full command of several languages', as if to suggest that Handel might be engaged in diplomatic activities in the manner of Agostino Steffani.[27] Strangely, Ferdinando lays little accent on Handel's music, in which he discerns only 'a more than middling talent'.

The eye-witness accounts by non-musicians relating to the early part of Handel's stay in Italy – for instance, those by Valesio and the Florentine Duke Antonio Maria Salviati (in a letter dated 19 October 1707) – identify him as a harpsichordist ('sonatore di Clavicimbalo'). We can be reasonably sure that this was how he too wanted to be regarded. If his prime interest had been opera, he would probably have spent less time in Rome, where the opera-houses were closed, and more time in Venice or Naples. He may have considered taking a position as a 'virtuoso' at a court or in a noble household, such as Corelli held from Ottoboni, but he would have ruled out (despite his great success at writing liturgical compositions for the Catholic rite, as evidenced by his music for a Carmelite service of Vespers)[28] any suggestion of becoming a *maestro di cappella* to a church, if only because of his staunch adherence to Lutheranism. Mainwaring's report of attempts to convert him are probably based on fact; if so, Agostino Steffani, who was a veteran of missionary activity in Germany, probably took a hand.

It is difficult to overestimate the benefit to Handel of his contact at source with Italian music. His encounters and experiences during those years had a profound influence on his development, moulding his own style and providing him with a stockpile of ideas on which he was to draw for the rest of his life: the subjects and librettos of operas and oratorios, which he borrowed and reworked; the marvellously 'old-fashioned' character of his ritornellos in vocal arias; the *concerto grosso* genre (and mode of scoring), which he cultivated long after it became unfashionable in Italy; favourite themes, re-used or paraphrased. It is harder to trace Handel's own impact on the country he visited. He enjoyed his greatest success in Naples, where his serenata *Aci, Galatea e Polifemo* was revived in 1711 and 1713; *Agrippina*, too, was revived at Naples in 1713 with additional arias by Francesco Mancini. In Bologna an aria from *Rodrigo* was originally selected in 1710 for inclusion in a prestigious pasticcio, *Il Faramondo*, but at the last moment was rejected. Another aspect demanding further clarification is Handel's relationship with the Neapolitan nobility and especially with the Viceroy of Naples, Cardinal Grimani. There has been much speculation, insufficiently backed by hard evidence, about the composer's alleged 'pro-Habsburg' and 'anti-papal' stance, which is seen as most manifest in *Agrippina*. But even if Grimani's recommendation and family connections were vital for Handel's access to the Venetian stage, the former's authorship of the libretto of that opera, and therefore Handel's presumed endorsement of its 'message', remain in doubt.[29]

3 Handel's London – social, political and intellectual contexts

William Weber

When George Frideric Handel touched English shores late in the year 1710, he arrived in a country that was in an alarming condition of social change and political turmoil. The composer immediately thrust himself into London's public life on its highest levels. He acted in a diplomatic as well as a musical capacity upon arriving there, emerged as the leading figure in one of the key cultural activities of the upper classes, and in so doing participated directly in the fast-moving changes that were taking place in English life.

What was going on in British politics at the turn of the eighteenth century was novel and forward-looking, but very dangerous. Britain was the first Western nation in which political dispute became public, uncensored, and driven by parties. Despite the triumph of Parliament over the Crown in 1688–89, the country remained deeply divided constitutionally, threatened by the prospect of a new civil war, and shaken by open-ended ideological conflict which was publicly promoted in uncontrolled pamphleteering. If anything, people from other countries saw the English as the wild men of Europe. But in many respects the political activities that began in this period marked the start of modern, ideologically defined political parties. While we must be careful not to cast this history in the terms of mid-Victorian Peelites and Conservatives, a new political order was being established in England at the turn of the eighteenth century.

Handel participated within these developments because he was the leading composer in London's operatic world. Since opera served as the most significant performing genre throughout contemporary Europe, it was by definition intimately linked with political elites and whatever was going on among them, and was affected by the internationalism of aristocratic life in this period, seen most specifically of all in the customs of the Grand Tour. The opera house represented the main venue, save the Houses of Parliament, where members of Britain's elites met most often and in the greatest numbers. It is therefore necessary to examine the founding and development of Italian opera companies in London from a political perspective.

However, 'politics' here does not refer simply to whether someone was a Whig or a Tory, or what posture he or she took towards a Government. Historians now approach political history from a much broader, less institutional perspective than they used to do, viewing politics as a set of social and cultural values and activities related to civic authority that cannot easily be disengaged from other areas of society or culture. They indeed start with the concept of 'political culture', the ideas and customs by which a society dealt with problems of authority in general, that can reveal as much about intellectual as political structures.[1]

Such a perspective helps us understand why the commentary on opera in London that was rampant in pamphlets, poems and essays during the first half of the eighteenth century was filled with a complicated array of musical, political, literary, social and personal meanings that can be quite difficult to sort out. A pamphlet of 1727, published during the legendary rivalry of the sopranos Faustina Bordoni and Francesca Cuzzoni, is unusually blunt:[2]

> Which of the two is the Aggressor, I dare not determine, lest I lose the Friendship of my Great Noble personages, who espouse some the one, some the other Party, with such Warmth, that it is not now, (as formerly) *i.e.*, are you High Church or Low, Whig or Tory; are you for Court or Country, King *George*, or the Pretender: but are you for *Faustina* or *Cuzzoni*, *Handel* or *Bononcini*. There's the question. This engages all the Polite World in warm Disputes; and but for the soft Strains of the Opera, which have in some Measure qualified and allay'd the native city of the *English*, Blood and Slaughter would consequently ensue.

The political situation at the time of Handel's arrival was essentially post-revolutionary in nature. The Civil War that began in 1641 set in motion a sequence of political upheavals that lasted until the defeat of the Jacobite rising in 1745, and the Battle of Culloden a year later, ended a fundamental division over the nature of the monarchy. (In that respect, the British experience is directly comparable to what happened in France between the late 1780s and the firming up of the Third Republic around 1880.) Neither the government that came about at the Restoration of 1660 nor the one after the Glorious Revolution of 1688–9 established a stable regime; the constitutional changes accomplished then and in the Act of Settlement of 1701 made the Hanoverian succession upon the death of Queen Anne a contested political issue. Historians see political stability emerging not simply from constitutional arrangements, but also from the opening up of English politics to ideological partisanship in ways found nowhere else in Europe at the time. The new order emerged from the failure of Parliament to pass a new law for censorship of the press in 1695, the explosion of pamphlets that came with the cessation of controls, and the vibrant political struggles that ensued within almost all areas of public life until the late 1730s, when some forms of censorship were re-introduced. Anyone active in cultural life – poet, playwright, musician or painter – was involved in these disputes, which divided Whig from Tory in fluid but sternly enforced lines of partisanship.[3]

Handel arrived when the crisis was coming to its peak. In March 1710 riots broke out in the City of London among Tories angry at the impeachment of Henry Sacheverell for a sermon he had delivered against the government at St Paul's Cathedral two years earlier. An extremist supported by many London clerics, businessmen and artisans, Sacheverell preached a stern sermon on the theme of 'the Church in Danger' at the 1711 Festival of the Corporation of the Sons of the Clergy. Many members of the Corporation, and most London clergy generally, must have sympathised with him, fearing that the anti-clericalism of Whigs and Latitudinarians would severely limit their authority and their financial perquisites.[4] During his first years in London, Handel seems to have been used by the House of Hanover in its preparations for the Succession, and, probably as a result of Hanoverian introductions, was warmly welcomed by the court. The change of government, from chiefly Whig membership to Tory in 1711, then divided his loyalties between the Hanoverians and the new cabinet, especially when in 1713 he was invited to set the Te Deum for the Thanksgiving following the Peace of Utrecht, a treaty to which the more war-minded Whigs objected strenuously.[5] That Handel moved through these troubled waters with such apparent poise suggests the extent of his political intelligence and independent fortitude.[6]

Important social changes were going on within the English elite groups at this time that bore directly upon developments in both politics and musical life. During the late seventeenth century noble and gentry families, and the many people who served them, began moving to newly built houses in the West End, in an area of Westminster roughly between the Strand and Hyde Park. Under the reign of Queen Anne the court ceased to serve as the focal point of daily life, either in political or social terms, as the place where anyone of consequence had to go.[7] That role was assumed by an array of clubs, public houses, coffee-houses, and theatres, most of them in the West End. The King's Theatre, which housed the premier opera companies, emerged as a key gathering-point, as *The Weekly Journal* said in 1725:[8]

> Musick is so generally approv'd of in *England*, that it is look'd upon as a want
> of Breeding not to be affected by it, insomuch that every Member of the
> *Beau-monde* at this Time either do, or, at least, think it necessary to appear
> as if they understand it; and, in order to carry on this Deceit it is requisite
> every one, who has the Pleasure of thinking himself a fine Gentleman,

should, being first laden with a Competency of Powder and Essence, make his personal Appearance every Opera Night at the Haymarket.

The *beau monde* was itself a social milieu that emerged in the new public world of politics and culture at the turn of the eighteenth century. It should in part be perceived in demographic terms, for it constituted a milieu significantly larger and less intimate than a court but at the same time one much smaller and more distinct than the upper classes of the mass metropolis such as developed in London and Paris in the second half of the nineteenth century. An increasing number of aristocratic and gentry families purchased or rented houses in London, and spent more of the year there, variously for political, social or cultural reasons. There resulted a group – a public – most of whose members knew most of each other by engaging in a closely linked set of social, cultural and political contexts. They at least knew *of* each other; as such, the group was different from a court, where one did know everyone, and also from the amorphous, highly segmented elite worlds that emerged in the subsequent growth of the capital cities, with the accompanying rise of mass politics and mass culture, in the nineteenth century.

During the eighteenth century it was in the capital cities, London and Paris most prominently of all, that a new culture of consumption developed, a product of the concentration of elites and the competitive tendencies that it produced among its members. While it may be argued that the origins of such a way of living were first found in Amsterdam, eighteenth-century London and Paris developed it on a much larger scale, since their courts were much closer at hand and state authority had much greater power than was the case in the United Provinces.[9] Some historians in fact see a redistribution of wealth taking place from the country to the capital cities, enabled by the state and consumed by the central elites.[10] The centrality of these cities within their societies made consumption a public phenomenon such as it had not been before, and from that came the economic power that made the dynamism of eighteenth-century musical life possible.

The *beau monde* was by no means co-extensive with the nobility. At its lower social end it included not only the baronetcy and relations of peers and baronets, but also both men and women whose professional roles led them into the aristocratic world – doctors, financial agents, high-level artists and musicians, cultural entrepreneurs, high-class prostitutes, and so on. This is not to minimise the centrality and the ultimate authority of the nobility in eighteenth-century England, in musical life as much as in society at large.[11] What it does mean is that the social life of this group avoided overtly caste-like conventions and favoured a fairly loose sense of social levels. While the nobility did of course 'pull rank' upon people of lesser social standing, they did so in *ad hoc* circumstances and avoided rigid traditions of social custom – clothing codes, for example, as well as strict separation between classes at the opera – that smacked of an older social order.

Thus there was no strict separation between nobles and commoners in the seating at the King's Theatre (or indeed at the Opéra in Paris); only in the top level of boxes did one find no titled people. By comparison, in Vienna the seats at the Burgtheater served as a wooden barrier between the two classes throughout the eighteenth century.[12] Modernity meant fluid relations between elites in the leading national capitals of Britain and France, and that may be why so careerist a musician as Mozart seems to have been planning a trip to London just before his death.[13]

Still, it is significant that peers of the realm served as Directors of the Royal Academy, and that some of them participated closely in its management. Historians have taken quite different points of view on the role of the nobility in eighteenth-century England; some emphasise the rigidity and conservatism of English life, others how middle classes came to the fore in a fast-changing society.[14] The early history of the opera companies at the King's Theatre suggests a middle-ground interpretation that sees a reinvigoration of aristocratic leadership in the context of the open-ended political world – noblemen taking new cultural and political roles in an unstable public arena. We must not forget how tiny and highly formalised the British peerage was by comparison with the titled classes in any other Western country; even with baronets included, it was possibly one-fortieth the size of its French counterpart. Nowhere else did so small a group of families have political authority vested in such strict legal terms within so powerful a state, and that is why French and Italian nobles looked in awe at their British colleagues, despite their reservations about the country's unstable politics. The respect that foreigners held for the London opera theatre gave a legitimacy to the unusually high fees that singers earned there and that set standards of pay internationally.

Party position was the most important fact of life for anyone in public life during the first three decades of the eighteenth century. Admittedly, Whigs and Tories did not differ socially or ideologically with any great consistency, and individual cases were riddled with contradictions. But conflict there was, especially among authors, all of whom had firm party identities at any one moment in time:[15] Curtis Price has demonstrated that even opera librettos made strong use of political implication in designedly ambiguous fashion.[16]

Musicians, however, were able to be more flexible in this regard, though not always with great comfort. The strength of Handel's independence was his seeming ability to mingle easily with both Whigs and Tories. In his early days in London he chiefly met Tories, but he clearly also came to know well such Whigs as the Duke of Manchester; good connections with Whig families became essential, since the peerage became overwhelmingly Whig by the early 1720s. The King's Theatre provided an important meeting-ground between members of the two factions. The Directors of the Royal Academy were almost entirely Whigs, most of them holding offices in the Royal Bedchamber, but the Subscribers, a larger group, included many prominent Tories.[17] In this fashion did the opera theatre fulfil a civic role in a time of contentious politics. In the quotation cited above from *The Weekly Journal* we find opera depicted in such terms, as a place where polite discourse would supplant faction and disorder, a place more aristocratic than the coffeehouse but still sharing its civic virtues.

It is important to remember that, despite the limitations put upon the British monarch, he or she still held potentially autocratic powers in many areas. The royal house disregarded the limitations of the Civil List, spending much more on the court than Parliament appropriated; the King faced no requirement for that body to approve the principal minister or cabinet, and in military affairs and foreign policy there was no legislative oversight whatsoever. By the same token, even though the court did not control the King's Theatre, far less use its productions for royal celebration, the Lord Chamberlain had direct and powerful authority over the London theatres, and the presence of the King was vital to the success of the opera companies. George I attended the opera regularly when he was in or near London, subscribed £1,000 per season and gave substantial gifts to leading singers, providing an indirect subsidy that was crucial to keeping the financially unsteady enterprise afloat.[18] In such a fashion did the Hanoverian monarchy succeed in fulfilling the expectations that there should be a major opera company in London and that the King should play a role in its promotion, while avoiding any direct public role as its patron. People assumed that a properly constituted opera company was impossible in a monarchy without the participation of the King, and we must admire how brilliantly George I finessed the issues that might have arisen over his participation.[19]

Another major factor that affected Handel's career, and the perception of his works, was religion. Religious implication was a given factor in both the librettos and the settings of Handel's oratorios, and Handel recognized the dramatic potential of religious ideas, both as a believer and as a craftsman.[20] Religion and politics were intricately intertwined in early modern British history.[21] Furthermore, religious issues were immediately relevant to the promotion of Italian opera in London.

Suspicion of Roman Catholicism figured importantly in English resistance to Continental opera. This factor operated quite out of proportion to the reality of the situation, of course. Catholics were neither numerous nor influential in England at the turn of the eighteenth century; though in some cases quite wealthy, members of that faith lived mostly in the north and tended to keep very much to themselves.[22] A small cenacle actually performed Gregorian chant in private services, chiefly at the ambassadorial chapels in London, and even published works on the subject, but they were so discreet about their activities that few outside their group ever knew about it.[23]

English Catholicism nonetheless became the most common popular scapegoat in England in the eighteenth century, as it had been since the Reformation. Almanacs instructed readers that Catholics had brought about the Great Fire of London in 1666, and crowds loved to go after Catholics violently and arbitrarily as late as the Gordon Riots of 1780. Traditional fears were put to a specific purpose in the early eighteenth century when pamphlets warned that French troops were about to impose the Pretender and the Catholic Church upon England. Linda Colley sums up these tendencies:[24]

> the prospect in the first half of the eighteenth century of a Catholic monarchy being restored in Britain by force, together with recurrent wars with Catholic states, and especially with France, ensured that the vision that so many Britons cherished of their own history became fused in an extraordinary way with their current experience. To many of them, it seemed that the old popish enemy was still at the gates, more threatening than ever before. The struggles of the Protestant Reformation had not ended, but were to be fought out over and over again. How could Britons hope to survive?

Fears of Catholic plots linked to the Pretender recurred in the pamphlets about Italian opera, as in the discussion cited above of the rivalry between Cuzzoni and Faustina in 1727:[25]

1. They come from *Rome*:
2. The Pope lives at *Rome*:
3. So does the Pretender.
4. The Pope is a notorious Papist;
5. So is the Pretender;
6. So is Madam *Faustina*,
7. And so is Madam *Cuzzoni*.
8. King *George* (God bless him) is a Protestant;
9. The Papists hate the Protestants;
10. The Pope hates King *George*;
11. The Pretender can't abide him.

12. But Madam *Cuzzoni* and Madam *Faustina*, love the Pope, and in all
     Probability the Pretender.
   Ergo **************
      From whence I infer, that it is not safe to have Popish Singers tolerated
   here, in *England*; but on the contrary, it would be a great Security to the
   Protestant Interest to have a Clause added to some Act of Parliament,
   obliging all Foreign Singers, Dancers and Tumblers, to adjure the Devil, the
   Pope, and the Pretender, before they appear in Publick.

That Faustina and Cuzzoni were discussed in such inflammatory terms
shows how vitally commentary on the opera served as a vehicle for discussing political issues.

Handel had a complicated set of relations with men of letters, since he
remained determinedly independent and avoided becoming embroiled
in the disputes of other artistic fields. The background to current literary
controversies centred on ideas that we have since associated with the
Enlightenment, a movement that arguably began in Britain. While the
term 'Enlightenment' is problematic, and is often used too loosely, diverse
currents of thinking developed in Britain between the 1690s and the
1740s that were sceptical of tradition, custom, the Church and orthodox
theology: these were quite comparable with movements that began in
France around 1720 and therefore deserve the appellation. In some cases
the new ideas amounted to religious freethinking that brought about
severe ecclesiastical reprimands, even trials for heresy or for treason. In
other cases 'enlightened' attitudes grew up among established thinkers,
mainly clerics, producing a situation quite different from that in France.
As John Pocock has argued, the English Enlightenment was far more conservative than its comparable manifestation in France.[26]

Handel had much more to do with the moderates than the extremists
in these matters, since he tended to move towards the mainstream in any
field where he was active. It is not surprising that, being a foreigner, he
kept his distance from the attacks on the Church of England made by
Whiggish, enlightened men of letters, even more so because some of them
also mounted a vigorous campaign against Italian opera. This campaign
had begun even before he came to London, and immediately after the first
production of an all-sung work in an Italian idiom in 1705. Unimpressed
by the dramatic merits of Italian opera, and disturbed by the rash of
popularity given to it by the public, the London *literati* feared that spoken
drama and English musicians would suffer from the fad, and instead
championed attempts at English opera. John Dennis opened the controversy in *An Essay on the Opera's after the Italian Manner* (1706) and *An
Essay upon the Publick Spirit* (1711); Joseph Addison and Richard Steele
gave it a more sophisticated tone with numerous pieces in the *Spectator*;

and pamphlets continued to appear from 1720 up to the early 1740s, spurred on particularly by the premiere of the *Beggar's Opera* in 1728.[27]

Handel also came into conflict with advanced thinking among men of letters when, beginning in 1732, he shifted the focus of his career from opera to oratorio. As Ruth Smith has shown, the oratorio subjects, librettos, and musical settings followed a moderate point of view theologically and, by implication, rejected contemporary freethinking.[28] Indeed, in his selection of the prefatory quotations printed in the *Messiah* wordbook, Charles Jennens alluded critically to John Toland's widely known 'enlightened' book of 1696, *Christianity not Mysterious*, when he stated bluntly that 'without Controversy, great is the Mystery of Godliness'.[29] Almost all of Handel's oratorio librettists were High Church Anglicans hostile to deism and the many new theological ideas of the time.[30] Here as elsewhere, Handel and his librettists followed the mainstream – or one might say *created* a mainstream – in musical and spiritual terms. Their accomplishment was to turn traditional theological notions to new ends in the extraordinary inclusiveness of the works' religious implications. While a few Dissenters objected to the oratorios, especially to their being performed in church, for the most part the works reached a wide public without serious opposition.

We must not let the many disputes in which Handel became embroiled blind us to the power and the imagination of his leadership within the musical world – indeed, within English public life as a whole. In directing London's opera companies and oratorio concerts, he broke new ground in establishing roles for the entrepreneurial musician independent of traditional patronage. That he depended upon the nobility in doing so was typical of the age, since we now know that aristocrats participated in early modern capitalism, for example by modernising agricultural development, promoting mining and making armaments from the ores. Handel's acumen as a businessman pointed into the future of musical commerce. Carole Taylor defined his role perceptively:[31]

> His transition from composer of Italian opera to composer of English oratorio involved a crucial transition from protégé, largely dependent on aristocratic largesse, to independent purveyor of his own works to a more broadly based public. By an ironic twist of fate, the Opera of the Nobility, set up to put Handel to rout, actually dealt a blow to their own form of collective aristocratic patronage. By indirectly sanctioning the running of the Italian opera by a professional, they opened the way to the more commercialized form of patronage by the general public that was to take hold in the second half of the eighteenth century.

The canonisation of Handel, which began even before his death, had implications both forward and backward historically, and it had a great deal to do with British history on a broad plane. On one hand, as I have argued elsewhere, the oratorios represented a healing of wounds opened up during the Civil War:[32] Anglicans and Dissenters came together within the Handelian tradition as they did in no other cultural context. On the other hand, the continuing performance of Handel's works – the oratorios, odes, masques and concertos especially – was the most important starting-point of 'canonic' repertories that were deemed to be great music in ideological terms. The social contexts within which the music persisted formed part of the broad political process between the 1740s and 1780s by which partisan divisions were fundamentally reconstituted and a new national consciousness emerged.[33]

The oratorios and odes contributed significantly in redefining the identities of the nation, the monarchy and the British people. Their performance histories grew out of the traditions established around Purcell's D major Te Deum and Jubilate at the start of the century, and around the extensive repertories of sacred works performed in public concerts or feasts. Such events spanned religious ceremony and entertainment in a fashion special to the age and to the evolution of England since the Civil War. They culminated in the founding of the Concert of Antient Music in 1776 and the presentation of the Handel Commemoration in Westminster Abbey in 1784. The dedication of George III to the promotion of Handel's music – itself an innovation, a King patronising a dead composer – encapsulated the new popular political role of the monarch and the sense of the nation that emerged in the 1780s.

4 Handel's London – the theatres

Judith Milhous and Robert D. Hume

Handel first came to London in his capacity as an opera composer, and that remained his primary occupation for more than twenty-five years. Consequently the 'theatre system' in London had a profound effect on the conditions in which he worked. The fledgeling opera company was far from stable when he arrived in 1710 and underwent several major revolutions in the course of Handel's life: confusing as these are, one must try to make sense of them if one is to understand Handel's often stormy career in the theatre.

London was (in theatrical terms) quite different from any other European city of its time. The multiple theatres that had flourished in Shakespeare's day had been abolished by the Puritans in 1642, and after Charles II was restored in 1660 he granted a pair of perpetual patents, creating a monopoly for two favoured courtiers. Neither Charles nor any of his successors could afford to create a court theatre or to patronise the arts on a lavish scale comparable to the promotion of masques by James I and Charles I before 1642. The London theatres were commercial enterprises dependent on daily ticket sales. The patent grants of the 1660s limited London to just two active theatre companies for more than fifty years: opera (or semi-opera, to be precise) was presented occasionally by the resident companies as part of their regular repertories. When Handel arrived, the patent theatres were Drury Lane (opened in 1674) and the Queen's Theatre in the Haymarket (opened in 1705). The Haymarket theatre was designed and built by John Vanbrugh, who had used government connections to force a genre separation that gave him a monopoly on Italian opera in 1708 and left London with only one company acting plays. Thus Handel was hired by a company in a new theatre that offered only the new all-sung opera imported from Italy, and did so in head-to-head competition with an English playhouse.

Almost nothing beyond the site size is known with any certainty about the Drury Lane theatre. A drawing by Sir Christopher Wren (the 'Wren section' at All Souls, Oxford) has traditionally been used as a basis for reconstructions, but there is actually no proof of any connection. Vanbrugh's theatre can be reconstructed at least in its general outlines.[1] (See Plate 1.) Both theatres were equipped for wing-and-shutter changeable scenery of

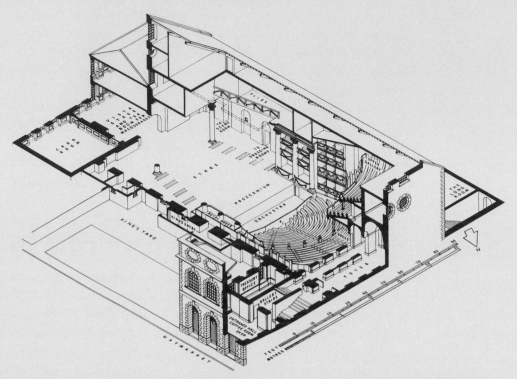

Plate 1   The Queen's Theatre, Haymarket, London, after the alterations of 1707–8: reconstruction by Richard Leacroft

the sort introduced in London by Sir William Davenant after 1660: they could mount elaborate scenic display and machine effects.[2] Both theatres were, by later standards, very small. No precise figures for capacity can be given because there were no individual seats except in boxes. The capacity depended on how tightly people were squeezed onto a bench, and how closely the benches were packed together. From attendance records we know that Vanbrugh's theatre held at least 670 in comfort (400 in pit and boxes, 270 in two galleries), and as many as 940 (500 in pit and boxes, 400 in galleries, 40 on stage) if absolutely packed. Later reports of audiences of 1,500 and 2,000 may be true, but reflect special arrangements for oratorios (rather than operas), with large amounts of seating on stage and in back-stage space.[3] Drury Lane's capacity was probably about the same at this time.

In 1714 a second acting company, housed in the newly rebuilt Lincoln's Inn Fields theatre, was established with the blessing of the new King. The capacity of this theatre was probably 1,200–1,400. The King's Theatre (as Vanbrugh's building was known after the accession of George I) was by this time associated almost exclusively with Italian opera; Drury Lane and Lincoln's Inn Fields staged spoken plays and musicals in English. In 1732 a new theatre at Covent Garden was opened by John Rich, who also owned the theatre at Lincoln's Inn Fields.[4] The two theatres were similar in size and technical capacity, but the availability of the old theatre in 1733 was to make possible the formation of the Opera of the Nobility, a company that opened in direct and disastrous competition with Handel.

Until 1708, when Vanbrugh engineered the monopoly that virtually bankrupted him in four months, opera had always been produced and financed by the English theatre companies.[5] Trying to run a company devoted solely to opera proved difficult. To avoid exhausting both singers and audiences, opera was usually given no more than two nights a week (Tuesday and Saturday) in a season from November or December through to June, a complete season averaging 50 nights.[6] The other theatres performed six nights a week for more of the year (averaging 180–200 nights); they competed directly on opera nights; and they were free to mount musical entertainments of all kinds, provided the language was English. Song, dance, pantomime, masques, instrumental interludes, and full-scale English operas (plus some 'Italian'-style, all-sung operas in translation) were part of the regular fare at Drury Lane and Lincoln's Inn Fields. In the 1720s (when advertisements become more detailed) we find the English theatres featuring entr'acte song, dance, and instrumental music night after night even when the 'mainpiece' was an ordinary spoken play rather than an opera or a musical. The craze for ballad opera started by John Gay's *The Beggar's Opera* in 1728 can be seen as an amalgamation, even a rationalisation, of earlier practices.

In these circumstances, opera management was an uphill struggle. Aaron Hill, the first manager Handel worked with, was summarily fired between the second and third nights of *Rinaldo*, Handel's first opera in London; Hill's successor Owen Swiney fled to the continent, unable to pay his debts, in 1713.[7] The company collapsed in the spring of 1717, the fad for foreign-language entertainment apparently over. But three years later Italian opera was back on the London stage, restored by its social appeal, and in particular by the enthusiasm of George I, a genuine devotee of opera.[8] The King granted a royal charter for a joint-stock company known as the Royal Academy of Music, designed to establish opera properly in London, and he provided a personal subsidy of £1,000 per annum.[9] The result was eight artistically glorious seasons, the standard by which the rest of Handel's career as an opera composer is measured. However, not enough attention was paid to long-term finances: by 1728 the company had run through some £20,000 in capital and had to go out of business, though the Directors allowed Handel and John Jacob Heidegger to use their stock of scenery and costumes.[10]

The exact basis on which Handel and Heidegger ran the 'Second

Academy' between 1729 and 1734 is not known: the likelihood is that their deficits were underwritten by patrons.[11] At just this time the ballad opera craze was drawing musically inclined theatre-goers off to Drury Lane and Lincoln's Inn Fields, and two unlicensed theatres (the 'Little Haymarket' across the street from Vanbrugh's theatre, and Goodman's Fields nearer the City of London) provided yet more competition. The scanty financial records that survive suggest that the Handel–Heidegger opera company struggled along, making little or nothing but probably losing no great amount.[12] The foundation in 1733–4 of a second company devoted to Italian opera, playing on the traditional opera nights, shifted the balance ruinously. At the end of that season the Opera of the Nobility took over the King's Theatre. Surprisingly, John Rich invited Handel to move to Covent Garden, where he assembled a company to do Italian opera and oratorios on nights vacated by the acting company (who had to be paid for doing nothing on those nights). The new partners survived three unprofitable seasons, but by that time the Nobility Opera was in a state of collapse: direct operatic competition had proved the last straw for a genre that in economic terms had always been marginally viable at best.

Most of the income for the opera company came from two sources: season subscribers and walk-in trade. The English theatres depended entirely on daily ticket sales at 4s for a box seat, 2s 6d for a place in the pit, 1s 6d in the first gallery, and 1s in the second. Opera prices were always higher, and settled in 1720 at 10s 6d for pit and boxes, 5s for the gallery. Even when the other theatres demanded 'raised' prices for special occasions, 5s was the top price: by comparison the opera was extremely expensive. Various subscription schemes were tried early in the century, but as of 1720–1 the Royal Academy established terms that were to remain the top price until the 1790s: 20 guineas for 50 nights. At this rate, 200 subscribers would have generated 4,000 guineas per season. The actual number of subscribers is unknown until 1732–3, when there were only 140 of them, 122 of whom paid 15 guineas in full. Even when there was a more solid base of subscribers, about half of the expensive tickets remained subject to the whims of walk-in customers, a precarious way of financing a season.

The Royal Academy was set up in 1720 on the unrealistic budgetary assumption that there would be a full house every night. No actual annual figures have survived, but hypothetical projections based on fragmentary evidence suggest that the company might have taken in £4,000 in subscriptions, £5,000 in daily ticket sales, £1,000 in royal subsidy, and another £1,000 in miscellaneous income – a total of £11,000 for a whole season. Income was not sufficient to meet costs. The largest item of expense was always singers. Back in 1708 Owen Swiney had chosen to introduce international stars into the London operas, hiring in the great castrato Nicolini from Italy for a mind-boggling 800 guineas per annum at a time when the top salary for an English actor was £150. The Royal Academy went further down the same slippery slope, reportedly paying as much as £1,500 per season to Senesino, Cuzzoni and Faustina *at the same time*.[13] A budget forecast made for 1720–1 and now preserved in the Portland Papers (University of Nottingham) allows £6,400 for singers; £1,000 for dancers; £2,500 for scenery and costumes; £2,500 for nightly expenses (including orchestra and house servants, among other items); £400 for new operas and another £200 for librettists; £400 for theatre rent; £300 for other staff salaries: a total of £13,700. What the company actually spent is not known, but the discrepancy between income and outgoings must have been upwards of £3,000 per season. What the Royal Academy paid Handel is likewise unknown. From the previous opera company he was owed £430 in 1712–13, but apparently collected only about £186.[14] His remuneration under the 'Second Academy' was rumoured to be £1,000 per annum, a sum that presumably included composition, directing the orchestra, and serving *de facto* as artistic director.

The average cost per performance for opera in the 1720s was *c.* £240; high salaries and production costs had to be amortised over a season of just fifty nights. At Drury Lane or Lincoln's Inn Fields the total constant and incident charge was well under £50 a day, and the company could write off costs against upwards of 200 performances each season. Small wonder that the opera struggled while the theatres were highly profitable (Drury Lane often boasted £3,000 net profits per annum in this period). The opera enjoyed enormous social glamour, but its economics did not really make sense. By contrast, the theatres could make a lot of money without capacity audiences, and their cash flow was such that they could remain profitable while judiciously hiring expensive singers and dancers, and investing heavily in fancy scenery and staging. Their orchestras were by no means contemptible, though smaller than that at the opera. The English theatres constituted a formidable counter-attraction. The early eighteenth century was not a great time for new plays: Colley Cibber, Susanna Centlivre, and Henry Fielding were the foremost professional playwrights in London during Handel's career. But the theatres offered nightly performances by such players as Cibber, Robert Wilks, Anne Oldfield, John Rich, and in later years Kitty Clive, all of whom were to become legendary figures.

How much the opera was hurt by direct competition from Drury Lane and Lincoln's Inn Fields is hard to say. Someone who wanted to see a fine musical production could go to *The Tempest* (set to music in 1674) or

Bononcini's *Camilla* ('Englished' in 1706) for far less money than the King's Theatre demanded for such hits as *Radamisto* or *Ottone*. Nonetheless, the nature of the attraction was different. The theatres relied on veteran actors and a repertory consisting mostly of proven English classics, mounting some fifty or sixty mainpieces per annum and adding an 'afterpiece' to make a double bill on most nights. The opera usually mounted between six and ten productions per annum, most of them 'new', and it depended heavily on imported superstar singers for audience appeal. Turnover among the singers was high from season to season: novelty was extremely important to an audience many of whose subscribers attended performance after performance.[15]

The theatres put up 'great bills' in the streets, advertised in London's newspapers, and distributed handbills at coffee-houses, taverns and the houses of favoured customers. The opera company's advertisements took pride of place in the daily papers. Few playbills survive (and none for the operas), but the newspaper advertisements are interesting for what they include and omit. Here is one that appeared in *The Daily Courant* for the premiere of Handel's *Alessandro* on 5 May 1726:

> At the King's Theatre in the Hay-Market, this present Thursday, being the 5th of May, will be perform'd, A New Opera call'd, ALEXANDER. No Subscriber, or any other Person with a Subscriber's Ticket, will be admitted without producing it at the first Bar. Gallery 5s. No Persons whatsoever to be admitted behind the Scenes. To begin exactly at Seven a-Clock. The Doors to the Pit and Boxes will be opened at Five.

Handel had been the most celebrated composer in England for more than a decade, but no matter: composers and librettists generally went unmentioned in publicity. Nor were singers named or roles specified: one would never guess that this performance featured the long-awaited London début of the great soprano Faustina. Opera was an in-group entertainment that relied on social appeal and word-of-mouth publicity. Probably most of the opera regulars knew or soon learned who had written the music: the dual-language librettos sold near the time of the premiere generally name the composer (as was the case with *Alessandro*), but not always (no name is given in the wordbook for *Scipione*, produced the same season). Handel was a very public figure, and even in the rather rudimentary newspapers of the 1720s he receives a lot of notice. But though the Royal Academy employed other composers (notably Bononcini), no one seems to have thought to publicise them. In this respect, they were probably following local theatrical practice: Drury Lane and Lincoln's Inn Fields hardly ever name a playwright in their bills, other than famous dead ones like Shakespeare, Jonson and Dryden. Lack of singers' names in the bills is easier to explain: the same small group usually performed together the whole season, and regular patrons must have known exactly who was available.

A particularly difficult factor to judge is the atmosphere of the London theatres, including the opera house, in the eighteenth century. Extant letter and diary commentary on performances themselves is scanty and general until much later in the century, and the newspapers did not publish anything we would regard as an opera review until nearly half a century after the end of the Royal Academy. Riotous disturbances, though they have received extensive commentary from later historians, were in fact extremely rare: if they had been the norm, there would have been less reason to record them as newsworthy. The likelihood is that later patterns of audience behaviour held true earlier as well. If so, then Handel's audience was more reminiscent of that found at cricket matches than at Bayreuth. In all eighteenth-century London theatres members of the audience seem to have felt free to come late; to wander about; to talk with friends in boxes; and to depart whenever they pleased. Liveried servants could sit in the second gallery for free, and their noisy behaviour led to regular threats to expel them and terminate the privilege.[16] The social and economic standing of the opera's pit and box patrons was on average far above those of the other theatres, but there is no reason to suppose that standards of attention and decorum were much higher. Although in the other theatres hearing the words was more important, the texts were often quite familiar. At the opera the constant flow of new productions required that at least the cognoscenti paid enough attention to be able to tell others whether it was good or not. Opera audiences were eager not to miss passages thus certified – to learn when to talk and when to listen. How many members of the audience arrived on time and listened attentively throughout is anyone's guess.

One of the most conspicuous changes in London theatrical entertainment during Handel's career was the boom in oratorios to which he so signally contributed in the 1730s and 1740s. Despite Handel's long association with the King's Theatre, oratorios were particularly welcomed at the other theatres. There were two reasons for this. Oratorios had English librettos, and few imported Italian singers could sing comprehensibly in English. The other factor concerned Lent. London theatres had always been dark during Passion Week, but early in Queen Anne's reign the Lord Chamberlain started to enforce a prohibition of all theatrical performances on Wednesdays and Fridays during Lent. This ban affected both spoken plays and operas, but it did not apply to concerts, and when oratorios developed the authorities evidently decided that such relatively pious, unstaged musical works could be tolerated. The result was great enthusiasm on the part of Drury Lane and Covent Garden for oratorio performances during Lent: the only alternative was a dark house and no income at all. A list of Handel's payments to John Rich for the use of Covent Garden on nineteen nights in 1735–6 is extant. From it we learn that Handel paid £19 5s 8d house rent on Wednesdays and Fridays in Lent, but £52 5s 8d on nights when oratorio or opera kept the regular actors off their stage – i.e. Handel had to compensate Rich for the £33 owed to actors on every performance night.[17] The potential profits were considerable. For *Alexander's Feast* in February 1736 Covent Garden charged 10s 6d for places in the pit and boxes, 4s for the first gallery, and 2s 6d for the second. At these prices a full house could generate upwards of £500. Unlike opera, oratorio could easily make its expenses, and it had the additional advantage of fitting comfortably into the English theatres.

The greatest single change in London professional theatre life during Handel's career affected him almost not at all. In 1737 Sir Robert Walpole succeeded in getting the 'Licensing Act' passed. It closed all theatres but the two holding patents and the opera house; it also imposed strict censorship on all texts to be performed in public, including those of Italian operas, which remained in place until 1968. So far as we know, however, opera and oratorio librettos received their licences with only the most desultory scrutiny. The real importance of the Licensing Act for opera was that it put all small theatres out of business, thereby removing a potential source of competition for the opera company.

Between 1711 and 1717 Handel worked for a series of shaky impresarios; from 1719 to 1728 for the lavishly funded Royal Academy of Music; from 1729 to 1734 as artistic director of a company whose financial auspices are unclear; and from 1734 to 1737 in some kind of partnership with John Rich at Covent Garden. Except during the early years of the Royal Academy, finance was a constant problem. With the exception of the rival Opera of the Nobility in the mid-thirties, opera in London was always essentially a commercial venture in these years, despite subsidies of various sorts. This remained true even during the relatively palmy days of the Royal Academy: it was not a court opera, despite George I's attendance and subsidy. The opera company performed in a public theatre that had been built as a private commercial speculation (designation as the Queen's/King's Theatre notwithstanding), and it had to compete directly against plays and musical entertainments at the English theatres. The opera's great drawing cards were social glamour and star singers. Handel's extraordinary abilities were certainly rewarded: he appears to have earned vastly more money as an opera composer than anyone else was to do in eighteenth-century England. But despite his fame, he had to accommodate himself to a theatre system and an English-speaking public that were less than wholly supportive of the Italian opera to which he was so passionately committed. We cannot be surprised that Handel eventually devoted his energies to English oratorio: the wonder is that he clung so pertinaciously to Italian opera for more than a decade after the financial collapse of the Royal Academy. Oratorios were popular, cost-effective, and highly suitable to the personnel and performance calendars of the English theatres: a concatenation of fortunate circumstances from which Handel was to profit handsomely the rest of his life.

5 Handel's London – British musicians and London concert life

H. Diack Johnstone

When Handel arrived in London in the last weeks of 1710, Henry Purcell had been dead for just fifteen years. His younger brother Daniel, though still active as a professional organist, was no longer a productive composer, and much the same is true of the long-lived William Turner (1651–1740), who, with John Blow (d. 1708), had been the most distinguished of Purcell's colleagues and contemporaries in the Chapel Royal. Likewise John Eccles, the leading English theatrical composer at the turn of the century, and official court composer from 1700 until his death in 1735, had by this time retired from the hurly-burly of life in the city and gone to live in Hampton Wick where, according to Hawkins,[1] he spent most of his time fishing. As for Jeremiah Clarke, one of the more impressive creative talents of the next generation, he had, seemingly for love, put a pistol to his head in late November 1707. Of those native composers still left and active on the London musical scene, much the most gifted were John Weldon (1676–1736) and William Croft (1678–1727), both of whom Handel must surely have encountered quite early on in his first visit.

A former organist of New College, Oxford, Weldon moved in 1701 to London where, as a rank outsider, he immediately succeeded in winning first prize (over the heads of both Eccles and Daniel Purcell, who came second and third respectively) in a celebrated competition for a setting of Congreve's masque *The Judgment of Paris*.[2] In 1708 he succeeded Blow as one of the two organists of the Chapel Royal, and not long after he was also appointed second composer for the Chapel, at which point he seems more or less to have dried up. Though he published a number of attractive songs, his church music, most of which had been written by 1715, is disappointing. Croft is altogether more important. A former Chapel Royal chorister and protégé of Blow, he was by 1710 firmly ensconced not only as principal organist and composer but also as Master of the Children there, and organist of Westminster Abbey as well. As a young man, he contributed a certain amount of incidental music to the plays at the patent theatres; he also wrote a good deal of fine keyboard music, many songs and some instrumental chamber music (mostly early), but it is for his church music that he is now chiefly remembered. His output was considerable and included four large-scale orchestrally accompanied anthems and a Te Deum. Handel would almost certainly have heard some of these pieces, and they may even have provided useful models for his own first efforts in this field. As regards the 'Utrecht' Te Deum and Jubilate, however, the more obvious exemplar was the famous Purcell setting of 1694.[3]

In the words of Thomas Tudway, another of Purcell's immediate contemporaries, but now organist of King's College, Cambridge, and Professor of Music in the University there, Purcell 'was confessedly the greatest Genius we ever had'.[4] In 1710, however, Handel's music was still unknown to the great majority of English music lovers, though some London theatre-goers at any rate would have encountered those extracts from *Rodrigo* which, earlier that same year, had been included in a revival of Ben Jonson's comedy, *The Alchemist*, as the work of an unspecified 'Italian Master'.[5] But Handel himself was by no means backward in coming forward. According to Mainwaring,[6] he 'was soon introduced at Court, and honoured with marks of the Queen's favour'. Indeed, it seems that, on 6 February 1711, less than three weeks before the triumphant premiere of *Rinaldo*, the birthday of Queen Anne was celebrated with[7]

> a fine Consort, being a Dialogue in *Italian*, in Her Majesty's Praise, set to excellent Musick by the famous Mr. *Hendel*, a Retainer to the Court of *Hanover*, in the Quality of Director of his Electoral Highness's Chapple, and sung by Signior *Cavalier Nicolini Grimaldi* and the other Celebrated Voices of the *Italian* Opera: With which Her Majesty was extreamly well pleas'd.

What the work was, however, we do not know. Handel's English Birthday Ode for the Queen, *Eternal source of light divine* (HWV 74), composed two years later, was probably never performed,[8] though it was clearly intended for court performance in the year of the 'Utrecht' peace celebrations.

Quite whom Handel met on that first visit to London we can only guess, but it must obviously have included John Jacob Heidegger (1666–1749), the Swiss impresario already intimately involved in the operatic life of the capital and with whom Handel's own career was, for so many years, to be so very closely connected. Another early professional associate must have been Aaron Hill, who produced the scenario for *Rinaldo* and was later, in 1732, to issue an impassioned appeal to Handel[9]

> to deliver us from our *Italian bondage*; and demonstrate, that *English* is soft enough for Opera, when compos'd by poets, who know how to distinguish the *sweetness* of our tongue, from the *strength* of it, where the last is necessary.

One English poet who knew how to do just that, and was indeed concerned to effect a rapprochement between English words and Italian-style music, was John Hughes (1677–1720), with whom, it is clear from a letter written by Handel at the end of July 1711, the composer was already acquainted.[10] Not long after this, and certainly before 1714, Hughes wrote the words for a cantata *Venus and Adonis,* which was doubtless one of the very first English texts set to music by Handel, while his contribution to Handel's first English dramatic masterpiece *Acis and Galatea,* would now appear to have been greater than hitherto supposed.[11]

When, in the late autumn of 1712, the composer returned to London determined this time to settle, he lived at first with a certain Mr Andrews at Barn-Elms, in an area where, some years later, Heidegger also lived in some style. Barn-Elms (Barnes) would then have been a rural retreat somewhat removed from the musical and artistic life of the metropolis. It was not long, however, before he was invited to take up residence at Burlington House, the palatial London home of Richard Boyle, Earl of Burlington, and in 1717 he removed to Cannons, the no less imposing mansion of James Brydges, Earl of Carnarvon and soon to become first Duke of Chandos. During his time at Burlington House, if not before, Handel would have come into contact with a lively and interesting literary and intellectual circle which included Alexander Pope and his friend John Arbuthnot, John Gay and Burlington's architect, William Kent, an essentially anti-Establishment group, tainted with Jacobitism.[12]

It was evidently soon after his return to England in 1712 that Handel first made the acquaintance of the men of the St Paul's and Chapel Royal choirs. If we may believe Hawkins, the composer frequently attended evensong at the cathedral and then stayed on to play the organ (of which he was said to have been 'very fond'); after that, he often repaired with the gentlemen of the choir to the Queen's Arms tavern in St Paul's Church-yard where he enjoyed an evening of convivial conversation, and yet more music.[13] Burney, commenting on the St Paul's connection, tells an amusing tale of how Handel 'used frequently to get himself and young Greene [i.e. Maurice Greene, then assistant organist of the cathedral] locked up in the church, together' and, with Greene acting as bellows-blower, 'in summer, often stript into his shirt, and played till eight or nine o'clock at night'.[14] The particular attraction of the St Paul's organ is said to have been that it alone among the large English instruments of the period had pedals, but this was not in fact yet the case, though it may well be that a set of 'pull-down' pedals were among the 'Amendments and Alterations' made to it in 1720. Handel's prowess as an organist was well known, and on 24 August 1724 the two eldest of the Royal princesses,

Anne and Caroline, who had by then become his pupils, visited the cathedral to hear 'the famous Mr. Handel' play.[15]

By this time too, Maurice Greene (1696–1755) had succeeded his teacher, Richard Brind, as organist of St Paul's. Much the most talented English musician of his generation, Greene was clearly destined for higher things, and in August 1727 he stepped naturally into Croft's shoes as principal organist and composer of the Chapel Royal. On the death of Eccles in 1735, he became Master of the King's Musick also. In the meantime, he had taken a doctorate of music at Cambridge, and 'in compliment to his performance' had been made (honorary) Professor of Music in the University. According to Hawkins, Greene 'courted the friendship of Mr. Handel with a degree of assiduity, that, to say the truth, bordered upon servility; and in his visits to him at Burlington-house, and the duke of Chandois's, was rather more frequent than welcome'.[16] Later, however, they fell out, so violently in fact that Handel, in Burney's words, 'never spoke of him without some injurious epithet'.[17] Quite what the reason was remains a matter of conjecture; certainly Hawkins' explanation – that it was Handel's discovery that Greene 'was paying the same court to his rival, Bononcini, as to himself' – does not ring true.[18] The break came, it seems, somewhere round about 1727, and may well have had something to do with their relative standing as composers at court. Certainly, the following extract from a spirited polemic in defence of Handel, first published in 1734, would appear to suggest that there was an element of pique involved:[19]

> You must know then, Sir, [that] I [Handel] once went to the World in the Moon [i.e. England] . . . [where] I was immediately admitted into the good Graces of the Court, and principal Grandees; who were all ravished with the Novelty and Exquisiteness of my Compositions: In consequence of which I was declar'd principal Composer to their O[per]as; and *should have enjoy'd* the same Station in the Court Chapels and Publick Temples, only that Place could not be conferr'd upon a Foreigner: Yet upon all Solemn Occasions, they were obliged to have Recourse to me for their Religious Musick, tho' their ordinary Services were all compos'd and performed by Blockheads that were Natives; they claiming from several Laws a Right hereditary, to have the Places in their Temples supply'd with Fools of their own Country.

Whenever the interests of the Royal Family themselves were directly involved, as for example at the Coronation of George II in 1727 and the wedding of Princess Anne seven years later, it was Handel, not Greene, who was called upon to hymn the event; in the latter case the two were openly in contention, because an anthem specially composed by Greene for the occasion was displaced by Handel's *This is the day which the Lord has made* (HWV 262).

Though Italian opera, all-sung, had been but lately (and somewhat precariously) established on the London stage at the time of Handel's arrival, the city enjoyed a teemingly active concert life. Thanks to the pioneering efforts of John Banister in the 1670s, London had become in fact the first city in Europe in which musical performances were commercialised, and auditors actually paid to listen. Among the venues in which concerts regularly took place was York Buildings in Villiers Street, then owned by Sir Richard Steele, the editor of *The Spectator*, and the first room in London specifically designed for the purpose. Located just off the Strand on a site now occupied by Charing Cross Station, it functioned from about 1680 until 1732 when, after a performance of Handel's *Esther* given there on 20 July of that year, it was apparently closed. Even more important throughout the whole of the eighteenth century was 'Mr. Hickford's Great Room', originally situated in James Street, quite close to the opera house in the Haymarket, and later (from 1739) in Brewer Street, in a rather newer and more fashionable part of town. The scene of the young Mozart's English debut in 1765, it survived until 1934 when the building was demolished to make way for the Regent Palace Hotel annexe.[20]

Virtually every reputable artist of the day played in one or the other, if not both, of these concert venues – but not, curiously enough, so far as is known, Handel. Though London audiences were obviously struck by the prodigious dexterity shown in the harpsichord solo passages incorporated in Armida's aria 'Vo' far guerra' in *Rinaldo*, it was not until he started to include organ concertos between the acts of his oratorio performances in the mid-1730s that Handel regularly appeared in public as a solo keyboard player. A newspaper advertisement for a performance of *Teseo* given on 11 May 1713 specifically mentions the addition of 'an Entertainment for the Harpsichord, Composed by Mr. Hendel on purpose for that Day' (which was a benefit for Handel himself),[21] but otherwise all we have are a few fleeting references to such occasional private musical entertainments as that hosted (and charmingly described) by Mrs Pendarves (later Mrs Delany) in April 1734, when Handel evidently 'played lessons and accompanied Strada and all the ladies that sang from seven o' the clock till eleven'.[22] Similar private performances were organised by various musically inclined members of the upper classes, most notably perhaps Viscount Perceval, first Earl of Egmont, but Handel is not known to have been involved, though he probably performed to private gatherings whilst living at Burlington House, and at Cannons.

In an entirely different category were the celebrated concerts promoted by Thomas Britton, the so-called 'musical small-coal man' who, from 1678 until his death in 1714, presided over a series described by

Hawkins as 'the weekly resort of the old, the young, the gay and the fair of all ranks, including the highest order of nobility'.[23] These took place in a long narrow room directly over his shop in Clerkenwell, with Handel, it is said, a frequent performer on the harpsichord. Among the other participants were John Hughes (who was also an accomplished violinist) and Johann Christoph Pepusch (1667–1752), a fellow German expatriate who, at the time of Handel's arrival, was probably the single most active figure on the London musical scene. Also prominent in London's concert life, though not so far as we know in the Britton series, were the German oboist and composer Johann Ernst Galliard, the French-born violinist and harpsichordist Charles Dieupart, the Italian soprano Francesca Margherita de L'Epine (whom Pepusch later married), the leader of the opera house orchestra William Corbett, and John Loeillet, its principal oboist and flautist (i.e. recorder player), the English harpsichordist (and violinist) William Babell, and Nicola Haym, an Italian 'cellist and composer who was soon to become closely associated with Handel, together with a host of lesser artists such as Thomas Clayton who had earlier (in 1705) been responsible for the first English opera 'after the Italian manner'. Other distinguished foreign performers such as Veracini and Geminiani followed shortly – both arrived in 1714 – and the first appearance of the latter at court is said to have been accompanied, at Geminiani's insistence, by Handel himself.[24] Later still, in 1729, the great Italian oboist and composer Giuseppe Sammartini also arrived.

In addition to the concert rooms, music was also regularly to be heard in the theatres, not only as 'First and Second Musick' performed before the play itself began, but also between the acts. Later in the century, mini-operas in English like Boyce's *The Chaplet* (1749) and Arne's *Thomas and Sally* (1760) were often tacked on to the end of the evening's theatrical entertainment, as 'afterpieces'. But the theatres themselves – Drury Lane, Lincoln's Inn Fields, the new Covent Garden Theatre from 1732, and the Queen's (later King's) Theatre in the Haymarket – were often used for concerts as well, chiefly it seems benefit concerts to which various members of the profession would contribute their services in support of a (sometimes necessitous) colleague. Necessitous colleagues were also looked after by annual concerts given in aid of the 'Fund for the Support of Decayed Musicians and their Families' (now the Royal Society of Musicians) founded in 1738, and generously supported by Handel, who was a founder member.[25]

For many eighteenth-century Englishmen, the charitable use of music was a happy way of salving their corporate social conscience, and from the 1740s onwards the various London charities (most notably, in a Handelian context, the Foundling Hospital, as also Mercers' Hospital in

Dublin) were assiduous in summoning music – generally either *Messiah* or the Handel Coronation Anthems – to their aid. Even earlier in the field were the Sons of the Clergy, whose annual festival service held in St Paul's Cathedral was presided over by Greene, and normally involved an orchestrally accompanied setting of the Te Deum together with a specially composed anthem performed by the combined choirs of St Paul's, Westminster Abbey and the Chapel Royal, accompanied by the largest band of instrumentalists to be heard on any suchlike occasion anywhere in the country. During the earlier part of the century, the Te Deum used was usually Purcell's 1694 setting, but the notion that this was replaced by Handel's 'Utrecht' setting in 1713 and that the two were thereafter alternately performed until 1743, when Handel's new 'Dettingen' Te Deum supplanted both, is no more than a myth which originated with Burney.[26] Indeed, there is no evidence of any music by Handel being performed at any Sons of the Clergy Festival prior to 1731.

By a curious coincidence, it seems that it was also in January 1731 that a work of Handel's (the 'Utrecht' Te Deum and Jubilate) was for the first time included in any of the programmes of the Academy of Vocal (subsequently Ancient) Music.[27] This was a prestigious semi-private concert-giving society which, like many other similar groups that sprang up in the period shortly after Britton's death, met regularly in one of the many London taverns with large rooms suitable for music: in this case, the Crown and Anchor Tavern in the Strand. Founded by Pepusch, Galliard, Croft and Greene together with a number of other (mainly Chapel Royal) musicians, the membership grew from a nucleus of thirteen (plus the choristers of St Paul's Cathedral) at their inaugural meeting on 7 January 1726 to as many as eighty-two by the 8th Subscription of 9 April 1730.[28] Included in that number were Bononcini, Senesino, Haym and Geminiani – but not Handel – Pier Francesco Tosi (the famous castrato, now in his seventies), Giuseppe Riva the Modenese ambassador in London, William Hogarth the painter, and the Lords Perceval, Paisley and Plymouth. Concerts were given fortnightly during the season from late autumn to spring and, while the Academy was evidently by no means averse to performing contemporary music (the works of its own composer members in particular), its primary concern, as is implied by the name it was shortly to acquire, was with music of the past. (In a memorandum dated 26 May 1731, the 'ancients' were defined as 'such as lived before the end of the Sixteenth Century'.)[29] A wordbook of 'such Pieces as are most usually performed by the Academy of Ancient Music' published thirty years later is an astonishing document which shows just how extensive was the range of early music in their repertoire; it also reveals the considerable number of Handel's works they had performed.

The Crown and Anchor Tavern, later a favourite haunt of Dr Johnson's (though he himself was notoriously unmusical), was a popular venue for concerts, and it was there, on 23 February 1732, Handel's forty-seventh birthday, that *Esther* was revived under the aegis of Bernard Gates, Master of the Children of the Chapel Royal, with repeat performances on 1 and 3 March, the latter for the Academy of Ancient Music, with which Gates was then also connected. The first two of these performances were, it appears, promoted by members of the Philharmonic Society (also known as the Society of Gentlemen Performers of Musick) which likewise met there, and which, as the 'Philarmonica Club', had earlier subscribed to the publication of *Rodelinda, Scipione, Alessandro* and *Admeto.* The Duke of Chandos is said to have been a member, and its orchestra was led by Michael Christian Festing, the leading English violinist of the period. Other flourishing London music clubs include the Castle Society which met initially in the house of John Young, the musical instrument maker and publisher in St Paul's Churchyard. Quickly outgrowing its accommodation there, it transferred to the Queen's Head Tavern in Paternoster Row and then, in 1724, moved just round the corner to the Castle Tavern from whence it took its name.[30] Also important as a venue for concerts were the Swan Tavern in Exchange Alley, Cornhill, the Globe Tavern in Fleet Street, and the Devil Tavern, Temple Bar, which, from 1731, housed the meetings of Greene's Apollo Society, a splinter group whose organisers had originally belonged to the Academy of Ancient Music.

Such tavern-based musical societies were by no means confined to the metropolis, and contemporary subscription lists show numerous similar groups operating in the provinces. Some, like the Musical Society at Oxford, subscribed to all of Handel's later publications, from *Atalanta* in 1736 to the *Grand Concertos* Op. 6 issued in April 1740; the latter was taken not only by several of the London clubs already mentioned, but also by music societies in Dublin, Canterbury, Salisbury and the 'Ladies Concert in Lincoln'.[31] In almost every case, one assumes, the name of Handel loomed large on the musical agenda, and especially so at the annual performances of the Three Choirs' Festival (founded *c.* 1715). Although it has been said that the first recorded performance of Handel's music outside London took place at Bristol in November 1727,[32] a tantalising reference to 'Hendel's Oritorio [sic], & some of his Anthems' by Claver Morris, a Wells-based west-country physician and keen amateur musician, in a diary entry for 1 May 1724 shows that this cannot be so.[33] Much the most important of all the provincial performances, however, and the only ones in which Handel himself was involved, were those which took place during his celebrated visit to Oxford in July 1733, when

Athalia had its first performance in the Sheldonian Theatre.[34] Four months prior to this, *Applebee's Original Weekly-Journal* of 7 April had informed its readers of the university's intention of presenting 'the celebrated Mr. Handel with the Degree of Doctor of Musick, at the Publick Act to be held there this Summer' and also that 'Signor Senesino is expected to be present on that Occasion'. In the event, however, neither happened, for not only had Handel in the meantime fallen out with Senesino, but he evidently also declined the offer of an honorary degree – on the grounds (so it was said) that his erstwhile friend Maurice Greene had, three years earlier, taken a doctorate in music at Cambridge. How ironic then that one of Greene's orchestral anthems, *O praise the Lord, ye angels of his*, should later find its way into Chrysander's monumental collected edition as the work of Handel himself.[35]

More or less coincident with all of this concert activity was the development of music at the various London Pleasure Gardens from the late 1730s onwards, and here too a great deal of Handel's music was performed. First to open its doors, in June 1732, was Vauxhall Gardens owned by Jonathan Tyers who, five years later, commissioned the well-known Roubiliac statue of Handel which is now in the Victoria and Albert Museum (but was then, in April 1738, sited just to the west of the orchestral bandstand in the Gardens). Here nightly concerts were given throughout the summer months, subject of course to the vagaries of the English climate, but Handel himself was never personally active there, save in 1749 when the Fireworks Music was publicly rehearsed at Vauxhall, an event which caused an enormous traffic jam on London Bridge. Just across the river to the north lay Ranelagh Gardens (opened 1742), whose vast circular Rotunda was impervious to the weather and attracted a rather more fashionable clientele, with musical performances featured not only in the evenings but sometimes in the morning as well. Also important, though rather less so from the purely Handelian point of view, were Marylebone Gardens, just to the east of Marylebone High Street and not far from the present Royal Academy of Music, Cuper's Gardens on the south side of the Thames opposite Somerset House, and, though some distance out of town, Ruckholt House near Low Layton in Essex.[36]

It was in the early 1730s too, and not long after his appointment as Musical Instrument Maker in Ordinary to the King, that the younger John Walsh (1709–66) became Handel's regular publisher. Although Walsh's father (who had founded the firm in 1695) had been responsible for the first edition of the songs in *Rinaldo*, another publisher, John Cluer in Cheapside, printed most of Handel's early operas and also the 1720 set of *Suites de Pieces pour le Clavecin* (HWV 426–33). Nevertheless, it was the Walshes who, from their premises in Catherine Street, just off the Strand, soon came to dominate the market and, by vigorous newspaper advertising, not to mention the innovative use of pewter plates and metal punches (as opposed to expensive copper plates and hand engraving), triumphed over almost all their early eighteenth-century rivals. The combined Walsh catalogue is enormous, and, excluding Handel, runs to well over 2,000 items by almost every major English and foreign composer of the period.[37] The Walshes both showed real entrepreneurial flair, and the son indeed is said to have died worth £40,000, some at least of which he owed to the genius of the man whose music it was now his business to promote.

As far as Handel's relations with his own English contemporaries are concerned, we are faced with a mass of floating tradition, the exact details of which are difficult to ascertain and impossible to verify. From various references in Burney, Hawkins and other subsidiary sources, however, one gains the impression that these relations were by no means entirely cordial. Indeed, if Burney is to be believed, Handel 'had a thorough contempt for all our composers at this time ... and performers on the organ too'.[38] Those who were wise were obviously at some pains not to challenge the great man on his own ground. And with some reason too, for when Greene, inspired perhaps by the success of *Esther* some six months earlier, first tried his hand at oratorio (*The Song of Deborah and Barak*) in the autumn of 1732, Handel promptly retaliated with a setting of the same biblical tale (HWV 51). According to Hawkins, Pepusch immediately 'acquiesced in the opinion of his [Handel's] superior merit, and chose a track for himself in which he was sure to meet with no obstruction, and in which none could disturb him without going out of their way to do it'.[39] Boyce was evidently of the same opinion, his characteristically generous nature being nicely illustrated by his reported attitude to Handel's own borrowings: 'He takes other men's pebbles and converts them into diamonds.'[40] Arne, on the other hand, is said to have been 'aspiring, and always regarded Handel as a tyrant and usurper, against whom he frequently rebelled, but with as little effect as Marsyas against Apollo'.[41]

Though Handel himself is described by Burney as 'impetuous, rough and peremptory in his manners and conversation, but totally devoid of ill-nature or malevolence',[42] it can hardly have been coincidence that the immensely successful first performance of *Alexander's Feast* at Covent Garden on 19 February 1736 was timed to take place on the evening of the same day as the Sons of the Clergy Festival that year, the one and only time that Greene (alone among contemporary musicians) was honoured with a Stewardship and thus made partially responsible for the administration of the charity; it was also the only time between 1731 and 1755 that a

Handel setting of the Te Deum was supplanted by one of Greene's. According to contemporary newspapers, the takings that year were about £200 down on what they had been the year before. It is all the more surprising therefore to find Greene listed among the subscribers to *Alexander's Feast* when, two years later, it first appeared in print. Needless to say, Handel did not reciprocate when, in 1743, Greene's own magnum opus, *Forty Select Anthems*, was also published by subscription.

He did, however, subscribe to a fair number of works by various other English contemporaries. Among them are Boyce's *Solomon* (1743) and *Twelve Sonatas* for two violins and continuo (1747), Chilcot's *Six Suites of Lessons for the Harpsicord or Spinet* (1734) and *Twelve English Songs* (1744), *Six Setts of Lessons for Harpsichord or Organ* [1743] by John Christian Mantel,[43] Nares's *Eight Setts of Lessons For the Harpsichord* (1747), Barnabas Gunn's *Two Cantata's and Six Songs* (1736), the first set of William Felton's *Six Concerto's for the Organ or Harpsichord* (1744), John Bennett's *Ten Voluntaries for the Organ or Harpsichord* [1757] and the first two books of John Christopher Smith's *Suites de Pièces pour le Clavecin* (1732 and 1737). Literary publications to which he subscribed (in addition to the works of Aaron Hill already mentioned) include the collections (all entitled *Poems on Several Occasions*) by John Gay (1720), Henry Carey (3rd edition, enlarged, of 1729), and Joseph Mitchell (1729 also), the last two of which contain eulogistic references to Handel himself.

Among the few English players whom Handel is said to have admired was the blind organist John Stanley (1712–86) who, together with John Christopher Smith, continued the annual Lenten oratorio seasons at Covent Garden (and later Drury Lane) for some years after the composer's death. And though he was not himself, it seems, one of the judges at the election of Thomas Roseingrave (1688–1766) as organist of his own local parish church (St George's, Hanover Square) in 1725, it may well be that Handel provided a subject for the candidates to extemporise upon, as he was also invited to do at the election of Roseingrave's successor in 1744.[44] It does, however, look as if he was called in to give his opinion of the new organ by Gerard Smith, just as, five years later, he was also to do with the rebuilt Schrider instrument at Westminster Abbey; though he had evidently been asked to comment on an almost identical Renatus Harris organ for St Dionis Backchurch in December 1722, it seems that, when it came to the actual trial (in June 1724), he was unable (or unwilling) to appear.[45] Another with whom he must from time to time have been closely associated was Greene's friend the violinist (and composer) Michael Christian Festing (d. 1752), who from 1737 led the opera orchestra, the band at Ranelagh and several of the City musical societies, and was, it seems, the moving spirit behind the establishment of the 'Fund for the Support of Decayed Musicians and their Families'. Abraham Brown, his successor as director of music at Ranelagh, ought also perhaps to be mentioned as having led the orchestra for the Foundling Hospital performances of *Messiah* in 1754 and 1758. Likewise Matthew Dubourg (1703–67), who succeeded Festing as leader of the King's Musicians in 1752: ten years earlier, when he was Master and Composer of State Music in Ireland, he had led the band during Handel's visit to Dublin.

English singers with whom Handel worked include several well-known names, most notably the tenor John Beard (*c.* 1717–91), for whom he wrote the title roles in *Samson* (1743), *Belshazzar* (1745), *Judas Maccabaeus* (1746) and *Jephtha* (1752); as a boy chorister of the Chapel Royal Beard also sang in the first London performances of *Esther* in 1732. Nor were his activities confined to the world of oratorio (or to the music of Handel either, for that matter). A former pupil of Bernard Gates at the Chapel Royal, he made his operatic debut as Silvio in the 1734 Covent Garden revival of Handel's *Il Pastor Fido*, and during the following years, he appeared in no fewer than ten Handel operas, creating roles in *Ariodante, Alcina, Atalanta, Arminio, Giustino* and *Berenice* (1735–7); he also took part in numerous ballad operas, pantomimes and other more serious pieces by Arne, Boyce, Lampe, De Fesch, J. C. Smith and others. Less distinguished, but similarly active in both opera and oratorio, was William Savage (1720–89), who first sang as a treble in *Alcina*, and then for two or three years as an alto before his voice finally settled as a bass; a competent organist (and composer too), he subsequently became Master of the Choristers of St Paul's, and on Handel's death in 1759 he was given the composer's ring by his executors.[46] The tenor Thomas Lowe, on the other hand, was best known as a popular theatre and pleasure gardens singer; nevertheless, he too was closely associated with Handelian oratorio from 1743 onwards and, though nothing like so versatile, it seems, as Beard, had no fewer than half a dozen roles (including the title role in *Joshua* and the part of Septimius in *Theodora*) specially written for him.

Also very much in the public eye during this period was the soprano Cecilia Young, who sang in the premieres of *Ariodante* and *Alcina* (1735) and married Arne two years later. Likewise Susanna Maria Cibber (Arne's sister) was not only a good mezzo-soprano, but was soon to become the finest tragic actress of her generation; the centre of a messily public marital dispute in 1738, she then left the stage, only to reappear in Dublin where she sang for Handel in 1741–2 and again later in London. (It was incidentally of her singing of 'He was despised' in the first performance of *Messiah* that Patrick Delany, husband of Handel's long-standing friend and admirer, is reported as saying: 'Woman, for this all thy sins be for-given thee!')[47] Nor must we forget the celebrated Anglo-Irish actress and soprano Kitty Clive, who made her reputation as Polly in *The Beggar's Opera*, and for whom Handel not only wrote the part of Dalila in *Samson*, but also a couple of little-known but nonetheless delightful English theatre songs.[48] Her protégée and pupil Miss Edwards was another soprano who sang regularly for Handel in the 1740s and also took part in plays as well. Among the later English male soloists were two basses: Robert Wass, who was the first Zebul in *Jephtha* (1752), and Samuel Champness, who sang Time in the 1757 premiere of *The Triumph of Time and Truth*.

Handel's chorus singers in his oratorios included performers drawn from the ranks of the Chapel Royal, Westminster Abbey and St Paul's Cathedral choirs (see Chapter 18), and it was entirely fitting that all three should be involved when, at his own request, the composer was finally laid to rest in the Abbey itself.[49] The treble line for the oratorio choruses, it appears, was usually provided by the boys of the Chapel Royal under the direction of Bernard Gates (1686–1773), who, as a bass singer himself, had been closely associated with the composer from his earliest days in London and, more or less inadvertently in 1732, presided over the birth of Handelian theatre oratorio in London. Among Gates's Chapel Royal col-leagues who also sang for Handel during the first ten years or so after his arrival was the great English countertenor Richard Elford (d. 1714), for whom Handel wrote the alto solo in the first version of the anthem *As pants the Hart* (HWV 251a), Francis Hughes (also an alto), and Samuel Weely (bass). On the secular front, he was associated, though only very briefly, with the long-lived English bass singer and composer Richard Leveridge (1670–1758), the contralto Jane Barbier, Mrs Ann Turner Robinson (soprano), and the Scottish tenor Alexander Gordon, who trained in Italy and returned to London in 1719 where he sang in the spring 1720 and 1723 seasons of the Royal Academy before abandoning his operatic career to become a scholar, author and antiquary.[50] But far more important than any of these was Anastasia Robinson (*c.* 1692–1755), who made her debut as a soprano in 1714 and later that same year sang Almirena in a revival of *Rinaldo*. In May 1715 she created the role of Oriana in *Amadigi*, but by the end of the decade her voice had dropped to contralto. As a member of the Royal Academy, she sang in all the operas between spring 1721 and summer 1724 when, two years after her secret marriage to the elderly Duke of Peterborough, she retired from the stage.

That Handel totally dominated the English musical scene during the period from 1710 to 1759 (and indeed for many years after his death) is undeniable, but that he somehow cowed his English musical compatriots into submission and stylistic servitude, as has so often been suggested in the past, is a nonsense which I have laboured elsewhere to expose.[51] They all spoke the common musical *lingua franca* of the era, a language ultimately rooted in Italy and perfected for general European usage by Corelli in the closing years of the seventeenth century, but one which, for all its confident self-assurance, did not totally inhibit the development of certain regional accents. Though the essential Englishness of the music of Handel's English contemporaries is undoubtedly easier to recognise than it is to define, he himself was by no means impervious to its charms, as is evident enough in some of the later works, *L'Allegro, il Penseroso ed il Moderato* in particular.[52] Even *Deborah*, the first of his oratorios to be written for the London theatre, shows strikingly English features in the (non-da capo) air 'How lovely is the blooming fair' and especially in the duet 'Smiling freedom, lovely guest'. Likewise the strophic setting of 'Ask if yon damask rose' and 'Ye verdant hills' in *Susanna*, while 'Queen of summer, queen of love', the opening chorus in Act 2 of *Theodora*, might almost have been written by Purcell himself.[53] Clearly the question of stylistic influence and cultural interaction is by no means as entirely one-sided as has generally been supposed.

6 Handel's London – Italian musicians and librettists

Lowell Lindgren

During the fifty years preceding Handel's half-century in London, Italian music gradually eclipsed the French, which had enjoyed much favour after Charles II returned from France in 1660. Purcell had abetted this change in taste, for he had 'faithfully endeavour'd a just imitation of the most fam'd Italian Masters; principally, to bring the seriousness and gravity of that sort of Musick into vogue, and reputation among our Country-men, whose humor, 'tis time now, should begin to loath the levity, and balladry of our neighbours'.[1] Italian music had overwhelmed the English as well as the French by 1714, when John Macky noted that the decade-old theatre 'for *Opera's* at the End of the *Pall-Mall*, or *Hay-Market*, is the finest I ever saw, and where we are entertained in *Italian* Musick generally twice a Week . . . The *English* affect more the *Italian* than the *French* Musick; and their own Compositions are between the *Gravity* of the first, and the *Levity* of the other . . . They have now a good many very Eminent Masters; but the Taste of the Town being at this Day all *Italian*, it is a great discouragement to them'.[2] This was true for instrumental as well as vocal genres. When reflecting upon the 'circumstances which concurred to convert the English Musick intirely over from the French to the Italian taste', Roger North (*c.* 1650–1734) found the decisive step to be the arrival of Corelli's sonatas and concertos, which 'cleared the ground of all other sorts of musick whatsoever' and 'are to the musitians like the bread of life'.[3] Corelli was the only Italian to be revered unreservedly by the English during Handel's lifetime. Handel of course had performed with him in Rome before he joined the throngs of admirers in England by utilising Corelli's works as models for some of his own.[4]

England's attractiveness to a foreign musician was summarised in 1713 by Johann Mattheson: 'In these times, whoever wishes to be eminent in music goes to England. In Italy and France there is something to be heard and learned; in England something to be earned; but, at best, in the Fatherland [i.e. Germany] music is something to be consumed.'[5] The ability to earn money – anything from a living wage to an immense fortune – was undoubtedly London's main attraction for Italians. Yet, since they were Roman Catholics and most English were not, London could be inhospitable, as it ultimately became for all of the Italians employed by Charles II in 1660–79 and by James II in 1685–8.[6] The few who arrived in the 1690s are known mainly from reports of public concerts, which were in their infancy in London (and were non-existent in Italy). The first two Italians featured at them were 'the Italian lady' and the castrato Pier Francesco Tosi, both of whom sang in London and returned to Italy in 1693.[7] A decade later, foreigners typically remained much longer, in some cases because the War of the Spanish Succession (1701–13) had severely reduced their opportunities for employment at home – as Handel must have experienced when he travelled in Italy during these years.

The ensuing paragraphs will briefly characterise the Italian instrumentalists, composers, librettists, singers, dancers and scene painters who flourished in London during Handel's half century in the city, then summarily note how British musicians, patrons and critics received them.

The first Italian musician who came to London in the 1700s and stayed until death was the Roman 'cellist Nicola Francesco Haym (1678–1729). When the violinist Nicola Cosimi was invited to serve the Duke of Bedford in 1700, he brought his friend Haym with him. The two arrived in March 1701 and were generously supported by the Duke, who was the dedicatee of the first musical opus published by each. They received further recompense for teaching and for playing at various noble homes, at public concerts, and between the acts of plays given at public theatres. Such opportunities for freelance musicians in a land that was free from military battles led one Italian to describe England as 'the terrestrial paradise'.[8] Haym subsequently earned his keep by playing in the opera orchestra, managing the career of his companion (the singer Joanna Maria, Baroness Linchenham), reworking scores for the London opera house, editing Italian literary works and opera librettos (including about ten set by Handel), serving the Earl of Carnarvon as 'cellist and composer (1715–18), publishing bibliographical studies concerning ancient medals and Italian books (1719–26), working as secretary or stage manager for the Royal Academy of Music (1722–8), and writing *A General History of Musick* (which was never published, and is not known to survive).

Names are known for about seventy other Italian instrumentalists who worked in Britain between 1710 and 1760, while Handel was there. They are mainly found on orchestral rosters,[9] in newspaper advertisements for concerts[10] and at the end of dedicatory prefaces in their published compositions. Such sources may provide only a surname, and they often supply the only known reference to a performer's stay in England. Thus we can often only surmise that those who came spent years rather than weeks

Table 6.1 A select list of Italian instrumentalists in London

Violinists	*Bass viol player*
Mauro d'Alay	Fortunato Chelleri
Attilio Ariosti	
Giovanni Stefano Carbonelli	*Contrabassist*
Pietro Castrucci	Stephano Storace
Prospero Castrucci	
Francesco Geminiani	*Lutenist*
Felice Giardini	Carlo Arrigoni
Niccolo Pasquali	
Giuseppe Passerini	*Oboists*
Francesco Scarlatti	Francesco Barsanti
Francesco Veracini	Antonio Besozzi
	Carlo Besozzi
'Cellists	Giuseppe Sammartini
Filippo Amadei	
Giovanni Antoniotto	*Trumpeters*
Giovanni Bononcini	Girolamo Bartolotti
Andrea Caporale	Giovanni Battista Grano
Giacomo Cervetto	Signor Manselli
Giuseppe Dall'Abaco	
Nicola Haym	
Salvatore Lanzetti	
Giovanni Schiavonetti	

or months in Britain. Since the evidence that survives is altogether sketchy, the total number who came may well have been twice or thrice the currently known number of seventy. As might be expected, most were string players: there were twenty-nine violinists and fourteen 'cellists. All the instrumentalists presumably also played the harpsichord, but those who were primarily or exclusively harpsichordists included Tommaso Gabrielli, Pietro Giuseppe Sandoni and Adamo Scola. The names of some of the most prominent instrumentalists are given in Table 6.1.

Too little is currently known about the London careers of most of these instrumentalists to determine whether they, like Haym, typically supplemented their performance activities with several other lucrative or lustrous endeavours. Like Cosimi and Haym, many gained esteem, and presumably a profit, by publishing their sonatas or cantatas, either shortly (e.g. d'Alay, Geminiani and Sammartini) or some years (e.g. Ariosti, Barsanti, Cervetto and Sandoni) after their arrival. Many earned money by teaching, and they customarily 'advertised' by means of their performances and publications rather than in newspapers. Some of the male performers managed the careers of female singers: among such pairs were Schiavonetti and Isabella Pilotti, the castrato Girolamo Polani and Maria Maddalena Salvai, Sandoni and Francesca Cuzzoni, d'Alay and Faustina Bordoni, and the harpsichordist and/or 'cellist Santo Lapis and Signora Lapis. During the 1750s grandiose, yet vain, hopes of earning a fortune must have led the librettist Francesco Vanneschi, the composer-instrumentalists Domenico Paradisi (Paradies) and Giardini, and the singers Regina Mingotti, Giuseppe Ricciarelli and Colomba Mattei to manage the London opera house in solo or joint ventures.[11] In a far more modest vein, Scola earned money by accompanying, teaching, preparing scores for publication, and making copies of scores. Perhaps the only performer whose activities rivalled Haym's in terms of variety was Geminiani, whose restless career involved many trips to Ireland and the continent, much dealing in paintings, the directing of a Masonic concert series in London, teaching, and publishing activities: seven musical works between 1716 and *c.* 1755, six practice manuals for musicians in 1748–60, and various arrangements of works by himself and by Corelli.[12]

The Italian composers who worked in London when Handel was there included at least fifty of the seventy Italian performers plus another twenty for whom no performance activity is known. The latter were mainly opera composers – e.g. Nicola Porpora (who was in London in 1733–6), Giovanni Battista Lampugnani (1743–4 or 5), Vincenzo Ciampi (1748–56) and Gioacchino Cocchi (1757–72) – who presumably played harpsichord continuo for their works. Like Handel, a significant number remained in Britain until death: these included Haym and Ariosti (d. 1729), Sammartini (1750), Pietro Castrucci (1752), Pasquali (1757), Prospero Castrucci (1760), Geminiani (1762), Gambarini (1765), Carbonelli (1772), Barsanti (1775) and Cervetto (1783). Elisabetta Gambarini (b. London, 1731) exemplifies the usual performer/composer duality: she sang in Handel's oratorio productions in 1746–7, published her harpsichord pieces and songs *c.* 1748–50, and composed a new ode for her benefit concert on 15 April 1761. Others might have remained in England if retirement (Cocchi and Paradisi), a scandal (Bononcini) or career-related reasons (including loss of favour in London) had not taken them back to the continent. As is well known, Handel extensively borrowed and transformed music by Italian composers, and these included at least one (Bononcini) with whom he worked in London.[13]

Only five Italians were active as librettists in London while Handel was there. Since almost all of 'their' texts were derived from librettos that had previously been produced in Italy, their hackwork mainly consisted of cutting out two-thirds of the recitative, then rewriting a little or a lot of the remaining one-third. Without such a reduction, a bored English public might have fled from the opera house, because the poetic artifice expressed in Italian recitatives was meaningless to them. In addition to such cuts, at least one-third of the aria texts were replaced, sometimes by 'suitcase' arias provided by composers or singers. Such work was apparently done without complaining by Nicola Haym (who might have done as many as thirty-five adaptations in the period 1706–29), Giacomo Rossi (who did four in 1711–13 and perhaps did several more for Handel after Haym died in 1729), Angelo Cori (who did nine in 1734–7) and Francesco Vanneschi (who presumably did many in 1741–59). Paolo Rolli, who adapted at least thirty-four between 1720 and 1744, complained about all aspects of the task. Since he was a *poet* who had been trained with Metastasio, he preferred lyrical fables to the super-charged histories demanded by English audiences, and he often lyrically (rather than dramatically) rewrote the works he adapted. He viewed his fellow adaptors – and most other mortals – with haughty disdain. His undoubted brilliance earned him the patronage of Princess (later Queen) Caroline, who chose him as the Italian instructor for her children.[14] Rossi and Cori had come to London to teach Italian, and they presumably continued to do so until they died in the city. Librettists of the day typically functioned as stage managers, and this was the role of the Secretary to the Royal Academy of Music, a post first held by Rolli (1720–2), then by Haym (1722–8). Cori and Vanneschi had similar duties, which ranged from prompting to managing.[15]

In the 1700s, the first Italian singer who came to stay in 'the terrestrial paradise' was the soprano Francesca Margherita de L'Epine (*c.* 1680–1746). During the 1703–4 season, this 'tawny Tuscan'[16] and the fiery yet 'fair *Toftida*'[17] (the English singer Catherine Tofts) each sang Italian arias between the acts of plays on different nights. According to a journalist who clearly detested foreigners, Christopher Rich, the manager of the Drury Lane Theatre, thus utilised L'Epine as 'his *Italian* Decoy-Duck, which he has lately paid through the Nose for, in order to draw Fools into his Nets with'. Resentment against the intruder climaxed bizarrely on 5 February 1704, when Tofts's maid bought oranges 'in order to pelt Mrs. *Lepine* off the Stage, while she was Singing to the Audience that knew not a Syllable of the Matter, out of their Senses; and this Mrs. *Lepine* took in d[amna]bly in Dudgeon that she should be so serv'd, after coming so many Miles to make Fools of 'em: which made the aforesaid Mr. *R*[*ich*] take off the Maid aforesaid, for Affronting the Gentlewoman aforesaid'.[18]

This 'Gentlewoman' was soon joined by other 'Italian Decoy-Ducks' and by 1709, when Tofts left London (for Venice!), they had virtually excluded English singers from London's fledgeling operatic endeavours. Tofts had been the star of *Arsinoe, Queen of Cyprus* (January 1705), the first opera sung throughout – 'in the Italian manner' – to be publicly staged in London. While it was being sung at Drury Lane in English, John Vanbrugh opened his new theatre in the Haymarket with *Gli amori d'Ergasto* (April 1705), 'perform'd by a new set of Singers, arriv'd from *Italy* (the worst that e're came from thence); for it lasted but 5 Days; and they being lik'd but indifferently by the Gentry, they in a little time marcht back to their own Country'.[19] When Haym's adaptation of Giovanni Bononcini's *Camilla* was produced in English at Drury Lane in March 1706, its cast included one foreigner, Joanna Maria, as Lavinia. Before the end of 1706, two others, L'Epine (as Camilla, the role sung by Tofts in March 1706) and the newly-arrived eunuch Valentino Urbani, had also sung in the opera. In December 1707 these three sang their roles partly, mainly or completely in Italian.[20] A year later they became mere accessories to the great eunuch Nicolino Grimaldi ('Nicolini'), who made his London debut in Haym's adaptation of Alessandro Scarlatti's opera *Pirro e Demetrio* (December 1708). Nicolini portrayed Pyrrhus in fifty-nine performances, and proved to be the mainstay for Italian operas during his seven seasons in London (1708–12 and 1714–17). Beginning in March 1710, audiences were treated to his realistic battle with the lion in *L'Idaspe fedele* (*Hydaspes*), which he performed forty-six times. Then he portrayed the Christian hero who overcame pagan witchcraft in forty-seven performances of *Rinaldo* (February 1711), the first London opera with music by 'Signor Georgio Frederico Hendel, Maestro di Capella di S. A. E. d' Hanover'. The original cast of *Rinaldo* included one Englishman and seven Italians: three eunuchs, three women and one bass. The English singer, a bass, is barely worth mentioning, for he sang only five lines of recitative.

The casts of the Italian opera companies in London during Handel's time in the city were dominated by the seventy-five women and sixty-five men who came from Italy. Two-thirds of the Italian men were eunuchs. Only seven tenors and five basses are known to have sung in serious works, but eleven of the men who sang in comic operas were presumably tenors or basses. Most Italian singers stayed in London for few seasons: 60 per cent stayed for only one or two, 70 per cent stayed no more than three, and 80 per cent stayed no more than four. The rapid turnover was undoubtedly caused by the clamour for novel voices, which were the focus of audience attention. Among the singers of the first rank who came, Faustina Bordoni and Farinelli (Carlo Broschi) stayed for three seasons, while Giovanni Carestini and Angelo Monticelli stayed for three and later returned for one more. Nicolino Grimaldi, Gaetano Guadagni and Antonio Montagnana (bass) spent seven in the city, while Giuseppe Boschi (bass), Francesca Cuzzoni, and Anna Maria Strada del Pò spent nine. Senesino (Francesco Bernardi) spent fourteen and Giulia Frasi spent twenty-eight, while Caterina Galli died in Chelsea, fifty-seven years after her first appearance in London.

The quality of the leading singers was by far the most significant contributor to the success of any Baroque drama. Thus it is not surprising that Vanbrugh, the manager of the opera house in spring 1708, proposed that his three main singers (Valentini, Tofts and L'Epine) should each have one share in the undertaking, while his three chief musical arrangers (Haym, Charles Dieupart and Johann Christoph Pepusch) should divide one.[21] From December 1708 until June 1717, Nicolini – rather than any score, stage design or dancer – was the *primum mobile*;[22] he was contracted to supply serious operas[23] and was lauded for his superb acting abilities.[24] No other Italian singer in Handel's London is known to have received any such contract or praise. Senesino starred as the principal male singer from November 1720 until Farinelli's vocal agility astonished all (even Rolli and Senesino) in October 1734. John Gay wrote to Jonathan Swift in February 1723 that 'Senesino is daily voted to be the greatest man that ever lived', and it seems likely that the anonymous versifier of *The Session of Musicians* (1724) astutely avoided naming the hero crowned at the end, so that the advocates for both Senesino and Handel could justifiably claim that their man had received the crown.[25]

Singers of the first rank did perform at noble homes and, during the summer season, at noble spas like Bath; but few are known to have interacted in other ways with Britishers. The only one known to have taught singing was Maria Gallia, who sang in London in 1703–10, then returned in 1722 'with a view of maintaining her Self by Schollars'.[26] Only a few are known to have married Englishmen: Anna Signoni Lodi married the violinist William Corbett in 1703;[27] Maria Manina married a Mr Fletcher *c.* 1715, then the musician Seedo (Sydow) in 1727; Celeste Gismondi, while at Naples in 1732, married a Mr Hempson, with whom she came to London, where she died on 11 March 1735. The most striking interaction of Italian singers with the English language and with British singers came about through their performance in English theatre works, most notably in Handel's oratorios. When Handel revived *Esther* and *Acis and Galatea* in 1732 and produced *Deborah* and *Athalia* in 1733, his casts consisted largely of Italians. One of them was the tenor Filippo Rochetti, who, beginning in 1724, had sung in works produced in English at the playhouses.[28] In later years Handel made use of many worthy Italians, such as Caterina Galli in 1747–54, Domenica Casarini in 1748, Gaetano Guadagni in 1749–53, and Giulia Frasi from 1749 until his death. Guadagni also sang the role of Lysander in John Christopher Smith's *The Fairies* (Drury Lane, February 1755).[29]

The foreign dancers who performed – usually between the acts – in London theatres during Handel's years in the city were mainly French, but about thirty-five women and twenty-five men from Italy also danced there. They did not equal the fame of the most noted French dancers, such as Marie Sallé (1707–56) who was in London in 1725–7 and 1734–5 (when she danced in four works produced by Handel), or Marie Camargo (1710–70) who was there in 1732 and 1750–4. Nor did they settle in England, as did the Viennese Eva Maria Veigel (1724–1822), called Violette, who arrived in 1746 and married the actor-manager Garrick in 1749.[30] The first group of Italian dancers came with a *commedia dell'arte* troupe in 1726–7, and sixteen dancers (some of whom were French) participated in one of its performances.[31] Very few Italian dancers appeared in London during the 1730s, but after 1740 they became frequent. Among the first were the Neapolitan Antonio Rinaldi, called Fausan (or Fossan or Fossano), and his wife, Signora Costantini.[32] When answering a query, Fleetwood, the manager of Drury Lane, admitted that the Fausans had attracted the large audiences that provided him with funds to pay his actors' salaries.[33] The Fausans head the list of names given on the title page of the first volume of *The Comic Tunes, &c., to the Celebrated Dances Perform'd at Both Theatres by Sig^r. & Sig^{ra} Fausan, Mons. Desnoyer and Sig^{ra} Barberini, Mons. & Madem. Michel, for the Harpsicord, Violin or German Flute. Compos'd by Sig^r. Hasse* (1741). By 1761, eight such volumes of tunes, mainly for dances performed at the opera house, had been published.[34] A pioneering study of them has identified the dancers who performed in 1740–59.[35] The published collections indicate the increasingly important role of Italian dancers and dance music in London's theatrical productions after Handel's 'retirement' from Italian opera in 1741.

Joseph Addison's ridicule of stage effects in Handel's *Rinaldo* is well known,[36] yet even Addison admitted that 'Scenes affect ordinary Minds as much as Speeches; and our Actors are very sensible, that a well-dress'd Play has sometimes brought them as full Audiences, as a well-written one'.[37] Handel must have insisted upon fresh and spectacular stagings for his London operas, because about fifteen of them had new designs and a relatively large number of special effects, which was extraordinary in an age that typically utilised stock sets and only a limited number of effects because audience attention, like production funds, was lavished instead upon the singers.[38] Handel conceivably collaborated with five Italian designers, whose work in London is, alas, only sketchily known. The first was Marco Ricci, the presumed painter of four pictures depicting 'opera rehearsals', two of which are conjecturally off-stage rehearsals of *Pirro e Demetrio* (December 1708).[39] (See Plate 7, p. 187.) Ricci, working together with Giovanni Antonio Pellegrini, first provided an 'entire Set of new Scenes' for the Queen's Theatre in April 1709, then designed the new sets for *L'Idaspe fedele* (March 1710).[40] The second was Roberto Clerici, who created his first set of scenes for the opera house in May 1716, then served as 'Engineer to the Royal Academy', according to the libretto for Giovanni Porta's *Numitore* (April 1720). The third was Giovanni Servandoni, who

Plate 2 Stage design by John Devoto, 1724, probably for a set
representing a Roman temple

reportedly created seven sets of scenes in London (perhaps all of them for
an opera of about 1723).[41] The fourth was John Devoto, whose long career
in London is known to have included only one Italian opera, probably
Lotario (December 1729).[42] (See Plate 2.) The last was Jacopo Amiconi,
who conjecturally worked at Covent Garden while Handel was there in
the 1730s.[43] Our information is much less sketchy for Antonio Jolli, the
only significant designer who worked in London when Handel was
writing oratorios rather than operas. According to information given in
opera librettos, he designed and painted all the scenes for *Rosalinda*

(January 1744), *Annibale in Capua* (November 1746), *Mitridate* (December 1746), *Bellerofonte* (March 1747) and *Semiramide riconosciuta* (May 1748). He apparently managed the King's Theatre at least during the 1747–8 season, because when he dedicated *Semiramide* 'To the Ladies' he declared that it would be 'the last Opera I shall bring on this Season'.

These, then, were the approximately 320 Italian instrumentalists, composers, librettists, singers, dancers and scene designers who in many ways dominated the musical life of Handel's London. Their endeavours were supported by other Italians in the city, including diplomats, such as Giuseppe Riva and Giovanni Giacomo Zamboni,[44] impresarios, most notably Giovanni Francesco Croza,[45] and many businessmen, among whom were those married to female singers: Casimiro Avelloni to Margherita Durastanti, Michele Palermo to Anna Dotti, and Aurelio del Pò to Anna Maria Strada. Handel was, of course, not the only successful foreigner from a country other than Italy: they included a significant number of instrumentalist-composers (e.g. Charles Dieupart, Matthew Dubourg, Johann Ernst Galliard, one or more members of the Loeillet family, James Paisible and Johann Christoph Pepusch). There were, however, very few singers, no librettists, and only two noteworthy scene designers (Joseph Goupy and Pieter Tillemans) from other countries. To these must be added many French dancers and one ubiquitous manager, the Swiss John Jacob Heidegger, who was inextricably involved with most operatic endeavours between 1707 and his death in 1749. But Handel and other non-Italians were much more highly valued if they, like Jakob Kremberg in 1697, could claim to have 'lately come out of Italy'.[46] A similar point was wittily made in the report of a benefit concert given at Salisbury in 1742 by a violinist named Kneller:[47]

> when the night came only fifty persons were present; the reader may perhaps wonder, but the reason may be soon assign'd for Kneller having so thin an audience; his name not flowing with vowels, occasioned the people to imagine him but an indifferent performer. It is a just remark, that if any person of merit in the musical world should unfortunately have his name end with a consonant, he seldom succeeds; on the contrary, a name that flows with an *ini*, an *ani*, or a *gobioni*, hardly ever fails of making a fortune.

How were British musicians affected by the influx of so many Italian competitors? They retained their primary roles at London playhouses, but lost them at the opera house and at concert venues. A few, all of whom were probably Roman Catholics, went to Italy to study and/or perform, and they – like Kremberg – sometimes advertised their Italian patina upon their return. Among them, the eldest who overlapped with Handel's stay in London was the countertenor John Abell (b. Aberdeenshire, 1659), who performed in Italy and elsewhere on the continent during at least four different periods in his life. He is first known to have 'newly return'd from *Italy*' on 27 January 1682,[48] and last known to have done so on 30 June 1715.[49] For Handel, the most significant British singer who had been in Italy was Anastasia Robinson (b. Italy, *c.* 1692), who sang at the London opera house in 1714–17 and 1720–4. The only British singer who returned after singing in Italian productions was the tenor Alexander Gordon (b. Aberdeen, *c.* 1692), who sang at Messina and Naples in 1716–18, had 'lately arriv'd from Italy' when he performed at a concert on 7 December 1719,[50] then sang for the Royal Academy of Music in 1720 and 1723.[51] Much less is known about the Italian experiences of instrumentalists. The violinist Matthew Novell, for example, refers vaguely to 'the time of my Forreign Travels' in the dedication of his *Sonate da camera* (London [1704]). The Dean and Chapter of St Patrick's Cathedral, Dublin, granted money in December 1709 for the Italian journey of the organist Thomas Roseingrave (b. Winchester, 1688), who could thereby 'improve himself in the art of music . . . that hereafter he may be useful and serviceable to the said Cathedral'.[52] In Venice, Roseingrave 'became very intimate with the young Scarlatti, [then] followed him to Rome and Naples, and hardly ever quitted him while he remained in Italy'.[53] The only British instrumentalist known to have settled in Italy was the flautist Robert Valentine;[54] he married Julia Baretti, and they had a family in Rome.[55] The most fascinating Briton who went to Italy was, however, the violinist William Corbett. He apparently led the opera orchestra at London in 1705–15, then settled at Milan in 1716 with his wife, Anna Lodi. He returned to London in 1724, when he played 'several Pieces on the Viol de Venere, a particular new Instrument, never yet heard of in England, after the New Manner of Signiora Faustina',[56] and in 1728, when he published *Le Bizarie Universali . . . Concertos in four parts . . . Composed by William Corbett, Delitante, on all the new Gusto's in his Travels thrô Italy, Opera VIII.* When he returned to stay in 1732, a scurrilous pampheteer accused him of having been a spy during his many years in Italy.[57] During Handel's entire career in London, Italians there were often suspected of espionage for the Pretender,[58] which sometimes adversely affected their conditions of employment.[59]

Why did so many Italians come to London to perform, compose or design during the half century beginning in 1710? Mainly because they could not resist English offers of lavish patronage. In early 1703, for example,[60]

> a famous young woman, an Italian, was hired by our Commedians [in London] to sing on the stage, during so many plays, for which they gave her 500 pounds: which part (which was her voice alone at the end of 3 Scenes) she performed with such modesty & grace, above all by her skill, as there

was never any (of many Eunichs & others) did with their Voice, ever
anything comparable to her. She was to go hence to the Court of the K[ing]
of Prussia, & I believe carryed with her out of this vaine nation above 1000
pounds, every body coveting to heare her at their privat houses, especialy
the noble men.

Although such gossip may often contain round figures that are quite
exaggerated, it does provide a good indication that Italians, even if they
were not first-rate, were given a luxurious reception in 'il paradiso terrestre'. Another early example is John Downes's assertion in 1708 that
'Madam *Delpine* since her Arrival in *England* [four years ago?], by Modest
Computation . . . got by the Stage and Gentry above 10000 Guineas'.[61]
Projected salaries are listed in extant documents for various operatic
seasons,[62] but they do not include the amounts that Italians earned from
dedicatees, from gentry who sponsored concerts in their homes, or from
patrons of the benefit performances for individual singers or instrumentalists. Nicolini, for example, who was paid 800 guineas for the
1708–9 season and reportedly earned another 800 for his benefit performance on 19 January 1709,[63] might have earned hundreds more from
private performances. Extant ledgers that record income and outlay, or
the names and contributions of subscribers, provide further evidence of
the immense sums spent on opera.[64] The dedicatee of a libretto or score
may have typically given the dedicator a rather large sum, and authors
must have earned far more by dedicating a work to more than one person.
Haym, for example, dedicated his edition of *La Gerusalemme liberata di
Torquato Tasso* (1724) to King George I, then dedicated the twenty plates
within the volume to twenty different noblemen. Another way to earn
money was to publish by subscription. For his collections of opera songs
in the mid-1720s, Handel garnered 120 subscribers for *Rodelinda*, 58 for
Scipione, 80 for *Alessandro* and 57 for *Admeto*, while Bononcini obtained
238 for his *Cantate e duetti* (1721) and Ariosti mustered 764 for his collection of six cantatas and six lessons for viola d'amore (1724). Ariosti's
number, which may be the largest for any eighteenth-century musical
print, includes 42 dukes and duchesses, 105 earls and countesses and 146
other lords and ladies; 133 of them are identified as subscribers to the
Royal Academy of Music.[65]

How did British literary critics react to the lavish patronage for all
things Italian? Since most of them were dependent upon the success of
plays for their livelihood, they launched frequent and bitter attacks upon
Italian opera when it was being established in London. John Dennis published several, the first of which was *An Essay on the Operas after the
Italian Manner . . . with Some Reflections on the Damage which they May
Bring to the Publick* (1706). A year later, Colley Cibber lamented in the

Epilogue to one of his plays, *The Lady's Last Stake*, that he would have to change his name to 'Seignior Cibberini' in order to survive the change in taste. Richard Estcourt parodied *Arsinoe*, *Camilla* and *Thomyris* in his *Prunella: an Interlude Perform'd in the Rehearsal, at the Theatre-Royal in Drury-Lane* (12 February 1708). Charles Gildon railed against 'prodigal Subscriptions for *Squeaking Italians* and cap'ring Monsieurs' in 1710.[66] Richard Steele and Joseph Addison lauded some singers and productions, but mainly ridiculed them in nine issues of *The Tatler* (1709–11) and fifteen issues of *The Spectator* (1711–12). In *Poetical Miscellanies* (1714), edited by Steele, the poems concerning opera include one addressed to the departing Nicolini ('Back to thy own unmanly *Venice* sail') and one in praise of Addison's successful tragedy *Cato* ('The Brood of tuneful Monsters you controul').[67]

But such venomous outbursts against the Italians had little effect. The only way to combat them effectively was to beat them at their own game, that is, to draw audiences back to the playhouses with entertaining pantomimes, English masques and English operas. The intent, according to Cibber's preface to his masque *Venus and Adonis* (Drury Lane, March 1715), was to 'give the Town a little good Musick in a Language they understand' and to 'reconcile Musick to the English Tongue'.[68] In January 1717, John Rich mounted Bononcini's *Camilla* in English at Lincoln's-Inn-Fields Theatre as his rival to *Rinaldo* in Italian at the King's Theatre. Since support for the expensive Italians had flagged, the new edition of the *Camilla* libretto included a shrewd address 'To the Nobility and Gentry':

> The Persons concern'd in the reviving of *English Opera's* lay before the Town the Scheme of their Undertaking . . . Their first and principal Design is to fix these Entertainments, and make them more lasting in *England*. It has been observ'd, that if we shou'd have the Misfortune to lose the best of the *Italian* Performers, either through Age, want of Health, or their Customary Inclination of returning to their Native Country, *Opera's* must necessarily fall. But it wou'd be happy if we had young People train'd up here in *England*, and instructed to sing after the *Italian* Manner; (and sure the Town will be willing to encourage such a Nursery, who may emulate those Excellent Performers:) This wou'd be a Means not only to establish but perpetuate these favourite Entertainments . . . Those *Artificial Voices*, which are the peculiar Product of *Italy*, may well be spared; and we are apt to believe the *English* will never regret the want of them in their own Country.

Rich likewise revived *Thomyris* in May 1717, and the same address was inserted into its libretto dated 1719. When the absence of the leading castrato, Senesino, meant that there was no Italian opera in autumn 1726,

Rich once again revived *Camilla*. In January 1728 he again revived *Thomyris*, then produced *The Beggar's Opera* by John Gay.[69] Since this ballad opera 'made Rich gay and Gay rich', many ballad operas were produced during the remaining three decades of Handel's career. But more important for Handel was the next attempt to establish 'English operas after the Italian manner'. The repertory included not only works by Thomas Arne, John Frederick Lampe and J. C. Smith the younger, but also unauthorised productions of Handel's *Esther* and *Acis and Galatea*, to which the composer reacted swiftly by mounting his own revised versions of the works and ultimately by writing the oratorios by which he is best known today.[70]

Italian musicians and theatrical artists were thus wooed to Handel's London by extraordinary emoluments. All new arrivals were keenly awaited, for they were expected to keep Londoners up to date by displaying the most recent Italian compositional styles and performance practices. Since English money was able to buy the *best* that Italy had to offer, it is not surprising that the English and non-Italian foreigners were increasingly relegated to back seats at London's opera house and concert venues after 1710. The only one who escaped this fate is Handel, who perhaps did so by spending half a decade in Italy just before he spent half a century in London. Yet even he might not have weathered all the whimsical changes of fashion if the Hanoverian monarchs (George I and II) had not remained his staunch supporters in all ways and at all times. He certainly would not have written the great works we know today if the finest Italians of the age had not been in London to inspire and perform them. Thus we should in no way regret the importation and influx of expensive Italians, because they produced and inspired many glorious works, and much of the money spent on them would not otherwise have been spent on the arts.

7 Handel's English librettists

Ruth Smith

None of Handel's English writers could be described as professional librettists in the sense of making their living by writing librettos, though all of them except the wealthy Charles Jennens (1700–73) had to earn their livings.[1] It is not certain whether oratorio libretto-writing was a money-earning activity; we do not know if librettists shared in composers' benefit nights, or if there was a royalty arrangement on the sale of wordbooks. As with other forms of writing, there could be an expectation of financial return from a dedication. Thomas Morell (1703–84) dedicated his first libretto, *Judas Maccabaeus*, to the Duke of Cumberland, 'as a compliment . . . upon his returning victorious from [quelling the Rebellion in] Scotland', and was rewarded with 'a handsome present'.[2] Some phrases of Handel's suggest that he may usually have paid his English librettists. Having received the second instalment of the libretto of *Belshazzar* he writes to the author, Charles Jennens: 'I profess my Self highly obliged to You, for so generous a Present', and once the final instalment has arrived, he reiterates his 'grateful acknowledgments for your generous favours',[3] which implies gratitude for something not only estimable but not ordinarily given. But libretto-writing was only one intermittent activity among many others for Handel's English collaborators; none was as fully engaged in this occupation as, for example, Paolo Rolli was with Italian opera librettos. Only John Gay (1685–1732) and Samuel Humphreys (*c.* 1698–1738), the earliest collaborators, were writers to the exclusion of other occupations. Jennens was a patron, connoisseur and heir to large estates; Newburgh Hamilton (*fl.* 1712–59) was steward to the third Earl of Strafford and his family; Thomas Broughton (1704–74), James Miller (1704–44) and Morell were Church of England clergymen, Broughton having a successful Church career which took him to a prebendal stall at Salisbury Cathedral. (Miller's career demonstrates that in the eighteenth century a clerical calling did not preclude secular literary activities.)

The librettists and literature

The librettists were very diverse individuals, but inasmuch as they had a common identity they would perhaps be best described as men of letters, well-educated contributors to the intellectual scene of their day. In their lives and work – including their librettos – they engaged with and gave expression to contemporary artistic, religious and political concerns. Jennens and Miller studied at Oxford University, Broughton and Morell at Cambridge. Only three of the librettists – Gay, Hamilton and Miller – had experience as playwrights, and that, perhaps unexpectedly, in the field of comedy. But all of the librettists were literary practitioners. Humphreys was a noted translator of foreign literature: before collaborating with Handel in oratorio, he had been providing translations for the wordbooks of Handel's Italian operas. Jennens was the driving force behind the Virgil commentary of his friend Edward Holdsworth, and in later life he published innovative editions of Shakespeare's plays. Morell was a distinguished classical scholar, editor and teacher, and was reputedly responsible for much of Hogarth's book on visual aesthetics, *The Analysis of Beauty*.[4]

Of all the librettists, Miller had the strongest literary standing.[5] His consistent and incisive criticism of the follies and vices of the age cost him his public favour as a playwright, and his mordant style would not have led one to expect him to produce the libretto of *Joseph and his Brethren*, an unequivocally sentimental drama. His satires now recall those of Alexander Pope, and in fact Pope drew on several of them. He was a tireless critic of bad art; like Pope and other writers of the time (including Handel's collaborator Aaron Hill), he passionately argued that good art strengthens a nation, that bad art corrupts it, and that degenerate artistic forms (masquerades, pantomimes) and foreign influences diluting national identity (such as Italian opera) were harming Britain. In *Harlequin Horace, or the Art of Modern Poetry* (1732) he mentions Handel in this regard. According to Miller,

> Since *Masquerades* and *Opera's* made their Entry,
> And *Heydegger* and *Handell* rul'd our Gentry;
> A hundred different Instruments combine,
> And foreign *Songsters* in the Concert join . . .
> All league, melodious Nonsense to dispense,
> And give us *Sound*, and *Show*, instead of *Sense*.

This is from the edition of *Harlequin Horace* published in February 1735. By the time of the next edition, later in the same year, Miller had revised his opinion of Handel: '*Heydegger* and *Handell* rul'd our Gentry' now reads '*Heydegger* reign'd *Guardian* of our Gentry', Handel no longer being damagingly associated with 'melodious nonsense'. Miller may have been influenced by hearing the revivals of *Esther*, *Deborah* and *Athalia* performed by Handel during March at Covent Garden. Certainly from this date he did not criticise Handel in print, and by 1739 in *The Art of Life* he was according him the highest praise, linking him with Pope, devoting thirteen admiring lines to an enthusiastic description of his *Saul*, and commending Handel's oratorios in a couplet that claims the composer as an ally in his reforming intentions:

> When such Delights your leisure Moments know,
> Virtue and Wisdom from Amusement flow.

With oratorio, Handel had produced the exact contrary of the debased pantomime forms against which *Harlequin Horace* had contended, and from having excoriated him, Miller eventually turned to writing for him.

The librettists and religion

Religion was as much a common tie between the librettists as literature. Those who were clergymen all published vindications of Christian doctrine, responding, like hundreds of their fellow clergy, to the new biblical criticism and deistical thinking which cast doubt on the integrity of the biblical text and hence undermined its authority – an interesting point in connection with Handel's oratorios, which largely drew their texts from the Bible (see Table 7.1, pp. 100–1).[6] Broughton, who published a massive 1,200-page encyclopedia of comparative religion,[7] took up a central challenge of the free-thinkers which is also central to the oratorios. From Matthew Tindal's *Christianity as Old as the Creation* (third edition published in the year of the first public performance of *Esther*) to Lord Bolingbroke's *Letters on the Study and Use of History* (published in the year of the first performance of *Jephtha*), God's directive to the Israelites to invade Canaan and destroy the Canaanites, and their efforts to obey Him, were repeatedly held up as appalling instances of the Old Testament's tendency to cite morally reprehensible behaviour as exemplary and to promote an idea of the deity irreconcilable with an ethical 'supreme Being'. The specific instance of the Canaanite invasion, which forms the groundplot of *Joshua*, was crucial because this was the Israelites' first military action as a nation, a precedent (good or ill according to the biblical reader's attitude) for all subsequent Israelite defences of their terrain and for all aggression in the name of religion – including the wars and conquests of eighteenth-century European powers. Broughton's answer to Tindal, *Christianity distinct from the Religion of Nature* (1732), is characteristic of the orthodox response in canvassing every possible justification: the Canaanites were wicked and deserved what they got; the conquest led ultimately to the Gospel; the innocent must expect to be destroyed along with the wicked in a national disaster; the innocent were rewarded in the afterlife; children were spared being taught idolatry by their parents; the Israelites were only instruments of deserved divine vengeance; and the whole event was an eternally useful lesson against idolatry.

Several of the librettists besides Broughton were equally devoted to the defence of orthodox religion. Humphreys wrote a colossal biblical commentary based on the work of all his major predecessors from the Church Fathers onwards, *The Sacred Books of the Old and New Testament, Recited at Large* (1735): this comprised three folio volumes, each of over a thousand pages, with an Introduction defending the Bible against charges of forgery and spuriousness. Jennens was a scholarly, evangelising supporter of the Church. He left legacies for the Society for the Propagation of the Gospel in Foreign Parts and a fund for lectures on the catechism; he gave money for the rebuilding of the church in his family's parish of Nether Whitacre, and arranged for the parish tithes (which were due to him as landowner) to be returned to the church. He funded the publication of a treatise against atheism, his extensive library was stocked with hundreds of volumes of sermons and theological works, and his picture collection contained an unusually high proportion of religious, especially biblical, subjects. Even the fireplaces of his mansion were, most unusually in English architecture at this date, adorned with reliefs of biblical scenes (the raising of Lazarus, and Daniel in the lions' den, both typifying the Resurrection), and to crown the monument which he erected to his friend Holdsworth he commissioned from the great sculptor Louis François Roubiliac a statue of Christian Faith which was unprecedented in English sculpture and is unique in Roubiliac's oeuvre.

Morell's commitment to the defence of Christianity is rather endearingly indicated by his commentary on Locke's *Essay concerning Human Understanding*, which he wrote, according to his handwritten note on the flyleaf, for the erudite Queen Caroline.[8] This note includes a list of books referred to in his commentary, and more than half of them are about religion rather than philosophy, the largest proportion pertaining to debates stimulated by deism. Locke's analysis of perception and ratiocination was for Morell a prompt to argue the claims of faith. As he himself wrote in his *The Christian's Epinikion* (1743):

> Can ye, ye deists, the Apostle hear
> With thankless Ear?

In the 'Prefatory Copy of Verses on Divine Poesy' prefixed to his *Poems on Divine Subjects, original, and translated from the Latin of Marcus Hieronymus Vida, Bishop of Alba (and M. A. Flaminius)* (1732, reissued

1736), Morell commends the defence of religion through poetry and modestly enrols himself in the tradition of 'sacred Bards' as an apprentice of his illustrious English predecessors – the names he lists include Isaac Watts, Abraham Cowley, Matthew Prior, Richard Blackmore, Alexander Pope, Edward Young and of course Milton. These authors, says Morell, had the satisfaction of settling men's minds in the secure basis of religion, and, even more rewardingly, their words evoke wonder and rapture in the reader, kindling a desire for union with God by giving a foretaste of its joy. Quoting Pope's *Essay on Criticism* the future author of *Theodora* and *Jephtha* prays:

> Oh! may some Spark of your celestial Fire
> Spread through my Soul, and fill its large Desire,
> That I at humble Distance may pursue,
> And keep my Duty, and my *God* in view.
> To teach vain Man a Lesson little known,
> *T'adore Superior Pow'r, and doubt his own.*

Morell was well aware of the issues at stake, and his divine poems and translations contribute directly to the orthodox defence of the evidence of miracles. 'The First Hymn of Vida. To God the Father' recounts the crossing of the Red Sea and the engulfing of the Egyptian army (the subject of *Israel in Egypt*), and Morell's extensive footnotes argue (with numerous supporting references) that the division of the sea *was* a miracle, and that through the Israelites' safe transit God was proving His power, His justice 'and his Mercy and Faithfulness to his People'. He describes the fall of Jericho with even more extensive footnotes, exhorting respect for God's power. His note to the account of the sun standing still for Joshua (two-thirds of a page) likewise declares its miraculous status: 'we cannot doubt of it, unless we renounce all human Faith, and the Evidence of our Senses'. In this insistence on the miraculousness of Old Testament history he is in the mainstream of anti-deist writing. Miracles, especially miraculous deliverances, are also central to the oratorio librettos.

The librettists and politics

Several of the librettists have left a distinct indication of their political views and in some cases their involvement in contemporary political life. They present an interesting conspectus of contemporary political identities.

Jennens was one of many English squires forced by the Roman Catholicism of King James II and his heirs into a genuinely agonising conflict, between loyalty to the Stuart family which had the hereditary (and, many believed, divine) right to rule, and an obligation to protect the English constitution and the Church of England. Political and ecclesiastical office-holders, from parish priests and magistrates upwards, had to swear allegiance to the crown. While James II and his immediate heirs were still alive, committed so-called Nonjurors refused to take the oath of loyalty to his successors on the English throne and (once the Protestant succession had been established in 1701) the oath abjuring loyalty to the Stuarts, thus effectively excluding themselves from careers in public life. Had he not been a Nonjuror, Jennens would certainly have been a magistrate, and he might have followed the family tradition of studying Law at Middle Temple. Nonjurors' political activity had to be either symbolic and polemical, or treasonable. Jennens steered an honourable course between subversion and passivity. No suspicion of treasonable involvement attaches to him, but he was the leading patron of Nonjurors of his generation, and some recipients of his generosity were probably Jacobites. He was an assiduous reader of opposition propaganda and helped to circulate it; and, within the bounds of legality, he declared his loyalty to the old regime. For example, his seal ring portrayed the head of Charles I; he collected, and displayed, a remarkable number of portraits of the Stuarts and their deposed descendants; and he crossed the names of the Hanoverian royal family out of the prayer books that he used in the chapel of his house at Gopsall.

Hamilton's associations with the aristocracy may have had a political bias.[9] His St Cecilia Ode (1720) was 'most humbly inscribed, by his lordship's most obliged, and most obedient servant' to Peregrine Marquess of Carmarthen, a Tory whose father, the second Duke of Leeds, was from 1716 to 1723 admiral and commander-in-chief of the Pretender's fleet. The third Earl of Strafford, his long-time master, was created Duke of Strafford in the Jacobite peerage in 1722 and was appointed as commander-in-chief of the Pretender's forces north of the Humber and one of the Lords Regent in the Pretender's absence; he was a leading conspirator in both the Atterbury Plot (1720–2) and the Cornbury Plot (1731–5) to restore the Stuarts, and was also involved in negotiations on behalf of the Stuart cause in 1725. As Strafford's trusted factotum, Hamilton was presumably aware of his master's consistently Jacobite allegiance. His choice of John Dryden's *Alexander's Feast* for Handel to set in 1736 is interesting in this connection, since it possibly has a Jacobite subtext.[10] However, two of his subsequent librettos had other political overtones. He dedicated his libretto of *Samson* to the Prince of Wales at the height of Frederick's campaign as leader of the Patriot opposition to the government of his father (King George II) and Robert Walpole. Again with a different political emphasis, his text for the *Occasional Oratorio* is a prayer for the defeat of the 1745 Rebellion. The Rebellion drew large numbers of Britons who were critical of the government temporarily to lend support to the crown; we cannot deduce any more definite picture of Hamilton's political allegiance from his last libretto than from any of his others, but they all reflect contemporary political consciousness.

Miller was recognised in his own time as a leading writer for the opposition against the 'court' administration, the government directed by Walpole and (after 1742) Lord Carteret. In 1734 the anonymous pamphlet *The Dramatick Sessions; or, The Stage Contest* aligned him with Henry Fielding, James Thomson, and Aaron Hill, all current or incipient opposition playwrights. His attacks on the government are impressive for both their quantity and their quality and, unlike some of his fellow critics of the political leadership, he proved resistant to attempts to buy him off, despite considerable penury. He was one of the most serious opposition writers, like Alexander Pope associating the tendency to national moral decline and corruption with the current expedient style of government. His most incisive shaft is one of the most swingeing of all the attacks on Walpole, the anonymous poetic satire *Are These Things So?* (1740; he also probably wrote one of its nine sequels, *The Great Man's Answer*). It adopts the persona of Pope himself to expose the first minister, in an open letter from 'an Englishman in his Grotto' to 'a Great Man at Court'. Typically Patriot criticisms of Walpole's policies and abuses of power end with suggestions of men better fitted to lead the nation, who bear fictitious names in the first edition but in the second (six weeks later) constitute a roll-call of opposition worthies. In 1741 Miller dedicated his *Miscellaneous Works* to the Patriot opposition's figurehead, the Prince of Wales. The subscription list, which includes a strong opposition side, also includes Handel.[11]

Morell's attempt to secure Queen Caroline's patronage and his dedication of his first libretto to the Duke of Cumberland suggest solidarity with the court. But in the 1730s he also nailed his banner, by contrast, to the Patriot opposition mast, and in the early 1740s he was a satellite of Prince Frederick's opposition circle. His attachment to the opposition cause is evident in some of his poems, now preserved in a manuscript in Yale University Library.[12] In 1731 *The Gentleman's Magazine* published his 'The Lord and the 'Squire. A Ballad', one of many literary repercussions of the almost bloodless duel between the dissident Whig leader William Pulteney and the court Whig Lord Hervey. This real-life fight was intensely political, originating in a particularly savage pamphlet duel in the larger campaign between the government and its chief hornet *The Craftsman*, a newspaper which was directed and largely

written by Bolingbroke and Pulteney.[13] Morell's ballad is firmly on the
opposition side, and makes a characteristically oppositionist thrust
against the government's corruption of the executive by patronage
(Pulteney had resisted such inducements). In his poem 'The Patriot'
(1732)[14] Morell eulogises Pulteney in even more deliberately partisan
terms, and in the language associated with his poem's title, as one 'Who
dares oppose Corruption, Pensions, Bribes . . . freely good, and obsti-
nately just'. Again in standard Patriot opposition mode, he depicts
Britain as a 'suff'ring Land' which Pulteney defends, Perseus-like, from
the government's 'vile Measures'. One of these measures, the Excise Bill
(1733), prompted 'A new ballad'.[15] Addressing 'my Countrymen', Morell,
like other writers against the Excise, takes the opportunity to condemn
the government for the depredation of civil rights, the destruction of the
constitution, and peace without honour.[16] He heads the ballad with
references to *The Gentleman's Magazine* which explain the political
context. These references, evidently added for the benefit of his wife, who
was reading the poem long after it was written, show the strength of
Morell's concern – years after the event – to have his alignment with the
Patriot opposition appreciated.

There are several indications that Morell was still within the opposition orbit, if not acting as one of its mouthpieces, during the late 1730s
and the 1740s. In 1737, after his expulsion from court, the Prince of Wales
moved into Morell's neighbourhood, and Kew House was thenceforth
Frederick's family home.[17] Morell dedicated his edition of modern versions of Chaucer's *Canterbury Tales* (1737) to Frederick as a wedding
present, and he is said to have tried to secure financial support through
the agency of the Prince's dancing-master, Desnoyers. His poem 'The
Widow'd Swan' depicts him strolling in the grounds of Cliveden, another
of the Prince's country homes, and includes, as part of the dying swan's
song, lines in praise of Frederick's integrity.[18] His poems include 'To my
Friend Mr Thomson, on his unfinished Plan of a Poem, called The Castle
of Indolence. – in Imitation of Spenser',[19] four aptly Spenserian stanzas
dating from 1742, when Thomson was one of the Prince of Wales's chief
writers. The poem which Morell was urging Thomson to complete has
itself been interpreted as a Patriot opposition work, in which 'indolence'
means political lethargy, the pursuit of private pleasure to the neglect of
public duty (akin to Pope's 'dulness')[20] – a clash of interests which Morell
himself was to explore in his librettos. Morell's political allegiances curiously interlock just at the point when he becomes Handel's librettist: in
later life he recorded that it was at Frederick's suggestion that he wrote a
libretto for Handel, and the result was the wordbook he dedicated to the
Duke of Cumberland, *Judas Maccabaeus*.[21]

Table 7.1 Libretto authors and sources

(a) Handel's English oratorios

Title	Librettist	Chief sources of libretto (OT: Old Testament; Ap: Apocrypha; NT: New Testament)
Esther (HWV 50a)	? Alexander Pope, John Arbuthnot	OT: Esther II–X; Ap: Esther XII–XVI; Jean Racine, Esther, trans. Thomas Brereton
Esther (HWV 50b)	Samuel Humphreys	HWV 50a libretto and sources
Deborah	Samuel Humphreys	OT: Judges IV–V
Athalia	Samuel Humphreys	OT: 2 Kings VIII–X; Racine: Athalie
Saul	Charles Jennens	OT: 1 Sam. XV–XX, XXVI, XXVIII, XXXI, 2 Sam. I, II; Abraham Cowley: Davideis; Roger Boyle: The Tragedy of King Saul
Israel in Egypt	? Charles Jennens	OT: Exod. I, II, VII, XV; 2 Sam. I, Pss CIII, CV, CVI, CXII, Job XXIX, Lam. I, II, Dan. XII; Ap: Wisd. of Sol. V, Ecclus XXVI, XLIV; NT: Phil. IV
Messiah	Charles Jennens	OT: Job XIX, Pss II, XVI, XXII, XXIV, LXVIII, LXIX, Isa. VII, IX, XXXV, XL, L, LIII, LX, Lam. I, Hag. II, Mal. III, Zech. IX; NT: Matt. I, XI, Luke II, John I, Rom. VIII, X, 1 Cor. XV, Heb. I, Rev. V, XI, XIX
Samson	Newburgh Hamilton	OT: Judges XIII–XVI; John Milton: Samson Agonistes, paraphrases of OT Pss VII, LXXX, LXXXI, LXXXIII, LXXXIV, LXXXVI, CXIV, CXXXVI, The Passion, On Time, On the Morning of Christ's Nativity, An Epitaph on the Marchioness of Winchester, At a Solemn Music
Joseph and his Brethren	James Miller	OT: Gen. XXXVIII–XLV; Charles-Claude Genest: Joseph; Apostolo Zeno: Giuseppe
Belshazzar	Charles Jennens	OT: 2 Kings XXIV, XXV, 2 Chron. XXXVI, Ezra I, II, V, VI, Isa. XVI, Jer. XXVII–XXIX, XXXII, XXXIII, XXXIX, Dan. I, V; Herodotus: Histories; Xenophon: Cyropaedia
Occasional Oratorio	Newburgh Hamilton	Milton: paraphrases of OT Pss II, III, V, LXXXI, CXXXVI; Edmund Spenser: Faerie Queene, Hymn to Heavenly Beauty, Tears of the Muses; libretto of Israel in Egypt
Judas Maccabaeus	Thomas Morell	Ap: 1 Macc. II–VIII; Josephus: Antiquities
Alexander Balus	Thomas Morell	Ap: 1 Macc. IX–XII
Joshua	?	OT: Exod. XII, Lev. XXIII, Num. IX, XIII, XIV, Joshua I, III–XI, XIII–XV
Susanna	?	Ap: Susanna
Solomon	?	OT: 2 Sam. XVI, XIX, 1 Kings I–XI, 1 Chron. XXII, XXVIII, XXIX, 2 Chron. I–IX

Theodora	Thomas Morell	Robert Boyle: *The Martyrdom of Theodora and of Didymus*
Jephtha	Thomas Morell	OT: Judges X–XII; George Buchanan: *Jephthes, sive Votum*
The Triumph of Time and Truth	? Thomas Morell	Benedetto Pamphili: *Il trionfo del Tempo e del Disinganno* (set by Handel 1708), trans. George Oldmixon (for performance in 1737 as *Il trionfo del Tempo, e della Verità*)

(b) Handel's English masques, music dramas, cantatas and moral odes

Title	Librettist	Chief sources of libretto
Acis and Galatea	John Gay, with John Hughes and probably Pope and Arbuthnot	Ovid: *Metamorphoses*, trans. John Dryden; Homer: *Iliad*, trans. Pope; Pope: *Autumn*
Alexander's Feast	Newburgh Hamilton	Dryden: *Alexander's Feast*
Ode for St Cecilia's Day	Newburgh Hamilton	Dryden: *A Song for St Cecilia's Day*
L'Allegro, il Penseroso ed il Moderato	James Harris, Charles Jennens	Milton: *L'Allegro and Il Penseroso*
The Story of Semele	? Newburgh Hamilton	William Congreve: *Semele* and poems; Pope: *Summer*
Hercules	Thomas Broughton	Sophocles: *Trachiniae*; Ovid: *Metamorphoses*
The Choice of Hercules	? Thomas Morell	Robert Lowth: *The Judgement of Hercules*

Collaboration with Handel

Handel did not, so far as we know, write any of his English librettos (see Table 7.1 for authors and sources of librettos). Nor do we have any record of his suggesting the topic for any of the oratorios which he composed. There is an intriguing note in his hand for a prospective oratorio about Elijah, but this idea had to wait another century to be realised.[22] He probably discussed possible topics or concepts of 'oratorio' (using the term in its widest sense) with any or all of his writers, but we have little documentary evidence of this. The fullest record of collaboration on a libretto, a series of letters from Handel to Jennens about *Belshazzar*, tantalisingly raises as many questions as it answers.[23]

The only instance so far known of Handel's selecting a text without the help of a collaborator seems to be his second St Cecilia ode (1739), which needed no librettist, since he set Dryden's text verbatim. He was not a proto-Wagner, nor was his collaboration with his librettists of a Strauss–von Hofmannsthal intensity: it would have been very unusual for its time if it had been. However, he could take a strong and determining part in shaping a libretto. He broke the textual units of Milton's *L'Allegro* and *Il Penseroso* into smaller sections than James Harris's draft had proposed in order to increase the variety and contrasts; and he asked for a third section which would provide a concluding equilibrium (though his suggestion of using Milton's 'At a solemn musick' was rejected by Jennens in favour of a more pertinent 'Moderato' written by himself).[24] More usually, so far as we can tell, Handel's involvement with his librettists' texts consisted of editing them, principally cutting them and occasionally changing individual words. It is often unclear to what extent this was a collaborative exercise. Not that Handel set everything he was offered. Neither John Upton nor Mary Delany managed to persuade him that an oratorio taken from Milton's *Paradise Lost* had possibilities, nor did he warm to Edward Synge's proposal and draft synopsis, inspired by *Messiah* and *L'Allegro*, for an unremittingly didactic work to be titled *The Penitent*.[25] But he did not have to be in at the start or even during the progress of a libretto's composition for it to be acceptable to him. *Messiah* was Jennens's idea, and the libretto was complete before it was offered to Handel.[26]

The relation of librettist to libretto – the librettist's 'input' – varied greatly. The original 1718 version of *Esther* was typical of the majority of later oratorio librettos, in being a newly written text dramatising the biblical and apocryphal narratives. The dramatisation involved embroidering or inventing incidents – usually at the suggestion of the source material – and paraphrasing Scripture. As later with, for example,

Samson, there was an intermediary source between the Bible and the libretto, in this case the choric drama on the same subject by Racine. *Samson* unobtrusively includes material from five other poems and psalm paraphrases by Milton, in addition to a condensed version of *Samson Agonistes* exceptionally well suited to the political circumstances and theatrical tastes of the day. The anthems inserted into the 1732 version of *Esther* represent the other and less frequent strain of libretto composition, using actual scriptural text. Only *Messiah* and *Israel in Egypt* consist entirely of texts taken from Scripture with only minor verbal adjustment, but here too the librettist shaped the works, by his selection, juxtaposition and sequencing of the biblical verses.[27] Most of the secular English works consist of selection and rearrangement of pre-existing texts, *Acis and Galatea* being the outstanding exception in which nearly all the words were specially written for Handel to set. Some of these librettos evolved piecemeal. The inspired alternation of passages from Milton's two poems to produce a sequence of contrasting moods in *L'Allegro* resulted from a series of amendments by Jennens and Handel to Harris's original plan. Harris's initial draft, as well as alternating the texts from Milton's poems, had specified particular musical treatments of several movements (see Plate 3), many of which were followed up by Handel. Newburgh Hamilton's mastery of the scissors-and-paste technique is evident in *Semele* (if the libretto was indeed his work).[28] Broughton altered Sophocles' *Trachiniae* almost out of recognition to produce a *Hercules* sufficiently decorous for his audience. At the other end of the scale, Hamilton rightly claimed in the preface to his libretto of *Alexander's Feast* that he had hardly tampered with the text (though Dryden's poem was only part of the evening's entertainment which Handel performed under its title).

The librettists' choice of theme was seldom novel. Precedents for their subjects (besides their immediate sources, for which see Table 7.1) can be found among Italian oratorios, Italian sacred cantatas, German Passions, European sacred drama, recent and contemporary English drama and verse – including fair-booth drolls – or English oratorios by other composers, or a combination of these. Deborah, David and Jonathan, Jephtha, and the Choice of Hercules had all been subjects of English musical compositions before Handel came to them. The Exodus, Joseph, David, Solomon and the Messiah were subjects of English eighteenth-century verse and drama. Saul and the witch at Endor, and Jephtha, were subjects of drolls performed at London fairs (at which all classes of society mingled) during the early eighteenth century. Saul's meeting with the witch at Endor had been the subject of Purcell's *scena* 'In Guilty Night'. Some topics were mooted in poems of praise addressed to Handel,

Song for a Base Voice with French. Horns

Mirth admit me of thy Crew,
To listen how ye Hounds & Horn
Clearly rouse ye slumbring morn,
From ye sides of some hear Hill,
Thro' ye high. wood echoing shrill.

    Chorus

Mirth, admit us of thy Crew,
&c &c &c &c echoing shrill.

    Recit: Beard

Or let me wander, not unseen
By Hedge-row Elms on hillocks green,
Right against the Eastern Gate,
Where ye great Sun begins his State,
Robed in flames, & Amber Light,
The Clouds in thousand Liveries dight.

    Song by Beard in ye Sicilian Taste

There ye Plowman near at Hand
Whistles o're ye furrow'd Land,
And ye Milkmaid singeth blithe,
And ye Mower whets his Scythe,
And every Shepherd tells his Tale
Under the Hawthorn in ye ~~Dale~~ Dale.
Thus past the day to bed they creep,
By whispring Winds soon lull'd asleep.

    Chorus Sicilian, to ye same Words.

        End of the first Act

Plate 3 A page from James Harris's *Allegro & Penseroso* (1739), an adaptation of John Milton's contrasting poems *L'Allegro* and *Il Penseroso*, subsequently revised and supplemented by Charles Jennens, and set by Handel in 1740. Harris from the beginning hoped that Handel would set his libretto, and named Handel's current oratorio soloists in his headings to movements (here, the tenor John Beard), as well as specifying or suggesting characteristic instrumentation and musical styles.

or in critiques of his work.[29] The contemporary Milton cult is reflected in the choice of *L'Allegro* and *Il Penseroso, Samson Agonistes* and *Paradise Lost* for complete works and the use of Milton's psalm translations for *Samson* and the *Occasional Oratorio*. As Jennens wrote sourly of the latter, 'it is transcribed chiefly from Milton, who in his Version of some of the Psalms wrote so like Sternhold and Hopkins that there is not a pin to choose betwixt 'em. But there are people in the world who fancy every thing excellent which has Milton's name to it.'[30]

The printed wordbook was an authoritative record of the libretto, usually being prepared for printing under the author's direction, and it constituted an essential element of the experience of the oratorio in the theatre. Members of the audience bought copies of the wordbook in the theatre in order to follow the text during the performance, as Fielding's *Amelia* attests: Amelia's unknown admirer in the first gallery 'procured her a book and wax-candle, and held the candle for her himself during the whole entertainment'.[31] Wordbooks were also sold in advance of the performance so that they could be studied beforehand. They contained information essential to full understanding and enjoyment of the performance. Some, after the manner of the similarly marketed opera librettos which often gave the larger narrative context of the part of the story being treated, provided a synopsis of the parts of the story which the librettist had chosen to omit. James Miller's *Joseph* is an example, obviating the charge occasionally made by modern critics that the librettist rendered the 'plot' unintelligible. In any case, most oratorio stories were very familiar to the audience, enabling the librettist who so wished to dispense with details of the action and provide a commentary on it instead. Printed 'stage directions' often compensated for the lack of visible action. Frequently the apportioning of text to characters had to be clarified by reference to the libretto, because soloists doubled minor and even major roles. For example, Esther Young created the roles of both Juno and Ino in *Semele* (aptly, since the plot involves the former disguising herself as the latter); given the absence of costume and action, this doubling would have been extremely confusing to the audience but for the wordbook.[32]

But what the audiences read did not always match what they heard. The librettists had a tendency to write too much (or, as they probably saw it, Handel provided too many notes), so portions of their texts were frequently not set. However, to make sense of the action, or just to indicate the complete 'ideal' text, the unused portions were printed with the rest, the omissions usually indicated by inverted commas around the passages involved. Conversely, as Handel's autograph material in the British Library shows, the librettist sometimes provided text which never appeared in print, either because Handel did not set it, or because, despite being set, it was discarded from the score before the libretto was printed. Such passages can adjust our idea of the librettist's contribution.[33]

The question arises: why did people write oratorio librettos for Handel? In England librettos had been regarded, ever since Dryden first provided and deprecated them, as one of the lowest forms of literary creation.[34] Both Morell, in his recollection of working with Handel,[35] and Miller, in his dedication of *Joseph*, disparaged libretto writing on the grounds of subservience to the musician, which resulted in what they regarded as second-rate literature. On his own account Morell good-naturedly wrote *Judas Maccabaeus* to oblige the composer, in part because he was flattered by princely encouragement. However, this was not the whole truth – he needed the money, as did Miller. But these and the other librettists for whom money may have been a motive had other sources of income and were able to earn by other forms of writing, so why did they diversify into oratorio?

The authors did not really view their librettos as negligently as they pretended, in the time-honoured fashion of the gentleman practitioner. It is no surprise to find Morell, an energetic and esteemed classical philologist, vigilantly scrutinising the printing of the wordbook for *Judas Maccabaeus*.[36] Similarly Jennens was incensed by the 'bulls' (printing errors) in the first edition of the libretto of *Messiah* and determined to expunge them in time for the first London performance: 'I have a copy, as it was printed in Ireland, full of Bulls; & if he [Handel] does not print a correct one here, I shall do it my Self, & perhaps tell him a piece of my mind by way of Preface.'[37] Winton Dean points to an errata slip in the first issue of the libretto of *Susanna*, and corresponding corrections in the second, as evidence of 'a finicky author with a passion for minute accuracy'.[38] Morell describes himself as willing to alter his metre at the composer's whim, but this should not lead us to suppose that he had a tin ear; a letter in the archives of his old college (King's, Cambridge) on Sophocles' versification proves his sensitivity to metrical variation and other details of aural effect.[39] In fact the English librettos for Handel are a standing refutation of the conventional contempt for song texts, because they consist of or derive from the greatest literature, including the Scriptures, Sophocles, Milton and Dryden. And the librettos do not compromise their sources. They contain the intellectual, emotional, political and spiritual preoccupations, questions and solutions of eighteenth-century authors and audiences. They make Handel's English works signal repositories of the prevailing ideas of their time and major conduits of eighteenth-century sensibility and thought.[40]

Handel was recognised by his English contemporaries as the country's leading composer. He achieved remarkable prominence on the London scene by any standards, and he was written about to a degree surely unmatched by any British composer until the twentieth century. Most of the people who volunteered or agreed to write librettos for him were admirers of his music, or part of his circle of acquaintance, or both (Jennens, James Harris, Mrs Delany, John Upton, Edward Synge, Newburgh Hamilton, Thomas Broughton, James Miller), as indeed his very first English librettists had been (the authors of *Acis and Galatea*, John Gay and his literary friends in Burlington's and Chandos's orbits). Hamilton, Jennens and Broughton had subscribed to his published operas before they wrote for him. It would appear that the many enthusiasts of high culture among Handel's librettists wrote for him at least in part because they admired his work and wanted to join in creating great art. This seems to have been what principally motivated such devotees as Mrs Delany, Harris and Hamilton – the splendid project of allying the music of their favourite composer, famed for his capacity for the sublime, with the highest achievements of the sublime in verse, the poetic masterpieces of Dryden and Milton. In selecting *Alexander's Feast* to 'give Satisfaction to the real Judges of *Poetry* and *Musick*', Hamilton was convinced, as he claimed in the jubilant conclusion to his libretto's preface, that 'it is next to an Improbability, to offer the World any thing in those *Arts* more perfect, than the united Labours and utmost Efforts of a *Dryden* and a *Handel*'. Miller deprecated his own efforts, but described Handel's oratorios as 'Refined and Sublime Entertainments' and the composer as 'the Great Master, by whose Divine Harmony they are supported'.

Of all Handel's librettists Jennens emerges as the most fervent admirer of his music, so it is no surprise to find him actively trying to promote the composition of a masterpiece by providing the words for it, as his letters to Holdsworth explain:[41]

> Handel says he will do nothing next Winter, but I hope I shall perswade him to set another Scripture Collection I have made for him . . . I hope he will lay out his whole Genius & Skill upon it, that the Composition may excell all his former Compositions, as the Subject excells every other Subject. The Subject is Messiah.

Some months later,

> I heard with great pleasure at my arrival in Town, that Handel had set the Oratorio of Messiah; but it was some mortification to me to hear that instead of performing it here he was gone into Ireland with it. However, I hope we shall hear it when he comes back.

His subsequent chagrin is largely due to his sense of Handel's failure to do *himself* justice in failing to do justice to the subject. A contemporary

writer attests that Jennens and Harris, at least, achieved the aim of propa-
gating great art. According to Joseph Warton in his essay on Pope (1756),
Milton's 'L'Allegro and Il Penseroso . . . are now universally known', but
this was not so before 1740: they 'lay in a sort of obscurity, the private
enjoyment of a few curious readers, till they were set to admirable music
by Mr Handel'.[42]

There might have been more personal motives for providing librettos
for Handel than that of giving a spur to his creative power. Most of the
librettists were keen to contribute to the major contemporary topics of
debate, religion and politics. It is interesting that Miller turned to writing
for Handel only after his own hitherto successful plays had been perma-
nently denied a hearing by an offended claque. The most astonishing
phrases in Jennens's letters to Holdsworth, about his willingness to col-
laborate once more with Handel (on *Belshazzar*), suggest that he had a
specific, individual purpose beyond the creation of great art. His state-
ments 'I must take him as I find him, & make the best use I can of him' and
'the truth is, I had a farther view in it' imply that he had an axe of his own
to grind; and I have suggested elsewhere that Jennens did indeed 'use'
Handel's oratorios to promulgate his deeply felt religious and political
views.[43] The topic and source of an oratorio could be the librettist's
choice; Hamilton's prefaces to *Alexander's Feast* and *Samson* imply that he
suggested these texts for setting. Librettists other than Jennens may have
had 'a farther view' in the words they provided for Handel to set.

Handel was not only a masterly artist, he was a famous one. Writing
oratorio librettos for him might not increase one's reputation in the
world of letters, but it increased one's audience. Handel's public ranged
from the royal family to the patrons of Vauxhall Gardens and from
London to Dublin to Edinburgh, and his work lasted (the repeated performance of his oratorios and operas was a novelty in early eighteenth
century England; musical works were seldom revived in their entirety).
The theatre was the most popular forum for serious secular writing, and
hence the most sought-after arena for writers with a message; and serious
music theatre works were less vulnerable to censorship than stage plays.[44]
For a writer with something to say to the educated, influential upper- and
middle-class London public, Handel's music could be an ideal vehicle.

PART II

The music

8 Handel and the aria

C. Steven LaRue

While in our own time Handel's choruses (particularly those in *Messiah*) are perhaps his best known vocal music, throughout much of his career it was his arias that generated the most public enthusiasm.[1] Partially owing to the relative neglect of the works in which arias are the most prominent element (the operas and cantatas) in the two centuries following Handel's death, and partially owing to rapidly changing tastes in the genres to which those works belong (both then and now), our appreciation of Handel's aria composition has suffered. Arias are the most important structural element in all of Handel's vocal works, however, and consequently they occupied more of his creative energy than any other form. As a result, Handel's arias provide us with a clear picture of his compositional development and also with insights into his aesthetic aims throughout his career.

Certainly part of our neglect of Handel's arias is the result of the fact that the vast majority of them are in da capo form, a form most commonly associated with *opera seria*.[2] Until quite recently, *opera seria* as a genre has been relentlessly criticised by both contemporary commentators and modern scholars alike; moreover, quite often the focus of the criticism has been the da capo aria itself. Essentially an expanded ternary form, the grand da capo aria (or five-part da capo, the type most commonly found in Handel's arias) takes the form A1 A2 B (B) A1 A2, in which A1 is the first stanza of text, A2 is a repetition of the first stanza, and B is the second stanza of text. Although the grand da capo represents one of the most sophisticated musical forms of the eighteenth century, the fourfold statement of the first half of the text in particular (involving the complete restatement of A1 A2 after B) has been the focus of a number of criticisms; because of the repetitiveness of the text, the da capo aria has often been seen as simply a vehicle for vocal improvisation and a shameless showcase for brilliant virtuoso singing rather than a form suitable for musical or dramatic expression.[3]

The importance of opera and the da capo aria to Handel's compositional development, however, cannot be overestimated. At the age of eighteen, Handel went to Hamburg to begin his long association with the Hamburg opera at the Theater am Gänsemarkt, first as orchestra member (violin and then harpsichord) and subsequently as composer. Years later, in his biographical sketch of Handel's life, Johann Mattheson described Handel's arrival at Hamburg in 1703 and his compositional skills at that time:[4]

> He composed at that time long, long arias, and almost endless cantatas, which still had not yet the right skill or the right taste, albeit a perfect harmony; he was, however, soon fashioned in quite another form by the high school of opera.
>
> He was a skilful organist: more skilful than *Kuhnau* in fugue and counterpoint, particularly *ex tempore*; but he knew very little about melodic writing before he got to the Hamburg Opera.

While Mattheson suggests that writing opera arias was fundamental to Handel's early compositional experience, there can be no doubt that Handel's experience in this genre continued to affect his compositional choices long after he abandoned opera composition altogether.

In *Almira*, Handel's only surviving opera score for Hamburg,[5] the wide range of formal aria types and musical styles, as well as the two languages used in the arias (German and Italian), reflect the diversity of stylistic influences that characterised German opera at that time. Even in Handel's score of *Almira*, however, the association of the da capo aria with opera, and particularly Italian opera, is clear. Of the German-texted arias, nearly half are in da capo form, and of these, one is in a shortened version of the form,[6] whereas almost all of the Italian-texted arias are in da capo form. The structure of the *Almira* libretto, particularly in terms of the placement of arias within scenes and the nature of the dramatic contexts in which arias appear,[7] also had a significant impact on Handel's early approach to opera composition. Although quite different in a number of ways from his practice in later Italian operas, Handel's arias for *Almira* exhibit both the conventions of the libretto and the dramatic characterisation that distinguish his aria writing throughout his career.[8]

By the time Handel wrote *Agrippina* for Venice late in 1709,[9] his extensive experience with the da capo aria and his cosmopolitan musical training made it possible for him to treat the form with a variety of musical styles. More significantly, the arias of *Agrippina* begin to show a differentiation from one another based not just on varied musical style in response to the immediate dramatic context, but on the relation of individual character to that context and the larger context of the opera as a whole. In the first four arias, for example, musical portraits of the characters Nerone, Pallante, Narciso and Agrippina are painted that define those characters throughout the opera.

Nerone's 'Con saggio tuo consiglio' makes it clear that his interest in becoming Emperor is solely due to his desire to please his mother; while the text could be set in any number of ways, the combination of siciliano features (compound time, minor mode) commonly associated with melancholy, and the ironic use of word painting for the phrase 'il trono ascenderò' ('I will ascend the throne'), in which 'ascenderò' is set to a descending-scale figure,[10] musically characterise Nerone as the weak character he proves to be throughout the opera. By contrast, Pallante's aria 'La mia sorte fortunata' (common time, G minor) establishes his strength and his self-confidence; in response to Agrippina's promise that if Nerone ascends the throne Pallante will receive her love, Pallante boldly exclaims that his fortune is great in a wide-leaping melodic phrase that enters immediately with the orchestra in a motto-like gesture. While Pallante is by no means an entirely heroic figure, his conventional heroic characteristics contrast sharply with his rival/collaborator Narciso, whose response to Agrippina's proposal (the same she made to Pallante) is a delicate F major aria in 3/8 time accompanied by recorders ('Volo pronto; e lieto il core'), in which Narciso sings of the happiness of his heart. Finally, after convincing Nerone, Narciso and Pallante to comply with her wishes, Agrippina sings of her power and of her initial triumphs in a mock-military aria in C major and common time ('L'alma mia frà le tempeste') that is particularly notable for its syncopated phrasing. While the march-like quality of the aria establishes Agrippina's mood, the phrasing lends a twist to it that makes it uniquely her own; far from being a stock military piece, her aria establishes her emotional state and her singular character.

All four arias from *Agrippina* described above are da capo or dal segno arias (dal segno is a variant of the da capo form in which the opening ritornello is abbreviated, or even sometimes elided completely, at the repeat of the A section), but all four differ from one another in terms of musical style. Handel's acceptance of Italian *opera seria* and its conventions made this aspect of aria composition enormously important; although the formal features of the aria were restricted, the musical content of the aria could be varied in terms of metre, mode, melody, rhythm, accompaniment, texture and word setting.

From the premiere of *Agrippina* until the 1730s, Handel's compositional attention was almost entirely devoted to Italian opera. With the huge success of his *Rinaldo* in 1711, Handel began what was to become a long career in writing Italian *opera seria* for the London stage. The height of this career fell in the period from 1720 to 1728, during which Handel wrote fourteen operas for the Royal Academy of Music, a publicly held company devoted to the presentation of authentic Italian opera in England. Within the scores that Handel wrote for the Royal Academy, his treatment of the da capo aria reveals a number of important aspects of both his technical skill in aria composition in particular, and his approach to the aesthetics of lyric expression in general.

By the time Handel wrote *Radamisto* for the Royal Academy in the spring of 1720, he had mastered the art of Italian opera and had developed his own personal operatic style. During its eight years of production, the Royal Academy company enlisted some of the finest opera singers to be found anywhere in Europe, giving Handel access to extended working relationships with his cast that he was to enjoy at no other time during his life. The results of this circumstance are evident in many aspects of Handel's operas from this period, and it is in the arias that many of the most subtle and most profound results can be found.

Handel's opera composition for the Royal Academy reflects a number of distinct and important changes of compositional approach. Intimately connected to these changes are the singers themselves; the relation between singer and aria type is closely associated with the relation between arias and the drama as a whole. Thus Handel's early Royal Academy operas have a musico-dramatic style that is distinct from his later Royal Academy works, on account of changes in the cast of soloists.

Changes in Handel's compositional approach to the Royal Academy operas particularly coincided with changes in personnel in the company's prima donna position. Margherita Durastanti, the Royal Academy's first leading lady (she had also been the creator of the role of Agrippina at Venice) was a thoroughly competent and experienced Italian singer who was capable of considerable vocal virtuosity and dramatic expression. Durastanti's versatility inspired Handel to cast her in a wide variety of roles, including a number of 'trouser' roles, and her arias reflect the dramatic range of her parts. When she took the title role in *Radamisto*, Durastanti could thus sing intimate love songs (such as 'Cara sposa'), heroic arias (such as 'Ferite, uccidete'), and melancholy arias (such as 'Ombra cara' or 'Dolce bene'). Handel's settings of these different types of texts reflect both Durastanti's versatility and his own ability to write in a number of different musical styles. The four arias mentioned above vary enormously in style, from a continuo-accompanied aria ('Cara sposa'), an old-fashioned type found in Handel's first opera, *Almira*,[11] to a heroic bravura aria ('Ferite, uccidete', described by Charles Burney as 'A spirited song in the style of the times'),[12] to a highly original melancholy aria ('Ombra cara'), to a siciliano aria ('Dolce bene'); nevertheless, all of these are, of course, da capo arias, and have in common the basic da capo formal structure.

Because of her ability to command a wide range of aria types and styles, the roles Handel wrote for Durastanti differ significantly from those he wrote for her successor, Francesca Cuzzoni. The German composer and theorist Johann Joachim Quantz describes Cuzzoni in the following terms, based on hearing her in Handel's *Admeto* in 1727:[13]

> Cuzzoni had a very agreeable and clear soprano voice, a pure intonation and beautiful *trillo*. Her range extended from middle c to the c above the staff. Her ornamentation did not seem to be artificial due to her nice, pleasant, and light style of delivery, and with its tenderness she won the hearts of her listeners. The *passagien* [melismas] in the allegros were not done with the greatest facility, but she sang them very fully and pleasantly. Her acting was somewhat cold, and her figure was not too favourable for the theatre.

Because the arias that Handel wrote for Cuzzoni within a given opera tend to be less varied in style than those found in Durastanti's roles, musical style becomes in itself a defining characteristic of Cuzzoni's roles. The siciliano, for example, was only one from a number of aria types which Handel employed for Durastanti, whereas in Cuzzoni's roles it became a regular musico-dramatic characteristic. Ironically, the first two Handel arias that Cuzzoni sang in London ('Falsa imagine' and 'Affanni del pensier' in *Ottone*, 1723) may have been written for Durastanti,[14] and, in spite of the fact that Cuzzoni is said initially to have refused to sing them, it was these two songs that, according to Burney, established her London career as 'an expressive and pathetic singer'.[15] With her very first London opera, therefore, Cuzzoni's stylistic strengths were established, and Handel began a long series of roles for her in which the siciliano became a symbol for the pathos inherent in her part, and came to reflect her particular abilities.

This is demonstrated by a comparison of Teofane's 'Affanni del pensier' in *Ottone* with Emilia's 'Mà chi punir desio' in *Flavio*, which was written specially for Cuzzoni later in 1723. Although these arias are found in quite similar dramatic circumstances (in *Ottone*, Teofane expresses her confusion about the identity of Ottone; in *Flavio*, Emilia is confused about whether her loyalties should be with her father or her lover), they display very different musical characteristics. Where 'Affanni del pensier' contains a complex contrapuntal accompaniment to Teofane's vocal line, 'Mà chi punir desio' is largely homophonic, giving primacy to the vocal line. In general, the sicilianos that Handel wrote for Durastanti ('Dolce bene' in the April 1720 premiere of *Radamisto*, 'Fatemi o Cieli' in the December 1720 revival of *Radamisto*, 'Oh dolce mia speranza' in the 1722 revival of *Floridante*) differ in kind from those he wrote for Cuzzoni ('Mà chi punir desio', 'Se non mi vuol amar' in *Flavio*), in that Durastanti's arias have independent accompaniments, often responding to the vocal phrases and/or creating an active counterpart to the voice, whereas in Cuzzoni's arias the orchestra simply accompanies the voice, harmonically supporting the vocal line and creating the context for numerous vocal appoggiaturas and suspensions. The concerto-like sicilianos written for Durastanti, therefore, gave way to the accompanied-song style of sicilianos written for Cuzzoni.

Here I have taken only one type of aria as an example, but the association of specific aria type with specific singer reflects a broader change in Handel's approach to opera composition in general, the results of which can be found in the operas written between 1726 and 1728. During this period another international star, Faustina Bordoni, joined the Royal Academy, and the introduction of her fiery virtuoso style into the company resulted in two new developments. First, she possessed a number of unique virtuoso abilities that had to be incorporated into her arias if Handel was to maximise her musico-dramatic potential. Quantz describes her singing as follows:[16]

> Her way of singing was expressive and brilliant (*un cantar granito*), and she had a light tongue, being able to pronounce words rapidly but plainly in succession. She had a facile throat and a beautiful and very polished *trillo* which she could apply with the greatest of ease wherever and whenever she pleased. The *passagien* could be either running or leaping, or could consist of many fast notes in succession on one tone. She knew how to thrust these out skilfully, with the greatest possible rapidity, as they can be performed only on an instrument.

Writing for Faustina therefore involved dealing with a new type of singer in a leading role and a new set of vocal techniques. Secondly, the nature of Faustina's vocal style and complementary dramatic style further codified Cuzzoni's role, in contrast, as a 'pathetic' heroine. Writing for Cuzzoni increasingly became a task of fully utilising her pathetic qualities.

This musico-dramatic distinction between Cuzzoni and Faustina is immediately apparent in *Alessandro*, the first Royal Academy opera in which the two stars shared the stage. The source for Handel's opera is Ortensio Mauro's *La superbia d'Alessandro*, a libretto which was set by Agostino Steffani for Hanover in 1690.[17] In the Hanover version the roles of Rossane and Lisaura were treated equally, even to the point of having their first arias consist of different verses to two virtually identical da capo arias,[18] but Handel's librettist (Paolo Rolli) gave them contrasted aria texts in the equivalent scene. As a result, Lisaura (Cuzzoni) dwells upon the thought that jealousy destroys the joys of love ('Quanto dolce amor saria') and Rossane (Faustina) sings of love's allurements and resultant anxieties ('Lusinghe più care').

This distinction between Lisaura and Rossane by means of separate aria texts resulted in very different musical treatments in which metre (3/8 / common time), tempo (andante / allegro ma non troppo), vocal style (lyrical, essentially conjunct melodic line with a number of suspensions and few melismas / comparatively disjunct melodic line with numerous complex vocal divisions), and the relationship between text and music (ironic / straightforward) are contrasted. Throughout the opera, Handel and Rolli portray Lisaura as a brooding, melancholy character whose emotional state climaxes in Act II Scene 2 with the aria 'Che tirannia d'Amore', in which she laments Alessandro's love for Rossane and Love's tyranny over herself in a siciliano aria loaded with expressive appoggiaturas and suspensions. By contrast, Rossane is portrayed as an outwardly coy but inwardly scheming woman of considerable spirit whose character is most clearly demonstrated in her aria 'Alla sua gabbia d'oro' later in the second act, in which she addresses Alessandro in a thinly veiled simile aria replete with staggeringly difficult vocal figuration.

By developing characters around the vocal and dramatic strengths of his two leading ladies, Handel demonstrates a distinct compositional approach that differs from that of the Durastanti years. In short, Handel developed two techniques in the Royal Academy operas. For singers with sufficient versatility, Handel could vary aria styles to suit specific dramatic contexts, as demonstrated in many of the arias written for Durastanti. Alternatively, Handel could suit the style to the specific singer, as can be found in many of the arias written for Cuzzoni and Faustina. Interestingly, these two approaches to aria composition could and did exist side by side: in the Royal Academy operas written for Cuzzoni and Faustina, there were also more musically varied roles for Senesino.[19]

While the preceding discussion has been largely concerned with musical style and its functions in the arias Handel wrote during the Royal Academy years, other aspects of his aria composition during this period are also significant. Throughout, Handel's arias demonstrate his sensitivity to text setting both in terms of overall *Affekt* and in terms of the musical treatment of individual words and phrases. Concerning overall *Affekt,* there are a number of instances in which the implications of the text are purposely ignored in the musical setting (Nerone's 'Con saggio tuo consiglio' from *Agrippina,* for example, or Lisaura's 'Quanto dolce' from *Alessandro*), often to provide ironic comment or to further an aspect of character development that is clearly being drawn by Handel in response to the dramatic situation, singer, or both. In other instances, individual lines within aria texts are moved around or repeated in order to suit Handel's desired musical expression ('Dolce bene' from *Radamisto* provides one example). In virtually all of his arias, however, Handel's care with the setting of individual words or phrases is apparent. By means of word repetition, the association of specific words with specific musical ideas, the emphasis on a particular word or phrase by means of extensive melismas, and the use of musical word painting, Handel could both manipulate and clarify the musico-dramatic meaning of his aria texts.

Form is another element of the aria that Handel manipulated in his scores for the Royal Academy operas, although significant deviations from the da capo form are used somewhat sparingly. On one hand, there are shortenings of the full-blown five-part da capo, such as the dal segno aria (see p. 113) and the cavatina (which consists of only the A section), that are not unique to specific operas or to Handel. On the other hand, there are alterations of form that are highly specific to the arias and scenes in which they occur, and one example serves to illustrate the astonishing impact that a change of form could have on the musico-dramatic effectiveness of an aria.

In *Tolomeo* (1728), Handel's last Royal Academy opera, the title-role character (played by Senesino) is the self-exiled son of Cleopatra who has disguised himself as a shepherd on the island of Cyprus. Seleuce, his wife, comes in search of him disguised as a shepherdess, but the King of Cyprus, Araspes, falls in love with her, and the King's sister, Elisa, becomes infatuated with Tolomeo. These circumstances result in husband and wife being separated until the very end of the opera. In the penultimate scene, Tolomeo appears in a soliloquy with a cup of poison. Given the choice between Elisa and death, Tolomeo has chosen death; but instead of poison, Elisa has given him a sleeping potion. In his recitative, Tolomeo contemplates his life and his impending death, and drinks the 'poison'; in his aria, 'Stille amare', he sings of the effects of the 'poison' and falls asleep. It is ostensibly a dal segno aria in the score, but Handel wrote out the repetition of the A section so that he could disrupt it before it was complete: after repeating the first eight bars of the vocal A section, Handel breaks away from the original, and Tolomeo, unable to complete his aria due to the effects of the sleeping potion, collapses on the stage four bars later.[20]

Handel's increased emphasis on the English oratorio from the 1730s onwards did not involve a complete break from his operatic past, and continuity is especially apparent in his attention to the aria. The full da capo form survived even in his later oratorios, and all of the important techniques that Handel developed in his opera arias during the Royal Academy period can be found in his later operas and oratorios. Throughout the repertory of the later period, Handel's attention to word setting, both in the treatment of individual words and the setting of entire aria texts, reflects his sense of the relation of music to drama, a sense that was perfected in his opera composition for the Academy. The arias in *Messiah* (1741–2), for example, display a sensitivity to the dramatic situations inherent in the texts (in spite of the works 'non-dramatic' libretto) that can only be described as operatic. From simple but effective word painting in the tenor aria 'Every Valley' (in which the word 'exalted' is consistently associated with a rising sequence, the first occurrence of the phrase 'and ev'ry mountain and hill made low' contrasts the high F on 'moun̲tain' with the low F on 'low', and the phrase 'the crooked straight and the rough places plain' juxtaposes oscillating conjunct motion with a held note) to the choice of compound time, extensive passages in parallel thirds and the use of sustained bass pedals in 'He shall feed His flock' – evocations of the pastoral arias that are found in both his operas and oratorios – it is clear that Handel's experience as an opera composer had continued to influence his approach to aria composition.

Handel also continued to explore the possibilities of varying the standard da capo form in his operas of the 1730s and in his oratorios. There are numerous examples of the substitution of modified da capo and non da capo forms (such as Orlando's famous rondo 'Vaghe pupille' at the end of Act II of *Orlando*, 1732–3) in the later operas where convention (and, in the case of 'Vaghe pupille', the source libretto[21]) suggested a straightforward da capo. On the other hand, while the modification of da capo forms, such as that in 'Stille amare' described above, can be attributed to Handel's desire to create a unique *Affekt* by bending convention in unusual dramatic contexts, he also used the da capo form as a starting-point for a very different type of formal manipulation. David Hurley describes a number of examples in which a movement that began as a da capo was modified during composition, in his study of Handel's compositional process in the oratorios.[22] Although the aria modifications that Hurley describes are largely devoted to shortening the full-blown da capo form, Handel's starting-point for many of his other arias in the oratorios was in fact the da capo scheme.

As in his most effective opera arias, however, Handel's most poignant oratorio arias combine an abstract musical symbolism with an intense dramatic situation. One of the most powerful dramatic situations for Handel seems to have been that in which a father is confronted by the death or impending death of his daughter. From the two most famous instances of arias relating to this situation, a number of interesting parallels can be observed. In the aria 'Su la sponda del pigro Lete' from Act III of *Tamerlano* (1724), Bajazet addresses his daughter with instructions to drink poison and wait for him on the banks of the river Lethe, the river of the underworld in classical mythology where thoughts of the past life on

Example 8.1   *Jephtha* (HWV 70/32)

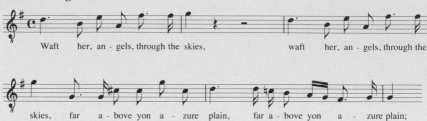

earth are purged by drinking from it. Handel's concern with the aria was such that he set it twice, the second time giving it both an undulating quality in the opening arpeggios (perhaps symbolic of the waters of the river Lethe) and a continuity (there are no times at which voice and orchestra rest together – as there were in the previous version – perhaps signifying the continuity between life and death) that create a musical sub-text to Bajazet's solemn words to his daughter.[23]

In *Jephtha* (1751), Handel's last oratorio, once again a father is confronted by the impending death of his daughter. Reflecting on the prospect of his daughter's sacrifice (the result of his own vow), Jephtha sings of her ascent to heaven in his aria 'Waft her angels through the skies'. The arpeggiation of Jephtha's first phrase and the rising melodic line of much of his vocal part in general is clearly symbolic on one level of Iphis's ascent to heaven. On another level, however, the angular nature of much of Jephtha's melody (see Example 8.1) and the alternation of rising and falling melodic phrases suggest both Jephtha's anguish and his welling of emotion (particularly for the repetition of the phrase 'glorious there like you to rise' in the B section) at the thought of his daughter's sacrifice. Like 'Su la sponda', 'Waft her angels' is a full da capo aria and, also like 'Su la sponda', 'Waft her angels' was extensively altered before Handel was satisfied with it.[24] Even more significant, however, is the fact that in spite of the nearly thirty years that separated the composition of these two arias and the fact that they were written for different genres, similar techniques are used by Handel to convey the complexity and intensity of the emotion being expressed.

While there can be no doubt that oratorio offered Handel considerable freedom from the strict five-part da capo form of the *opera seria*, it is equally clear that the da capo continued to exert a powerful influence on Handel's aria composition throughout his career. His continued use and modification of the da capo aria is certainly most evident in the 'dramatic' oratorios, where the parallels with opera are clear. Even in a non-dramatic oratorio such as *Messiah*, however, in which the reflective nature of the libretto and the lack of a continuous plot sharply differentiate it from Handel's operas, it is interesting to note that for the description of Christ's rejection by the Jews in the aria 'He was despised', Handel used the five-part da capo form, and that his first version of 'Rejoice greatly' was also cast in da capo form.[25] Thus in two of the most emotionally intense arias of the work, Handel continued to employ the da capo form.

From the standpoint of musical construction, the da capo aria quite clearly provided the foundation for Handel's career in aria composition. From an aesthetic standpoint, however, the da capo aria's association with opera is evident in all of Handel's compositions: even when he was no longer bound by convention to write da capos, Handel employed the form at moments of intense drama and/or emotion. Far from being a restrictive form that catered to the performer rather than the composer, the da capo aria appears to have been for Handel a symbol of drama and of the strongest individual expression of emotion. Although it was not suitable to every type of musico-dramatic expression, the personal, individual emotions that characterised opera in Handel's day were expressed almost exclusively in terms of the da capo aria. For Handel, therefore, the form was associated with a type of musical expression to which he devoted the majority of his creative life.

Given Handel's career and the importance of the aria to his compositions, it is somewhat ironic that he is best remembered today for the 'Hallelujah' chorus from *Messiah*. While there is no denying the significance of the choruses in many of his vocal works, for Handel the aria formed the foundation of his stylistic development and his compositional career. It is appropriate, therefore, that the Handel monument at his grave in Westminster Abbey represents the composer at work not on one of his famous choruses, but on the aria 'I know that my Redeemer liveth'.

9 Handel's compositional process

David Ross Hurley

For the sheer number of issues that it raises and potentially illuminates, the investigation of Handel's compositional process constitutes a particularly bountiful field of inquiry.[1] It has yielded new insights into Handel's concept of musical style and structure, his approach to text and drama, and his interactions with singers and librettists. As a result of recent studies we can identify many of Handel's creative tendencies: his attempts upon revision to mitigate thematic garrulousness and to achieve a continuous musical surface, his use of 'cut and paste' techniques akin to eighteenth-century *ars combinatoria*, his concern with musical imagery and drama and with the roles of specific singers in the creation of the operas and oratorios. Yet more remains unknown than known about Handel's compositional process, and even the most basic of received views must sometimes be questioned.

Such is the case with one of the traditional models for Handel's compositional procedures, invoked whenever the genesis of a work must be described, which is generally stated roughly as follows: 'Handel began composing by writing down a skeleton score, drafting the principal melodic lines and bass for arias and choruses (the lines for accompanying instrumental parts were left blank), and writing the recitative texts between the set pieces. At a later stage, he went back and "filled up" the score, providing music for the recitatives and writing out the orchestral parts.'

An unfinished early version of an aria in *Belshazzar* casts doubt on the universality of this paradigm. This fragment,[2] an incomplete setting of 'The leafy honours of the field', was abandoned after the vocal cadence to the dominant.[3] It is reproduced in full, from Handel's autograph, in Plates 4–6. If we assume that Handel intended to compose a full da capo aria, the fragment represents the entire first half of the A section. Now the puzzling fact is that the fragment is completely orchestrated and includes dynamic markings and revisions that one would normally assign to the 'filling up' stage or later, thus defying our received view of Handel's typical music-writing procedures. This example raises a host of questions. Should the received model of Handel's music-writing methods simply be abandoned, or merely qualified? Or does the fragment at hand represent an exception that requires explanation – for example, that Handel was working from a pre-existing draft, or that the aria contains unique features that might explain its exceptional treatment? In fact, there are several possible explanations, which I will discuss in turn, but the likelihood of each must be weighed against the evidence derived from studies of the compositional process.

1. If 'The leafy honours' represents an anomaly, the exception could be explained if Handel were working from an extensive pre-existent 'draft'. This raises the question of exactly what the term 'draft' means in Handel studies. In the musicological literature 'draft' often denotes a pre-compositional piece that serves as the basis for a new piece. There is little evidence that Handel ever created such drafts *that were intended to serve as pre-compositional drafts from the beginning*. Certainly almost anything – a completed composition, a rejected work, works by others – might serve Handel as model or raw material for new compositions. But there is little evidence, if any, to suggest that Handel prepared pre-compositional drafts before setting down a piece in the autograph score. Some sketches survive (which we will consider below), but these are generally brief, and could hardly explain the relatively developed and finished appearance of the 'Leafy honours' fragment. In Handel studies the term 'draft' is more commonly used to refer to a composition that was drafted into the autograph, but not completely orchestrated, and abandoned before or during Handel's 'filling up' stage.

If a surviving pre-compositional item served as the source for 'The leafy honours', I have failed to locate it. The possibility that this was nonetheless the case cannot be ruled out – there are certainly instances in which Handel copied from pre-existent works – but this hypothesis is not essential to the history of this particular aria.

2. At least one other reason why this aria might have required special treatment when it was written down concerns the particularly important role of the orchestra and of dynamics, which must be understood in the light of Handel's use of musical imagery. The opening text ('The leafy honours of the field') evokes a pastoral setting, which is represented in musical terms by 3/8 metre and occasional pedals, as well as the key of F major. However, the 'furious driving wind', a metaphor for Belshazzar's debauchery, imposes upon the pastoral landscape: the *forte* marking and the register have much to do with the effectiveness of its musical representation. It could well be that the important role of this element explains why Handel might have wished to record the orchestral material from the beginning, and even to make revisions (such as adjusting the register of the music for 'furious, driving wind') before reaching the end of the aria. Indeed, the musical imagery (including the falling triplets for 'in giddy

Plate 4 Handel's first setting of 'The leafy Honours of the field' (*Belshazzar*), in the composer's autograph, beginning. (British Library RM 20.d.10, fol. 61v)

Plate 5 Handel's first setting of 'The leafy Honours of the field' (*Belshazzar*), in the composer's autograph, continuation. (British Library RM 20.d.10, fol. 66r)

Plate 6 Handel's first setting of 'The leafy Honours of the field' (*Belshazzar*), in the composer's autograph, conclusion of fragment on staves 1–3, with part of Handel's second setting below. (British Library RM 20.d.10, fol. 66v)

dissipation fly') must belong to an early creative layer of the piece; it is not the sort of writing that one later 'fills in'.

3. There can be no doubt that Handel did, indeed, set out many pieces in skeleton score, filling in the orchestral parts after completing the whole. In many of the oratorio autographs Handel included dates for the completion of specific acts in skeleton draft and the dates of 'filling up'.[4] But this paradigm does not apply throughout Handel's oeuvre, or necessarily to every item within a given work. Steven LaRue has found that in the Royal Academy operas Handel composed the arias in all parts as he worked, rather than drafting melody and bass-line only.[5] The most obvious explanation for this difference is that the arias in the operas are relatively lightly scored in comparison to those in the oratorios. It is reasonable to assume, then, that even in the oratorios arias that were lightly scored could have been written down in all parts from the beginning. Because the first version of 'The leafy honours' is scored for voice, bass, and *violini unisoni* it would not have been odd or even unusual if Handel had written down all these parts from the beginning of the aria.

We shall not know which of these explanations is the true one unless more evidence comes to light. In any case, the fragment for 'The leafy honours' underscores the limits of our knowledge about Handel's compositional process; even the most cherished of our notions must be abandoned in certain cases. The lesson to be learned is not that paradigmatic models should be abandoned altogether, but that in a field comprised of so much *terra incognita* we must constantly be open to revising our models and introducing new ones. For knowledge to proceed we must constantly question what we think we know. In what follows I will attempt to advance various models that cover central issues of Handel's compositional process. I want to stress, however, that I do not wish to establish one model as 'normal' and another as 'atypical'; at this stage in Handel studies it is wisest to speak not of 'the compositional process' but of 'compositional processes'.

In an oft-quoted passage written in 1954, Gerald Abraham inaugurates a discussion of Handel's musical style by likening Handel's propensity to begin composing from a 'borrowed' datum to the practice of improvisation:[6]

> it is clear that a large proportion of [Handel's] published work originated in private improvisation, however polished and worked up after being set on paper. There is ample evidence that Handel frequently began to compose by playing the harpsichord, starting from the first favourite cliché that came under his fingers . . . and allowing it to grow into something that was usually in the end absolutely his and his alone.

A rigorous critique of Abraham's theory might begin by trying to delineate the issues raised by the term 'improvisation', for there are surely differences between eighteenth-century usage of the term (as a matter of practice with no value judgement assigned to it), Abraham's understanding of Baroque improvisation (informed, but coloured by a need to save Handel for the vestiges of what might be called the 'Cult of Originality' – the Romantic view that a composer's work must be entirely original in order to be a work of genius) and our own understanding of improvisation.

For the moment, however, I would like to avoid these matters and ponder a momentous issue sparked by Abraham's observation: to what extent can Handel's compositional process be described as 'spontaneous' (the view I believe that Abraham meant in part to propagate); or conversely, to what extent did Handel plan a work or aspects of a work before the 'event' of composition? Such questions are perhaps ultimately impossible to answer. The relationship between planning and spontaneity is apt to be a fluid one, changing from piece to piece, or even from moment to moment during the act of composition, and we cannot expect the state of the autographs to detail all, or even a majority, of Handel's mental processes. But certain questions are worth asking, even if they cannot be definitely answered, for the sake of the light they shed upon other questions. By pursuing the unanswerable I hope to achieve two goals: first, to uncover at least two of the many possible models that capture aspects of Handel's compositional process; and secondly, to distinguish, similarly, between two distinct kinds of Handel fragments. The fact that my examples are drawn from oratorios that Handel composed in 1744, *Hercules* and *Belshazzar*, argues that these particular models for Handel's compositional process coexisted chronologically: Handel did not, in this case, change from one practice to the other over time.

Abraham's observation on Handel's style suggests that borrowed material is in a sense extraneous to improvisatory or spontaneous compositional processes; borrowings are the materials with which such processes work, but obviously are not products of those processes. This is equally true of other pre-compositional materials such as sketches, whose nature deserves our scrutiny. The term 'sketch' refers to musical ideas, generally brief, that Handel jotted down more than likely before setting out to compose a piece in score, though some sketching may have taken place during the process of composing. The bulk of Handel's surviving sketches, along with rejected drafts, detached sections from other autographs and Handel's handwritten extracts from works by other composers, resides now in the Fitzwilliam Museum, Cambridge.[7] The paper types and layout of the sketches suggest that for sketching Handel randomly used empty staves on rejected drafts or other scrap pages and sometimes unused music sheets: the pages concerned were often contemporary with his composing scores, but occasionally he used up space on folios that were years older. It is generally assumed that Handel's sketches survive merely by chance, and that many sketches must have been lost,[8] but this has by no means been proven. There is in fact little surviving evidence that Handel sketched extensively.

Handel's method of sketching distinguishes him from Bach, the greatest number of whose sketches seem to be memory aids, written at the bottom of recto pages in the composing scores to record the immediate continuation of the music for the next page while the ink dried.[9] A certain number of Handel's sketches possibly served as memory aids, but others show the composer in the process of creating material that would be used in the main autograph.

For the time being, I wish to focus on one common type of sketch and what it tells us: this type has passages of important melodic material, often brief – sometimes merely two to four bars of melody.[10] Many of Handel's melodic borrowings[11] also often consist of short two- to four-bar resemblances that are nonetheless significant enough to merit pointing out, and there are many shared features in the use of such borrowings and sketches. The very existence of such sketches and borrowings would seem to indicate that Handel began composing by collecting or creating melodic material – a common practice in tonal composition.[12]

The fact that Handel prepared sketches of this sort but did not intentionally prepare long drafts might suggest that the actual formal creation of a piece, once the main melodic ideas were decided upon, could be done more or less 'automatically', thus explaining why Handel could compose directly into the final autograph score. This was due, no doubt, in part to the universality of certain musical techniques in the early eighteenth century, such as pre-existent tonal plans (for the A sections of da capo arias), methods of sequential repetition, and melodic combination and re-ordering.[13]

Handel sometimes changed his mind about the 'working out' of musical ideas as he composed. At times such changes of inner structure were significant enough to alter the outer form of the complete movement.[14] We can thus suggest one tentative model for Handel's normative compositional process in which melodies are worked out before the fact and musical forms result from 'spontaneous' processes – precompositional melodic creation followed by spontaneous formal creation.[15]

The interplay of compositional forethought and spontaneity according to this model can be seen in a series of fragments for the duet 'Joys of freedom' in *Hercules*. All four versions of this duet derive from an Italian chamber duet, *Beato in ver* (HWV 181), a single-movement work written in October 1742, two years before *Hercules*.[16] Analysing the wealth of material created and sifted for a single piece illustrates both the abundance of Handel's imagination and his difficulty in this particular instance in deciding how the piece should continue.

Scored for soprano, alto and continuo, *Beato in ver* is a da capo structure that follows Handel's most typical harmonic plan, its A section ending in the tonic (A major), its B section ending in the mediant minor (C♯ minor).[17] As in many of Handel's arias, the A section departs from conventional five-part da capo form[18] in several ways. There is no opening ritornello, for example, and the A section does not divide into two halves either harmonically or in terms of textual repetition. In fact, the A-section text is stated four times rather than twice, and there is no strongly articulated cadence to mark the A section's midpoint.

All versions of 'Joys of freedom' from *Hercules* draw upon melodic, harmonic, and even contrapuntal aspects of *Beato in ver*, but not the

Example 9.1 'Joys of freedom' (*Hercules*, HWV 60/30), opening

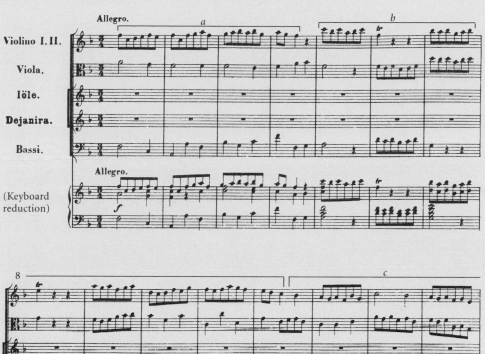

form, scoring or key of the model. In the extensive opening ritornello of 'Joys of freedom' we can identify four major melodic ideas: *a* (1–4), *b* (5–12), *c* (12–20), *d* (20–25). (See Example 9.1.) The first two melodic ideas (*a* and *b*) are apparently original in 'Joys of freedom', but *c* and *d* derive from *Beato in ver*, though their order of appearance has been changed; *d* was the first thematic event in *Beato in ver* (bars 1–4) and *c* first appeared eight bars later (bars 12–16). (See Example 9.2.)

In 'Joys of freedom' Dejanira's first vocal statement not only harmonically redirects the thematic ideas, which now move from tonic to dominant, but also changes the order from that of the ritornello to *a, b, d, c*. Having reached the dominant at this point, *d* serves as a medial ritornello

Example 9.1 *(cont.)*

in the new key. The next vocal section, featuring Iole and with a new text, repeats the new ordering (*a b d c*), followed by counterpoint on *d* for both voices (95–109) – their first moment of interaction in the duet. This last passage corresponds roughly to bars 16–23 of *Beato in ver*, although there are harmonic differences: the Italian duet concluded in the dominant (E) before moving through the subdominant (D) and modulating to other keys, whereas 'Joys of freedom' concludes in the tonic (F) before moving to the subdominant (B♭). Even though the oratorio duet and its Italian model differ formally, therefore, Handel nonetheless returned to the original for melodic and contrapuntal material at a major structural point.

Example 9.1   *(cont.)*

All versions of the *Hercules* duet share these first 110 bars, but we must examine independently Handel's various solutions for the continuation. It is fascinating that Handel's difficulty with the composition apparently began at this point. In terms of tonal organisation, by bar 102 'Joys of freedom' has unfolded as a completely typical A section, lacking only a concluding ritornello: the first statement of the text (by Dejanira), as noted, reaches the dominant in bar 56 (*HG* vol. 4: p. 178, bar 6), followed by an abbreviated ritornello in the dominant key; the second statement of the text (by Iole) reaches a strong close on the tonic by bar 102. But, in spite of the structure so far, Handel apparently did not intend to cast the

Example 9.2 Duetto *Beato in Ver* (HWV 181), opening

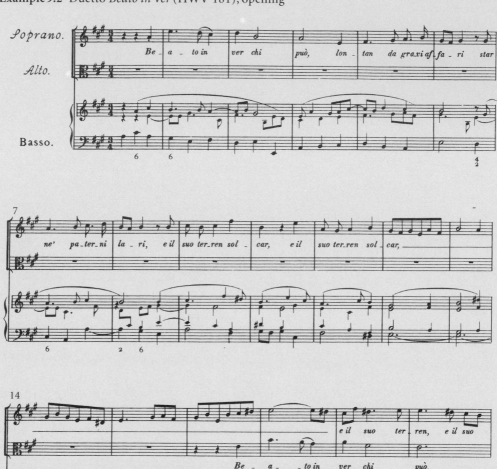

duet in da capo form at any stage: he did not wish the piece to conclude before providing an opportunity for the voices to sing together in an extended passage. Having completed A1 and A2 in the solo sections (with the actual 'duet' beginning at the end of A2, when the voices finally sing together at bar 95), the duet now needed a concluding section or sections – at least an 'A3', as it were – for which there is no prescribed formal plan. There were several compositional options, and Handel tried different structural schemes before he reached his final solution.[19]

In the first version Handel continued with imitation on thematic figure *a* for the two voices in the subdominant, Bb major. (See Example 9.3.) This is followed by a variation of *b* (based on bars 37–40, themselves a variation of bars 9–12), which is restated and ornamented over a C pedal. (See Example 9.3, bars 116–23). Finally, there are two ideas derived from *Beato in ver*. The first is imitation on *c* (Example 9.3, bars 123–33), which corresponds to several places in *Beato in ver*.[20] In 'Joys of freedom' this material occurs over an F pedal which moves to Bb and Eb. Second, the fragment ends with eight harmonically unstable bars whose tonal direction is unclear. Fittingly, the prominent melodic motive in these bars (marked 'x' on Example 9.3 at its first occurrence, bars 134–5) comes from an unstable part of the B section of *Beato in ver*.[21] Handel abandoned his first version of 'Joys of freedom' at this point.

Having reached the tonic already in bar 102, Handel must have wished to achieve sufficient harmonic interest in the new section to justify extending the composition beyond a point at which, in a cavatina, or after the A section repeat in a da capo aria, the piece might have ended. One possibility was to allow the next portion of the duet to take on some of the character of a B section, hence Handel's use of material from the B section of *Beato in ver*. Unless the length of the piece were to become unwieldy, however, it had to be composed in such a way that it could end convincingly in the tonic without sounding tonally redundant – this is not a relevant problem in aria B sections, which end in contrasting keys, and are completed by the repeat of the A section. We may discover why Handel's first contribution to the duet proved unsatisfactory after we have examined his next attempt.

The second version (Example 9.4) follows the first one in many particulars. The first six bars are almost identical (up to bar 116), except that the imitative entrance of the top voice occurs a bar later. In bar 117, however, Handel makes a tonal shift, presenting *a* in F where the first version had featured material derived from the end of *b* in Bb. In bars 121–5 Handel employs the beginning of *b* rather than its end. The melodic unit *c* appears over an F pedal, somewhat as in the first version (Ex. 9.3, bars

Example 9.3 First version of 'Joys of freedom', bars 111 ff.

* Handel probably deleted the middle notes of the triplet groups.

Example 9.4   Second version of 'Joys of freedom', bars 111 ff.

124–31). Rather than introducing *x*, however, Handel next moves to the dominant key and presents *c* over a C pedal leading to a cadence (*d*) in C major, which is echoed by the orchestra.

A comparison of the first two versions clearly shows that Handel thought afresh about the tonal structure of this section. The dominant, which occurred as a prolonged pedal (but not as a key area) moving to the tonic early in the first version, is reserved until its appearance as a key area near the end of the second version. The solution offered by the second version, however, emphasises the dominant perhaps too strongly. Like the end of A1 earlier in the duet, the cadence to the dominant key area is followed by a three-bar ritornello in the new key. In order to conclude the piece Handel would have had to write a new section – in effect, an A4 – to return to the tonic and balance the modulation to the dominant. Handel rejected that plan as well. Coming after A1/A2, this second version was not only formally and harmonically redundant, mirroring exactly the

Example 9.4 *(cont.)*

progression to the dominant in A1, but the requisite statement returning to the tonic that would have been needed after bar 146 might have resulted in too lengthy a composition.

The third version retains much of the earlier part of the second version (to bar 134). Thereafter it offers new material over a dominant pedal. (See Example 9.5.) This thematic idea is not really 'new' in the larger context of the duet, however; it derives from bars 29–30. This leads to imitation on *c* (beginning with a brief reference to *b*) at first over the tonic, then spun out over another dominant pedal. After a strong cadence to the tonic in bars 155–6, the 'head-motif' of *c* gives way to *x*, which appears over yet another C pedal, again moving towards the tonic at the end.

Certainly the dominant is strongly felt in this third version but, with only a passing reference in bar 150, it is never established as a key area as it had been in the second version; instead the dominant serves to emphasise the tonic key. Yet after he has established the tonic in bars 147 and 156,

Example 9.5   Third version of 'Joys of freedom', bars 134 ff. (preceded by
bars 111–33 as in Ex. 9.4)

Example 9.6 Final version of 'Joys of freedom', bars 141 ff. (preceded by bars 111–33 as in
Ex. 9.4 and bars 134–40 as in Ex. 9.5)

Handel moves back to an area of prolonged dominant harmony (or at
least, as in the latter, an area of dominant-weighted harmony). The
cadence to the tonic near the end of the draft (bars 167–8) is therefore one
among the many within this section.

In the more pithy final version (Example 9.6) the sweet-sounding
thirds and sixths ('how sweet they steal upon my ear'; bars 142–6) are
altered from the preceding version, followed by a common-time adagio
cadence (147–50), and ending finally with a varied return of the ritornello. This final version is directed towards a strong return to the tonic
near the end, withholding emphasis of the tonic within A3 until this
point. The remarkable changes – the *fermata* that arrests the rhythmic
momentum with the change to a common-time adagio and an abandonment of the previous melodic material – provide dramatic emphasis for
the return of the tonic key. Handel's final solution provides a striking
close indeed.

The autograph of this duet, then, shows an array of formal options that
Handel actually considered as he developed the movement. On the whole
the contrasts in tonality and structure among the various versions
are particularly striking, whereas the basic melodic material, in spite of its

re-ordering and the differences in its development, remains essentially the same until the 'written-out cadenza' at bars 147–9 of the final version. The compositional history of this duet could thus support the view that melodic or thematic content tends to be a planned and reasonably fixed aspect of composition for Handel, but details of harmonic direction as a determinant of formal structure – in this case even the outer form – were not worked out in advance, thus indicating a more intuitive aspect of Handel's creativity. 'Joys of freedom' provides a fascinating illustration that compositional choice, in a section whose modulation plan was not predetermined by convention, resulted in significant formal changes as Handel composed.

This model does not tell the whole story, however. Even if Handel seems often to have decided on his primary melodic material before he began to compose a given piece in the autograph score, on many occasions his original melodic material proved unsuitable and he changed it, introducing new material, during composition. There exist cases in which thematic material was significantly reworked, or rejected and replaced. At the same time, there are many cases in which internal alterations do not affect outer form. In Handel's time, after all, the text in vocal music often determined such stereotyped outer forms as the da capo aria. Handel sometimes chose a different form from that dictated by the text, and he sometimes required changes of text from his librettists. Nonetheless, the choice of outer form, like melodic sketching, must often, perhaps typically, have been a pre-compositional act, and in many cases Handel maintained this pre-compositional formal choice even if he made other revisions. For an illustration we must return, in the manner of a da capo repeat, to 'The leafy honours' from *Belshazzar*.

One of the most salient ways in which Handel's second setting of this aria differs from the first, incomplete, one is the richer scoring – Handel adds a part to be shared by third violin and viola – but the new orchestration does not fully explain other fundamental musical changes. It seems at first that a reasonable hypothesis for the composer's abandonment of his first version of 'The leafy honours' at the arrival of the dominant marking the end of the first half of the A section might be that he was dissatisfied with his approach to the dominant. But this turns out not to be the case. Indeed, Handel's new setting maintains almost exactly the features of the last part of the first version: the C major section which begins with the text 'in giddy dissipation fly', with its giddy triplets, its lengthy melisma, and its cadence to the dominant. In spite of very slight changes near the end,[22] both the tonal plan and the form of the fragment are retained in the second version, in contrast to Handel's procedures in 'Joys of freedom'.

For the most part, Handel's revisions to 'The leafy honours' focus rather on earlier parts of the aria, beginning with elaboration and expansion of the opening ritornello. This process of expansion involves in part the appropriation of borrowed passages, identified by John Roberts, from the aria 'Và col canto lusingando' from the cantata *Clori, Tirsi e Fileno* (HWV 96) of 1707.[23] The treatment of the material in the new setting, however, differs from that of the source, and it is this treatment that demands our scrutiny, beginning with the opening ritornello.

On a broad scale, the changes in the new setting serve to tighten the relationship between the ritornello and the vocal A section of the aria – a fairly common type of compositional revision in Handel's autographs that has been discussed by Paul Brainard.[24] Perhaps more important for our purposes, however, are the local ramifications of the changes within the ritornello itself. On this immediate level, the alterations seem to have two main musical goals: to provide more melodic and rhythmic drive; and, relatedly, to reduce the regularity of phrase structure, which had involved predictable patterns of repetition in the first draft of the orchestral opening. (See Example 9.7.) Originally the phrase structure of the ritornello was:

8 bars $(4 + 4) + 4 (2 + 2) + 8 (2 + 2 + 2 + 2) + 6 (4 + 2)$

Within these predominantly regular phrase groupings, bars 1–4 were immediately repeated in bars 5–8 (with an octave transposition in the bass); bars 9–10 (derived from 'Và col canto' bars 61–2) were duplicated in 11–12 (lowering the bass-line an octave); bars 13–14 and 17–18 were repeated an octave lower in 15–16 and 19–20, respectively. Only the final six bars of the first version are irregular and unpredictable.

The alteration of the ritornello in the new version does much to mitigate the pervasive regularity of phrase structure and repetition from the first version. The opening eight bars are expanded to ten. The passage consisting of triplets followed by a dotted crotchet that was stated in bar 9–10 of the original is lowered by a third and, after repeating it, Handel adds another statement at the original pitch level, expanding the original four-bar passage to six bars. After the next motif (*z*, later used to depict the 'furious driving wind') has been stated and restated at various pitch levels, Handel adds two bars ultimately derived from 'Và col canto' bars 8–9 (second version, bars 19–20). The resulting phrase structure is less predictable than in the original:

10 bars $(4 + 4 + 2) + 6 (4 + 2) + 8 (2 + 2 + 2 + 2) + 8 (2 + 4 + 2)$

The new version also involves some reworkings of melodic material, as examination of the opening melody of the ritornello in Example 9.7

Example 9.7 'The leafy honours' (*Belshazzar*, HWV 61/17a), ritornello

discloses. The original consisted of a four-bar phrase which was repeated exactly, apart from the change of anacrusis from C to F. In the final version Handel retains the first two bars, but rewrites the last two bars (in a manner that follows 'Và col canto', bars 2–3), so that the melodic goal at bar 4 is A rather than C. When the opening four-bar phrase is repeated, Handel uses demisemiquavers rather than triplets, increasing the rhythmic drive. Next, he adds two new bars which complete the melodic ascent to C. The rhythmic variation of bar 3 in bars 7–10, combined with the melodic ascent, is perhaps mimetic in nature, suggesting an increasing flurry of wind. Together with the transposition of material at bar 11 of the second setting, these changes reduce the melodic emphasis on the note C, which occurred every two to three bars in the original. The melody of the new version is accordingly somewhat more directional and less static in its component parts than the first, although the prolongation of C is (more subtly) maintained. Whether or not the new setting represents an 'improvement' upon the original, its expressive aim has changed: Handel has moved away from the predictable pastoral repose of the fragment, to the increased irregularity of the second setting.

The changes between the two settings are of course not limited to the orchestral introduction. While Handel naturally rewrites passages in the vocal body of the aria that re-state material from the ritornello (such as the vocal statement of the head-motif) so that corresponding passages match, he also sometimes transforms music that is unrelated to the ritornello. The new setting of 'before the furious driving wind', for instance, discloses another fundamental change of melodic material. (See Example 9.8.) Whereas in the first version the accompaniment figure depicting the wind enters right away, in the final version it is reserved until after the voice has stated the line of text once – probably an indication of Handel's concern that the text should be heard in performance before its musical depiction begins. The melody of the new version, though it retains much of the pitch content of the original (in the first three bars of Example 9.8), has more character of its own; unlike the draft, it is not merely a counter-melody to the 'wind' motif.[25] This is particularly noticeable in the second half of the passage, where the tail of the melody is repeated against the 'wind' in the accompaniment, as opposed to the arpeggiated melody of the original.[26]

The fragments for 'Joys of freedom' and 'The leafy honours' embody two distinct types of fragments that are found among Handel's compositional material. The 'Joys of freedom' fragments illustrate that Handel sometimes abandoned a composition because he was unsure of its continuation, but was quite satisfied with how the piece had progressed up to a certain point. The early version of 'The leafy honours', on the other

Example 9.8 'The Leafy honours'   (a) Original setting, bars 34–41

(b) Second setting, bars 41–50

hand, was apparently abandoned at least in part because the piece as written required changes, whether for the sake of the immediate context or to lay ground for a better continuation, or both. Similarly, the compositional model exemplified by 'The leafy honours' is in a sense the opposite of that shown by 'Joys of freedom': for in the former Handel alters original melodic material, but (as far as can be seen) not the form. It is tempting, therefore, to suggest a second model for Handel's compositional method in addition to the one outlined on page 128: changeable melodic material within predetermined and 'fixed' formal creation. Admittedly 'The leafy honours' illustrates this model only to an extent, for most of the original melodic ideas are retained in the setting; changes in details of the inner structure, however, do not seem to change the outer form. Although these two models cover any number of examples (here I have illustrated them with one example of each), there are many cases that lie between them, or beyond both, thus requiring different formulations. Some pieces share passages in which the bass-line is the unchanging element.[27] In other cases the changes are so extreme that we must speak of unrelated settings (such as the two versions of 'Will the sun forget to streak' from *Solomon*).[28]

In addition to teaching us about the composer at work, then, the study of Handel's compositional process constantly forces us to play devil's advocate with our paradigms. A single model can never explain all cases, for models serve to summarise tendencies, and not as fixed rules. Strict adherence to any single paradigmatic model inevitably misleads us.

Robert Oppenheimer has argued for the necessity of maintaining both old and new theories in the sciences, and certain of his remarks are relevant here:[29]

> To what appear to be the simplest questions, we will tend to give either no answer or an answer which will at first sight be reminiscent more of a strange catechism than of the straightforward affirmatives of physical science. If we ask, for instance, whether the position of the electron remains the same, we must say "no"; if we ask whether the electron's position changes with time, we must say "no"; if we ask whether the electron is at rest, we must say "no"; if we ask whether it is in motion, we must say "no." The Buddha has given such answers when interrogated as to the conditions of a man's self after death; but they are not the familiar answers for the tradition of seventeenth- and eighteenth-century science.

Similarly, if we ask whether Handel composed spontaneously, we must answer 'yes'; if we ask whether composition for Handel involved forethought and planning, we must answer 'yes'; if we ask if Handel's revisions alter musical form while maintaining essential melodic content, we must answer 'yes'; if we ask if Handel abandons his original melodic ideas in the course of revision, the answer is 'yes'. The fact that our brief overview of Handel's compositional processes has revealed differing tendencies merely reflects the multiplicity of techniques and styles at Handel's fingertips. Only with the help of different models extracted from analyses of individual pieces – models that, viewed from a certain distance, may seem paradoxical – can we begin to capture the creative acts of such a versatile composer.

10 Handel and the idea of an oratorio

Anthony Hicks

In seventeenth-century Italy the term 'oratorio' was applied to certain vocal musical works having characteristics in common but often quite different in scale and style.[1] The fact that the word did not appear in the title of a work did not necessarily debar it from being considered a member of the genre. Almost any vocal work having a non-liturgical religious text, written for more than one singer and of greater extent than a single aria or chorus, could be considered an oratorio. Since the form was largely confined to Catholic Italy, the texts were invariably in Italian or Latin, and generally there was an implication that the work was dramatic – that is, the singers, at least when performing solo, represented named characters, whether historical, mythical, supernatural or allegorical. The text might include narration, sung either by a single voice or shared among a number of singers, thus setting the work at a distance from pure theatrical drama, while by no means precluding highly personalised emotion. The best-known example of an oratorio of the mid-seventeenth century, Giacomo Carissimi's *Historia de Jepthes*, has several narrative solos, but the main characters of Jephtha and his daughter are impersonated consistently by a tenor and a soprano, and the Israelites by the chorus. Their music is powerfully expressive, and clearly designed to involve the listener in the events of the tragic story and its effects on the participants.

By the end of the century oratorio had spread to other countries and had become more settled in form. The term implied a substantial vocal work on a religious text, for several singers and an orchestra, divided into two parts and taking over an hour – often more than two hours – to perform. In the hands of Italian composers and librettists, who continued to be in the forefront of developments, the role of the narrator faded and oratorio became entirely dramatic. The drama, however, was invariably contained within the words and the music, not realised in stage action, and not normally performed in a theatre. An oratorio for a grand occasion might nevertheless be presented in what would now be called a 'semi-staged' manner, with painted back-cloths to help the audience visualise key moments in the story. Handel's *La Resurrezione* was so presented at a Roman palace in 1708, in a style that followed established precedents.

Oratorio outside Italy, and particularly in Protestant countries, was slow to catch on. Suspicion of the effects of music, and of the treatment of religious themes in words other than those of unadulterated Scripture, no doubt hindered its acceptance. In Germany, however, there had been a tradition of musical settings of the New Testament Gospel narratives, particularly those dealing with Christ's Passion and Resurrection, since the late sixteenth century. These *Historiae*, as they were called, were composed in a chant-like style, but Heinrich Schütz (1585–1672), in his masterly settings of the Easter and Christmas stories (1623 and 1664), the Seven Last Words of Christ (1645) and three of the Passion narratives (1665–6), began to explore and realise in music the expressive and dramatic qualities of the texts. Of these, Schütz's Christmas story, with its instrumental accompaniments and its vocal ensembles representing the angels, the shepherds, the three kings and the high priests, comes closest to Italian oratorio, but the work was still called *Historia* and was largely a setting of the relevant portion of Luke's gospel, with a tenor Evangelist supplying the narration. A related form was the *actus musicus*, also containing a mix of impersonation and narration, but making freer use of non-biblical text. The earliest example, Andreas Fromm's *Actus musicus de Divite et Lazaro*, published in Stettin in 1649, uses narration only as a prologue, the rest of the work consisting of non-biblical dialogues for the various characters interspersed with reflective solos and choruses mostly based on chorales. Though not so titled, Fromm's work has with some justice been called 'the first German oratorio'.

The first formal use of the term 'oratorio' for a work in German appears in 1704 with Reinhard Keiser's setting of a text by C. F. Hunold, the libretto of which bears a title beginning *Der blutige und sterbende Jesus, wie selbiger in einem Oratorio musikalisch gesetzet*, though more than a decade earlier a lost work by N. A. Strungk had been informally described as 'ein Oratorium, die Auferstehung Jesu' [an oratorio, the Resurrection of Jesus].[2] Keiser's oratorio was produced in Hamburg, where there had previously been a vogue for sacred opera, beginning in 1678 with Johann Theile's *Der erschaffene, gefallene und aufgerichtete Mensch*, which, however, had faded by the 1690s. This in itself was a continuation of an earlier tradition inaugurated by Emilio de' Cavalieri's *Rappresentatione di anima, e di corpo* of 1600 (in vernacular Italian and introducing the new style of monodic recitative into a sacred dramatic work) and brought to Germany with S. T. Staden's *Seelewig*, published in Nuremberg in 1644. German oratorio, as performed in Hamburg in the first decade of the eighteenth century, and presumably as first experienced by the young Handel, could therefore draw upon a wide range of established patterns. Hunold emphasised the relationship of *Der blutige und sterbende Jesus* to

Italian forms 'without the Evangelist', but in contrast to Italian practice the early Hamburg oratorios were confined to the Passion story and generally performed in secular buildings during Holy Week; it was not until Johann Mattheson began composing oratorios for performance in the cathedral in 1715 that a wider range of subjects was introduced.

The extent to which Handel was interested in these developments must remain conjectural, as he made no contribution to them while he was working in Germany.[3] His one exercise in the German passion tradition (*Der für die Sünde der Welt gemarterte und sterbende Jesus*, HWV 48) was a setting of an influential libretto by the Hamburg pietist poet Barthold Heinrich Brockes (1680–1747), first set by Keiser in 1712. Brockes's text used the device of the Evangelist to tell the story, but the narration is a rhymed text derived (without direct quotation) from all four Gospels, and thus allowed for performance outside a strictly liturgical context. Much of the commentary is given to the symbolic Daughter of Zion, and emphasises the sufferings of Christ as proof of his devotion to mankind. Handel composed his setting around 1716, almost certainly in London (where Handel's ventures outside the world of the opera house were largely devoted to English church music). The sense of distance is reflected in Handel's setting of Brockes's text, which is always worthy and occasionally moving, but reveals little sense of spiritual involvement. Though the music was later to play a significant part in Handel's first exploration of English oratorio, the work was an isolated exercise in a form which appears to have held little interest for him.

The two oratorios which Handel wrote in Italy in 1707 and 1708 were more significant pointers to future developments. The quasi-operatic idiom into which the form had settled, especially in Rome where public performance of opera was barred by papal decree, was congenial to Handel and there are signs that his librettists were glad to co-operate with him in creating striking effects. The title of the first, to a libretto by Handel's patron Cardinal Benedetto Pamphili, seems originally to have been *La Bellezza ravveduta nel trionfo del Tempo e del Disinganno* ('Beauty repentant in the triumph of Time and Enlightenment') but is usually given as *Il trionfo del Tempo e del Disinganno* (HWV 46a).[4] In form it is an unstaged drama for four allegorical characters which becomes explicitly religious as the action unfolds. Beauty (Bellezza) is tempted by Pleasure (Piacere) with the promise that she will retain her outer attractiveness, but Time (Tempo) and Enlightenment (Disinganno) convince her that this will fade; only the inner beauty of a soul devoted to God is eternal. The arguments and allusions of the libretto are sometimes obscure, but the composer responds to the various images in the arias with appropriate musical inventiveness. Tensions between the characters develop, and physical action (such as the shattering of Pleasure's false mirror) is occasionally suggested. The scene that takes most ingenious advantage of the concept of unstaged drama is that in which Beauty is introduced to the palace of Pleasure. Amid marble sculptures of youths a 'graceful young man' (*leggiadro giovinetto*) 'awakens wondrous delight with enchanting sound': the sound in question was the composer himself playing the organ, first in a short sonata with orchestral accompaniment, and then in Beauty's subsequent aria. There could be no better illustration of the way unstaged drama can float between the dramatic action realised only in the listener's mind and the actuality of the performance in concert; in the case of the Sonata the composer himself becomes momèntarily the centre of both the real and the notional action.

Handel's next work in oratorio form, *La resurrezione* (HWV 47),[5] was composed about a year later. It was designed to celebrate Easter Day, and Carlo Sigismondo Capece's libretto is a poetic dramatisation of the appropriate passages of the Gospel narratives, mixed with other aspects of Christian tradition. Commissioned by Marquis Francesco Maria Ruspoli, the most important of Handel's Roman patrons, and first performed at his residence, the Bonelli Palace, on Easter Sunday (8 April) 1708, it formed a sequel to Alessandro Scarlatti's Passion Oratorio,[6] composed to a libretto by Cardinal Pietro Ottoboni and performed at the latter's palace on the preceding Wednesday. Much of the Cardinal's text for Scarlatti consists of vernacular paraphrases of the Lamentations of Jeremiah (the Latin Vulgate version of which is the basis of the Tenebrae services of Holy Week), interspersed with comments from the three allegorical characters. The work is therefore reflective in style, as may be thought appropriate to its subject. By contrast, the treatment of the resurrection story by Handel and his librettist is defiantly dramatic, and its presentation was almost theatrical: the performers appeared in a specially constructed set, with back-cloths depicting key moments in the story.[7] The discourse of the three mortal characters from the Gospel story, Mary Magdalene, Mary Cleophas and John, reveals the anxious mood of Christ's followers the night before the resurrection and their joy on the day itself, while the theological significance of the event is expounded in fiery exchanges between Lucifer and an Angel. The device of allowing the overture to end darkly on a half-close, to be followed immediately by a brilliant opening aria for the Angel, was the result of a pre-performance revision almost certainly instigated by Handel himself. Such formal freedom was probably available only in non-staged works, and shows Handel's keenness to involve his audience in the dramatic situation. Though the libretto includes many passages of doctrinal exposition (Capece skilfully keeps within the common ground of the

Protestant faith of the composer and the Catholic faith of his patron and audience), it is the characters and their personal predicaments that create the strongest impression and are expressed most forcibly in the music.

There was one other musical product of Handel's Italian stay which was to have later significance for oratorio, though not then combined with it: his choral music for the church. (See Chapter 11.) Throughout the seventeenth and eighteenth centuries most composers who were involved with opera also cultivated a simultaneous interest in church music, because it allowed them to develop and demonstrate compositional skills which could not be used to any great extent in a form conceived primarily for the display of the solo voice. Church music could certainly include passages of solo vocal display, but it also gave opportunity for large-scale choral movements, sometimes built with strict counterpoint, sometimes with massive block harmonies, often combining these and other styles. The composer generally had considerable freedom to choose how he set the biblical or liturgical texts, though he may have been expected, and indeed may have wished, to have regard for earlier precedents. In the world of opera, composers could be pushed towards what was new and fashionable by extra-musical developments in literary and artistic tastes. These influenced church music too, but in that genre the composer also had a sense of working within an ancient tradition, where respect for predecessors was of value, and new contributions could be seen as extensions of the tradition.

Thus by the time Handel left Italy in the early months of 1710, his compositional experience had already encompassed all those elements that he would later be able to develop in English oratorio; but he had not yet had the opportunity to bring them together. His skill in church composition was further extended under the influence of a tradition he had not previously encountered. During his first years in London he not only composed Italian operas, but made important contributions to English church music, including the 'Utrecht' Te Deum and Jubilate (HWV 278, 279) of 1713, and gracefully adopted the style of the English court ode in the Birthday Ode for Queen Anne (HWV 74), probably written in the same year. In these compositions Handel often re-worked music from the Latin psalm settings and other works that he had written in Italy, just as in his London operas of this period he re-used music from his Italian operas and cantatas, but there is much that is fresh in the music, reflecting a specifically English influence. The setting of Brockes's Passion text already mentioned seems to have followed this batch of English choral works, and to have been sent to Germany for performance. It was his first quasi-dramatic work with a true chorus, but most of the music is for solo voices and the choral numbers are not expansive, especially when compared to those in the English works; as is common in Passion settings, many of the choruses simply represent the utterances of the crowd or the assembled disciples.

In the summer of 1717 Handel returned briefly – but productively – to the kind of personal patronage he had enjoyed under Ruspoli, this time working for James Brydges, Earl of Carnarvon and later Duke of Chandos, at Cannons, near Edgware. Brydges's remarkable employment of a group of vocal and instrumental musicians for church services and major domestic occasions gave the composer opportunities not otherwise available to him and of momentous consequence. Within a year Handel had composed eleven anthems and a Te Deum for performance at the small church of St Lawrence, Whitchurch, which served as Brydges's private chapel until the chapel in Cannons itself was opened in 1720. At the end of this period, in the spring and summer of 1718, came two major dramatic works. One was *Acis and Galatea* (HWV 49), basically in the style of the short English masques produced in London between 1714 and 1716 as an antidote to the Italian opera,[8] yet comprehensively transcending them both technically (in its use of the five soloists as choral voices) and emotionally. The other was *Esther* (HWV 50a), the first English oratorio.

The circumstances which gave birth to this new musical form remain frustratingly obscure. Even the accepted date of composition for *Esther* rests solely on the heading of one of the earliest manuscript copies[9] – 'The Oratorium Composed . . . in London 1718' – which casts doubt on the assumption that the work was composed at Cannons. (Edgware would not then have been regarded as part of 'London'.) No record of the first performance has been found, and the authorship of the libretto remains uncertain.[10] There were, however, specific reasons why Handel might might have been prompted to contemplate an English oratorio at this time, and why the subject should have been the story of Esther. There was, first, a musical imperative. With the Brockes Passion Handel had generated a substantial score which both he and his admirers would have liked to hear, but which could not be performed in England in its original form; a way out of the dilemma would be to rework at least some of the music in a new English context. (He had already begun this process in *Acis and Galatea*.[11]) Secondly, the subject of Esther arose from the biblical plays which the French dramatist Jean Racine (1639–99) had written for performance by the girls of Madame de Maintenon's school at St Cyr: *Esther* (1689) and *Athalie* (1691). Racine had modelled these on ancient Greek tragedy, and had included choruses set to music by Jean-Baptiste Moreau; these, he said, were integrated into the action and praised the true God just as their ancient equivalents had praised the pagan divinities. *Esther* was probably more suited to genteel domestic performance than *Athalie*, with its disturbing portrait of the murderous Queen Athalia, and in any case an English version of Racine's *Esther* by Thomas Brereton, published in 1715, was conveniently to hand, with a preface recommending that, though the sacred subject precluded stage performance, the work could well be performed privately in the houses of 'those chearfully virtuous Families, which are sometimes pleased to recreate themselves'. An English oratorio at Cannons was therefore an appropriate sequel to the secular masque *Acis and Galatea*.

The 1718 *Esther* has no act divisions; its six scenes seem to be designed to run without a break (a characteristic it shares with *Acis and Galatea*). The recitatives are in metrically irregular rhymed verse, perhaps suggested by the 'tuneable speech' devised by Congreve for his opera libretto *Semele* (published in 1710), but lacking the latter's felicity of language; it was not a precedent followed in later English oratorios, where heroic couplets or unrhymed iambic pentameters are the norm for recitative. The distribution of arias and ensembles among the various soloists seems arbitrary in comparison with the careful patterns generally found in opera, and there is no coherent exposition of the story; each recitative contains just enough information to generate a context for the next set piece, but a broader view of the conflicts that underlie the drama is lacking. Nine numbers (seven arias and two choruses) take music from the Brockes Passion, some being substantially altered; the score is more remarkable for its innovations in the instrumental accompaniments (including a solo oboe over pizzicato strings and a fully written-out harp obbligato) and for the expansiveness of the new choral numbers. Both these features are combined in the alto solo 'Jehovah crown'd' and its choral continuation: horns appear for the first time in an English vocal work – probably the same instruments which had rung out over the Thames a year earlier in the Water Music – and the choral section ('He comes to end our woes') powerfully mixes tight counterpoint and homophonic exclamation. Both in this and in the lengthy rondo with solo trumpet that ends the oratorio (perhaps never performed complete)[12] Handel seems to exploit freedom from the constraints of the operatic aria by writing movements that are almost excessively extensive (as also in the final chorus of the Chandos Te Deum from the same period). Though *Esther* was to have no direct successor for another fifteen years, during which Handel returned to Italian opera with renewed intensity, it had established the potential of oratorio as a medium in which several types of music could be explored and united. *Acis and Galatea*, with its more controlled choral contributions, showed that the masque, or some related form, could perform the same service in the secular sphere.

Neither *Acis and Galatea* nor *Esther* were totally forgotten before Handel himself brought them before the London public in 1732. Copies of the scores circulated among private collectors, a few songs were printed, and there may well have been more performances than the documentary record suggests. Were it not for a diary kept by a west-country physician and amateur musician we would not have known that the music society at Wells in Somerset tackled *Acis* ('Hendel's Pastoral') in February 1719 and *Esther* ('Hendel's Oritorio') in April 1724;[13] other such private and provincial performances could have taken place without notice in the 1720s. Thus when *Acis* was given at Lincoln's Inn Fields on 26 March 1731 'at the desire of several persons of quality' for the benefit of the tenor singer Rochetti, it may not have been an exceptional event, but merely the first to receive a press announcement; presumably it had Handel's approval – or did not need it – and it passed without comment.

The performance of *Esther* by the Children of the Chapel Royal under their master Bernard Gates at the Crown and Anchor Tavern on 23 February 1732 was undoubtedly exceptional. It was given 'in action' under the auspices of the Philharmonic Society, as was the repeat performance on 1 March; a third performance on 3 March was promoted by another private society, the Academy of Ancient Music. The libretto printed for the Philharmonic Society performances is entitled *Esther; an Oratorio or Sacred Drama*. Viscount Perceval (later Earl of Egmont), a member of the Society, called it an 'oratoria or religious opera' and found it 'exceeding fine'.[14] These performances, not in a theatre, and technically not public, avoided the objections to staged religious drama, and could be seen as part of an old tradition of using dramatic performance as part of the religious and moral instruction of the young participants (of which Racine's *Esther* and *Athalie* were already a late manifestation).[15]

The next part of the story is well known. Those who had seen the Crown and Anchor performances – notably the Princess Royal – urged Handel to bring *Esther* before the general public. According to Burney, the first hope was that it could be staged in a theatre, but the Bishop of London (in his capacity as Dean of the Chapel Royal) forbade the use of the Chapel Royal boys in such a performance.[16] (Such a ban would have been entirely in line with precedent; there is no need to attribute it to the personal attitude of Bishop Edmund Gibson.) In theory Handel could have adapted the work to reduce the choral element and performed it entirely with adult singers, but since the choruses were part of its attraction, and a staged sacred work would still have been unacceptable in a public theatre, such a course would hardly have been given serious thought. The preferred compromise was to perform it without action, which was in any case normal practice for an oratorio. To make the work into a full evening's entertainment, as would usually have been expected for an opera, Handel expanded it, taking the opportunity to insert two of the anthems he had written for the coronation of King George II and Queen Caroline in 1727 and composing new music to suit the members of his opera company who assumed the solo roles. Samuel Humphreys provided the additional text required, notably a new opening section clarifying the motivation of the action. The result was a three-act choral oratorio, somewhat inchoate in style, but unquestionably dramatic in inspiration and musically richer in its variety of movements than was possible in contemporary opera. The performance at the King's Theatre on 2 May 1732, with the 'Musick . . . disposed after the manner of the Coronation Service'[17] brought English oratorio into the public arena.

The novelty of the production secured full houses for the six performances, and the recorded comments – rare, as usual – immediately indicate a diversity of opinion which came to apply to oratorio in general. The Earl of Egmont noted that *Esther* was composed 'in the church style', suggesting that the choruses had made the greatest impact on him, while the anonymous author of the pamphlet *See and Seem Blind* (probably written in May 1732) was not impressed:[18]

> Han't you been at the *Oratorio*, says one? Oh! If you don't see the *Oratorio* you see nothing, says t'other; so away goes I to the *Oratorio*, where I saw indeed the finest Assembly of People I ever beheld in my Life, but, to my great Surprize, found this Sacred *Drama* a mere Consort . . . *Senesino* and *Bertolli* made rare work with the English tongue you would have sworn it had been *Welch* . . . I like the one good Opera better than Twenty *Oratorio's*: Were they indeed to make a regular *Drama* of a good Scripture story, and perform it with proper Decorations, which may be done with as much reverence in proper Habits [costumes], as in their own common Apparel; (I am sure with more Grandeur and Solemnity, and at least equal Decency) then should I change my mind, then would the Stage appear in its full Lustre, and Musick Answer its original Design.

The author expressed more enthusiasm for the series of operas in English which were being promoted at the Little (or New) Theatre in the Haymarket in the 1731–2 season, and which were to have an effect on Handel's performances. On 17 May the English company at that theatre, led by Thomas Arne and featuring his sister Susanna (later Mrs Cibber) as one of the leading singers, produced the Cannons version of *Acis and Galatea*, 'being the first Time it ever was performed in a Theatrical Way'. This event, coupled with the success of *Esther*, seems to have prompted Handel to make a new version of *Acis and Galatea*, weaving substantial extracts of the Cannons version of 1718 and other works into a framework provided by his *Aci, Galatea e Polifemo* (HWV 72), a cantata written for a Neapolitan wedding in 1708. Passages derived from the cantata were left in their original Italian, and many of the other numbers were translated into that language as best suited the mix of Italian and English singers involved: Handel presumably wished to spare the Italians the criticism they had encountered in *Esther*. His 'new' *Acis*, first performed on 10 June 1732, was presented as a serenata, a half-way house between opera and oratorio. In continental Europe this was a well-established form, usually an original composition written to celebrate a royal or political event; but in Britain it was largely unknown, its place being taken by the celebratory ode. The 1732 *Acis* followed the serenata form superficially, being secular in subject and presented with little or no action in a standing set; but it was in three acts instead of the usual two, was largely pastiche, and had no celebratory reference. The choruses were sung by the soloists, reinforced with extra tenors and basses. On the whole the 1732 *Acis* seems an odd and slightly desperate compilation if regarded solely as a response to Arne's production of the 1718 version. It may be that Handel saw it more positively as a sequel to *Esther*, a conscious attempt to create a large-scale unacted dramatic work corresponding to an oratorio, but on a secular subject.

During the rest of the 1730s Handel still regarded the production of Italian opera as his prime concern, despite the formation of a rival opera company in 1733 which, besides drawing away some of his audience, caused him to move his activities in autumn 1734 from the King's Theatre to John Rich's new theatre in Covent Garden. Meanwhile he continued to build a varied repertory of English choral works. The oratorios *Deborah* (HWV 51; first performed at the King's Theatre, 17 March 1733)[19] and *Athalia* (HWV 52; Sheldonian Theatre, Oxford, 10 July 1733) were the immediate successors of *Esther* in different ways. *Deborah*, like the 1732 *Esther*, is partly pastiche, drawing on several of Handel's early works composed in Italy as well as the Brockes Passion, and draws on the two Coronation Anthems not used in *Esther*; there is nevertheless much new music, especially choral, of high quality. A new feature (developed more extensively in later oratorios) is the use of the chorus to portray different peoples, here the Israelites and the Priests of Baal; the former are represented by the standard forms of the church style – rich harmony and well-crafted counterpoint – while the music for the heathens is generally based on dance forms, with catchy rhythms and simpler harmonies. The Priests' chorus 'O Baal! Monarch of the skies', dominated by unrelenting triplet figures on the strings, is barbaric in effect; in later oratorios Handel painted unbelievers more sympathetically. *Athalia* connects with *Esther* in being based on Racine's second and more powerful biblical play, but the music is all newly composed, with little re-working of earlier material.[20] It does not, however, move beyond its predecessors as much as might be expected: the anthem-style choruses lack the harmonic and melodic interest of the coronation music, and many of the arias, though intrinsically beautiful, seem detached from their dramatic context. In 1734, to celebrate the marriage of his pupil Anne, Princess Royal, Handel re-used much of the music very effectively for his only true serenata, *Parnasso in Festa*[21] (HWV 73; King's Theatre, 13 March), where its qualities can be more easily enjoyed. Several newly composed numbers of high quality give the serenata an individual flavour which raises it above mere pastiche. In 1735 Handel introduced a new feature in his oratorio concerts: the organ concerto, perhaps brought to mind when he perused the score of *Il trionfo del Tempo e del Disinganno* for musical ideas used in *Deborah* and *Parnasso in Festa*, and re-discovered the movement for organ and orchestra that he had composed in 1707.

Handel's new willingness to compose works in English gave an opening to all his admirers to suggest English texts to set, or to offer texts of their own: in contrast to the traditions of Italian opera librettos, no precedents constrained their form. Thus in the later 1730s Handel no doubt received many suggestions for, or offers of, English texts, and he seems deliberately to have chosen as widely as possible in regard to both genre and librettists. His setting of Dryden's *Alexander's Feast* (first performed at Covent Garden, 19 February 1736) was encouraged by Newburgh Hamilton, a minor poet and playwright who supplied additional lines from his own ode *The Power of Music*, written (like Dryden's) in honour of St Cecilia, the patron saint of music. This was Handel's first attempt at setting an admired English poem, and his magnificent response to that challenge gained him a classic status as a British composer which his Italian operas could never have achieved. Within two years Roubiliac's statue, showing the composer as Apollo and with the score of *Alexander's Feast* prominent at his feet, had been installed in Vauxhall Gardens, and the complete score of the ode, with a portrait of the composer, had been published by Walsh with a lengthy and distinguished subscription list.

Alexander's Feast is mainly an account of the feast celebrating Alexander the Great's conquest of Persia, at which the playing of the musician Timotheus controls, all too easily, the emotions of the conqueror, finally inducing him to burn the city of Persepolis. The concluding stanza draws away from this classical scene, and tells – perhaps too briefly – of the coming of St Cecilia, her invention of the organ and, by implication, a new 'sacred' music, which, unlike that of the pagan Timotheus, has beneficent rather than pernicious effects.[22] Handel's setting, especially notable for its powerful and formally innovative choruses, ignores Dryden's subversive sub-text: the section in which

Alexander orders the destruction of Persepolis to avenge slaughtered Greeks is intensely thrilling, free of any hint that the act is a pointless outrage. The composer also makes up for the poet's failure to define the superiority of Cecilia's music by supplying a magnificent choral fugue ('Let old Timotheus yield the prize') with four subjects, presumably beyond Timotheus's limited compositional technique.

Handel returned to English oratorio in 1738, writing two works in quick succession, both of which suggested new paths of development. *Saul* (HWV 53; King's Theatre, 16 January 1739) is in the line of musical dramas already defined in the earlier oratorios, but with a better sense of coherence and purpose. Charles Jennens, the librettist, was a man of wide cultural interests.[23] He saw the potential of oratorio more clearly than Handel's earlier collaborators and, having supported Handel since the mid 1720s, he also understood what brought out the best in the composer. There are awkward moments in the verse, and some good ideas – such as the contrasted characters of Saul's two daughters – are not followed through convincingly; but the libretto gave Handel the framework to create a true tragedy in music, in which Saul's growing jealousy of the young David undermines his authority as Israel's king and threatens the safety of his nation. The music is highly atmospheric, whether in the glitter of the procession welcoming David's defeat of Goliath, or in the grim darkness of Saul's visit to the Witch of Endor, and leaves little doubt that Handel saw, and wanted his audience to see, a living drama played out in the ideal theatre of the mind. Jennens's attempt to vivify David's condemnation of the Amalekite who reports the death of Saul by bringing in the voice at the start of the aria suggests that he, too, was equally concerned to stimulate the imagination.[24]

Yet oratorio did not need to have dramatic form. The second work composed in 1738, *Israel in Egypt* (HWV 54; King's Theatre, 4 April 1739), was the first of Handel's two scriptural oratorios, a genre that turned out to be less fruitful for Handel himself, though it led to the production of what later became his most popular work. In 1737 Handel had composed a long and austerely grand anthem for the funeral of Queen Caroline (HWV 264). From this arose a three-part oratorio on a text which, for the first time, was taken directly from the Bible. The Funeral Anthem, with minimally adapted text, became Part 1, and Part 3 was a new setting of the Song of Moses (Exodus 15, vv. 1–21); for Part 2 Handel set a selection of texts describing the Ten Plagues and the Exodus of the Israelites from Egypt. The subdued pathos of the opening anthem did not blend well with the choral exuberance and colourful brass-dominated orchestration of the newly composed sections, and the work, despite a published appreciation, received only a limited run of performances.[25]

Handel used the occasion of the feast of St Cecilia (22 November) in 1739 to pair *Alexander's Feast* with a setting of Dryden's shorter and earlier ode *A Song for St Cecilia's Day* (HWV 76), but the two works taken together are somewhat indigestible and the coupling was not repeated. Meanwhile his circle of friends was pressing him to unite his music with another English poet of even more exalted reputation.[26] From James Harris came the idea of a work setting alternating extracts from John Milton's two short poems celebrating the contrasted joys of 'L'Allegro' ('the merry man' or the extrovert) and 'Il Penseroso' ('the thoughtful man' or the introvert). Handel showed immediate interest and asked Jennens to add a resolution to the debate provided by 'Il Moderato' ('the moderate man'). The result was *L'Allegro, il Penseroso ed il Moderato* (HWV 55; Lincoln's Inn Fields, 27 February 1740) – never given a generic description, though it is a species of ode, being both secular and reflective. In responding to Milton's images of the active and the contemplative life with equal intensity, Handel made Jennens's added arguments for a balance between the two viewpoints almost redundant, and in later years Handel dropped this final part; but it is hard to lose the duet in which the two voices representing Allegro and Penseroso are at last united in harmony.

Jennens's greatest act for Handel was to compile the text of *Messiah* (HWV 56), conceived as a work for performance in London in Passion Week but first performed in Dublin at Neal's Music Hall on 13 April 1742, the climax of a highly successful season in which both sacred and secular works had been equally prominent.[27] The libretto, entirely scriptural, achieves much by simple means: Parts 1 and 2 cover the whole of Christ's life on earth, His conquest of death, and His ascension into Heaven; but only the section dealing with the Nativity is directly narrated. Otherwise the gospel story is largely told through the Old Testament texts held to justify the claim of Jesus to be 'Messiah' or 'Christ', the anointed one foretold by the prophets. Narrative force is thus maintained, the listener's involvement being held by the emotional power of the music (especially in the Passion section of Part 2), while at the same time biblical prophecy is vindicated.[28] Part 3 is reflective, taking on (perhaps too ambitiously at times) the great Pauline texts proclaiming the significance of Christ's redemptive sacrifice, and moving from the quietly radiant assurance of 'I know that my Redeemer liveth' to the Apocalyptic vision of the Lamb glorified by the hosts of Heaven.

Though well received in Dublin, where the performances were given for the benefit of local charities, *Messiah* encountered objections when first performed in London (Covent Garden, 23 March 1743), partly on account of its combination of a scriptural text and its specifically doctrinal content, but even more for its presentation in a theatre by singers associated with the stage.[29] Thus Handel treated the work cautiously throughout the 1740s, at first announcing it only as 'A New Sacred Oratorio' and keeping its performances towards the end of Lent, nearest to Easter. In 1750 he gave the first of what became a series of annual charity performances at the newly built chapel of the Foundling Hospital, an organisation devoted to the rescue of abandoned children. These helped audiences to appreciate the oratorio's unique blend of liveliness and spirituality, qualities which soon gained for it a ubiquitous and deserved popularity which remains undiminished.

The success of the Dublin season was consolidated on Handel's return to London, by the excellent reception given to a new oratorio based on Milton's *Samson Agonistes* which Handel had mostly composed in the autumn of 1741, just before his Dublin visit. It was revised and completed in London for its first performance at Covent Garden on 18 February 1743. The idea for *Samson* (HWV 57) had been sown as early as 1739. On 24 November 1739 Lord Shaftesbury reported to James Harris that on the previous evening Shaftesbury's brother-in-law James Noel [30]

> read through the whole poem of Samson Agonistes, and whenever he rested to take breath Mr Handel (who was highly pleas'd with the piece) played I really think better than ever, & his harmony was perfectly adapted to the sublimity of the poem.

Further encouragement came from the poet Elizabeth Tollet.[31] The adaptation of the poem for musical setting was finally provided by Newburgh Hamilton, who noted in the preface to the libretto of *Samson* that Milton's original poem, though dramatic in form, was not intended for the stage:[32]

> But as Mr Handel had so happily here introduc'd *Oratorios*, a musical drama, whose subject must be Scriptural, and in which the Solemnity of Church-Musick is agreeably united with the most pleasing Airs of the Stage: It would have been an irretrievable Loss to have neglected the Opportunity of that great Master's doing Justice to this Work; he having already added new Life and Spirit to some of the finest Things in the *English* language.

Hamilton thus neatly defined the appeal of oratorio to a cross-section of the public wider than that for Italian opera. The 'Airs of the Stage' offered by opera were there, but sung in English and supplemented by the 'Solemnity' of the choruses; and the use of subjects from Scripture, which in itself implied presentation without action, broke down the resistance of those who would normally reject stage entertainments as frivolous, if not actually sinful. Milton's *Samson Agonistes*, as a poetic rather than a theatrical drama, was peculiarly suited for treatment as an oratorio. The action, centred on the last hours of Samson 'eyeless in Gaza', is static, but the musical contrast of the choruses for the hedonistic Philistines and the sober Israelites is an enlivening element, as is the touch of sexual interest provided by the appearance of Dalila, happily made allowable by Samson's outright rejection of her flattery. Here then was a formula for oratorio, with clear audience appeal, to which Handel could adhere with confidence.

In fact he was determined to expand his horizons. The English works he had produced up to 1740, as we have seen, were by no means confined to sacred themes, and it must have seemed reasonable to him that he should continue to offer a variety of forms, as he had done in both London and Dublin. In July 1743 his copyist and business manager Christopher Smith reported somewhat despondently to Lord Shaftesbury that Handel had rejected all offers to become involved with the Italian opera and was composing a new work 'from Dryden's words' (actually Congreve's). Smith wondered 'how the Quality will take it that He can compose for Himself and not for them when they offered Him more than ever he had in his Life.'[33] The new work, *Semele* (HWV 58; Covent Garden, 10 February 1744), was produced 'after the manner of an oratorio', and many of the 'quality' were clearly not prepared to take it. Charles Jennens described it as 'a baudy opera'.[34] Mrs Delany and a few of her friends liked it, but reported that 'all the Opera people were enraged at Handel' and that her husband (the Revd Patrick Delany) would not attend, 'it being a profane story'.[35] The new biblical oratorio *Joseph and his Brethren*, produced in the same season (HWV 59; Covent Garden, 2 March 1744), was better received despite the verbal infelicities of James Miller's libretto. Handel stubbornly offered the same combination of secular and sacred the following year in his last, troublesome season at the King's Theatre,[36] with *Hercules* (HWV 60; 5 January 1745) and *Belshazzar* (HWV 61; 27 March). The decision to compose Thomas Broughton's impeccably classical libretto for *Hercules* suggests that Handel was still determined to 'write for himself', since he can hardly have assumed that it would be any more successful than *Semele*; and it was not. The objection once again was that *Hercules* was an 'English opera', and Jennens explained that it failed 'for want of the top Italian voices, Action, Dresses, Scenes and Dances, which us'd to draw company'.[37] This cannot have been Handel's own view: he would not have composed *Semele* and *Hercules* if he had not regarded oratorio as having established a format in which secular subjects could also be validly treated, and indeed the quality of these two musical dramas confirms his faith in the form. Yet clearly there was a substantial constituency in his audiences hostile to this view: for them it was only the 'sacredness' of oratorio and its potential for religious sublimity that made it acceptable as theatrical entertainment. Handel would not have denied this potential, and never held back from true oratorio composition; but his vision was wider, and the music for his last secular dramas showed that sublimity could be achieved outside the religious sphere.

After 1745, presumably in the light of public reaction, Handel created no further secular works in oratorio form.[38] The Jacobite rebellion of 1745–6 inevitably influenced public entertainments, and Handel, having set a note of cautious optimism in the semi-pastiche *Occasional Oratorio* (HWV 62; 14 February 1746, Covent Garden: this was the venue for all of Handel's subsequent seasons), made a deliberate bid for popular appeal with *Judas Maccabaeus* (1 April 1747). The librettist Thomas Morell designed it as a compliment to William, Duke of Cumberland, under whose command the rebels had been crushed at Culloden, but sensibly avoided too triumphalist a mood by incorporating pleas for unity and peace within a generally celebratory framework. Handel's easily tuneful music was enough to secure the work instant success, and guarantee its popularity with future generations. But, as in 1743, Handel was not content to allow one work, however successful, to set a formula. The bellicose *Joshua* (HWV 64; 9 March 1748) appears to imitate certain elements of *Judas Maccabaeus*, but that may be because the anonymous libretto was written close to the events of the Jacobite rising (the recitative preceding 'See the conqu'ring hero comes' makes poor sense in context and seems to refer directly to the Duke of Cumberland) and it may have been supplied to Handel some time before he set it. Morell's own sequel to *Judas Maccabaeus*, *Alexander Balus* (HWV 65; 23 March 1748 – though composed before *Joshua*), is a story of blighted love which could easily have formed a plot for an *opera seria*, but there is no *lieto fine* and Handel movingly sustains the elegiac mood to the end.

The last four newly composed oratorios are all highly individual masterpieces.[39] The librettos of *Susanna* and *Solomon* (HWV 66 and 67; 10 February and 17 March 1749) appear to have the same anonymous author, and both involve a depiction of an ideal marriage, but *Solomon* (composed first) is a celebration of universal ideals – of enlightened rule, of equal justice, of pious worship. To see it merely as a flattering picture of Georgian England (or as a pointed contrast to the reality of that regime) is diminishing: the gorgeousness of its music speaks to any age. In *Susanna* the straightforward tale of Susanna falsely accused of adultery by two Elders of the community, finally vindicated through the intervention of the young Daniel, blends humour with strength. *Theodora* (HWV 68; 16 March 1750), perhaps the most extraordinary of the group, has a libretto by Morell based on a non-Biblical tale of two Roman martyrs. It touches on such issues as freedom of thought, the moral validity of suicide to avoid rape, and the clash of religion and state authority; the music sublimely portrays the spiritual nobility of the martyred lovers Theodora and Didymus, and the contrasting characters of the pagan and Christian communities. *Jephtha* (HWV 70; 26 February 1752) is more conventional oratorio fare, but of remarkable power in the scenes when Jephtha is faced with sacrificing his daughter in order to fulfil a vow made to gain divine support in battle. Morell goes too far, however, in softening the expected tragic ending by use of alternative post-Biblical interpretations. It is dramatically appropriate for Iphis, the innocent daughter, to be saved from sacrifice and live instead 'in pure and virgin state for ever', but not for this outcome to be treated as entirely happy.

There is scant evidence that Handel's audiences understood these last works or found them much to their taste. Lady Shaftesbury thought that *Susanna* would not meet her approbation, 'being in the light operatic style':[40] she had correctly discerned one element of the oratorio, but the seriousness of the choruses, of Susanna's own music, and of (for example) Daniel's 'Chastity' aria obviously eluded her. Handel's disappointment at the indifference shown to *Theodora* is on record,[41] and the work was heavily cut both before and after the first performance. Further cuts were imposed for the revival in 1755, and the single-performance revivals of *Solomon* and *Susanna* in the same period were similarly treated. In the oratorio seasons from the period of Handel's blindness (1753–59) we see a narrow canon beginning to emerge, swiftly consolidated in the decade after his death: three oratorios (*Messiah, Samson* and *Judas Maccabaeus*) usually received two performances each season, while the rest of the repertory was revived only occasionally or not at all. In the nineteenth century the amateur choral movement stimulated the addition of *Israel in Egypt* (Parts 2 and 3 only) to the main canon, but otherwise the picture hardly changed for two centuries.

To suggest that an artist is out of step with his own time may often be romantic fancy, but the failure of most of Handel's oratorios and musical dramas to hold a place in the repertory, despite unstinted acceptance of his status as a great composer, clearly indicates some problem of perception. According to Hawkins:[42]

> The applause bestowed on the oratorios of Handel, was at least equal to that of the best of his operas; but, such was the taste of the town, that he was constrained to give these entertainments a dramatic form; for he was used to say, that, to an English audience, music joined to poetry was not an entertainment for an evening, and that something that had the appearance of a plot or fable was necessary to keep their attention awake. Perhaps he might be mistaken in this opinion; and the success of Israel in Egypt,

> L'Allegro ed Il Penseroso, and Messiah seem to indicate the contrary;
> nevertheless it determined his conduct with respect to these
> entertainments, and frequently induced him to have recourse to some small
> poet for his assistance in forming a drama, which, without regard to
> sentiment or language, or indeed anything but the conduct of the drama,
> was to be the mere vehicle of his music; and such, for instance, are the
> oratorios of Esther, Saul, Susanna, and many others.

There is confusion in this comment – *Israel* and *L'Allegro* were not especially popular in Handel's lifetime – but Hawkins's report of Handel's opinion and his questioning of its validity are worth noting. What the succession of oratorio-style works suggests is that it was Handel himself, not his audiences, who most valued 'the appearance of a plot or fable'. Such an attitude is hardly surprising for a composer who had been primarily a composer of opera for most of his working life. Though it was the sacred nature of the subjects which initially justified the performance of dramatic oratorios without stage action, Handel saw that unstaged presentation opened possibilities of musical expression on the large scale which could not be accommodated in opera; he probably also saw the further practical advantages of not having to deal with sets, costumes, stage action and the caprices of expensive Italian singers, and of not having to share overall control of performances with librettists and scenic designers. In Handel's mind the idea of an oratorio opened out into a form which could encompass works sacred and secular, dramatic and non-dramatic. By 1743, when *Semele* was composed for presentation 'after the manner of an oratorio', 'manner' had clearly become separable from content.

The presentation of dramatic works in oratorio form nevertheless created problems for audiences of Handel's time and for their successors, especially in the case of secular dramas where the justification of oratorio-style performance – sacredness of subject – was absent. Works in which the presumed action is vividly invoked, by stage directions in a published wordbook and by apt gesture in the music, set up expectations that are inevitably frustrated in concert performance. It is hardly coincidental that the two dramatic oratorios which remained regularly performed after Handel's death and which became standard choral repertory in the nineteenth century were *Samson* and *Judas Maccabaeus*, in both of which the events of the story are largely narrated, and little attempt is made either in the text or in the music to encourage visual imagination of the action. In the twentieth century, however, the perception of Handel's oratorios has altered markedly, tilting in favour of the specifically dramatic works. Prejudice against the public representation of sacred stories, and against the theatre in general, has vanished (in the Christian tradition, at least), and a sceptical view is taken of the notion that religious drama is any more or less morally improving than secular. The staging of the English oratorios and music dramas in Britain from the 1930s onwards, at first mainly by amateur groups, was an important step towards a change in attitude, and inspired a new critical approach set out with persuasive brilliance by Winton Dean.[43] At the same time the dissemination of music through recordings and radio broadcasts, as well as performances of operas in concert, has made the once alien concept of unstaged (and even unseen) music drama quite familiar. In the last decades of the twentieth century the works that Handel cast in oratorio form have gained a recognition in both performance and critical study which (with the exceptions already noted) they never received from the audiences for whom they were ostensibly written. It may well be that Handel's idea of an oratorio, and the extent to which he successfully realised it, is more clearly and more widely understood today than it ever was in his own lifetime.

11 Handel's sacred music

Graydon Beeks

Handel was involved in the composition of sacred music throughout his career, although it was rarely the focal point of his activities. Only during the brief period in 1702–3 when he was organist for the Cathedral in Halle did he hold a church job which required regular weekly duties and, since the cathedral congregation was Calvinist, these duties did not include composing much (if any) concerted music. Virtually all of his sacred music was written for specific events and liturgies, and the choice of Handel to compose these works was dictated by his connections with specific patrons. Handel's sacred music falls into groups of works which were written for similar forces and occasions, and will be discussed in terms of those groups in this chapter.

During his period of study with Zachow in Halle Handel must have written some music for services at the Marktkirche or the Cathedral, but no examples survive.[1] His earliest extant work is the F major setting of Psalm 113, *Laudate pueri* (HWV 236),[2] for solo soprano and strings. The autograph is on a type of paper that was available in Hamburg, and he may have written it there in late 1706 to take with him to Italy; alternatively, he may have written it at Rome early in 1707 on paper brought with him from Hamburg.[3] The jagged vocal lines for the solo soprano are typical of his early style and may be related to Mattheson's comment that Handel knew a great deal about fugue and counterpoint but 'very little about melody' in this period.[4]

Although Handel travelled extensively during his time in Italy, his sacred music was all written for performance in Rome and its environs on commission from two of his primary Roman patrons, Cardinal Carlo Colonna and Marquis Ruspoli. These works can be divided into liturgical and non-liturgical, the former having texts with fixed places in the Roman Catholic order of worship. It is worth remembering that works from either category could, given the right circumstances and proper dispensations, have been performed not only in a church service but also in a private performance of chamber music which might otherwise have been essentially secular in character.

Of the non-liturgical works, two have Italian texts. *Ah! che troppo ineguali* (HWV 230) consists of a recitative and aria for soprano and strings, and is probably a fragment of a lost Marian cantata written in 1708 for an unknown purpose.[5] *Donna, che in ciel* (HWV 233), an extended Marian cantata for solo soprano, chorus and strings, was written for the annual celebration of the delivery of Rome from an earthquake on 2 February 1703, and may have been performed on the anniversary of that event in 1708 or 1709.

The motet *Silete venti* (HWV 242) is a setting of a Latin text directed to Jesus rather than to Mary, and is scored for soprano, oboes, bassoon and strings. The type of paper used in the autograph score indicates a date of composition around 1724, and it may have been written in London for Cardinal Colonna in Rome. It is an appealing work and has been the only one of Handel's solo motets to join the standard concert repertoire. Several movements were used again by Handel in the 1732 version of *Esther* (HWV 50b): the extensive 'Allelujah' from the motet was the only movement to retain its original text.

The Roman liturgical works were primarily appropriate for the service of Vespers. This early evening service consists of a series of psalms, each followed by scripture readings and prayers appropriate to the specific day or feast, and the Magnificat. Each psalm would have been preceded and followed by a brief antiphon, again to a text proper to the day. In contemporary Roman practice, all portions of the service could be spoken or chanted, but they could also be set to music in a style which continued the tradition of Renaissance polyphony (the so-called *stile antico*), or in more up-to-date style for solo voices, with or without chorus, accompanied by orchestra with basso continuo. The psalm texts, of which five were designated as proper for Vespers (depending on the day of the week), tended to be set for larger forces while antiphons, which changed from service to service, were generally chanted or set for solo voices. Works designated 'motet' were more appropriate for use in the Mass, specifically during the Elevation of the Host and the distribution of the Eucharist, but under the right circumstances they, too, could be performed during or at the end of Vespers.

Handel's Latin psalm settings are large-scale, multi-movement works for soloists, chorus and an orchestra of strings with occasional use of oboes; bassoons were apparently unavailable. The techniques employed in the choruses vary from chordal homophony to imitative polyphony. Handel's occasional use of chorale-like themes in long notes, while undoubtedly related to techniques he had learned in his studies with Zachow, reflected a favourite usage in Rome in which the melodies were frequently drawn from Gregorian chant. The arias are not written in da capo form, but rather in one or another of the forms usually employed by Italian composers to emphasise the parallelism of the psalm verses (e.g.

A B or A B A′ B′). The rest of Handel's Roman church music is for solo voices accompanied by strings and occasional wind instruments, and ranges from short antiphons to extended, multi-movement motets and a single Marian antiphon.

Handel's first Italian sacred work, *Dixit Dominus* (HWV 232), a setting of Psalm 110 for soloists and five-part chorus and string orchestra, is one of his youthful masterpieces. It was completed at Rome in April 1707 and possibly written for Cardinal Colonna. It was presumably performed at Vespers for an appropriate festal celebration, perhaps even Easter. The scale and sheer energy of the writing are captivating and the technical challenges for performers are formidable. It is unfortunate that we know nothing of the performing forces for which it was written. Handel condensed the music and tightened its structure when he used some of it again later in English works such as the Cannons Anthems and *Deborah* (HWV 51).

Handel next wrote three smaller works for soprano and strings for his other principal Roman patron, Marquis Ruspoli, to be performed in the Church of St Anthony of Padua at Vignanello, the Ruspoli summer home near Rome. The motet *O qualis de coelo sonus* (HWV 239) was performed on Whit Sunday, 12 June 1707, while the motet *Coelestis dum spirat aura* (HWV 231) was heard the next day on the Feast of St Anthony of Padua. The Marian antiphon *Salve Regina* (HWV 241) was probably performed after Vespers on Trinity Sunday, 19 June 1707. The soloist for all these works may have been the soprano Margherita Durastanti, who created the title role in *Agrippina* at Venice in 1709, and later sang for Handel in London in 1720–4 and again in 1733–4.

Almost immediately after the Ruspoli pieces Handel composed another series of sacred works for Cardinal Colonna, at least some of which were performed on 16 July 1707 in the Church of the Madonna di Monte Santo in Rome to celebrate the Feast of Our Lady of Mt Carmel, the patron saint of the Carmelite Order of which the Colonna family were patrons.[6] The D major setting of *Laudate pueri* (HWV 237), partly based on music from the the F major setting but expanded to include chorus, five-part strings and oboes, was completed on 8 July 1707. It would have been appropriate for either First or Second Vespers, and is associated in surviving performing material with two specifically Carmelite antiphons from First Vespers (*Haec est regina virginum* HWV 235, and *Te decus virgineum* HWV 243), and the Carmelite motet *Saeviat tellus inter rigores* (HWV 240). Both HWV 237 and HWV 240 require a virtuosic soprano with secure high notes (the solo part in the latter rises to top d‴).

Handel's final sacred work from the Italian period is his setting of Psalm 127, *Nisi Dominus* (HWV 238), which was completed on 13 July

1707. Despite the fact that the forces expand from five parts to double chorus (with double orchestra) for the doxology, *Nisi Dominus* is both a gentler and a less rambling work than the earlier *Dixit Dominus*. The question of whether these two works, and even the *Salve Regina*, can also have been performed in connection with the Feast of Our Lady of Mt Carmel has generated a good deal of discussion, and attempts to perform all of the possible repertoire within the context of Second Vespers, for which only the three psalms would have been proper, using the rubric of 'substitute antiphons', have not met with entire critical approval, in part because of the discrepancy in scale between *Dixit Dominus, Nisi Dominus* and the other works.[7] Nevertheless, in whatever context they were first performed, the psalm settings must have made a profound impression on their early listeners and Handel was prepared to employ musical material from them later in England when the occasion arose.

Handel's remaining sacred music was written for the liturgy of the Church of England as set out in *The Book of Common Prayer*. The English Reformers had created two services, Morning and Evening Prayer, out of the eight Roman Catholic Offices. Each included a portion of the Psalms, Lessons (Scripture readings), Collects (prayers) and Canticles.[8] In addition, after the Third Collect a place was provided for an anthem, the text of which was not specified but was to be drawn from the Bible or the Prayer Book and to be appropriate to the season or specific feast day being celebrated.

The majority of Handel's English sacred works were written for the Chapel Royal, the institution responsible for meeting the ecclesiastical needs of the Monarch and the Court.[9] It consisted in Handel's day of the Officers serving under the Dean, the Gentlemen and Children, Composers, instrumental musicians, and various servants. At full strength the Chapel choir had twenty-six Gentlemen (of whom ten were priests) and ten boy choristers, but for a variety of reasons the actual numbers were generally lower. For most of the period of Handel's association there were two Composers, two Organists, a viol player, and a lutenist.

Handel supplied music for three sorts of services for the Chapel Royal. The nature and venue of those services, together with the number and type of musicians available for them, determined what he wrote. For the routine services, held in the small chapel at St James's Palace when the Court was in London, the boys and about ten to thirteen men were generally available, since the Gentlemen of the Chapel Royal attended in alternate months and, even allowing for the use of deputies, some places were bound to be unfilled at any given time. The regular instrumental resources available were limited to organ, viol (or possibly 'cello), and lute.

Somewhat more elaborate were occasional festal services of Morning Prayer at the Chapel Royal, generally including orchestrally accompanied canticles and anthem. In the reigns of George I and George II these were generally limited to celebrations of the King's safe return to London from visits to Hanover or Kensington. For these services string players from the Royal Musicians were employed, although whether all twenty-four of them performed is not clear. Occasionally oboe and bassoon players were imported from the opera or theatre orchestra, and for events requiring the performance of a special Te Deum and Jubilate, members of the Royal Trumpeters were sometimes employed.

Most elaborate of all were the great services of national rejoicing or mourning which might call for the full resources of the Chapel Royal, King's Musicians and Royal Trumpeters, and occasionally could command even larger forces. These services were usually held in buildings larger than the Chapel Royal at St James's Palace. Services of thanksgiving for great military successes, which were quite frequent during Queen Anne's reign, were generally held in St Paul's Cathedral. Coronations and royal funerals were traditionally held in Westminster Abbey. Royal weddings, which had been infrequent in the years leading up to Handel's arrival in England, had no fixed abode: the location and nature of the celebration generally depended on the dynastic importance of the specific wedding.

Handel probably wrote his first piece of Anglican church music soon after the beginning of his second visit to England in autumn 1712. It was almost certainly *As pants the Hart* (HWV 251a), which is likely to have been intended for a routine Chapel Royal service at St James's Palace during the period the Court was in London from December 1712 to May 1713.[10] It is written in the genre of the traditional English verse anthem with separate movements for soloists and chorus, the whole accompanied by organ, with viol or 'cello, and probably lute. The music reflects both English and German traditions of the seventeenth century, and is the least Italianate of all Handel's sacred compositions.

HWV 251a is the first of five versions of *As pants the Hart* (HWV 251a-e) which Handel prepared for varying occasions over the next twenty-five years.[11] Each setting but the first contains some material adapted from earlier versions and some newly composed music. The one element common to all versions is an opening chorus built on a point of imitation with which Handel would probably have been familiar from his studies with Zachow, and which also appears in the music of a number of composers including Antonio Caldara and John Blow. The version which Handel employs, with its initial leap of a minor third, is also found as the opening to the first sonata of Henry Purcell's *Sonnata's of Three Parts*

Example 11.1 (a) Henry Purcell, Sonata I (1683), opening

Violin I
Violin II

Basso*

* The basso continuo part, which broadly doubles the other parts, is omitted here.

(b) Handel, *As pants the Hart* (HWV 251a/1), opening

Voices*

Continuo
[Organ and
Cello or
Gamba]

* The opening entry is marked by Handel for 'Mr Eilfurt' (Richard Elford)

(London, 1683), and this source is very likely to have been familiar to both the composer and his listeners. (See Example 11.1.)

Handel's next contribution to Anglican church music, the 'Utrecht' Te Deum (HWV 278) and Jubilate (HWV 279), was on a much larger scale. By the end of 1712 it was clear that a peace treaty would shortly be signed at Utrecht which would put an end to Britain's participation in the ten-year-old European conflict now known as the War of the Spanish Succession. He was asked, apparently at the instigation of Queen Anne, to provide orchestrally accompanied Canticles for the great Service of Thanksgiving which would be held to mark that event.[12] William Croft (1678–1727), the principal composer to the Chapel Royal, provided the anthem, which was not orchestrally accompanied.

Handel completed the Te Deum on 14 January 1713 and the Jubilate sometime later.[13] The music was publicly rehearsed on 5, 7, and 19 March, and at least once more in May before being performed in St Paul's Cathedral at the elaborate official Thanksgiving Service on 7 July. Somewhere between forty and fifty performers probably took part, consisting primarily of members of the Chapel Royal and the Queen's Musicians; perhaps half were singers.[14]

Although provision had been made for the singing of Canticles since the earliest edition of *The Book of Common Prayer*, use of orchestral accompaniment in the setting of the Morning Canticles had been a relatively recent development in England. Only a handful of such pieces are known to have been composed prior to 1713, all written for specific events of public rejoicing. It is, then, hardly surprising that Handel's 'Utrecht' Te Deum and Jubilate betray a debt to Purcell's comparable setting written for the St Cecilia's Day celebrations in 1694, and to Croft's version written for the Thanksgiving Service in February 1709, both in general outline (including divisions into movements and the use of five-part texture with divided soprano parts) and in certain specific details. Handel's setting, however, is more spacious. His use of the woodwind instruments (with independent oboe parts in the tutti sections and obbligato parts for flute and oboe in vocal solo movements), and the higher proportion of choral involvement, make Handel's setting strikingly different from his models. The 'Utrecht' Te Deum and Jubilate were immensely popular, together with Purcell's Cecilian setting, throughout the eighteenth century, and although they shared the stage with Handel's 'Dettingen' setting of the Te Deum after 1743, they were only gradually replaced by it. They were printed by John Walsh *c.* 1732, the first of Handel's sacred works to achieve publication.

Queen Anne died on 1 August 1714 and the new King George I, accompanied by his son George August (later King George II), arrived in London on Monday, 20 September. The following Sunday, 26 September, they attended a service at the Chapel Royal where '*Te Deum* was sung, compos'd by Mr. Hendel, and a very fine Anthem was also sung'.[15] The remainder of the Royal party arrived nearly a month later and attended the Chapel Royal on the following Sunday, 17 October, where 'Te Deum, with another excellent thanksgiving piece with music composed by the famous *musico* Mr Handel, was sung on account of the joyful arrival of the Princess of Wales and the young Princesses'.[16]

All of these occasions required festal celebrations of Morning Prayer, and on at least one of them Handel's D major Te Deum (HWV 280, generally known as the 'Caroline' Te Deum because of its traditional association with the Princess of Wales, later Queen Consort of George II) was sung. It is substantially shorter than the Utrecht setting, and comparable in scale, scoring, and external details to Purcell's D major setting, departing only in the use of SAATB choruses and the addition of a solo flute (in one movement only) to the Purcellian orchestra of trumpets and strings. The most striking aspects of this setting are found in the outstanding writing for the two alto soloists, Richard Elford (1676–1714) and Francis Hughes (*c.* 1666–1744), the lack of imitative counterpoint in the choral sections, and Handel's use of the chorus to round off solo movements.

A piece which can almost certainly be paired with the 'Caroline' Te Deum is the anthem *O Sing unto the Lord* (HWV 249a), which is scored for a comparable orchestra, contains solos for Elford, and a movement with flute; in addition, it contains solos for bass voice and requires an oboe. At some stage Handel marked the second, and possibly third, movements for deletion, which was musically unfortunate but may have been forced by some practical expediency. He also replaced the second half of the fifth movement (the duet 'O Worship the Lord') with a chorus, to good dramatic and musical effect. With the exception of the Utrecht Canticles, none of these early Chapel Royal compositions seems to have been well known during Handel's lifetime, even though he revived the 'Caroline' Te Deum at least twice.

In July 1717 Handel joined the household of James Brydges, who had become Earl of Carnarvon in October 1714 (and would subsequently become First Duke of Chandos in April 1719), at his country estate of Cannons located at Edgware, Middlesex, some fifteen miles north-west of London. Brydges was immensely rich, having amassed a fortune estimated at around £600,000 in the course of his employment as Paymaster General to Queen Anne's forces abroad during the War of the Spanish Succession. He was currently engaged in converting the Elizabethan manor house of Cannons into a stately – not to say ponderous – example of Palladian style. In the course of this project he also arranged for his workmen to rebuild the local parish church of St Lawrence, Little Stanmore (also called 'Whitchurch') in the Italian Baroque style, complete with a tripartite gallery at the west end where he could sit with his family, servants and bodyguards. The church was re-opened for services by Easter 1716, and included a new single-manual organ by Gerard Smith which stood in the 'Organ Room' at the east end of the church behind the communion table, with enough space around it for up to twenty-four musicians to gather.[17] St Lawrence's also served as Brydges's domestic chapel until the chapel in Cannons house was finally completed and opened in August 1720, by which time Handel's association with Brydges had ceased. One of Handel's responsibilities was to provide music on occasion at St Lawrence's for the Sunday morning services attended by Brydges.

On Handel's arrival the so-called 'Cannons Concert' included some eight to ten players, most of them Italians drawn from the ranks of the opera orchestra, and perhaps five singers, all of them English. This ensemble would increase in size, although not without some cutbacks along the way, until by New Year 1721 it included six violins, a viola, 'cello, double bass, oboe, bassoon, trumpet and flute to accompany a chorus of three trebles, a [male] 'contralt', two 'counter tenors', a tenor, and two basses.[18] After that date the Duke of Chandos halved the size of his musical establishment in response to his losses in the collapse of the South Sea Bubble, and most of the dismissed musicians found work in the London opera orchestra. There were further retrenchments and by the mid-1720s musical activity at Cannons had virtually ceased.

In 1717–18 Handel composed twelve sacred works for Brydges – a Te

Deum and eleven anthems including a setting of the Jubilate.[19] The anthems are multi-movement works consisting of arias, duets and choruses, with an occasional recitative: all but one begin with a two-movement instrumental sonata.[20] The texts are drawn exclusively from the Psalms, but the verses employed are not always consecutive or even from the same Psalm.[21] It is sometimes said that these anthems – variously called 'Anthems for Cannons' and (less appropriately) 'Chandos Anthems' – are derived as a genre from the Lutheran cantatas of his teacher Zachow, and are thus closely related to the early cantatas composed by Bach. This is true only in the most general sense and they are, in fact, much more closely related to Handel's own Italian psalm settings and to the English verse anthems of Croft and other followers of Purcell, which betrayed strong Italian influence. Handel apparently chose as his specific models a set of six anthems setting verses from the Psalms which had been written by Nicola Francesco Haym (1678–1729) and had been presented to Carnarvon with a dedication dated 29 September 1716.[22] Haym was also a 'cellist in the 'Cannons Concert'.

Nine of Handel's works would presumably have been sung as anthems, while *We praise Thee, O God* (HWV 281) and *O be joyful in the Lord* (HWV 246) would have served as Canticles. *O come let us sing unto the Lord* (HWV 253), which begins like the Venite but sets only five verses from Psalm 95 before branching out into verses from other Psalms, seems unlikely to have qualified as the Invitatory (opening chant for Morning Prayer) and was probably also performed as an anthem. The time constraints on services at St Lawrence's must have been less restrictive than those at the Chapel Royal, and Handel's later Cannons Anthems in particular are quite extended.

In the works written for Brydges Handel both composed new music and re-used music from earlier works, often substantially rewritten in its new context. Many of these earlier works, including the Italian psalm settings and secular chamber duets, would not have been known to his listeners. A few, including the 'Utrecht and' 'Caroline' Te Deum settings, must have been familiar to some, and it is possible that the transcription of the 'Utrecht' Jubilate for the smaller Cannons forces (HWV 246) was the result of a specific request.

The first eight of Handel's Cannons anthems were written in pairs, each including one penitential and one celebratory work; there is no indication, however, that these pairs were meant to be performed at a single service. For the music Handel could draw on ideas from his previous English and Italian works. In the early anthems he was clearly challenged by the need to adapt music originally written for larger ensembles to the smaller Cannons forces, in most cases consisting of canto (i.e.

soprano-register voice), tenor and bass, accompanied by two or three violins and single 'cello, double bass, oboe, bassoon and organ continuo. They are full of a sort of musical sleight-of-hand in which some of the original vocal lines are taken over by instruments – especially the oboe, which was still somewhat of a novelty in English church music, where anthems had previously been accompanied either by strings or by organ alone – and the bass line is often separated into four constituent elements of bassoon, 'cello, double bass and organ, each being employed separately or in varying combinations.

The first pair of anthems are reworkings of the two anthems Handel had previously provided for the Chapel Royal. *As pants the Hart* (HWV 251b) – particularly notable for its opening chorus and the duet 'Why so full of grief, O my Soul' – seems to have become the best known of the set,[23] while *O sing unto the Lord* (HWV 249b) includes the duet 'O worship the Lord', subsequently used in the Chapel Royal Anthem *I will magnifie Thee* (HWV 250b), and the vocal fugue 'Declare his Honour unto the Heathen', whose theme is also used in both the Brockes Passion (HWV 48) and the Concerto Grosso Op. 3 No. 2 (HWV 313). The second pair of anthems, *Let God arise* (HWV 256a) and *My Song shall be alway* (HWV 252), add an alto to the ensemble. HWV 256a, which contains a striking borrowing from *Dixit Dominus*, is one of the best of the set, while HWV 252, which borrows extensively from the 'Caroline' Te Deum and the Brockes Passion, seems to have given Handel a great deal of trouble and is perhaps the least satisfactory.

The third pair of anthems consists of *O be joyful* (HWV 246), an adapted transcription of the 'Utrecht' Jubilate, and *Have mercy upon me* (HWV 248), an effective setting of verses from Psalm 51 which contains several musical borrowings from the 'Utrecht' Te Deum. The music of the final pair, *I will magnifie Thee* (HWV 250a) and *In the Lord put I my Trust* (HWV 247), contains much vigorous writing but lacks some of the variety that is found in the earlier three pairs. These anthems do not call for a 'cello, indicating that Haym may have been temporarily unavailable, and in their original versions require only a tenor soloist; at some point early on, two additional solo movements were added to HWV 250a, one of them for soprano.

The remaining three anthems and the 'Chandos' Te Deum (HWV 281) were probably written singly, although in some ways *O Come let us sing unto the Lord* (HWV 253) feels like a companion piece to the Te Deum. All four expand the vocal forces to include two (and, in the case of the Te Deum, three) tenors and, while technically assured and containing many memorable moments, they often seem unnecessarily extended, as if Handel had felt constrained to provide solos for each of his singers and sometimes two for his principal tenor. The instrumental scoring is also less adventurous, although the use of recorders in HWV 253 and HWV 255 provides variety.

Arguably the most interesting of the four is *The Lord is my Light* (HWV 255), with graphic depictions of natural phenomena (e.g. the waves of the sea, thunder and lightning) which look forward to *Israel in Egypt* (HWV 54). *O praise the Lord with one Consent* (HWV 254), which like HWV 247 sets the psalms in Tate and Brady's versifications rather than the versions of the *Book of Common Prayer*, also contains music of a consistently high standard which was later to be used extensively in *Deborah* (HWV 51). In the 'Chandos' Te Deum Handel borrowed from the portions of the Utrecht and 'Caroline' settings which he had not already re-used, and the presence of the trumpet encouraged the use of a type of rondo-like chorus which appears again in the finale to *Esther* (HWV 50a),[24] Handel's English oratorio from the Cannons period which itself resembles an extended anthem.

In the Cannons Anthems Handel honed his skills in setting the English language and developed his sense of proportion in the construction of choral movements. The instrumental and vocal fugues are related to the composer's increased interest in fugal composition during this period, and may also reflect a spirit of friendly competition with his sometime colleague at Cannons Dr Johann Christoph (John Christopher) Pepusch (1667–1752), who was already noted for his mastery of learned contrapuntal devices.[25] These anthems were seldom performed during Handel's lifetime, and only one was published before 1784, although they survive in a surprisingly large number of earlier manuscript copies. Handel consequently felt free to draw upon their music for choruses and, occasionally, arias in his later anthems and oratorios.

Handel renewed his contact with the Chapel Royal in the early 1720s, being appointed 'Composer of Musick for his Majesty's Chappel Royal' on 25 February 1723. William Croft still remained as the Chapel's principal composer, as well as organist and master of the choristers, and he was assisted by John Weldon (1676–1736), who had also been serving since the death of Blow in 1708. The exact nature of Handel's duties is unknown, but they cannot have been extensive since he was primarily concerned with London's Italian opera company, the Royal Academy of Music, in these years. He prepared four works for the Chapel Royal during the remainder of George I's reign, all re-using music from earlier Cannons compositions, transposed down by either a tone or a semitone. This feature presumably reflects the difference in pitch between the organ at Cannons, which now appears to have been near modern pitch at $a' = 433$, and that at the Chapel Royal, which was considered especially high even in the eighteenth century.[26] There is some indication that Handel may have undertaken his Chapel Royal compositions at this period in part to check the attempts made by Maurice Greene (1696–1755), organist of St Paul's Cathedral since 1718, to acquire royal patronage.

The first reappearance of Handel's music in the Chapel Royal seems to have been at a service on Sunday, 7 October 1722 to celebrate the King's safe return to St James's Palace from his summer stay at Kensington following the discovery of the Atterbury plot. Handel may initially have prepared a second verse-anthem version of *As pants the Hart* (HWV 251d) for this service. This was largely a revision of HWV 251a with some reference to HWV 251b, but was probably never performed. It seems very likely that when Handel discovered that an orchestra of oboe and strings would be available for this service, he prepared a second orchestral version of the same work (HWV 251c). This latter is primarily an expanded arrangement of HWV 251d, but it is clear that Handel drew ideas from the other two versions as well. It may have been performed with a revised version of the 'Caroline' Te Deum – in which an oboe may have taken over the original trumpet solos.[27]

The text of *As pants the Hart* was printed in 1724, in a volume of texts of anthems 'as the same are now performed in his Majesty's Chapels Royal', but Handel's music was not copied into the Chapel Royal partbooks and it apparently never entered the regular Chapel Royal repertoire.[28] A fifth version of the anthem (HWV 251e), consisting of HWV 251c with the addition of newly written settings of 'Now when I think thereupon' and 'For I went with the multitude' – the latter incorporating the Lutheran chorale 'Christ lag in Todesbanden' – together with a concluding 'Allelujah' borrowed from *Athalia* (HWV 52) of 1733, was incorporated into 'An Oratorio' for Handel's theatre benefit night in 1738.[29]

Handel next contributed an anthem for the service on Sunday 5 January 1724 celebrating the King's safe return from his visit to Hanover. Evidence points strongly to this having been *I will magnifie Thee*, HWV 250b, which may have been performed with another revival of the 'Caroline' Te Deum. For HWV 250b Handel borrowed music from four of the Cannons Anthems (HWV 250a, 249b, 253 and 252) and rearranged it for the larger Chapel Royal forces. This anthem, unlike others written for the Chapel Royal in this period, seems to have been taken up soon by other choirs: documentary evidence and surviving performing material indicate that some version of it was performed in London, Oxford, and Dublin during the 1730s, 40s and 50s. Handel also borrowed material from it for the conclusion to the oratorio *Belshazzar* (HWV 61) in 1744, and it is just possible that certain members of the oratorio audience were meant to recognise it.

Handel's final contributions to the Chapel Royal in the reign of George I were the anthem *Let God arise* (HWV 256b) and the A major Te Deum (HWV 282). These are arrangements and abridgements of their Cannons counterparts HWV 256a and HWV 281, and feature extensive bassoon solos. They were almost certainly first performed on Sunday 16 January 1726 to celebrate George I's safe return from Hanover, following a particularly bad Channel crossing. All of these later Chapel Royal works are more compact than their Cannons counterparts, mainly because the time constraints on the Chapel Royal services were apparently greater. The enforced concision often works to the benefit of the music, and these pieces deserve to be better known.

George I died at Osnabrück on 11 June 1727: it took several days for the news to reach London and for his son to be proclaimed as George II. On 11 August the coronation was announced for 4 October, and after several postponements it duly took place on the 20th of that month. Croft died at Bath on 18 August and on the same day the Bishop of Salisbury recommended Greene as his successor. Weldon, the likeliest choice to provide music for the coronation, appears to have given up composition by this date, but Handel, who already held court office as a composer to the Chapel Royal and had become a naturalised British subject on 27 February 1727, was both eligible and available. Furthermore, he was of the same generation as the new King and Queen and had known them since his days in Hanover; they may, in fact, have insisted on his participation in the coronation. Apparently some sort of compromise was arranged, the details of which are not known, by which Handel provided the music for the coronation; Greene assumed Croft's regular duties as composer and organist to the Chapel Royal, together with responsibility for the ongoing operation of that institution; and Bernard Gates became Master of the Choristers.[30]

Coronations were important dynastic events and were governed by precedent even more rigidly than other Court activities. The texts of the anthems, assembled from various Psalms and the Books of Kings and Isaiah, were prescribed from previous coronation services, although some cuts and other alterations were made in 1727 by the Archbishop of Canterbury and, apparently, Handel himself. Handel had presumably attended the coronation of George I in 1714, where he could have heard Croft's orchestrally accompanied anthem *The Lord is a Sun and a Shield*. He may also have looked at the scores of the anthems written by Purcell and Blow for the coronation of James II in 1685, the last occasion on which a Queen Consort had been crowned. From these sources he would have learned that the style of large-scale anthem deemed appropriate for coronations was the 'full' anthem accompanied by orchestra, including occasional passages for a semi-chorus or solo voices but containing none of the arias, duets and trios found in his earlier Chapel Royal music.

Handel's four Coronation Anthems satisfy these requirements perfectly, and his use of large blocks of choral sound accompanied by strings, oboes, bassoons, trumpets and drums indicates that he intended to take advantage of the augmented forces available (including perhaps twelve trebles, forty adult singers including members of the Chapel Royal and Westminster Abbey choirs, and some eighty instrumentalists) as well as the size and resonance of Westminster Abbey. Each anthem fulfilled a specific function within the coronation liturgy, although there is some disagreement about their exact placement. The most likely order is: *Let thy Hand be strengthened* (HWV 259) for the Recognition (which would explain its lack of trumpets, since the players might have been elsewhere in the Abbey at that point); *Zadok the Priest* (HWV 258) for the Anointing; *The King shall rejoice* (HWV 260) for the Crowning of the King; and *My Heart is inditing* (HWV 261) for the Queen's coronation.

Zadok the Priest has been performed at every succeeding coronation of a British monarch; it quickly became the most famous of the four anthems and was used for innumerable charity and benefit concerts and services during the eighteenth century. It is most striking for the blaze of sound at the initial entrance of the chorus following a twenty-three-bar string introduction which generates almost unbearable harmonic tension. *Let thy Hand be strengthened*, an altogether gentler piece and the only one not in the 'trumpet key' of D major, is most memorable for its turn to the relative minor at the words 'Let justice and judgment be the preparation of thy seat'. *The King shall rejoice* is perhaps the least individual of the group, while *My Heart is inditing*, with its move to the dominant and secondary dominant harmonies during the two inner movements, is the most varied and presented a suitable homage to the new Queen. Handel re-used much of the music from the Coronation Anthems in his oratorios of *Esther* (1732) and *Deborah* (1733), and it seems clear that the reference was meant to be recognised in its new contexts.

Handel's next official composition for the Court of George II was the anthem *This is the Day which the Lord hath made* (HWV 262), written to celebrate the marriage of his pupil Anne, the Princess Royal, to Prince William of Orange in the French Chapel at St James's Palace. The wedding was originally scheduled for 12 November 1733 but when the bridegroom contracted smallpox it was postponed until 14 March 1734. Greene, who had provided music to celebrate the King's safe return from Hanover in 1729 and 1732, apparently assumed that he should also provide the wedding anthem. He accordingly composed one which was publicly rehearsed on 27 October 1733 and for which he was paid. On 30 October, however, it was announced that Handel would compose the anthem, which was rehearsed before the royal family in early November.

Since this was the first royal wedding to have been celebrated in London in over half a century, the ceremony and the anthem itself were on a lavish scale. The choral writing and orchestral scoring resemble those found in the Coronation Anthems, and as many as seventy-five performers may have been involved, including the full complement of the Chapel Royal and the King's Musicians, together with some twenty-five 'additional' participants.[31] The arias for bass, tenor and soprano, as well as the opening chorus, borrow extensively from the oratorio *Athalia* (HWV 52), which had not yet been heard in London. This music was in turn re-used in the serenata *Parnasso in festa* (HWV 73), which the Royal Family and the Prince of Orange heard at the King's Theatre in 1734, the evening before the wedding.

Two years later Handel provided the anthem *Sing unto God* (HWV 263) for the marriage of Frederick, Prince of Wales, to Augusta, Princess of Saxe-Gotha, in the smaller Chapel Royal at St James's Palace on 27 April 1736. The music is on a suitably smaller scale, with the chorus reduced to four parts and the trumpets restricted to the first and last movements. The performing forces were perhaps comparable to those employed in the Chapel Royal anthems of the 1720s. Handel adapted the music of the concluding chorus from one in *Parnasso in festa*; the next year he re-used the other two choruses and one of the arias from the anthem in his oratorio *Il trionfo del Tempo e della Verità* (HWV 49b). The Prince of Wales had supported the Opera of the Nobility from its inception in 1733, and the wedding seems to have marked a rapprochement with Handel; the Prince subsequently supported Handel's activities until a renewed coldness set in over his support for Lord Middlesex's opera endeavours in the early 1740s.[32] The marriage led to the birth of a son in 1738 who, as King George III, played a significant part in the posthumous propagation of Handel's music. Handel apparently provided a condensed version of HWV 262 and HWV 263 for the proxy wedding of the younger Princess Mary (1723–72) to the Landgrave of Hesse-Cassel in the Chapel Royal at St James's on 8 May 1740, but no copies survive of this setting.

At the end of October 1737 Handel returned from Aix-la-Chapelle, to which he had travelled in search of a cure for the 'Paraletick Disorder' which had afflicted him the previous spring. Shortly thereafter, on 20 November, Queen Caroline died, and Handel completed her funeral anthem, *The Ways of Zion do mourn* (HWV 264), on 12 December, having spent perhaps a week on its composition. She was buried in King Henry VII's Chapel in Westminster Abbey on 17 December: the music at her funeral service was performed by singers from the Chapel Royal, Westminster Abbey, and St George's Chapel, Windsor, accompanied by the King's Musicians and additional instrumentalists. The number of performers was given variously as between 140 and 180, but is more likely to have approximated to the number involved in the 1727 coronation.

Caroline had been Handel's patroness and supporter for nearly forty years, since his days at Hanover, and the Funeral Anthem is both a personal and a formal work. It is a fully choral anthem with orchestral accompaniment, in the manner of the Coronation Anthems (though without trumpets and drums), to a text compiled from several books of the Old Testament by Edward Willes, Sub-Dean of Westminster Abbey. What is perhaps most striking about the music is Handel's extensive use of Lutheran chorale melodies (a practice he continued in his later oratorios and anthems). Also notable are citations of music by Johann Philipp Krieger (1649–1725), Heinrich Schütz (1585–1672), and especially Jacob Handl (Gallus) (1550–91), whose well-known funeral motet *Ecce quomodo moritur justus* is recognisably quoted at the words 'but their name liveth evermore'. These references seem clearly intended to acknowledge Caroline's German heritage, but may also reflect Handel's renewed contact with German musical traditions. The following year Handel employed the Funeral Anthem, suitably re-texted and with an added introductory symphony, under the title 'The Lamentation of the Israelites for the Death of Joseph' as the first part of his oratorio *Israel in Egypt* (HWV 54).[33] It may have been that, as with the use of the Coronation Anthems in *Esther* and *Deborah*, he intended the borrowed music to be recognised by at least some members of his oratorio audience. In any case, music serving the function of an anthem had by this time become an established element in his oratorios.

Great Britain entered the War of the Austrian Succession in 1742, and on 27 June 1743 an allied army defeated the French in a battle at Dettingen, in which George II led his troops in person. Handel began composing a Te Deum (HWV 283) on 17 July, following it with the anthem *The King shall rejoice* (HWV 265) written between 30 July and 3 August. It looks as though Handel wrote these pieces in anticipation of a large-scale public Thanksgiving celebration at St Paul's Cathedral, similar to the one in 1713 that had followed the Peace of Utrecht. Certainly the scoring, length and general style of the two works would have made them more appropriate for a larger venue than the Chapel Royal at St James's where they were eventually performed on 26 September, in the context of a smaller service of thanksgiving to celebrate the King's safe return.[34]

The Dettingen Te Deum became a great favourite and eventually supplanted the Utrecht setting almost entirely during the nineteenth century.

The music often strikes modern listeners as unnecessarily loud and predictable, embodying the worst of what Samuel Butler referred to as
Handel's 'Big Bow-Wow' style. Yet it cannot be denied that some
moments, such as the entry of the unaccompanied trumpets following
the words 'We believe that thou shalt come to be our judge', never fail to
make an impression. By contrast, the Dettingen Anthem disappeared into
almost complete obscurity after the four rehearsals and single performance of 1743. However, two choruses from it were heard in Handel's
new oratorios of 1744: the final chorus in *Joseph* (HWV 59), and 'And
why? Because the King' to a new text ('Bless the glad earth') in *Semele*
(HWV 58), from which it had, in fact, originally been adapted.[35]

Handel's last occasional work for the House of Hanover was the
Anthem on the Peace, HWV 266, written in 1749 to celebrate the Peace of
Aix-la-Chapelle which concluded the War of the Austrian Succession.[36] It
was performed before the King and the Royal Family on the official Day of
Thanksgiving, 25 April, in the Chapel Royal at St James's, and is scored for
soprano and two alto soloists, four-part chorus, flute, oboe, bassoon and
strings, with the trumpets and drums entering only in the second and
final choruses. It was performed with the 'Caroline' Te Deum, HWV 280,
perhaps with the oboes reinforcing the trebles in the choruses in the
manner of the oratorios. The first movement of the anthem, 'How beautiful are the feet of them', was newly composed, based on music from the
duet and chorus to the same text written for the 1742 Dublin version of
Messiah (HWV 56), combined with instrumental material derived from
the Chapel Royal version of *As pants the Hart* (HWV 251c). For the
remaining movements Handel added trumpets and drums to the chorus
'Glory and Worship are before him' from his earlier Chapel Royal anthem
I will magnifie Thee (HWV 250b), and re-used music from an aria (recomposed) and chorus (re-texted) from the *Occasional Oratorio* (HWV
62), before concluding with the chorus 'Blessing and Honour . . . Amen'
from *Messiah*.

Handel's final piece of sacred music was written not for a service of
worship but rather for a benefit concert, held on 27 May 1749 in the newly
completed but incompletely furnished chapel of the 'Hospital for the
Maintenance and Education of Exposed and Deserted Young Children',
generally referred to as The Foundling Hospital.[37] Handel had become
deeply involved in the work of this newest of London's major charities,
founded in 1739 by Thomas Coram, eventually becoming a Governor and
directing annual benefit performances of *Messiah* there from 1750
onwards. In its original form the Foundling Hospital Anthem (HWV
268) was fully choral, opening with the elaborate chorus 'Blessed are they
that considereth the poor', which includes music adapted from a move-

ment in the Funeral Anthem as well as a setting, in the style of a chorale prelude, of the tune 'Aus tiefer Not schrei ich zu dir' to the words 'O God who from the suckling's mouth'. This was followed by another chorus from the Funeral Anthem and a chorus from *Susanna* (HWV 66) – both with adapted texts – and the 'Hallelujah' chorus from *Messiah*.

Handel later revised and expanded the anthem, probably in connection with plans for the formal dedication of the Foundling Hospital Chapel in 1751, adding solo arias for the tenor Thomas Lowe and the alto castrato Gaetano Guadagni, as well as a duet for two trebles. In the event, the chapel was not opened until 16 April 1753, when the revised version of the anthem was performed together with the 'Caroline' Te Deum and one of Handel's settings of the Jubilate. It was performed again on 24 May 1759 as part of a memorial concert for Handel at the Hospital under the direction of John Christopher Smith the younger, the programme of which also included the four Coronation Anthems.

The Foundling Hospital Anthem can be seen as an apt summation of Handel's career as a composer of sacred music. The fact that it was composed for a benefit concert rather than for a service of worship illustrates the broadening definition of sacred music that can be observed in London over the first half of the eighteenth century in the use of the Coronation Anthems (as well as certain of the Cannons and Chapel Royal Anthems) in non-liturgical contexts. In the Foundling Hospital Anthem the movements adapted from the Funeral Anthem, together with the duet for two treble voices, testify to Handel's ties to both the Hanoverian Court and the specifically English Chapel Royal. The use of a Lutheran chorale tune illustrates Handel's increased interest in the musical traditions of his native Germany after 1737, as a complement to his essentially Italianate style. Finally, the juxtaposition in the anthem of arias for the playhouse singer Lowe and the opera singer Guadagni with the most recognisable chorus from *Messiah* sung by men and boys from the Chapel Royal, is emblematic of the fluid mixture of sacred and secular which was characteristic of much of Handel's church music written in the 1730s and 40s, and which formed the basis of his English oratorio style.

12 Handel's chamber music

Malcolm Boyd

The term 'chamber music' is normally understood today as referring to music for two or more instruments with a single player to each part. Anyone invited to a concert of chamber music might expect to hear works for string quartet, wind ensemble, violin and piano and so on. If the programme turned out to consist entirely, or even largely, of vocal pieces the modern concert-goer might well feel let down in his or her expectations.

This would not have been the case in Handel's lifetime. Chamber music (musica da camera) would then have been understood as including those genres, vocal as well as instrumental, which were not encompassed by church music (musica da chiesa) or theatre music (musica da teatro). The identification of 'chamber music' with works for small instrumental ensembles (or with the ensembles themselves) is the product of a later age, when the string quartet and allied genres (as well as the ensembles that performed them) assumed a leading role in domestic music-making and, to a considerable extent, in public concert-giving. One result of this has been that the sonatas and other instrumental works of Handel and his contemporaries have in modern times been not only heard, but also studied and discussed, separately from the vocal genres with which in the eighteenth century they would have shared a platform – and this despite the fact that the two principal vocal genres are frequently referred to specifically as the *chamber* cantata and the *chamber* duet.[1] The present chapter will focus on some of the structural and textural features that the instrumental and vocal chamber works of Handel have in common.

It is, unfortunately, typical of the complexities surrounding the history of Handel's instrumental music that a chronological survey of his chamber works must begin with the uncertainties raised by the six trio sonatas for two oboes (or, more likely, oboe and violin) with continuo, HWV 380–5. According to the historian Charles Burney, a manuscript containing these works was acquired in Germany by Lord Polwarth (later Earl of Marchmont), who gave them to his flute teacher in London, the virtuoso Carl Friedrich Weideman.[2] Burney stated that they were composed when Handel was 'only ten years old' and that when Weideman showed the manuscript of them to the composer they elicited from him the much-quoted remark: 'I used to write like the D[evi]l in those days, but chiefly for the hautbois [oboe], which was my favourite instrument.' Coming at third hand and at a distance in time of up to sixty years, Handel's remark is not easy to construe. Was he acknowledging authorship of the sonatas? How closely did he examine the manuscript that Weideman showed him? Did 'those days' refer to his pre-teen years? Did he, in fact, make the remark at all?

This is not the place to review the authenticity of Handel's various instrumental chamber works,[3] but the authorship, and indeed the composition date, for these sonatas is uncertain. It is unlikely that they are by Handel, and the same applies to three of the most popular violin sonatas, in F major, A major and E major (HWV 370, 372–3). For the same reason the still finer Trio Sonata in G minor for two violins HWV 393 must also remain outside the discussion.[4] The six sonatas that Weideman owned are now rejected by most Handel scholars;[5] they are worth looking at here since they all show very clearly the classic four-movement structure that became the norm for sonatas in the late Baroque period and is found in many of Handel's.[6] Each one begins with an Adagio in common time which develops an opening idea, typically using dotted rhythms, in suave counterpoint through a sequence of related keys. This is followed by a fugal Allegro (Alla breve in the case of the third sonata) and a brief slow movement in a related key. The last movement is usually an Allegro in the binary form of a dance, with each of its two sections marked for repeat; the exception here is in the last sonata, which ends with a Vivace not in binary form.

The term usually employed for this structure in both sonatas and concertos is 'da chiesa', used this time not to indicate the milieu for which a particular work was intended (although that was doubtless the original reason for the appellation) but simply as a convenient label for the structure itself, and for a style not dominated by dance movements but by more 'serious' andantes and allegros. The structure is also sometimes referred to as 'Corellian', although the overall structures that Corelli used in his sonatas and concertos are considerably varied; he did not himself use the term 'da chiesa' for any of his published sets. Of the thirty-eight 'abstract' instrumental works (i.e. those without dance movements as their basis) in his Opp. 1–6 only fifteen show a clear slow–fast–slow–fast (S–F–S–F) sequence of movements, and many of these fall short of the classic *da chiesa* pattern outlined above, especially by having all four movements in the same key (a feature associated more with the sonata *da camera*). The best one can say, on the basis of their publication dates, is that Corelli seems to have moved towards what we usually understand as the *da chiesa* structure in his abstract trio sonatas Opp. 1–4, but this observation is not confirmed by the first six solo violin sonatas of Op. 5 or by the first eight concertos of Op. 6, which include no four-movement examples at all. The acceptance of the classic *da chiesa* structure as a norm owed more to Corelli's pupils and followers, including Geminiani, whose music was often heard alongside Handel's in London.

Of Handel's thirty firmly authenticated sonatas, exactly half adopt the classic S–F–S–F sequence; the proportion rises to 65 per cent if we exclude the Op. 5 trio sonatas, which were mostly assembled from earlier music not originally intended as sonata material. Like Corelli's, Handel's sonatas of this type frequently depart from the classic norm as far as their internal structure is concerned. In the earliest of them, the Trio Sonata in G minor HWV 387, for instance, it is the second movement and not the third that switches key (to B♭ major); the third movement is unusually long, in four sections on the pattern *A–B–C–A*, and with each section marked for repeat.

If we may trust in a note which Handel's friend and librettist Charles Jennens entered into the manuscript copy that he owned – now found at Manchester[7] – this sonata was 'Compos'd at the Age of 14', in other words, in 1699–1700. By that time the chamber cantata in Italy had also achieved what might be described as its 'classic' make-up. The *cantata da camera* had superseded the madrigal after about 1620 as the most important genre of secular vocal music, usually scored for solo voice (typically soprano, whether female or castrato) and continuo (sometimes with one or more other instruments as well). Its subjects could be classical, historical, satirical or humorous, but were predominantly amatory in a pastoral setting. In the later period Arcadian texts prevailed, reflecting the literary tase of the aristocratic patrons who commissioned and promoted cantatas. Beginning in the early seventeenth century as a more or less free unfolding of melody (*arioso*) over a repetitive but rhythmically unfettered bass, the cantata developed, much like the sonata, as a variable sequence of musically defined sections in which recitative and aria gradually became more sharply differentiated. The final stage in the separation and regular alternation of the two elements, together with a reduction in their number as the lyrical element increased in length, coincided more or less with the formation of discrete movements in the sonata and their formal alternation of slow and fast, a process completed in both genres during the last two decades of the century.

The cantatas of Alessandro Scarlatti exist in large enough numbers to serve as an indicator of the preferred structures. Of the 783 cantatas listed in Edwin Hanley's catalogue, 317 (40 per cent) use what may be termed the 'classic' structure of recitative–aria–recitative–aria (R–A–R–A) and 60 (7.5 per cent) the shorter form of A–R–A;[8] these percentages would certainly be much higher if notice were taken only of those cantatas written after 1695. While it would be simplistic and misleading to suggest a parallel between cantata recitative and sonata slow movement on the one hand, and between aria and fast movement on the other, the pattern of four 'movements' is not the only thing the two genres have in common. One notes also the tonal unity of the sonata and the cantata (at least in the hands of the Italians): they both begin and end in the same key. Some sonata slow movements (particularly the second of the two) may be said to resemble recitatives in so far as they are comparatively short, are neutral in melodic interest and serve mainly as a link to the next fast movement. Slow movements are also frequently tonally 'open' (beginning and ending in different keys) or else they end with a Phrygian cadence inviting resolution in the succeeding fast movement; many sonatas may thus be said to consist of two slow–fast pairs, recalling the two recitative–aria pairs of the cantata.[9] As Michael Talbot has pointed out, there is a tendency for the second of the cantata's two arias to be lighter, or at any rate more relaxed, than the first;[10] in a similar way the last movement of a sonata (often in the style and structure of a dance) contrasts with the weightier counterpoint of the second movement.

The fact that one genre is texted and the other not must have tended to disguise the similarities between them, even when they were heard as part of the same concert. But Corelli's audience would surely have recognised a resemblance to cantata structure in his Trio Sonata in A minor Op. 3 No. 8, where a Phrygian cadence at the end of the third movement (Largo) is followed by an Allegro in a neat da capo form. A still more striking evocation of the vocal genre occurs in Handel's Flute Sonata in D major HWV 378; the third of its four movements is in the nature of a lightly decorated recitative, ending with a Phrygian cadence which leads into the binary-form Allegro. The movement is short enough to quote in full (Example 12.1). The fact that no other Handel chamber sonata includes a slow movement quite like this one has not prevented scholars from accepting the work as genuine, despite the attribution to 'Sr. Weisse' (identifiable as Johann Sigismund Weiss, brother of the famous lutenist Silvius Leopold) in the sonata's only known source.[11]

This sonata is thought to date from about 1707, during the period that Handel spent in Italy, and is perhaps the earliest of all his solo sonatas. It was during his Italian years also that he composed most of his chamber cantatas, producing a corpus of work which served as a training-ground (indeed, as a storehouse) for his later Italian operas, but which remains too little known in the recital room to-day.[12] The 'classic' R–A–R–A structure of the *cantata da camera* was, of course, imposed by the text (even if poets – most of them anonymous – were responding to musical needs), and it is therefore not surprising to find that Handel adopts it for no fewer than forty-two of his eighty-seven authenticated solo cantatas;[13] indeed, one might have expected a higher number than this. What is perhaps

Example 12.1   Flute Sonata in D major (HWV 378), 3rd movement and opening of 4th
             movement

more significant is the fact that only four of the forty-two date from the
years after his Italian journey, whereas half of those using the second most
popular pattern, of three sections (A–R–A), date from the London years.
This confirms a tendency for the number of cantata sections to decrease
as arias became longer, but it may also reflect an English antipathy
towards recitative.

While the broad structures of Handel's solo cantatas show few depar-
tures from the Italian norm, they are in some respects as unorthodox as
their instrumental counterparts, the solo sonatas. They depart most
strikingly from precedent when they fail to observe the principle of tonal
unity that had prevailed in the Italian cantata from its very beginnings
and which was almost universally observed by Handel's contemporaries
in the genre. It is extremely unusual to find other composers beginning
and ending a cantata in different keys; indeed, when this does occur it
often turns out to be an indication that the work in question is incomplete in the source. Even those cantatas (the majority) that begin with
recitative and immediately move away from the tonality of the opening
will start with the tonic or dominant chord of the key in which they end.[14]
No fewer than fifty-three of Handel's solo cantatas, however, are tonally
open, and this number includes works that begin with an aria. (It does not
include examples which are tonally 'closed', but which end in the opposite
mode.) Was the composer unaware of the convention? Was he aware of it,
but chose to ignore it? If so, why?

Plate 7   *The Opera Rehearsal* by Marco Ricci. The picture had several versions: this one may show a rehearsal for *Pirro e Demetrio* in London, autumn 1708, in which case the singer would have been Nicolini and the 'cellist possibly Haym. (Handel did not arrive in London until two years later.) The practical arrangements depicted are also applicable to contemporary cantata performances, in which string bass instruments could be part of the continuo accompaniment, reading the music over the shoulder of the harpsichord player.

In fourteen cantatas Handel begins in one key and ends in its relative major or minor; in more than twenty others the movement is to a key a perfect fourth or perfect fifth away. In other words, the majority of 'open' cantatas end in a key closely related to that of the beginning, but there are many which range much more widely. Some of these can be accounted for as revisions of more conventionally conceived works. The second version of *E partirai, mia vita?* HWV 111b, for example, which begins in F minor and ends in A minor, is a London revision of a cantata written in Italy which originally began in C major. Both versions exist in Handel's autograph, so we can be quite sure that a concern for tonal unity played no part in determining the nature of such revisions. But Handel could be just as extreme when composing a new cantata. *Ditemi, o piante, o fiori* (HWV 107), copied for Marquis Ruspoli in Rome in August 1708, begins in E minor and ends in F major – near neighbours in the chromatic scale but distant relatives in the tonal spectrum. A similar tonal polarity, but in the opposite direction, is found in *Del bel idolo mio* (HWV 104), copied for Ruspoli in the following year; this begins in B minor and ends in B♭ major – a conjunction of keys with several particularly strong resonances in later music.[15]

It might be thought possible to explain the 'progressive tonality' of these and other cantatas in dramatic terms, by observing that the situation at the end of the work is different from what it was at the beginning. Winton Dean has argued that 'many of the operas – not all, but including most of the outstanding ones – preserve a careful balance between tonal areas, major and minor modes, and flat and sharp keys',[16] and a predilection for dramatic texts is one feature that distinguishes Handel's best cantatas from those of other composers. There are, however, too many anomalies for an equation to be made between dramatic intensity and tonal design in the cantatas. One of the most operatic among them, *O numi eterni* (HWV 145), which begins with Lucretia's call for vengeance on Tarquin and ends with her suicide, is tonally closed, while the two modulating cantatas mentioned above (HWV 104 and HWV 107) typify the general run of Arcadian cantata texts, presenting a simple amatory situation in an idealised pastoral setting. Possibly Handel's fondness for tonally open structures may be understood as part of the adventurous approach to chromaticism and tonality that characterises his Italian period; Colin Timms has suggested that he may have been influenced by Alessandro Marcello, who alone, it seems, among the Italians was also unorthodox in this respect.[17]

If the continuo-accompanied cantata with a standard design of three or four sections may be said to be the vocal analogue of the solo sonata, the two genres are in certain respects very different as far as texture is concerned. There is, to begin with, no equivalent in the cantatas of the fugal or invention-style movements such as those that occupy second place in the sonatas HWV 363, 365, 366 and 371: by the time that Handel arrived in Italy in 1706 the vogue for long and contrapuntally elaborate *cavate*, such as we find at the end of some of Scarlatti's recitatives, had evidently passed. Also, the internal structure of the da capo aria (which far outnumbers all other types in Handel's cantatas, as in everyone else's) results in a two-strand texture unlike that of the typical sonata movement. Most continuo arias begin with an introduction (or ritornello) in which the bass foreshadows the opening vocal phrase, and thereby establishes a singing style which it maintains throughout the rest of the aria; in the non-fugal sonata movement the bass is differentiated from the solo instrument from the start. This does not prevent the occasional migration of material from cantata to sonata: the main theme of the last movement of the Recorder Sonata Op. 1 No. 2 (HWV 360, 1725–6) is also found in the cantata *Qual ti riveggio, oh Dio* (HWV 150); the aria 'Se non giunge quel momento' from *Filli adorata e cara* (HWV 114) supplied the bass for the first movement of another Recorder Sonata, Op. 1 no.4 (HWV 362). It was not only for his later operas that Handel found the cantatas of his Italian years a useful quarry.

In some cantata arias Handel chose not to match bass and vocal line, but rather to contrast them. The bass of 'Son come navicella' in *Lungi dal mio bel nume* (HWV 127a), for example, represents the troubled sea on which the singer finds himself tossed like a small ship (Example 12.2a), and the resultant texture is close to that found in several sonata movements (Example 12.2b).

Most of Handel's chamber cantatas were composed in Italy, particularly for Roman patrons such as Marquis Ruspoli and Cardinal Pamphili.[18] The chamber duets were once thought to have been written for the most part at Hanover, where Handel served as Kapellmeister in succession to Agostino Steffani, an acknowledged master of the genre whose influence on Handel has long been recognised. But we now know that Handel was familiar with Steffani's duets from early 1707 at least, and that six or seven of his twenty-one surviving duets date from his Italian years.[19]

If the continuo cantata may be said to be the vocal equivalent of the solo sonata, a still closer relationship exists between the chamber duet and the instrumental trio sonata. It is important at this point to distinguish between the duet cantata (*cantata a due*) and the chamber duet (*duetto da camera*) proper. In the first of these, of which Handel's *La terra è liberata* ('Apollo e Dafne', HWV 122) is a notable example, two characters engage in dialogue; except for the inclusion of at least one duet, the musical ingredients (mainly recitative and da capo arias) are the same as in the solo cantata. In the chamber duet both singers sing the same words; there is usually no recitative and no solo aria; and da capo structures are at a premium.

The duet *Troppo cruda, troppo fiera* (HWV 198, dating probably from the Hanover years) is an unusual example of the S–F–S–F sonata structure applied to the chamber duet. The text consists of two quatrains only:

Troppo cruda, troppo fiera
　è la legge dell'amor,
ma la speme lusinghiera
　radolcisce ogni rigor.

Infiammate, saettate,
　ma lasciatemi sperar;
a chi spera, o luci amate,
　non da pena il sospirar.

[Love's precepts are too harsh and stern, but hope soothes and sweetens all severity. Inflame and pierce me, O lovely eyes, but let me hope; sighing brings no pain to one who hopes.]

Example 12.2   (a) Cantata, *Lungi dal mio bel nume* (HWV 127a), aria 'Son come navicella' (extract)

(b) Recorder Sonata in A minor (HWV 362), opening of 2nd movement

Handel seizes on the antithesis in the first stanza to create a slow–fast, minor–major pair of 'movements' which find many parallels among the sonatas;[20] there is, as usual, no recitative. The first two lines of the second stanza form a tonally open Adagio, beginning in B minor and ending in E minor with a Phrygian cadence which leads into the final Andante. This remarkable movement is not only particularly expressive of the text, with broken phrases and rests for 'sospirar', but also incorporates thematic elements from earlier in the duet. The text of the duet has obviously deter-

Example 12.3 (a) Trio Sonata in G minor (HWV 390), 2nd movement (extract)

Example 12.3 (b) Duetto, *Troppo cruda, troppo fiera* (HWV 198), 2nd section (extract)

mined the character of the music, but once the Affekt has been embodied in a musical idea, the working-out of that idea proceeds on 'abstract' lines, just as in a sonata.

The only other chamber duet to approach the classic structure of the instrumental sonata is *Giù nei Tartarei regni* (HWV 187, composed in Italy), in which the third section is, most unusually, a brief recitative *a due*. More often, the text suggested two- or three-section musical schemes. Some of the tripartite duets, such as *Se tu non lasci amore* (HWV 193) and the two settings of *No, di voi non vuo fidarmi* (HWV 189 and HWV 190), share the F–S–F design of some of the sonatas of the period, but on the whole the most striking parallels between the chamber duets and the trio sonatas are textural rather than structural, which makes it the more surprising that Handel and his publishers seem never to have taken over movements from the duets into purely instrumental pieces.[21] Were it not for the presence of a text, it might not be obvious which of the two extracts quoted at Example 12.3 is from a sonata and which from a chamber duet.

The vocal and instrumental repertories in Handel's chamber music complement each other in a quite remarkable way. Although he went on composing cantatas and duets for highly professional Italian singers in London, the vocal music is associated particularly with his years in Italy and Hanover; it survived wholly in manuscript. The instrumental music, on the other hand, is associated almost entirely with Handel's years in England, and nearly all of it appeared in print (though not always with Handel's approval) during the 1730s, when it was probably taken up by amateur performers. In his early years Handel may have written 'like the Devil' for the oboe, but as an instrumental composer he arguably learnt as much from engaging in the vocal genres of cantata and chamber duet.

13 Handel as a concerto composer

Donald Burrows

London, where Handel spent his mature career, can be regarded as the historical home of the public concert. John Banister's concerts in 1672 have a claim to being the first-ever series of such concerts, though Banister may previously have attempted a similar venture in Oxford. During Handel's lifetime benefit concerts, usually involving a mixed programme of instrumental and vocal items, were a regular, if occasional, part of the London theatre programmes. Hickford's concert room was an established concert venue, and was one of the places attended by a visiting Frenchman in the mid 1720s:[1]

> While we are on the subject of music, I must tell you about the public concerts in London, which are poor stuff compared with ours. We heard one which took place in a low room, decorated throughout but with dirty paint, which is usually a dance-hall; there is a platform at one end that you climb a few steps to get on to, and that is where the musicians are placed. They played some sonatas and sang English and German ballads: you pay 5 shillings for these inferior concerts. We attended another concert on the first floor of a coffee-house, where the violins from the opera house play every Thursday. They were all Germans, who play very well but rather inexpressively; one of them played the German flute excellently. We also saw a clergyman playing the cello.

Music clubs, meeting in concert rooms of various sorts (often in taverns), were a feature of life not only in London but also in provincial cities: sometimes the performers were entirely professional musicians, but often they seem to have mingled with gentlemen amateurs – as in the combination of foreign string players and a clerical 'cellist in the description just quoted. For these societies, Handel's orchestral music – the so-called 'Oboe Concertos' Op. 3, the *Concerti Grossi* Op. 6 and the Organ Concertos Op. 4 and Op. 7 – became part of the regular repertory. Charles Burney said of Op. 4 that 'Public players on keyed-instruments, as well as private, totally subsisted on these concertos for near thirty years.'[2] He was referring to the use of the printed editions, the source of the 'opus' numbers by which these concertos are familiar to us today. The keyboard part for the concertos, as printed by London's leading music publisher John Walsh, could be played as a solo (on organ or harpsichord) without orchestral accompaniment, but sets of accompanying orchestral parts were also published. Handel himself prepared the concerto-sets Op. 4 and Op. 6 for publication, and he no doubt anticipated that they would be bought and performed by Britain's concert-giving societies. However, while we naturally associate orchestral music principally with free-standing concert performances today, Handel did not, so far as we know, ever give a concert-room programme of orchestral music or write any concertos specifically for such performance. The vast majority of his concertos he performed in the context of his opera or oratorio nights at the London theatres, and he composed them for that purpose. Most of the remainder can be accounted for in terms of probable performance under some form of private patronage.

Handel grew up during an interesting period in which the orchestra as we now know it was only just becoming established as a regular institution: the foundations were laid in the period *c.* 1660–1700 with Lully's court opera orchestra in France and the orchestras of large Italian churches, particularly in the Papal cities of Bologna and Rome.[3] The evolution of musical genres appropriate for orchestral performance naturally accompanied that of the orchestra itself. Torelli and Corelli are key figures in the development of concerto composition, though in rather different genres: Torelli's strength lay in concertos for solo instrument with orchestra, while Corelli favoured concertos featuring a full ensemble, usually contrasted with a small group of soloists. (The word 'concerto' itself carried an ambiguity – or duality – of meaning, involving concepts of contrast and competition but also, and alternatively, of 'playing together'.) In addition, overture forms from opera were detachable for development as independent orchestral pieces: the Italian 'Sinfonia' (three movements, Fast–Slow–Fast) and the French 'Ouverture'.

In the longer term, and in the wider European context, it was the opera house that demanded the continuous and extended employment of instrumentalists that sustained the development of a genuine orchestral ensemble. Even in London, where various opportunities in public concerts, large-scale church services and court odes encouraged the occasional development of orchestral music in the 1690s, it seems that it was the establishment of the Italian opera company at the Queen's Theatre, Haymarket, in the following decade that led to the creation of London's first professional orchestra in the modern sense. The presence of a number of talented foreign instrumentalists in London (many of them refugees from the continental war) was an important factor in the situation. They included string players, some of them no doubt using instruments from the contemporary golden age of violin-making, and these formed the basis of the ensemble: the opera orchestra may well have been the first in London to have a modern-looking bass section with 'cellos and double basses. But the immigrants included some talented wind instrumentalists as well, in particular the oboe players Kytch and Galliard.

The 'modern' form of orchestra as it had developed by about 1700 was based around a substantial body of strings (a well-equipped opera house orchestra would have about twenty-five, and special church services in Italy might involve more than 100), but court institutions often had smaller establishments that teetered between a chamber ensemble and an orchestra. The court at Hanover, to which Handel was appointed in 1710, provides a typical example, employing about sixteen musicians under a Konzertmeister. Of these, three (described as 'French musicians') were fairly well-paid and were presumably competent soloists (string players or possibly oboists), while the rest no doubt constituted rank-and-file players – *ripienists*. The instrumental ensemble employed by James Brydges at Cannons was yet smaller than this. One has only to recall J. S. Bach's famous memorandum to the town council in Leipzig in 1730 to realise that his 'orchestra' there had only one or two players to each string part for the performance of his weekly church cantatas. Furthermore, the works that we refer to as cantatas were as often as not described by the composer (following an older usage) as 'concertos', a word that we now associate with orchestral works involving a full ensemble. In fact, such usage was only just beginning to firm up in the first two decades of the eighteenth century, accompanied by a clearer distinction between instrumental chamber works (sonatas) and orchestral pieces (concertos). However, the separation between chamber and orchestral genres could become blurred in practice: composers (or their publishers) sometimes pointed out that their concertos could be performed by just a string trio with continuo, while on the other hand trio sonatas could be performed with an orchestral multiplication of string players on each part. The practical interpretation of even such famous pieces as Bach's *Brandenburg Concertos* is affected by the circumstances of their creation for ensembles that, in terms of size, were in the no-man's-land between chamber and orchestral genres. Most of Handel's concertos originated in association with theatre performances, so they do not present this ambiguity: they are orchestral in conception. But there are some that possibly fall into the chamber-ensemble category and, at the other extreme, a few that were written for what we might call super-orchestras involving any and every player that Handel could find for the occasion.

If we take the repertory of Handel's orchestral music as a whole, there is no doubt about the genre to which he contributed most: the orchestral introductions to his operas and oratorios are nearly all written in the

Ouverture ('French overture') form, of which the main components are a
grand dotted-rhythm opening followed by a faster section which begins
fugally, or at least with imitative entries of the same theme from different
instruments. By the 1690s this form of overture was sometimes also
adopted for Italian opera, even by Italian-born composers, particularly
when they were working abroad and in circumstances where allusion to
the French taste seemed appropriate: there are examples from Bononcini,
and in the operas that Steffani wrote for Hanover. The Ouverture form
was almost exclusively followed by Handel to introduce his theatre works,
both Italian operas and English oratorios, and he had become wedded to
the French overture form already in his first Hamburg opera, *Almira*.
Handel's overtures are a rich repertory, immensely varied in mood, thematic material and construction. The form was also transferable to the
keyboard. Handel included one Ouverture in a keyboard suite from his
published *First Collection*: keyboard versions of his theatre overtures were
published in a cumulative series during Handel's lifetime, ending up with
a grand collection of no fewer than sixty-five overtures, and the composer
himself made some of the arrangements.

Apart from the intrinsic variety arising from the use of different thematic material, the overtures display an imaginative range of constructional ideas. The Ouverture was normally written to a binary scheme, the
first section ending in or on the dominant (or relative major, for minor-
key movements).[4] The second section of a binary movement usually
begins in the dominant (or equivalent) key and gradually works back to
the tonic, but the allegro sections of Handel's overtures normally begin in
the tonic key, and very often with clear tonic harmony as well: in most
cases, you could play the allegro as a complete self-standing movement.
(As a result, the opening section functions more as an introduction to the
allegro.) However, in the overture to *Rinaldo*, Handel's first London
opera, he follows up the cadence at the end of the first section by beginning the imitative movement in the dominant, leaving the fugal 'answer'
to return him to the tonic, reversing the normal fugal procedure.[5] In the
subsequent working-out Handel uses Italian-style violin solos as episodes
between re-statements of the main subject.

The Ouverture form was extensible in various ways. The style of the
opening could come back again at the end of the faster section (the direction 'Lentement' at the return indicates the pace of the opening, which
does not usually carry an additional tempo indication). And then extra
movements could be added at the end: the famous 'Minuet in *Berenice*'
originated in just this way. Dance-rhythm movements, whether explicitly
entitled as dances or not, were in fact a common resource for extending
the French overture, and in its grandest form the 'Ouverture' could

develop into a full-blown suite. This happens in Handel's most famous 'large orchestra' works, the *Water Music* (*c.* 1717) and *Fireworks Music* (1749), where the French overture introduces a substantial sequence of movements, some in dance rhythms and some not. The musical contents of the *Water Music* can in fact be interpreted in terms of three separate suites, one based in F major and featuring horns, one in D major adding trumpets, and a suite with more chamber-type scoring in G minor and G major. Unfortunately, we shall never know whether this distinction was exactly what Handel intended, because his autograph of the *Water Music* is lost and the secondary copies disagree on the order of movements. Perhaps this does not matter too much, because the *Water Music* and the *Fireworks Music* were extrovert pieces intended to entertain the crowds (including Royalty) on large-scale open-air occasions. This is not to say that the quality of the individual movements is deficient: in some ways the opening movements of the *Fireworks Music* constitute Handel's most impressive contribution to the French overture genre.

An alternative model to the French overture for orchestral music lay with the Italian concerto, of which the two principal strands were seen in influential publications that came from Amsterdam during Handel's first years in London: 1711 saw the publication of Vivaldi's *L'estro armonico* concertos Op. 3, and 1714 (the year after the composer's death) Corelli's *Concerti Grossi* Op. 6. Perhaps rather surprisingly, Handel showed little interest in the solo concerto on the pattern that was developed in so masterly a manner by Vivaldi. Nevertheless, the three-movement scheme (fast–slow–fast) upon which Vivaldi built was used by Handel, who had encountered it at first hand during his years in Italy (1706–10) if not before. As with the French overture, however, Handel tended to show a preference for adding extra movements, a practice which often presented a challenge to establishing a good musical balance for a concerto as a whole, once the symmetry of the three-movement scheme had been broken.

Corelli's concertos certainly had an influence on Handel, but not immediately. The influence is clearest in Handel's own Op. 6 concertos, written in 1739, by which time Corelli's Op. 6 had acquired a 'classic' status in London: an indication of this is the fact that a full score of Corelli's concertos was published there in 1740 – the first-ever publication in Europe of orchestral music in score (published editions hitherto had appeared only as sets of part-books for individual instruments). In contrast to the three-movement concerto scheme that developed in the hands of Torelli, Albinoni and Vivaldi, Corelli's concertos were multi-movement works, in many cases with short movements forming aggregations to become larger musical units. There was no entirely regular pattern from one concerto to the next, but some of the concertos can be seen as expansions of the four-movement sonata structure (slow–fast–slow–fast), and this pattern itself provided one starting-point for Handel's concerto writing, especially in circumstances where the performing group was essentially a large chamber ensemble.

It happens that the work which is probably Handel's earliest surviving concerto is constructed to exactly this four-movement plan. The concerto in G minor for oboe and strings (HWV 287) was until recently known only from an edition published in Leipzig in 1863, whose title-page proclaimed that it had been composed by Handel in Hamburg in 1703. The music is certainly not in Handel's mature style and contains little thematic material that can be related to the composer's other works, which is always an important consideration when assessing the authenticity of such a self-referring composer as Handel. For Handel, as for several other major composers, oddball works of uncertain provenance have been explained from time to time as 'early works', but a defence of authenticity on that basis is insecure: the pieces concerned can turn out to be misattributed in the source, or even the work of a later forger. Thus this concertos claim to be a genuine work of Handel's has been regarded with some scepticism, but the discovery of an early eighteenth-century manuscript source from north Germany has made the attribution more plausible.[6] If the concerto was indeed written in 1703, it is a pioneering work in the oboe concerto genre: other early examples (by composers such as Telemann, Albinoni, Giuseppe Valentini, Alessandro Marcello) date from well after 1710. For the model of Handel's musical style in his Hamburg years we have the score of *Almira*: as far as comparisons can be made between an opera and a concerto, the harmonic language and phrase-construction of HWV 287 have some similarities with the music of this opera. Furthermore, the choice of solo instrument may remind us of the anecdote in which Handel is reported as saying that he wrote particularly for oboe in his early years,[7] and the music itself seems to embody the mixture of French and Italian styles that was characteristic at Hamburg. The opening movement, for example, while not actually a French overture, opens with French-style dotted figures treated antiphonally by the strings, though the subsequent working out of the music is more Italianate, with clearly defined ritornellos for strings delineating the landmarks in the key-scheme. Even the headings to the third movement seem to reflect a dual stylistic influence: the choice of a Sarabande seems French-inspired for a slow movement, but the tempo direction (Largo) is Italian. The interplay of material between oboe and violins in the two Allegro movements is quite effective, but the lower string parts are less interesting than we would expect from the later Handel: it looks as if, after the first twenty bars of the first Allegro, the composer gave up trying to inject any contrapuntal interest into the bass part and resorted to simple chordal accompaniment.

Another printed source, though this time from Handel's lifetime,[8] gives us two further concertos for oboe and strings. One (HWV 302a) is demonstrably a compilation (probably not by Handel) from music that he composed in London *c.* 1717, but the other (HWV 301) may be an authentic work from Handel's Hamburg or Italian years. Like HWV 287 this follows the four-movement scheme and has a 'character' piece (a Siciliano) as its Largo third movement. This time, however, the opening movement is in a more suave Italianate style. If genuine, HWV 301 seems most likely to be another Hamburg work. The one indisputable example of a concerto from Handel's Italian years is HWV 288, a work that Handel headed 'Sonata a 5'. This title refers to the number of parts in the scoring: solo violin with four-part accompaniment. In spite of the 'Sonata' title, there seems little doubt that Handel thought of the accompaniment in orchestral terms, and he scored the upper parts for violins and oboes in unison.[9] The work was composed in Rome *c.* 1707, and the intended soloist may well have been Corelli, who led the orchestras for Handel's oratorios *Il trionfo del Tempo* and *La Resurrezione.* The Sonata is written to the Italian three-movement scheme, though the first movement is a flowing Andante rather than a fast movement. The central Adagio is notated in simple minim chords, and we are left to imagine how (or indeed whether) the soloist ornamented the given part: the finale is a lively and extended movement with a genuine cadenza for the soloist, unaccompanied except for the final bars, in which the orchestral violins provide a simple harmonic accompaniment to the lead-in to the closing ritornello.[10]

A similar three-movement form is found in the 'Sonata del Overtura' to *Il trionfo del Tempo,* which could well be played as a separate concerto. Here the balance of movements is the reverse of that in the *Sonata a 5*: there is an extended first movement, while the final movement is a simple binary piece. The first movement is richer, both in ideas and the execution of them, than any of the other works considered so far. It opens with a fugal exposition which provides good ritornello material, and the working-out of the movement makes full use of contrasts between soloists and full orchestra: the soloists are the 'classic' string concertino of two violins and 'cello (with continuo) in some places, and a pair of oboes in others. The final phrase of the movement closes onto a diminished seventh chord that also forms the opening of the adagio second movement: this sort of linkage, while uncharacteristic of independent concerto works, is to be found in the three-movement Sinfonias that introduced contemporary Italian operas and oratorios. It is not surprising that

Handel re-used this fine first movement in a slightly adapted form for his second Roman oratorio, *La Resurrezione*.[11] Within the body of *Il trionfo del Tempo* there is also Handel's first 'organ concerto', in the single- movement 'Sonata' for organ and orchestra: this uses the solo organ as one concertino element along with solo violin and oboes, and the clear-cut ritornello form of the movement is the closest Handel came to the Vivaldian style.[12] Some of Handel's orchestrally accompanied cantatas from the Italian period (e.g. HWV 78, 82, 99, 143), begin with orchestral introductions in one or two movements and often headed 'Sonata', but it is interesting that others (HWV 83, 96), and also Handel's two Italian-period operas, begin with French overtures. According to an anecdote related in Mainwaring's biography of Handel, the overture to *Il trionfo del Tempo* as it now stands was deliberately written as an Italian-style movement after Corelli complained that he had difficulty in interpreting Handel's first, French-style, attempt at an overture for the work.[13] HWV 336, a French overture known only from later sources but certainly composed by Handel, uses in its second section the same main thematic material as the Sonata to *Il trionfo del Tempo*, and it is tempting to regard this as being possibly the contentious 'original' overture to the oratorio. There are reasons for doubting this connection,[14] but nevertheless HWV 336 is probably an Italian-period orchestral piece.

Next in chronological sequence probably comes HWV 312, a three-movement work of which the first movement is in B♭ major and the last in G minor, framing a central Largo featuring recorders among the solo instruments. On the evidence of the score, this concerto seems to fall exactly into the area between genuinely orchestral writing (in the later sense) and the idiomatic use of an expanded chamber ensemble. Handel's autograph of the work is lost, and the earliest copies suggest that the two viola parts were probably originally written in different clefs (and may have been given French designations). In this feature and others the concerto is rather similar to those written by Francesco Venturini, a musician active at the Hanover court and, in the absence of any specific documentary evidence about the origin of HWV 312, it seems reasonable to associate the concerto with the period of Handel's Hanover appointment. It is certainly not as Italianate in style as Handel's Roman orchestral pieces, yet the style is broader than that of the probable 'Hamburg' works: presumably Handel adapted his style, as developed through his accumulated experience in Hamburg and Italy, in order to accommodate the somewhat French taste in music that was cultivated at Hanover under the Konzertmeister J. B. Farinel.

HWV 312 was published in London in 1734, as the first in the set of six concertos printed by Walsh as Handel's Opus 3. It is very doubtful indeed whether this collection was produced under any sort of supervision (or even co-operation) from the composer, and it contains a rather disorganised repertory of works composed long before 1734. Six was a conventional number of instrumental works to bring out within one published collection, and the rather random contents were no doubt simply what Walsh could manage to scrabble together to make up the set. Furthermore, Walsh's title page was based on that for Corelli's famous Op. 6 concertos and gave the false impression that the works within would be string-orchestra concertos based on the concertino/concerto grosso scoring, while in fact the concertos that followed were far from uniform and reflected the diverse forces for which Handel created them.[15] In contrast to the 'Hanover court' scoring and three-movement scheme of Op. 3 No. 1, HWV 315 (Op. 3 No. 4) is a French-overture piece written for the London opera house orchestra: it formed the 'second overture' (probably played before Act II) at the orchestra's benefit-night performance of Handel's opera *Amadigi* in 1716. When Handel added extra movements to the basic two-movement scheme of the French overture, he usually kept the additions fairly modest if the piece was to be used as an overture to a full dramatic work,[16] but he regularly added more extensively to the basic design when the overture could be regarded as a free-standing orchestral work. Here he gave the opera orchestra three extra movements – a graceful andante, a more serious minor-key movement and a flowing minuet-type finale whose middle section was attractively scored with a middle-register tune for strings and bassoon, a striking texture that is also found in the quieter movements of the *Water Music*. HWV 313 (Op. 3 No. 2) originated at much the same time, and was probably also written with the opera orchestra (or a comparable group) in mind.[17] This concerto could be regarded as basically a three-movement concerto (Vivace featuring *concertino* violins – Largo – fugal Allegro) with a couple of dance-style additions, thus once again drawing on both Italian and French traditions. But the overall style of the music, into which ideas from various influences have been fully integrated, is individually Handelian. And, although there is a genuinely orchestral breadth to the music, the second and fourth movements preserve some of the intimacy of chamber-style scoring, particularly in the well-judged accompaniment to the oboe cantilena in the second movement.

Op. 3 No. 3 (HWV 314) is constructed from instrumental movements written during Handel's 'Cannons' period, *c.* 1717–18. The first two movements are the overture from one of the Cannons (Chandos) anthems and the short Adagio comes from a contemporary Te Deum, while the final movement is arranged from a keyboard fugue that Handel wrote at the same period. The arrangement of the last movement is so incompetent that it cannot be Handel's work, and it is doubtful if the scheme of this concerto as a whole carries Handel's authority in spite of the genuineness of the individual components. This tends in turn to cast suspicion on Op. 3 No. 5 (HWV 316), which has three movements derived from overtures to 'Cannons' anthems. However, this concerto exists in an important early manuscript copy, and has to be taken more seriously: it seems that in this case Handel really did construct an independent instrumental work by taking some fine Cannons music and adding two new movements. Whether the result was intended to be 'orchestral' is another matter: the work is called 'Sonata' in the manuscript, and most of the music was originally conceived for the chamber-scale ensemble employed by James Brydges. In his printed edition Walsh attempted to give a more orchestral appearance to the Cannons-period music by supplying a part for viola (an instrument not represented in the scoring of the originals) which simply doubles the bass part an octave higher.

Op. 3 No. 6 (HWV 317) has the most complicated history. The first movement is a residue from an attractive three-movement concerto that Handel wrote *c.* 1722. From this concerto Handel detached the first movement for separate use as a sinfonia in his opera *Ottone* (1722) and he re-worked the music of the last movement as the second section of the Ouverture to the same opera. As a result, the original concerto was broken up, and indeed the autograph of the last two movements ('HWV 338') is still physically separated from its companion.[18] It was only towards the end of the twentieth century that the original concerto was re-assembled in performances: the more delicately scored central movement (with solo violin, solo flute, and an archlute in place of harpsichord in the continuo) proves to be an effective foil to the more energetic outer movements. Another concerto that Handel composed at about the same time (HWV 331, in F) is in two movements and re-works music from two of the most substantial movements from the *Water Music*, for an orchestra including horns as well as the usual strings, oboes and bassoon. The parent movements came from the D major ('trumpet') section of the *Water Music*, and it is difficult to judge the concerto independently in view of the popularity of the original: in the second movement (Alla Hornpipe) particularly we miss the alternation of trumpet and horn timbres and we have to settle for less colourful contrasts between strings, woodwind and horns. If the *Water Music* had never existed, we would have liked the concerto well enough, though even so we might have found the succession of two movements in the same key and the same ternary (*da capo*) structure rather unimaginative.

In Walsh's publication, Op. 3 No. 6 consists of two movements – the first movement from the 'Ottone' concerto (in D major) followed by a D minor organ concerto movement. There seems to be no authority for connecting the movements as a concerto, beyond their appearance together in Op. 3, and it looks as if the coupling was a rather desperate expedient on Walsh's part to make up a sixth concerto for the set. The D minor movement was apparently originally a free-standing piece and is obviously of interest to us as the first published organ concerto movement by Handel, and indeed the only movement of this type that we know Handel to have written by 1734, apart from the Sonata in *Il trionfo del Tempo*. Like the earlier Sonata, the D minor movement is also related to a piece for solo keyboard that exists in a number of forms: it looks as if Handel came to the genre of the keyboard concerto by way of 'orchestrating up' one of his well-tried keyboard pieces that could accommodate the additional element of contrast between soloist and orchestra. The keyboard piece on which the second movement of Op. 3 No. 6 is based goes back in some form probably as far as Handel's Hamburg years,[19] but the actual organ concerto version may have been quite recent in 1734: it may have originated for performance in the overture to *Il pastor fido*, an opera that Handel revived in that year, as an alternative to the orchestral movement based on the same theme that occurs in the overture,[20] or it may have been put together for performance during the interval of one of Handel's oratorio performances in Oxford in 1733. Hawkins and Burney both claimed that Handel first introduced organ concertos into his oratorio performances during the Oxford visit,[21] but there is no multi-movement organ concerto that we can date as early as 1733. Rather, the serious launch of the Handel organ concerto as a genre seems to have come in his Covent Garden theatre season of 1734–5 where, in the course of his oratorio performances in the spring of 1735, he produced four concertos (HWV 290–3, later published as Op. 4 Nos. 2–5) to enliven his presentations of *Esther*, *Deborah* and *Athalia*. Their creation was also probably stimulated by the acquisition of a new instrument, described at the time as[22]

> a new large Organ, which is remarkable for the Variety of its curious Stops, being a new Invention, and a great Improvement of that Instrument.

Even so, the instrument was probably not, in absolute terms, sufficiently loud to compete with the theatre orchestra; the scoring of the concertos leaves the organ with a clear road for solo passages, either by silencing the orchestra completely or by marking the orchestral accompaniment down in volume.

As for the form of the concertos, Handel seems to have shown a preference for the four-movement (slow–fast–slow–fast) pattern derived from the chamber *sonata da chiesa*, and one concerto (HWV 293) was actually constructed by adapting a transcription of one of Handel's sonatas for recorder and continuo (HWV 369), though this description hardly does justice to the way that the opening to the sonata's last movement cunningly became the soloist's *answer* to a new opening orchestral two-bar ritornello. HWV 291 is not, in the literal sense, completely an organ concerto, since the organ shares the honours with solo violin and 'cello. In HWV 292, which is the most substantial of the four concertos, Handel takes the three-movement form (Allegro–Andante–Allegro) and inserts a recitative-like Adagio after the Andante: a movement in a similar style also occurs as the third movement of HWV 290. The last movement of HWV 292 originally ran into a 'Hallelujah' chorus, whose theme dictated the shape of the concerto movement's subject: when the concerto came to be published in the Op. 4 set, this time with Handel's active co-operation, in 1738, he provided an alternative orchestral ending to the movement.[23]

To make up the six concertos of Op. 4, Handel added two concertos that he had composed for performance with *Alexander's Feast* in 1736: one of them (HWV 289, Op. 4 No. 1) originated as a genuine organ concerto, but the other (HWV 294) was for harp, accompanied by recorders and muted strings. In the original version (and even as published) the solo part in the latter concerto, following the harp range, went too high for the notes on contemporary English organs: however there is an early manuscript copy incorporating revisions to the solo part that bring it within range, so it seems probable that Handel also performed the concerto with solo organ, perhaps accompanied by unmuted strings and oboes instead of recorders. For *Alexander's Feast*, also, Handel composed an orchestral concerto in C major (HWV 318), employing the conventional string concertino as a foil to the full orchestra. It can be regarded as a three-movement concerto with an extra movement added, and in this case the addition is not entirely happy: the constant return of the theme in the same (tonic) key in the final Andante seems rather a let-down after the dynamism that has been built up in the previous movements.

The publication of Op. 4 marked the start of a short series of publications of Handel's instrumental music that the composer seems to have taken seriously. A number of orchestral movements (in origin, and more surprisingly, also in style) found their way into the trio sonatas published as Op. 5 in February 1739. There were seven sonatas (in place of the more conventional six) in Op. 5 and it is tempting to think that No. 4 (HWV 399) was included by mistake, for every single movement is orchestral in origin, beginning with a group of movements that had a rather complicated previous history in the overtures to *Athalia* and *Parnasso in festa*, and including the magnificent Passacaille originally written for the opera *Radamisto* (1720). The sonata concludes with a couple of shorter

movements derived from dance-rhythm orchestral pieces from Handel's
operas of the 1730s, and another nine movements of a similar type found
their way into other sonatas in Op. 5.

These movements were thus not available for use in the set of orchestral concertos that Handel composed in September–October 1739, but in
any case it is doubtful if Handel would have wanted to use them in that
context. While the Op. 5 sonatas are undoubtedly effective, they lack the
seriousness and breadth of vision that Handel brought to his twelve
Concerti Grossi Op. 6. Two explicit stimuli lay behind the composition of
these concertos: Handel needed a repertory of concertos for his next
theatre seasons (particularly because his forthcoming season was to be
based mainly around English works, and therefore needed some novelties
to compensate for the lack of visual interest that would have been provided by operatic staging), but he also saw the opportunity to crown his
series of publications of instrumental music with a set of orchestral concertos of a type that (as he must have foreseen) would find a ready market
in Britain's concert world. But we may also suspect a deeper motivation,
for he took the composition unusually seriously. Normally he would dash
off a concerto a couple of days when the relevant oratorio performance
was imminent: in the case of Op. 6, he sat down for a month to devote the
sort of energy that normally went into the composition of an opera or
oratorio to the production of these twelve concertos. He paid the same
kind of attention to the details of craftsmanship as Mozart did nearly half
a century later in his 'Haydn' quartets. Borrowings and self-borrowings in
the thematic material were thoroughly absorbed by recomposition into
the new works.[24] In contrast to the Op. 3 concerto set, Handel seems to
have both initiated the publication and watched over the details of the
production of Op. 6: although printed and sold by Walsh, the concertos
were 'Publish'd by the Author' with an 'Englished' title (*Twelve Grand
Concertos*), and Handel even provided the detailed figuring for the basso
continuo part.[25] This conscious production of masterpieces – for indeed
the concertos are one of the peaks in Baroque instrumental music – suggests that Handel's motives in composing his own 'Op. 6' included an
intention to match Corelli's famous Op. 6 Concerti Grossi with works of
equal quality. Handel's set bore the same opus number and had the same
number of concertos as Corelli's, and in general terms Handel followed
the serious, multi-movement model of Corelli's classic pieces, with fairly
regular employment of the concertino/full orchestra contrast in order to
provide textural light and shade. He also followed the Corellian model by
conceiving the concertos for string orchestra, though when it came to
using them in his oratorio performances he added oboes (and probably
also bassoons) to the tutti; he inserted composed oboe parts into the score

of some concertos and we may guess that the wind players were given some sort of 'tutti' parts in the others.

Like Corelli, Handel aimed to give his set of concertos as much variety as possible, while keeping within the multi-movement form, the classic string-orchestra scoring and a general seriousness of style. In one respect Handel's set provided distinctly more variety, for in the twelve concertos Handel repeated only one key (F major), while Corelli's set included three concertos in D major, four in F major and two in B♭ major; Handel also divided the honours equally between major and minor keys, while the proportion in Corelli is 10:2. In these concertos Handel carried the integration of *da chiesa* and *da camera* genres to a level where the distinction becomes irrelevant, if not actually meaningless. There are dance-rhythm movements (indeed, Concerto 8 starts with an allemande, as if it is going to be an orchestral dance suite) and character pieces, but they are presented with a *da chiesa* seriousness: there are light-hearted movements, but no lightweight ones. The pervasive influence of dance-rhythms in Baroque music was by now so well established that they could be used without frivolous associations while, on the other hand, fugue could be treated with an orchestral levity, as in the 'one-note' subject of the second movement in No. 7. In concertos 5, 9 and 11 Handel drew upon previously composed movements of his own, borrowed from two organ concertos composed in 1739[26] and two recent overtures,[27] but this was because the music fitted his schemes and not because his inspiration and energy were flagging: concertos 10 and 12 are among the best of the set.

Having delivered his orchestral masterpieces to the world, Handel seems to have lost any further interest in publishing sets of original instrumental music, though he continued to produce new concertos to accompany his oratorio performances during the remaining twelve years of his active composing life. The later organ concertos, published posthumously as Op. 7, contain some of Handel's finest movements. In HWV 306 and 310 can be found two of Handel's best ground-bass movements, the former making full use of the two manuals and pedals that were available on the organ that Handel used at Lincoln's Inn Fields when he performed there in 1740.[28] Many other movements show that there was still plenty of vitality left in the old forms. HWV 308 (Op. 7 No. 3), composed in January 1751 and probably Handel's last instrumental work, is a particularly impressive achievement, hinting at a *rapprochement* of the Baroque ritornello with modern 'pre-classical' styles and forms, yet also managing to conclude with a graceful old-fashioned minuet without incongruity. But it is unfortunate that Handel never prepared these later concertos for publication, for each of them has some gap that the composer covered by improvisation: this is especially regrettable in the case of the second movement of HWV 309 and the last movement of HWV 311 – both attractive, lively pieces in which sections of some organ episodes were not notated at all.

As well as continuing with the composition of organ concertos, Handel developed another concerto genre in the 1740s which had not claimed his attention before: the *concerto a due cori* involving two wind-instrument 'choirs' (oboes and bassoons, sometimes with horns, in each 'choir') and strings. The idea of contrasted *cori spezzati* was of course not new: it was a principle of scoring for rich instrumental and/or vocal forces that we associate with the Gabrielis in late sixteenth-century Venice, and had been applied to the Baroque concerto by Vivaldi in five concertos 'in due cori'. Handel executed the idea in terms of the late Baroque orchestral style, and we may suspect that he was working to some model that has yet to be identified. There are constructional similarities between the three concertos HWV 332–4: they are all in five or six movements and begin with a movement somewhat in the French Ouverture style, followed by a triple-time non-fugal movement. The musical content of the concertos is extrovert to the point of exuberance, and includes arrangements of music from oratorio choruses, even including some that were current in Handel's performances of the period. A similar extrovert style is apparent in two other concertos (HWV 335a, 335b), also from the later 1740s, whose first movements appear to be trial runs for the *Fireworks Music* Ouverture. With the *Fireworks Music* (1749) and the Organ Concerto HWV 308 (1751) Handel made a good musical exit in the principal orchestral forms of the late Baroque: the *Fireworks Music* is a French overture-suite on a grand scale, while the organ con-certo is effectively an Italianate three-movement concerto (the middle movement being an organ improvisation) with an additional minuet.

14　Handel and the keyboard

Terence Best

Handel is remembered above all as a great composer for the human voice, the creator of operas, cantatas, anthems and oratorios; but in his lifetime he was also renowned as a brilliant keyboard player. As well as displaying his gift for improvisation, for which he was particular admired, he composed some superb music for keyboard instruments. The organ concertos of his later years were written for public performance, but his harpsichord music was no doubt composed for his own pleasure, the enjoyment of his friends and the instruction of his pupils; most of it was written by the time he was thirty-five, and was concentrated into two comparatively brief periods of his life.

The first of these periods covers his earliest years up to 1706, which is not surprising when we consider that the training he received as a boy in Halle from the excellent Zachow laid considerable emphasis on music for keyboard instruments. Zachow's world was that of the seventeenth-century German Protestant organist, whose art was based on the solemn counterpoint of the Lutheran chorale, on the well-wrought fugue, the church cantata, and sets of variations on choral tunes, with some light relief in suites and chaconnes in the French style. Earlier in the century French composers had developed a true harpsichord idiom distinct from that of the organ, involving among other techniques the *style brisé* accompaniments used by lutenists; but although their influence on German keyboard music after 1650 was considerable, initially conveyed through the works of Froberger, the distinction between the textures and figurations appropriate for the harpsichord and those for the organ was hardly observed in Germany. Most of the keyboard music which Handel knew and studied as a boy could be played on either instrument, or on the clavichord, an instrument which was almost unknown in France but which may have given the young Handel his first experience of the keyboard – Mainwaring relates that 'He had found means to get a little clavichord privately convey'd to a room at the top of the house. To this room he constantly stole when the family was asleep.'[1] While J. S. Bach took a keen interest in French music, studied it directly from original sources and imitated it in many of his harpsichord works (especially in the oddly named 'English' suites), Handel adopted French elements at one remove,

Example 14.1 Reincken, Suite No. 4 in C
         (a) Allemande, bars 10-15

         (b) Courante, bars 19–29

filtered through the music of his immediate predecessors, such as
Pachelbel, Kuhnau, Reincken, Georg Muffat, Johann Krieger and Zachow
himself. So, unlike Bach, he never wrote for the keyboard any example of
that quintessentially French movement, the courante in 3/2 time, with its
subtle cross-rhythms hesitating between 3/2 and 6/4, which had a pedi-
gree going back to Chambonnières and Louis Couperin, and had also
been cultivated by Froberger. Handel's courantes, like those of his more
recent German models, are usually in 3/4,[2] with an uncomplicated rhythmic structure which allows a free flow of two- or three-part counterpoint
and a smooth melodic line; he also adopted very early in his career his
predecessors' predilection – also borrowed from the French – for unifying
the allemande and courante of a suite by constructing them from the
same material. Example 14.1 shows these features in a suite by Reincken,
Example 14.2 in one by the young Handel. The movements in Example

Example 14.2   Handel, Partita in G (HWV 450)
(a) Allemande, bars 14–17

(b) Courante, bars 31–8

14.2 belong to a Partita in G (HWV 450) which, with a Suite in C (HWV 443), must be among Handel's earliest surviving compositions. No autographs now exist of any of his keyboard works that were composed before about 1712, so we have no physical means of dating the large number of pieces which survive in eighteenth-century copies; but HWV 443 and 450 show by their frequent awkwardness of technique, their obvious imitation of respected models, and their occasional flashes of real inspiration and originality, that they must be the work of a very young man. Perhaps they are contemporary with the musical notebook, bearing Handel's initials and the date 1698, which was in his possession until his death, but was lost in the first half of the nineteenth century.[3] It contained music by Zachow, [Johann Friedrich] Alberti, Froberger, Krieger, Kerll, Ebner and Strungk, all of them German composers, whose influence can be seen in the young Handel's work; he particularly admired the music of Johann Krieger, a copy of whose *Anmuthige Clavier-Übung* (1698) he took with him to England, and gave to his friend Bernard Granville, who wrote of it:[4]

> The Printed Book is by one of the Celebrated organ-Players of Germany. Mr Handel in his youth formed Him Self a good deal on His Plan & said that <u>Krieger</u> was one of the best writers of His time for the Organ, & to Form a good Player, but the Clavicord must be made use of by a beginner, instead of organ, or Harpsicord.

The last remark is interesting as the only comment we have by Handel about the teaching of keyboard technique.

Mainwaring says of Zachow that 'He had a large collection of Italian as

Example 14.3

(a) Kuhnau, Partita V (publ. 1962), Praeludium, opening

(b) Handel, *Prélude e Capriccio*, Prélude (HWV 571/1), opening

Example 14.4

(a) Muffat, Toccata 9 (publ. 1690), Presto section

(b) Handel, Partita in G, Preludio (HWV 450/1), bars 25–7

well as German music: he shewed him [Handel] the different styles of different nations';[5] but it is clear from his early works that Handel's keyboard style was formed under a predominantly German influence. Examples 14.3–14.6 show how closely he imitated these older masters in his youthful compositions.

Typically French-style movements (including the Lullian overture) appear after 1680 in publications of suites by Muffat and other German

Example 14.5

(a) Zachow, variations on 'Jesu, meine Freude' (copy dated 1703), Variation 1

Var. 1

(b) Handel, Suite in D minor, Aria con Variazioni (HWV 449/5), Variation 6

Var. 6

Example 14.6

(a) Pachelbel, Variations on 'Alle Menschen müssen sterben' (publ. 1683),
Variation 6

Var. 6

(b) Handel, Suite in D minor, Aria con Variazioni (HWV 449/5), Variation 3

Var. 3

composers, and Handel's use of a modified form of the 'chaconne-rondeau', in which the opening section recurs regularly as a refrain (HWV 453/5, 486), had a precedent in Muffat's noble G minor Passacaglia, published in 1690; while preludes consisting wholly or partly of plain chords marked 'arpeggio', of which Handel wrote many examples, have precedents in works by Richter, J. C. F. Fischer and others.

There is a substantial body of harpsichord music that we can assign

Example 14.7

(a)   (b)   (c)

Example 14.8 Handel, Suite in D minor, Sarabande (HWV 437/4)

with reasonable certainty to this early period of Handel's apprentice years in Halle and in Hamburg, a period which ended with his departure for Italy in 1706 at the age of twenty-one. There are at least eleven suites, five chaconnes, and numerous other single movements variously called Prelude (or Preludio), Allegro, Capriccio, Sonatina.[6] Much of this music may have been composed in Hamburg, where to earn his living he not only played in the opera orchestra but also gave harpsichord lessons, and we may surmise that as part of this task he wrote music for his pupils. These works have a number of common features: (1) the close relationship between the allemande and courante in a suite, with the curious quirk that the matching is sometimes more exact in the second half of the two movements (e.g. in HWV 439); (2) frequent use of certain cadence-figures (Examples 14.7a, b, c) which are found in profusion in his opera *Almira* of 1704 but appear only rarely in later works; (3) the dignified sarabande in 3/2 time, with a rhythm of ♩ ♩♪.♪♩ ♩: eight examples exist, five of them in keyboard works; there are two in *Almira*, one of which was reworked for the oratorio *Il trionfo del Tempo e del Disinganno* of 1707, and finally flowered in the superb aria 'Lascia ch'io pianga' in *Rinaldo* (1711), the last such movement in Handel's work. Example 14.8 is the beginning of the fine sarabande in HWV 437. This type of movement seems to have been a special creation of his early years: no one else wrote sarabandes quite like them, nor did Handel himself after *Rinaldo*; when in later years (*c.* 1717) he revised the one in his Suite in B♭ (HWV 440), he changed its notation to 3/4.

These pre-1706 works survive in some German copies (another pointer to their early date) and in a few made by the scribes who worked

Example 14.9 Handel, Suite in G minor, Allemande (HWV 439/1), bars 38–40

for him in England;[7] some were published many years later in the English collections of his suites.[8] Four single pieces (HWV 577, 481, 574 and 490) were published by Witvogel in Amsterdam about 1732, and reprinted by Walsh in 1734; a contemporary recorded that Handel said they were composed 'in his early youth.'[9]

Although there are some awkward passages which reveal their creator's immaturity, we can nevertheless see in these early works increasing confidence and mastery of compositional technique. Example 14.9, a passage from the allemande of HWV 439, is remarkable for its fluent and graceful keyboard writing, its sophisticated combination of counterpoint and *style brisé* which exploits the harpsichord's sonorities perfectly; and the boisterous eight-page gigue which concludes the same suite, though too long for its material, shows us an exuberant and confident young composer flexing his muscles both musically and physically, for it requires considerable technical skill to play it. By 1706 he was undoubtedly an outstanding player of keyboard instruments and an experienced composer for them.

Handel spent the next four years in Italy. Here there was no call for him to write keyboard music, because his attention was directed to cantatas, opera and (for a short time) church music, so it is no surprise that we have little evidence of harpsichord compositions being written down during these years; only the Sonata in G for a two-manual harpsichord (HWV 579) may be dated to the Italian period on stylistic grounds. Yet he often played the harpsichord (and organ), and dazzled the Italians with his virtuosity; the Gigue from HWV 439 could indeed have had that effect, but for such displays extemporisation was presumably more than adequate to satisfy his hearers. It is now that we begin to find documentary evidence of the reaction of contemporaries to his playing. Francesco Valesio noted in his diary that a 'Saxon' had played the organ at the church of St John Lateran in Rome on 14 January 1707 'to the astonishment of everyone':[10] although the performance took place on the organ, Valesio described the person as a harpsichord player and composer (see p. 41 above). A French visitor, Denis Nolhac, who attended this performance and confirms that the Saxon was Handel, records an entertaining incident which happened the previous day at a reception given by some of the Pope's musicians. After refreshments were served, Handel went to the harpsichord with his hat under his arm, and in this uncomfortable posture began to play, 'd'une manière si savante', as Nolhac put it, that everyone was amazed. Some of those listening, knowing that he was a Lutheran and therefore probably in league with the Devil, suspected that there was a supernatural influence at work which had something to do with the hat. This amused the cynical Frenchman, who went over to the harpsichord and told Handel what was being said, speaking in German so that the Italians should not understand; Handel joined in the game by dropping the hat, as if by accident, and played even better than before.[11]

An Italian's belief in Handel's diabolic connections as revealed in his keyboard virtuosity is also suggested in the first of Mainwaring's two accounts of his playing during these Italian years. It describes the meeting with Domenico Scarlatti in Venice:[12]

> He was first discovered there at a Masquerade, while he was playing the harpsichord in his visor. SCARLATTI happened to be there, and affirmed that it could be no-one but the famous Saxon, or the Devil.

Scarlatti figures in Mainwaring's other account, the description of the competition between the two musicians in harpsichord and organ playing which Cardinal Ottoboni is supposed to have organised in Rome. The harpsichord contest seems to have been inconclusive, but Handel won handsomely on the organ. Mainwaring comments (probably from first-hand experience, as he could have heard Handel play in England):[13]

> HANDEL had an uncommon brilliancy and command of finger: but what distinguished him from all other players who possessed these same qualities, was that amazing fulness, force, and energy, which he joined with them.

The next phase of Handel's life began in the spring of 1710, when he returned to Germany, to his new post at the Electoral Court in Hanover. On 4 June, in a letter to her grand-daughter, the Electress referred to him as 'un Saxon qui surpasse tout ce qu'on a jamais entendu sur le clavecin'; ten days later she wrote again of 'Hendel qui joue à merveille du clavecin, dont le prince et la princesse électorale ont beaucoup de joie'.[14]

Later that year Handel made his first visit to England; a ten-year-old girl, Mary Granville, who with her brother Bernard was to be among his closest friends in later life, heard him play. She later wrote 'In the year '10 [1710] I first saw Mr Handel ... we had no better instrument in the house than a little spinet of mine, on which the great musician performed wonders.'[15] Before long he had laid the foundation of his fame in England by composing *Rinaldo*; his genius as an opera-composer and his skill as a harpsichordist came together in this work, for in the final aria of Act II, Armida's 'Vo' far guerra', there are blank spaces in the score marked 'Cembalo', during which Handel extemporised on the harpsichord. The idea may have suggested itself to him because the main theme of the aria derives from the keyboard Sonata HWV 579 which he had written some years before. Walsh published a text of these solo passages in the third edition of the *Rinaldo* music (21 June 1711), described as 'the Harpsicord Peice [sic] Perform'd by Mᵣ Hendel',[16] Handel probably supplied it to Walsh, as it has many features of his harpsichord style; but we may guess that it did not represent everything that he played on the spur of the moment.

After another stay in Hanover, Handel settled in England in 1712. For the next five years he was busy with opera, and choral works for the court and ceremonial occasions. He may have composed a few harpsichord pieces at this time (the evidence of the paper of the autographs is inconclusive), but not many. There is one contemporary reference to such a work: *The Daily Courant* of 11 May 1713 announced that at a benefit performance of *Teseo* on 16 May there would be several new songs, 'and particularly an Entertainment for the Harpsichord, Compos'd by Mr. Hendel on purpose for that Day'. What the piece was we do not know.[17]

Suddenly, about 1717, he returned to the composition of keyboard music, which he had hardly touched since leaving Hamburg eleven years before. This was the period of his engagement at Cannons, so there must have been some situation which either required keyboard composition, or simply facilitated it. Perhaps with opera temporarily in abeyance he had time for other things; a steady flow of harpsichord pieces came from his pen and it is likely that some of the trio sonatas later published as Op. 2 belong to this period. By now his style had matured, and the Italian experience which had broadened his horizons shows in this area of his work as it had in vocal music. He still composed suites, but of a less conventional kind; in the allemandes and courantes he has mostly abandoned the close thematic linking that he had used in the earlier period, and when he does hint at it, it is in much more subtle ways. In only one case are these movements followed by the traditional sarabande and gigue; two suites have a gigue but no sarabande; one allemande–courante pair is followed by nothing at all; and there are a number of sonata-type movements in the Italian style, which have no connection with the conventional suite. There are sets of variations, some 'arpeggio' preludes, a powerful Largo in the French overture style, and eleven fugues which display a remarkable variety of techniques, ranging from a smooth counterpoint with predominantly quaver movement, suitable for

Example 14.10   Handel, Fugue in B♭ (HWV 607), bars 59–63

Example 14.11   Handel, Suite in F minor, Allegro (HWV 433/2), bars 109–16

performance on the organ (Example 14.10), to the extrovert one in F minor, where the subject enters in full chords, creating a thrilling effect on the harpsichord (Example 14.11).

This sudden flurry of keyboard composition seems to have been completed by the end of 1717: early in the following year an important manuscript containing most of these pieces (as well as some of those from the earlier period) was written by various copyists who were working for Handel at the time; it was commissioned by his friend and admirer Elizabeth Legh of Adlington Hall in Cheshire, and is now in the Malmesbury Collection.[18] Another manuscript copy from about the same time has a smaller selection, but with largely similar texts, and is now in the Boston Museum of Fine Arts.[19]

Whatever reasons Handel had for composing these works, for a time he seems not to have contemplated publication; but soon the London publisher John Walsh forced his hand. Having acquired copies of a substantial number of pieces, Walsh printed them, probably in 1719 or 1720, apparently in collusion with the Amsterdam firm of Jeanne Roger. The plates were undoubtedly prepared by Walsh: the music-engraving is in his style, and many movements have English titles such as 'Allmand', 'Corrant', 'Jigg'; one is a 'Sonata for a Harpsicord with Double Keys' (our old friend HWV 579), but the edition has Jeanne Roger's name on the title-page: *Pieces à un & Deux Clavecins Composées Par M.ͬ Hendel. A Amsterdam Chez Jeanne Roger.*

It is not clear exactly when the Roger/Walsh edition was published.[20] What is certain is that in June 1720 Handel took out a Royal Privilege which protected his work for fourteen years, and he then issued his own authoritative edition of keyboard pieces, as *Suites de Pieces pour le Clavecin . . . PREMIER VOLUME*, on 14 November 1720, printed by J. Cluer. It seems to be a riposte to the pirated edition, for in a prefatory note the composer says:

> I have been obliged to publish some of the following lessons because
> surrepticious and incorrect copies of them had got abroad. I have added
> several new ones to make the Work more usefull which if it meets with a
> favourable reception: I will still proceed to publish more reckoning it my
> duty with my small talent to serve a Nation from which I have receiv'd so
> Generous a protection.   G. F. Handel

Now known as the 'first set of suites', or the 'eight great suites', the 1720 collection (HWV 426–33) is familiar to all lovers of Handel's music, and has been published in several excellent modern editions. Handel composed seven new movements for the publication, and revised and re-ordered many of the existing ones, which included sixteen that appeared in the rival publication. It represents the best of his music for the harpsichord, because in spite of the promise to 'publish more' he wrote little more new harpsichord music of significance.

The 1720 collection has a remarkably wide range of styles, reflecting the cosmopolitan nature of Handel's musical experience up to that time; alongside traditional elements of the Franco-German suite which Pachelbel or Kuhnau would have recognised, there are the fugues (five of them were included), movements in Italian style, and a substantial French overture adapted from the orchestral one composed for the Cantata *Clori, Tirsi e Fileno* (HWV 96) in 1707. Although the word 'Suites' occurs on the title-page, and stands at the head of each work ('Suite première pour le Clavecin', etc.), there is no attempt at a traditional suite structure, such as we find in Bach,[21] and this variety is one of the most striking features of the collection. Suite 1, in A, has an 'arpeggio' Prelude, an Allemande, a Courante and a Gigue, but no sarabande. Suite 2, in F, has none of the conventional suite movements at all: it begins with a florid Adagio in the Italian style, followed by an Allegro of similar inspiration, another Adagio in three-part counterpoint, and one of the fugues; it originally had another binary Allegro, but this was cancelled before publication. Suite 3, in D minor, was mostly new-composed: it has a toccata-like Prelude based on earlier pieces, one of the fugues, an Allemande and a Courante which are new, a revised and shortened version of the variations from the early Suite HWV 449 already quoted, and a brilliant Presto which derives from a whole series of antecedents including the finale of the overture in *Il Pastor Fido*. (This music also later formed the basis for Handel's first published 'organ concerto' movement, in Op. 3 No. 6: see Chapter 13, p. 203.)

Suite 4, in E minor, is the only one originally composed with the four traditional movements (Allemande, Courante, Sarabande, Gigue), but for the 1720 edition it was expanded by placing one of the fugues at the beginning. Suite 5, in E major, has a new prelude, an Allemande and a Courante which are perhaps Handel's finest, followed by the famous set of variations, known later by the romantic but spurious title of 'The Harmonious Blacksmith', composed in two G major versions about 1717 but now revised and transposed to E to go with the two dance movements. Suite 6, in F♯ minor, is again highly individual: a new Prelude leads to a dotted-rhythm Largo in the French style, a fugue and a Gigue. Suite 7, in G minor, is a larger structure, starting with the French overture and finishing with a sparkling Passacaille; between them are what could be taken to be the traditional four movements of the suite, but the first two are called simply Andante and Allegro, and the Andante has only the 4/4 metre in common with a true allemande. Suite 8, in F minor, has an expressive Prelude newly written for 1720, the fugue already quoted in Example 14.11, then an Allemande, a Courante and a Gigue.

The 1720 set of suites is justly famous, and it was one of the best-known collections of harpsichord music of the eighteenth century. Its contents show Handel's originality and independence of mind, and his gift for drawing on different musical influences and unifying them by the power of his genius; the technical difficulty of many of the pieces (stretches of a tenth are common) is proof of his own proficiency at the keyboard.

The suites did not use up all of his keyboard music that existed in 1720, nor did they include all the movements that had appeared in the Roger/Walsh publication. Some of these unused pieces are of excellent quality, such as the Prelude and Sonata from HWV 434, while others are less mature works which originated in the pre-1706 period. Perhaps Handel really did intend to compose some new music. In the event he wrote very little: only a fine suite in D minor (HWV 436), composed some time between 1722 and 1726, and a few unimportant single pieces, probably written for his pupils, were forthcoming before Walsh again went in for a pirated edition. His 'Second Volume' of Handel's suites appeared first in a limited edition about 1727; it contains all but three of the pieces from his own earlier volume that Handel had not used in the 1720 edition, along with the new D minor suite, a Suite in G of doubtful origin (HWV 441), and an overlong and obviously early Chaconne (HWV 442/2). It is a scrappy production, omitting the Sarabande from HWV 439 because it had already been used in the 1720 volume (in Suite 7), and adding the rejected final Allegro from HWV 428 as a 'Preludio' to HWV 441, transposed to G. The text not only reproduces the errors of the earlier volume but adds many more; it is no wonder that having first engraved his imprint at the foot of the title-page Walsh had it blocked out when the copies were printed, perhaps because of the existence of Handel's Privilege. After a reprint about 1730, the edition was republished *c.* 1733–4, with changes in the order of the pieces and the full imprint revealed.

This 'Second Volume' of suites is inevitably inferior to the first volume of 1720; much of the music is from the pre-1706 period, and in places Walsh's text is corrupt. Handel had, after all, composed little of substance for the keyboard since 1720, though he made some fine arrangements of a number of his opera overtures.[22] He must have known that the volume was to appear, since Walsh advertised it, and he may even have been involved in the re-arrangement of the order of the pieces; but he cannot have checked the text, even cursorily: among many errors, the very first chord (the beginning of HWV 434) has its bass note missing. The relationship between the composer and his publisher in the years 1731–5 is still obscure, but Walsh certainly issued a good deal of Handel's instrumental music in those years,[23] including some more keyboard works: in 1734 the four pieces 'composed in his early youth',[24] and in 1735 the *Six Fugues or Voluntarys for the Organ or Harpsicord* (HWV 605–10),[25] which are those left over from the eleven fugues written in 1717, the other five having appeared in the 1720 collection.

In the mid-1720s Handel had become music-master to King George I's grandchildren (his initial duties were to Princesses Anne and Caroline),[26] and also gave instruction to the younger John Christopher Smith, who was then in his teens. For these pupils he wrote down some figured-bass exercises to be realised at the keyboard, which can still serve as a comprehensive course in continuo-playing.[27] Later Handel had Princess Louisa as a pupil, and in 1739, when she was fifteen, he composed for her two suites which revert to the traditional allemande–courante–sarabande–gigue pattern (HWV 447, 452); these are small-scale but exquisitely crafted works. Apart from such tasks Handel no longer felt any need to compose harpsichord music. As a keyboard player a new activity had opened up for him in the 1730s: his oratorio performances at the London theatres involved the introduction of the organ to accompany the chorus, and in inventing the organ concerto to complement these performances he was in one sense striking out in a new direction, yet at the same time following a path which had brought him fame in earlier years, that of keyboard virtuoso. These concertos had antecedents in obbligato organ parts which Handel had written nearly thirty years earlier for two arias in his first oratorio *Il trionfo del Tempo e del Disinganno* and one in the motet *Salve Regina* (HWV 241), both composed in 1707. In the concertos, following his habit of recycling music

Example 14.12

(a) Handel, *Prélude e Capriccio*, Capriccio (HWV 571/2), bars 16–19

(b) Handel, Organ Concerto in G minor, Op. 4 No. 1, Allegro (HWV 289/2), bars 142–6

Allegro

which had served its purpose in earlier guises, he re-used phrases, figuration and themes which are found in his harpsichord works; there is no perceptible difference of style or keyboard technique in his compositions for the two instruments, an approach that his old German masters would have understood: Example 14.12a is a passage from Handel's early Capriccio in G, Example 14.12b one from the Organ Concerto Op. 4 No. 1 of 1736.

Hawkins gives the best description of the impression Handel created when he played the organ:[28]

> As to his performances on the organ, the powers of speech are so limited, that it is almost a vain attempt to describe it otherwise than by its effects. A fine and delicate touch, a volant finger, and a ready delivery of passages the most difficult, are the praise of inferior artists: they were not noticed in Handel, whose excellencies were of a far superior kind; and his amazing command of the instrument, the fullness of his harmony, the grandeur and dignity of his style, the copiousness of his imagination, and the fertility of his invention were qualities that absorbed every inferior attainment. When he gave a concerto, his method in general was to introduce it with a voluntary movement on the diapasons, which stole on the ear in a slow and solemn progression; the harmony close wrought, and as full as could be expressed; the passages concatenated with stupendous art, the whole at the same time being perfectly intelligible, and carrying the appearance of great simplicity. This kind of prelude was succeeded by the concerto itself, which he executed with a degree of spirit and firmness that no one ever pretended to equal.

The organ concertos must have been played on chamber organs, usually with only one manual. However, the grandest of the concertos, Op. 7 No. 1 (HWV 306), which was played at the theatre in Lincoln's Inn Fields in 1740, requires two manuals and pedals: the latter were probably 'pull-downs' mechanically linked to the lowest notes of the manuals, since continental-type pedal-boards were unknown in England at the time. The specification of a contemporary single-manual organ (possibly a little larger than the one Handel used in the theatre) was recommended as 'being every thing that is necessary for a good and grand Organ' in a letter from Handel to Charles Jennens in September 1749. Handel prescribed one manual with a compass from GG to d''' and the following stop-list: an open diapason, a stopt diapason, a principal, a twelfth, a fifteenth, a great tierce and a [4'] flute.[29] Only once in the concertos does he give an indication of registration: for the quiet second movement of Op. 4 No. 4 (HWV 292), the autograph specifies open diapason, stopt diapason and flute; this is a 'soft organ' combination in the English tradition.

What sort of harpsichord did Handel play? The obvious answer is that he used German or Flemish ones in his youth, Italian ones in Italy, and Flemish or English ones in England; and since the German keyboard music of his youth was played as required on the harpsichord, clavichord or organ, he belonged to a tradition in which fine distinctions between types of instrument, and in the music that should be composed for them, were not contemplated. Musicians used whatever was to hand, as they have often had to do throughout history.

When he composed his most important harpsichord works, about 1717, he was probably living at Cannons. In 1720 Johann Christoph Pepusch made an inventory of the instruments owned by Brydges: these included a two-manual Joannes Ruckers harpsichord with a spinet built into one side, a two-manual made by Tabel in London, and a spinet by Thomas Hitchcock, all at Cannons; a spinet and another two-manual harpsichord were in Brydges's London house in Albemarle Street, and Brydges also owned an English harpsichord with gut strings.[30] The two-manual harpsichords would have had the standard disposition of two 8-foot registers and a 4-foot. They may not have had a lute-stop, though the device was known at the time: one is found on a Hitchcock harpsichord which is believed to date from about 1725.[31]

What instruments Handel actually owned is still a matter for speculation. Three have been proposed at various times as candidates for the 'large Harpsicord' which he bequeathed to Smith in his will:

(1) a two-manual Joannes Ruckers harpsichord of 1612, the property of the Royal Family, which was at Windsor Castle in the nineteenth

century, and is now at Fenton House, Hampstead. Doubts have been expressed about its claim to be the one mentioned in Handel's will, chiefly on the grounds that such an instrument would not have been called 'large' in 1750, when the will was written: by this time instruments by Shudi and Kirckman were in common use – on 11 December 1755 Mrs Delany wrote that Handel had played a new Kirckman harpsichord at a friend's house.

(2) a two-manual Andreas Ruckers harpsichord, made in 1651 and now in the Victoria and Albert Museum, which was presented by the firm of Broadwood in 1868 as 'Handel's Harpsichord'. Russell[32] gives in some detail the evidence for its being Handel's; doubt is cast on it by an advertisement in *The Public Advertiser* of 15 February 1769: 'also at Mr Pugnani's is to be sold an Harpsichord of J.[=Joannes] Rucher, of the late Mr Handel's'.[33] That Handel was believed to own a Ruckers is supported by Hawkins's statement that he had 'a favourite Rucker harpsichord'.[34]

(3) there is an important painting of Handel with a harpsichord, the famous one by Philippe Mercier from about 1728. It shows the composer seated next to a single-manual instrument which looks remarkably like one by William Smith which is now in the Bate Collection in Oxford. This has two 8-foot registers.[35]

All three instruments have GG as their bottom note, like English spinets, and English harpsichords before the arrival of Tabel. This fits the compass of Handel's keyboard works, which never go below GG. The two Ruckers instruments have no GG♯, a note Handel never uses. The top notes are f''', f''' and g''' respectively, although Handel does not use notes above d'''.

Whether any of these instruments belonged to Handel is at present an open question. What is clear is that, in addition to spinets and single-manual harpsichords, he knew and played two-manual instruments with the classical disposition of two 8-foot registers and one 4-foot; and although only four of his surviving pieces (HWV 466, 470, 485, 579) specify two keyboards, the autograph of his arrangement of the overture in *Amadigi* has 'pian' and 'forte' markings, which can be realised only on a two-manual instrument. All his keyboard compositions can be performed very effectively using the resources which two manuals provide; we can be sure that his predilection for powerful and dramatic effects means that the more sonorous a harpsichord was, and the more resources it had, the more he liked it – though he also 'performed wonders' on Mary Granville's little spinet. The strength and beauty of his music transcend the limitations of any one particular instrument, or of any one particular type. Handel, ever the pragmatist, would have thought that there was nothing strange in that.

PART III

The music in performance

15 Handel and the Italian language

Terence Best

There is plenty of evidence that Handel was a good linguist. According to one eighteenth-century account he[1]

> was possessed of a great stock of humour; no man ever told a story with more. But it was requisite for the hearer to have a competent knowledge of at least four languages: English, French, Italian and German; for in his narratives he made use of them all.

Ferdinando de' Medici, in a letter of recommendation to Carl Philipp von Neuburg in Innsbruck in 1709, wrote that among Handel's many talents was a 'gran pratica delle lingue' (an 'excellent knowledge of languages').[2] As well as his native German (and some Latin learnt at school), he had a good command of French, a necessary skill in those days for all educated Germans, whose own tongue was in some circles considered unsuitable for formal discourse. He wrote French stylishly in letters to his compatriots such as Telemann, Mattheson and his own brother-in-law in Halle;[3] in addressing the latter as 'Monsieur mon très Honoré Frère' he was following the same cultural tradition as his fellow German King George II of England, who, as his wife Caroline lay dying and urged him to marry again, uttered the immortal words 'Non, non, j'aurai des maîtresses'; and, according to Mainwaring, when Cuzzoni grew temperamental about singing an aria in *Ottone*, it was in French that Handel threatened to throw her out of the window.[4] Of his English many stories are told; it is clear from contemporary accounts that he spoke it fluently, although probably with a German accent and occasional oddities of grammar; but when he put pen to paper, his command was total: his letters are admirable examples of elegant eighteenth-century English,[5] and most people agree that apart from a few well-known lapses of accentuation he set the language beautifully to music.

But what of Italian? No German composer of the early eighteenth century could have escaped contact with Italian as used in music, not only in the growing but still quite novel employment of tempo marks such as 'Andante' and 'Allegro', but in its wider use as the language of the foremost opera tradition in Europe. Handel had come across Italian music in his youth in Halle,[6] and it is the language of thirteen of the arias in his first

opera *Almira*, composed in Hamburg in 1704.[7] It is not surprising, therefore, given his natural linguistic ability, that by the end of the four years he
spent in Italy from 1706 to 1710, composing continuously to Italian texts,
he should have acquired such proficiency in the language that Ferdinando
de' Medici thought this particular talent worthy of special comment.

However, although we may imagine him conversing easily with his
Italian friends and patrons and with the singers, instrumentalists and
librettists with whom he had to deal day by day, there is evidence in his
setting of Italian texts, both in the works he composed in Italy and in the
operas written later in London, that he had an insecure grasp of certain
aspects of grammar and syntax. The changes he made as he copied from a
source-libretto were very often intentional, but sometimes they look
more like grammatical errors, and it is not always as easy as it might seem
to decide which is the case; yet it is an important matter for those who edit
or perform his works.

We will take as a case-study Handel's opera *Tamerlano* (1724), which
provides excellent examples of the problems. The work was first composed to a libretto adapted by Nicola Haym from an original written by
Agostino Piovene and set to music by Francesco Gasparini in Venice in
1711. After completing the score, but before the first performance of his
opera, Handel acquired a copy of another version of the libretto, also set
by Gasparini and performed under the title *Il Bajazet* in Reggio Emilia in
1719; he set parts of the 1719 text, and the new music was grafted on to
the *Tamerlano* score before the first performance. There can be no doubt
that Handel paid close attention to the details of the texts that he set, and
a useful subject of future research will be to try to establish how many of
the alterations that were made to the source-librettos, as they were
adapted for his use, were the work of the composer himself, rather than of
the librettist who worked with him. It was probably a joint effort; many
last-minute corrections in the autographs show the care that Handel
bestowed on this aspect of his craft. Haym says in his dedication in the
London wordbook of *Tamerlano* that he has not written something new,
but has adapted the earlier piece for the London stage, and in fact his
contribution was limited to cutting lines of recitative, running scenes
together, and writing the text of a number of new arias and duets; Handel
may well have had a hand in the original adaptation of Piovene's libretto,
and certainly participated when it came to the later insertion of parts of
the 1719 text. Haym must have prepared a complete libretto, which served
as the printer's copy for the text of the 1724 wordbook; it is significant
that the wordbook does not include some late corrections made by
Handel in the autograph, nor does it reproduce those readings of the
autograph which we will conclude are mistakes.

If we can identify such mistakes, are we justified in correcting them, or should reverence for the composer's *Urtext* persuade us to leave them unaltered? There is not always an easy answer, and scholarly opinion is divided. There are rare examples in English-text works: the Prayer Book text from Psalm 41 v. 1, 'Blessed is he that considereth the poor and needy' was set by Handel as 'Blessed are *they* that considereth the poor and needy' in the Foundling Hospital Anthem (HWV 268), for the obvious reason that it was hoped that the benefactors of the Hospital would be many; but although the sentence is now ungrammatical, to tamper with its creates a problem, since the notes would have to be altered if 'considereth' were changed to 'consider', which is shorter by one syllable.

The errors in Italian are of a different order, in that they usually concern wrong endings of polysyllabic words in secco recitatives, so a correction involves no alteration to the number of notes, and the change in vowel sounds is not musically significant, as it might be on a long melisma in an aria. A brief survey of a tricky point in Italian grammar is necessary at this point, because it confused Handel just as it confuses many students of the language today. In modern Italian it is customary to address someone with whom you are not familiar or intimate in what is called the polite form, which is the third person singular of the verb: so 'you speak' is 'Lei parla'. This aspect of the Italian verb can be excluded from the present examination, as it is not found in Handel's opera librettos (or in others up to Verdi); people are addressed, in the older literary tradition influenced by classical French, either as 'tu', in the second person singular ('parli'), or as 'voi', in the second person plural ('parlate'), when the addressee is being spoken to less familiarly. The third person singular is, however, common in its subjunctive manifestation ('parli'), with the optative meaning of 'let him speak' or 'he must speak'. The problem is that, in the singular, verbs have different combinations of the '-a' and '-i' endings according to the conjugation to which they belong: in those of the 'parlare' group, the indicative 'you speak' is 'parli', the imperative 'speak' is 'parla', and the subjunctive 'let him speak' is again 'parli'; verbs of all other conjugations have a different system: so, with 'servire', for example, the indicative 'you serve' is 'servi', the imperative 'serve' is also 'servi', while the subjunctive 'let him serve' is 'serva'.

It is therefore very easy for a foreigner to slip into the wrong conjugation and produce a form ending in '-i' when it should be in '-a'. So, in the second line of Act I Scene 2 of *Tamerlano*, Andronico orders that Bajazet be taken care of for Asteria's sake, and says 'servasi Asteria in lui' – 'let Asteria be served through him'. This is a correct subjunctive, and must have been so written in Haym's libretto, since it is the reading of the 1724 wordbook (see Plate 8): the source-libretto has a different verb-form

6 TAMERLANE. [Act. I.

SCENE II.

ANDRONICUS, and to him TAMERLANE.

And. *Truſt him not out of Sight, this deſperate Man!*
In him you ſerve Aſteria: She muſt be
Kind to a Lover, that does love her Father.

Tam. *Now— Prince, the Greeks*
They, now, have placed the Empire in my Power,
And 'tis a Gift from Tamerlane to you;
Aſcend the Throne—— And know that Tamerlane
Uſurps not the Dominions of another;
He, when he conquers, conquers to oblige,
And does but take to Give.
I do declare you Emperor,
And at your Pleaſure, now, you may ſet out
And find Bizantium yours.——
And. *Oh! my good Lord,*
Great is the Gift, and Great the Giver— but——
Tam. *But you decline the Offer?*
And. *Not ſo my Lord;*
But at a Moment's warning to be gone!
Fain would I near the World's great Victor ſtay
Read Conqueſt's Rules; and learn the Trade of War.

Tam. *Andronicus,*
I freely do conſent, nay, more I wiſh it;
I rather fear'd to find the Marks upon you
Of an impatient Zeal for Governing——
But now your Stay muſt be of help to me,
Muſt help me to ſubdue a ſtubborn Foe.
And. *What Enemy remains for you to Conquer?*
My Lord!—All the whole Tide and Current of my Blood—

Tam.

Atto I.] *TAMERLANO.* 7

SCENA II.

ANDRONICO, *e poi* TAMERLANO.

And. Non ſi perda di viſta il diſperato;
Servaſi Aſteria in lui, e nel ſuo amante
Ami la figlia almen l'amor del Padre.
Tam. Prencipe: Or ora i Greci
Han poſto in mio poter il voſtro Impero;
Ond' io vi rendo il Trono. Il Tamerlano
Non uſurpa l'altrui, vince, e lo dona.
Io vi dichiaro Imperator: Potrete
Partir a voſtro grado.
Ite a Biſanzio——

And. Ah! mio Signor, è grande
Il dono, e il donator; ma——
Tam. Il rifiutate?
And. No, Signor; ma sì preſto
Dividermi da voi?
Deh! laſciate, che apprenda
Vicino ancora al vincitor del Mondo
Il meſtiero dell' Armi.
Tam. Andronico: il conſento, anzi lo bramo.
Temeva impaziente
La brama di regnar; ma il voſtro indugio
Deve ſervirmi a vincere un nemico.

And. Qual nemico rimane?
Signor: Tutto il mio ſangue——

B 4 *Tam.*

Plate 8 The text of Act I Scene 2 of Handel's opera *Tamerlano*, as it appeared in the wordbook for the first production 'Printed and Sold at the *King's Theatre* in the *Hay-Market*' (1724), with Italian text and English translation on facing pages

here, 'serviamo Asteria' – 'let us serve Asteria' – so the 1724 text is Haym's own. In writing the autograph Handel had a lapse of concentration, and wrote 'servisi', which would be right if 'servire' belonged to the other conjugation; 'servisi' can make no sense at all, since 'servi' is a second person indicative or imperative – you can say 'serviti' ('serve yourself'), but not 'servisi' with a third person pronoun. Handel's principal copyist John Christopher Smith senior, who wrote out the performing score,[8] evidently knew little Italian, as many mis-readings in his manuscripts show; at this point he and the other scribes who made copies of *Tamerlano* reproduced Handel's error, because their source was of course the musical autograph and not the libretto; and 'servisi' is still there in the first modern edition of the opera, published by the Händelgesellschaft in 1876 as volume 69 in the complete edition of Handel's works, and edited by Friedrich Chrysander. To insist on retaining Handel's reading would be a mistaken form of piety, as fidelity to the text must surely have as an important criterion the question of what was actually sung. There can be little doubt that the individual part copied out for Senesino, who sang Andronico, contained the error and read 'servisi', because this is the reading of all the musical sources; but Senesino was, after all, an Italian, and it is most improbable that he would have sung a word which he would instantly have recognised as wrong. What do singers do when they see a misprint in their copy? They correct it – at least we hope they do. Senesino may have pointed out the error, and if he did we may imagine him being told, in one of Handel's four languages, to sing the right word; but no one bothered to correct it in the copy, still less in the score. Of course, Senesino may have made the correction without comment, in view of Handel's legendary bad temper at rehearsal.

The first two lines of the B section of Bajazet's first aria, 'Forte e lieto', read in the source-libretto, as set by Gasparini in 1719, 'Se non fosse il suo cordoglio, tu vedresti in me più orgoglio' – 'if it were not for her grief, you would see more pride in me'. The conditional tense 'vedresti' – 'you *would* see' – is crucial to the sense, because in this aria Bajazet is explaining to Andronico what he *would* do (commit suicide) if the thought of his daughter did not hold him back; in the A section he has said 'Forte e lieto a morte andrei' – 'Bravely and joyfully would I go to my death'. The 'vedresti' of the B section is correct in the 1719 wordbook, in Gasparini's score and in the 1724 wordbook; but in the autograph (copied by all the other musical sources) Handel wrote 'vedesti' – he omitted the 'r'. By sheer coincidence this is not a meaningless word, but a perfectly valid form of another tense, the past definite, meaning 'you saw'. There is, however, no way that the idea of 'you saw' could replace 'you would see' without totally destroying the sense of the whole aria, so it must be an oversight. Again, the tenor Borosini, who had sung Bajazet in Gasparini's version, including these very words, would surely have corrected the text as he sang in Handel's opera.

These two examples show Handel being either careless in copying, or genuinely confused about details of Italian grammar, and an editor should have no hesitation in correcting them, as Chrysander did with 'vedesti' but not with 'servisi'. It must be said in passing that among Chrysander's virtues was a reasonably observant eye for errors in the Italian, and he makes some perceptive corrections; but he is inconsistent – it seems that sometimes he had assistance with Italian texts, and sometimes not – and since he based his edition of the operas largely on Smith's performing scores, he often reproduces the copyist's own frequently faulty Italian, even when the autograph, which he consulted as well, is correct.[9] A particularly disastrous example is in Act II Scene 10 of *Tamerlano*, where at a climactic moment Bajazet says to Asteria 'che per figlia non ti ravviso più' – 'for I no longer look upon you as my daughter'. The autograph is correct, but the 'o' at the end of 'ravviso' is scratchily written and could easily be misread: Smith wrote 'ravvisi' – 'you look' – instead of 'ravviso', and Chrysander follows him, even though in other places in this opera he observes that Smith has made a mistake and corrects it; and in every modern performance of which I am aware, both live and on record, Bajazet's powerful denunciation of his daughter has been made a nonsense through the retention of Smith's error.

We must, nevertheless, be very cautious when we correct Handel's text, because sometimes he seems to be well aware of what he is doing, as the next example shows. Having been engaged to sing in the London operas, Borosini arrived in London in September 1724, about six weeks before the *Tamerlano* premiere on 31 October; roughly the same time had elapsed since Handel had completed the first version of the score on 23 July. Borosini brought with him a copy of Gasparini's 1719 score, and a copy of the associated wordbook,[10] which Handel and Haym had not yet seen – as explained above, the text used hitherto by composer and librettist had been the Venetian wordbook of 1711. The magnificent scene of Bajazet's death, now universally admired as one of the peaks of *opera seria*, derives from this second libretto, and Handel revised the end of Act III to incorporate it; there is some evidence that the scene was actually inspired by Borosini himself.[11] The dying emperor, who has taken poison, addresses a poignant farewell to his daughter, saying that his only grief is that he is leaving her in misery and suffering. The text of the 1719 wordbook, Gasparini's score and the 1724 wordbook is as follows:

> Tu resta, ahimè, che dir non posso: in pace. Tu resti, figlia, negli affanni: e questo è il solo affanno mio.

> You must stay behind, but, alas, I cannot say 'in peace'. You are left behind, daughter, in suffering: and this is my only grief.

What has to be observed is the change in the form of the verb 'restare': first he says 'resta', which is the imperative – he is telling her that she must stay behind and not follow him into death; then 'resti', the indicative – he is now thinking of the consequences of her obeying him. The change is subtle, and perhaps not entirely convincing, but it cannot be a misprint in the 1719 wordbook, since Gasparini's score has the same reading, and clearly it was the text that Haym and Handel used, as it is also in the 1724 wordbook, and was initially in the autograph. Handel evidently had to give the passage some thought: copying the text from his source, he duly wrote 'resta' for the first appearance of the word, and 'resti' for the second; then he noticed what must have seemed to him to be an inconsistency, so he went back to 'resta' and altered the 'a' to 'i', so that 'resti' now occurs both times.

There are two possible explanations: first that, unsure as before about the finer points of difference between these endings in '-a' and '-i', he decided that 'resta' was wrong, so corrected it to match the other reading;

or second, that he knew very well what the difference was and decided that to have 'resti' both times made better sense, and gave a simpler but stronger meaning to the passage. We cannot exclude the second possibility, and since the corrected reading makes grammatical sense, there can be no justification for changing it, and we must read 'resti' as he left it.

The next example throws up a different set of problems. Among the texts newly written by Haym was one for a duet between Irene and Tamerlano towards the end of Act III. Irene has been consistently betrayed by Tamerlano, to whom she is betrothed, because he has been pursuing Asteria instead; but now that Asteria's plot to kill Tamerlano has been revealed and Irene has saved his life, he is reconciled with her and has promised that she shall be his queen. The duet was composed by Handel – the music is in the autograph and was copied into the performing score – but was dropped before the first performance, and so it does not appear in the 1724 wordbook; consequently, since it is not in either of the earlier librettos, there is no source for its text other than the autograph and the copies which derive from it.

It is one of those pieces in which the two voices sing the same thoughts, but with the pronouns reversed, of the type 'I love you' – 'Yes, you love me'. The A section is clear:

IRENE: Vedrò ch'un dì si cangerà del mio penar la crudeltà.
TAMERLANO: Vedrai ch'un dì cangiar saprò del tuo penar la crudeltà.

IRENE: I will see that one day the cruelty of my suffering will change.
TAMERLANO: You will see that one day I will be able to change the cruelty of your suffering.

but the B section is confused:

IRENE: Mia fede allor il premio avrà, se saprai amar chi amarti sa, chi amarti sa, etc.
TAMERLANO: Mia fede allor il premio avrà, se saprai amar chi amarmi sa, chi amarti sa, chi amarti sa, chi amarmi sa.

Irene's words translate as 'My fidelity will then have its reward, if you will be able to love the one who loves you', which makes perfect sense; but Tamerlano's words are obviously garbled, with both 'amarmi' and 'amarti', each given twice. Either his words should be the same as Irene's, which is unlikely in view of the style of the A section, and the appearance of 'amarmi' as an obvious antithesis of Irene's 'amarti' (in any case Tamerlano cannot speak of his fidelity having its reward, since until now he has been faithless); or the text should be 'Tua fede allor il premio avrà, se saprò amar chi amarmi sa' – 'Your fidelity will then have its reward, if I will be able to love the one who loves me.' Handel must have followed the wrong line of the libretto as he composed this passage, but he twice got 'amarmi' right. Smith, writing the performing score, realised that something was wrong, and wrote 'amarmi' all four times, but made no other corrections.

Here the editor must surely reconstruct the correct text from his own deduction; Chrysander, to his credit, did just that (*HG* vol. 69, p. 124), except that he printed 'che' for 'se' in Tamerlano's part. It seems that Handel failed to notice that the Italian words he wrote did not make sense. In this case, of course, the question of what was actually sung does not arise, because this duet was never performed; but if it had been, it is hardly likely that the singers, and the composer, would have failed to notice the error and correct it.

My final example is from Asteria's aria 'Cor di padre', which originally ended Act II, but was moved to the beginning of Act III before the first performance.

The A section reads thus in the 1711 and 1719 wordbooks:

> Cor di padre, e cor d'amante,
> Salda fede, odio costante
> Pur al fine vi placò.

'Father's heart, lover's heart; unswerving loyalty [to my father and lover], undying hatred [for Tamerlano], has [=have] indeed placated you in the end.' The loyalty and hatred are perhaps thought of as one simultaneous impulse, hence the singular verb – although this usage is odd.

Haym, or Handel, changed the past tense of the verb, 'placò', to the future, 'placherà', that is, 'has placated' becomes 'will placate', but the syntax remains the same; to make room for the extra syllable, 'fine' was shortened to 'fin'. Handel first wrote 'placherà' throughout, then altered it to 'placherò', a reading followed by the 1724 wordbook; this means 'I will placate', which alters the syntax of the sentence and leaves the meaning rather obscure: now all the elements of the first two lines, the father's heart, the lover's heart, the unswerving loyalty and the undying hatred, are grouped together, referred to as 'you' ('vi'), and are the objects of the verb 'placherò'. Handel probably made the change to preserve the rhyme with the last line of the B section,[12] which runs

> Sol non è pago il mio core,
> Perché dice il mio timore
> Ch'ambedue vi perderò.

but he evidently failed to see that by so doing he was dislocating the syntax. However, if we think of Asteria as the person whose actions will placate her father and lover, it can just be made to make sense, and we have no option but to leave it as it stands.

Example 15.1   Handel, *Almira*, aria 'So ben che regnante' (HWV 1/6)

de - gna   di   te   il _____   mon - do,   il _____   mon - do non ha.

Example 15.2   Gasparini, *Il Bajazet*, Act I Scene 5, recit. 'Ama il Tartaro Asteria'

co - me   mai   po - trò di - re,

So we must conclude from the evidence that while Handel was thoroughly at home in Italian, and especially in the literary language used in these librettos, it is clear that his knowledge was not such that every last grammatical and syntactical detail was second nature to him, and in modern editions and performances a little remedial action is sometimes necessary.

How well did Handel set the Italian language to music? The answer is that, as with English, he did it superbly; there are just occasional misjudgements over the correct stressing of words in recitative, but they are few (e.g. 'ra_dice' instead of 'radi_ce' in *Agrippina*, Act II Scene 18, and 'umi_le' instead of 'u_mile' in Act II Scene 4 and Act III Scene 13 of the same opera). His earliest surviving Italian settings are the thirteen arias in *Almira*, composed before he went to Italy. Already in these pieces we can see that he had a firm grasp of the basic principles, although his inexperience is revealed in an example from the first of them, Fernando's 'So ben che regnante' in Act I Scene 2, with its awkward emphasis on the definite article 'il' (Example 15.1).

Italian composers follow certain rules in setting their language to music, and Handel was not slow to learn them:

1. In secco recitatives the normal accentuation of the words is observed, so that stressed syllables fall on the strong beats of the bar. An exception is made when a word which ends with a stressed syllable ('potrò', 'perché') is followed by another which begins with one (e.g. 'potrò dire'); in this case the stresses of the first word are frequently reversed in the music, as in this example from Gasparini's *Il Bajazet*, Act I Scene 5 (Example 15.2) and another from the same opera, Act I Scene 1, (Example 15.3): here the 'il' after 'perché' does not count as a separate syllable, as the vowel is elided.

Handel understood the principle very well; Example 15.4 (*Tamerlano*, Act I Scene 1) is his own setting of the words of Example 15.3. In this

Example 15.3   Gasparini, *Il Bajazet*, Act I Scene 1, recit. 'Prence, lo so'

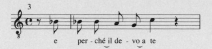

e   per - ché il de - vo a te,   più, dol - ce il   sen - to.

Example 15.4   Handel, Tamerlano (HWV 18), Act I Scene 1, recit. 'Prence, lo so'

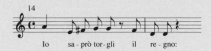

e   per - ché il de - vo a te

Example 15.5   Handel, *Rodelinda* (HWV 19), Act II Scene 2, recit. 'Rodelinda, sì mesta'

Io   sa - prò tor - gli   il   re - gno:

Example 15.6   Gasparini, *Il Bajazet*, Act I Scene 3, aria 'Co' sguardi'

or   la mia va - ga stel - la,   e il

Example 15.7   Gasparini, *Il Bajazet*, Act II Scene 12, aria 'No, che del tuo gran cor'

no,   non vò   per - do - no.

instance he may have had Gasparini's score in front of him as he penned the passage; but he observes the rule elsewhere, as in Example 15.5, from *Rodelinda*, Act II Scene 2.

2. In arias Italian composers use a more flexible and subtle pattern of stressing than in recitatives: where the dramatic or musical effect requires it, we frequently find on a strong beat words which in ordinary speech or recitative are by nature unstressed ('il', 'la', 'di'), as in Example 15.6 from Gasparini's *Il Bajazet*. Verdi's 'La donna è mobile' and 'Di quella pira' are well-known later examples; furthermore the unstressed syllable which occurs at the end of most Italian words invariably falls on a strong beat at cadences: see Example 15.7, also from *Il Bajazet*. Example 15.8 is an

Example 15.8 Handel, *Tamerlano*, aria 'No, che del tuo gran cor' (HWV 18/24)

non vò per-do - no.

Example 15.9 Handel, *Agrippina*, aria 'Col peso del tuo amor' (HWV 6/33)

e la tua spe - ne.

instance form Handel's *Tamerlano*. Example 15.9, from *Agrippina*, shows both of these features, and there are hundreds of other examples.

Handel adopted these conventions as to the manner born. The early awkwardness in setting Italian that we observed in *Almira* was swept away as soon as he arrived in Italy; even the earliest works that he composed there, such as the cantata *Da quel giorno fatale* (Il delirio amoroso, HWV 99), show that he rapidly acquired a fluency of technique equal to that of native composers. His gift for assimilating the style of the country in which he happened to be is revealed as much in this aspect of his art as in the music itself. The Italian language became for him the means by which his music expressed the whole range of human feeling and experience, until in due course he found another tongue equally suitable for the purpose, the one spoken in the land in which he finally made his home.

16 Handel and the orchestra

Mark W. Stahura

Studies of Handel's compositions have in general understandably stressed his use of and sensitivity to the human voice: studies of his orchestral works have, also understandably, dwelt on the Concerti Grossi and other purely instrumental works. Yet the orchestra was the under-pinning for the vast majority of his compositions – for all of the operas and oratorios, for example, which are the heart of his output. It was the working musical ensemble at the core of Handel's career, but apparently he did not consider it a viable separate concert 'instrument': in his own performances, the orchestra was merely a part of a larger entertainment, featured at times, but never self-sufficient.

We know almost nothing about the orchestra at Hamburg's Theater am Gänsemarkt, where Handel's first surviving major work involving orchestra was performed. Johann Mattheson, Handel's mentor and friend in Hamburg, tells us only that the orchestra used just one harpsi-chord, and that he (Mattheson) favoured orchestral direction from the keyboard.[1] *Almira* (HWV 1, 1705), the only surviving Handel score from this period, uses an orchestra of two upper wind parts (mainly oboes, occasionally recorders), one bassoon part, three trumpets, timpani, and strings (up to three violin parts, one viola part and basso continuo). It is not known how many string and woodwind players performed each part, or how many other realising continuo instruments were present. Even further from view is knowledge of the workings of the orchestra in terms of the division of continuo labour, or the extent to which the full string section may have been reduced occasionally to concertino players.

We are rather more fortunate in information concerning Handel's compositions from his Italian years (1706–10), as evidence survives about the orchestral forces for his Roman oratorios and church music. For the oratorio *Il trionfo del Tempo e del Disinganno* (HWV 46a) in 1707, a copyist's list for producing the orchestral parts indicates how many parts were copied and how many pages of music each contained, but not how many players read from each book.[2] If we assume two players to a part for both strings and wind, an orchestra of possibly twenty-six strings (8/6/4/8 – the 'cello and string bass parts are lumped together in the copyist's accounts) and four oboes is indicated. Handel certainly played keyboard continuo (presumably alternating harpsichord and organ), and more continuo players (lute, 'cello or double bass) could have read over his shoulder. There are no indications for other realising instruments, or for more than one realising instrument at a time: the organ was used only exceptionally, with a fully written concerto-like part separate from that for the string bass line. For *La Resurrezione* (HWV 47) the next year, a pay-list for the orchestra shows as many as twenty-two violins (the division of these is not given), four violas, six 'cellos, five string basses, four oboes, two trumpets, and one trombone.[3] This was probably the largest orchestra that Handel ever used for an opera or oratorio.

Original orchestral parts for his Latin church music, composed in 1707, re-surfaced during the 1980s.[4] It is possible that this material is incomplete, lacking 'cello and string bass parts for four of the six works. It is equally likely, however, that these players read over the shoulders of the keyboard player(s), and thus needed no separate parts. Presuming again two players per part, Handel's orchestra for these works was quite small: apart from the minimally-scored *Saeviat tellus* (HWV 240, for which only a concertino violin part and a vocal part survive), the instrumental group varied from three to five violins on each violin line[5] and two to four violas: as in the *Trionfo* list, the continuo contingent is impossible to measure, since various instruments could easily have grouped around the realising continuo player(s),[6] but we do not know how many or what kind of instruments were involved. Similarly, we do not know whether the two oboe parts to *Laudate pueri* (HWV 237) were read by one or two players each.

No comparable detailed evidence survives concerning the orchestras that Handel had available for the two operas he wrote in Italy, *Rodrigo* (HWV 5, 1707) for the Cocomero Theatre in Florence and *Agrippina* (HWV 6, 1709/10) for the Teatro S. Giovanni Grisostomo in Venice. The score of the former requires only two oboes (doubling on recorders) and strings, the latter adding two trumpets and timpani to this group. The four recorder parts called for in *Agrippina*'s 'Volo pronto' could have been covered by oboists if the oboe parts were played by two players per part. Otherwise, other instrumentalists could have covered the two extra recorder parts, a not unusual procedure.[7]

Handel arrived in London in 1710 to find an established, though financially precarious, opera orchestra waiting for an accomplished composer like himself. The surviving lists of the opera orchestra around this time vary slightly in certain details. In the period 1709–11 the violins vary between nine and twelve in number, and the distribution of these violinists is variable: one list puts only four players on first violin and six on second, while another reverses the ratio, and adds two mysterious 'ripieno' players at the at the bottom of the ranks.[8] Numbers of violas remain stable at two, but 'cello/bass players range between four and seven (some players were competent on both instruments, making a firm division of these numbers somewhat slippery). Two oboes, three bassoons (four on one list), one trumpet, and one harpsichordist round out the standing ensemble. Handel added to this group for his first London opera, *Rinaldo* (HWV 7a, 1711), using four trumpets and timpani, and calling for three recorders (which were certainly covered by players of other instruments, probably the oboists and one bassoonist). From the start, Handel varied the make-up of the orchestral scoring in London to suit his creative ideas and dramatic needs.

When opera in London faltered in 1717, Handel joined the household of James Brydges, the Earl of Carnarvon. During this period (1717–19) he composed and performed *Acis and Galatea* (HWV 49a) at Cannons, the Earl's home at Edgware. The extent of the Earl's private patronage of musicians at Cannons can be derived from his household accounts: in 1718, the probable year for the performance of *Acis*, his establishment could have mustered an orchestra of just four violins, two 'cellos and one double bass, two oboes, one flute/recorder (other players could probably also double on recorder), and sometimes one trumpet and one bassoon (possibly covered by a player doubling with another instrument).[9] The score of the first version of *Esther* (HWV 50a), probably written for Carnarvon *c.* 1718 but possibly not performed until later, requires slightly larger forces: from the somewhat augmented Cannons establishment Handel probably had the services of six violins, one viola, two 'cello/basses, two oboes, one trumpet, one bassoon (plus one of the oboists who could double on bassoon when needed), and at least one rehearsal keyboard player.[10] The score also calls for two horns and a harp. *Esther* requires substantial instrumental resources: in general, single-handed patronage in England could provide only limited orchestral forces, and few occasions on which to use them.

In 1719–20 the Royal Academy of Music was officially established as a permanent opera company in London, and fortunately documentation from the financial preparations for the formation of the company's orchestra survives. Handel was appointed from the start as the 'Master of the Orchestra', and these lists presumably reflect his opinions about the size and proportions of a proper opera orchestra, as well as the anticipated limits of the Academy's budget. The prospective orchestra was larger than that for the opera company of the previous decade, including seventeen violins in three divisions (8/5/4), two violas, four 'cellos, two double basses, four oboes, three bassoons, one trumpet and one theorbo.[11] Compared with the 1710 orchestra, both the top and bottom of the texture are filled out. The separate listing of the 'third' violins, commonly but not frequently called for in Handel's scores, leaves us guessing about their role when no designated third violin part is present in the score. Adding these lowest-paid violinists to the second violins brings the balance nearly equal (8/9) for the great many movements with only two violin parts, and certainly improves on the sometimes odd balance of the violins (4/7 in one source) in the lists of the 1709–11 London opera orchestra. It appears likely that the third violins joined the seconds when no separate line was written.

Evidence of Handel's London orchestra is sporadic and less detailed after 1720, until nearly the end of Handel's career, but it seems to indicate some growth in the violin section and variations in the continuo group. Pierre-Jacques Fougeroux, who heard three Handel operas under the composer's direction in 1728, describes the orchestra as having twenty-four 'violins' – the total certainly includes violas – three 'cellos and two double basses, and two harpsichords.[12] The wind contingent is not accurately described by Fougeroux: 'some' flutes and trumpets, and three bassoons. Sir John Clerk in his diary lists Handel's opera orchestra in 1733 at 'above 24' violins (which again must include violas), four 'cellos, two basses, two oboes, four bassoons, two harpsichords and a theorbo.[13]

A copyist's list for writing orchestral parts for the pasticcio *Didone abbandonata* that Handel produced in 1737 provides less firm evidence about Handel's orchestra, since (like the Roman list for *Il trionfo* and the Latin church music parts referred to above) it does not indicate how many players used each part. The *Didone* list implies fourteen violins (8/6; four Violin I and three Violin II parts copied), two violas (one part copied), three or four oboes (three parts copied, two for Oboe I and one for Oboe II), two French horns (two parts copied), three or four bassoons (two parts copied, but some doubling seems probable), and an unknown number of 'cellos and basses. Only a lead 'cello part was copied; the other continuo players must have read from the harpsichord score(s).[14] The smaller violin contingent is surprising, unless one considers the possibility of three players sharing a part, which could raise the violin numbers as high as twenty-one (12/9).

The last evidence of the size and constitution of Handel's orchestra is very specific. Pay-lists from his 1754 and 1758 charity performances of *Messiah* at the Foundling Hospital survive in the archives of the Thomas Coram Foundation in London, naming all of the performers for these occasions.[15] (See Plate 12, p. 272.) These lists provide the only incontestable testimony about Handel's orchestra between 1720 and the end of his life. Although the occasions were charity performances, the presence of names of established professional musicians in the lists of players gives us confidence that these groups were essentially the same as his theatre orchestra at the same period.

Wind numbers remain the same in both lists (four oboes, four bassoons, two horns, two trumpets and timpani). The lists suggest that only one player – an organist? – was responsible for realising the continuo line. (See Chapter 18 for further consideration of this matter.) The string numbers are more interesting. The division of the violins is not given, but between 1754 and 1758 the total number of players drops from fourteen to eleven. This later number is comparable to the violin section that Handel first used in London, in the *Rinaldo* orchestra. There were also fewer viola players in 1758, their number dropping from six to three. 'Cello numbers remain stable, but the number of double bass players jumps from only one in 1754 to three in 1758. Thus in 1758 the string texture lightened on top and strengthened at the bottom. It is certainly tempting to ascribe these changes to Handel, but the direction of these performances was effectively in the hands of J. C. Smith the younger, and there is a strong possibility that the changes in the 1758 orchestra reflect his, and not Handel's, tastes.

The composition of Handel's orchestras, from the evidence outlined, is summarised in Table 16.1. Several consistent patterns stand out. The violins are divided fairly equally, which runs counter to the expectation that the firsts, having the more dominant line, would dominate the numbers as well (they did have the better-paid players, however). 'Cellos and basses, by comparison, are quite few in number, being outnumbered four to one by violins in some of these lists. The doubling of the wood-wind instruments was considered normal, at least in England, with extra doubling on the first wind line when the numbers are odd (hence the extra first oboe part for *Didone*). Brass parts, by comparison, were apparently not doubled in the opera orchestra. Instruments for realising the continuo part vary from one harpsichord to two during the 1720s (see below for further discussion of this), and a theorbo joins the opera orchestra at least by the beginning of the Royal Academy in 1720. The return to a single realising instrument for the late *Messiah* performances is somewhat surprising, and may relate to particular circumstances in the 1750s.

Throughout his career Handel worked with instrumentalists of the highest calibre. The lead violinists for Handel's orchestra in Rome were Arcangelo Corelli and Matteo Fornari: they were the best known among many other star players in the group. His London orchestra was pan-European: prominent players from the Italian peninsula included the principal violinists Pietro and Prospero Castrucci, the 'cellists Nicola Haym and Filippo Amadei, and the bassist Giuseppe Saggione; from France the oboist Jean Loeillet and the harpsichordist Charles Dieupart; from German-speaking lands the violinist Johann Christoph Pepusch

Table 16.1 Handel's orchestras

	1707a	1707b	1708	1710	1718	1720	1728	1733	1737	1754/58
Violins[a]	14 (8:6)	2–10	22	12[b] (6:4:2)	4/6	17 (8:5:4)	} 24	} 24+	? 14 (8:6)	14:12
Violas	4	0–4	4	2	0/1	2			2	6/3
'Cellos	} 8[c]	?	6	} 4–7[c]	2/1	4	3	4	?	3/3
Double basses		?	5		1/1	2	2	2	?	1/3
Oboes	4	0–4	4	2	2/2[d]	4	?	2	3–4	4/4
Bassoons	0	0	0	3	?1/2	3	3	4	3–4	4/4
Trumpets	0	0	2	1	0/1	1	?	0	0	2/2
Timpani	0	0	0	0	0	0	0	0	0	1/1
Misc.	0	0	1tbn	0	0/2hn, hp	0	0	0	2hn	2hn/2hn
Continuo:										
harps	1	0	1	1	1/1+	1	2	2	?2	?0/0
theorbo						1	1	1		
organ		1–2								1/1

Notes:
1707a=*Il trionfo del Tempo*
1707b=Latin church music
1708=*La Resurrezione*
1710, 1720, 1733, 1737=London opera
1718=Cannons (*Acis/Esther*)
1754/58=*Messiah* (Foundling Hospital)

a figures thus: (8:6) indicate the break-down into sections = Violin I: II: (III)
b these figures vary somewhat in lists from 1709–11
c 'cello and bass parts are not clearly differentiated in these lists
d one oboe part

Flute/recorder players are not listed separately: these instruments were probably doubled by oboe or bassoon players. The *Esther* figures include instruments that occur in Handel's score, but for which no players can be identified from the Cannons establishment.

and the flautist Carl Friedrich Weideman; and from Holland the oboist (and bassoonist) Jean Kytch. Some of these players (the Castruccis, for instance) came to London after working with Handel elsewhere: Handel drew them to London. Others, drawn to London before encountering Handel personally, found secure careers in orchestras under Handel's direction.

Such information as is summarised in Table 16.1 is valuable, but it tells us only the raw size and constituency of his band, not how it was used. Handel encountered some variety of orchestral practice when he moved from place to place in his career, especially in the vital area of orchestral leadership. Johann Mattheson, as mentioned above, favoured orchestral leadership solely from the harpsichord. As Handel's friend and mentor in Hamburg, this would certainly have carried some weight with the relatively inexperienced Handel. Furthermore, since Handel was also primarily a keyboard player, keyboard leadership had obvious allure for him.

This unified leadership was not found in Rome, however. The concert-master (leading violinist) had a much more important position in Italian opera and oratorio orchestras than in Germany or England.[16] It was common in Italy for the concert-master to lead the orchestra, while the principal keyboard player took care of the singers. The concert-master was given a 'short score' part, containing the music for the continuo part below the violin line(s), to facilitate this dual responsibility for direction.[17] The leader's music was called the 'concertino' part, and this is a standard element in itemised lists of performing parts for Italian orchestras of the time.[18] In the original parts for Handel's Latin church music, the 'concertino' part to each work is a short-score violin part, having no indication that the 'concertino' title refers to any concertino/concerto grosso division of the upper strings.[19] For both *Il trionfo del Tempo* and *La Resurrezione* the leader of the orchestra was Arcangelo Corelli: the 'concertino' part mentioned in the *Trionfo* copyist's list was Corelli's directing part, containing probably the first and second violin lines and the continuo line.

In England Handel once again found that the keyboard player had firm control of the performance. Burney's anecdotes about Handel in rehearsal indicate no Italian-style shared leadership, and there are no listings of Italian-style 'concertino' parts for a concert-master/conductor.[20] Yet Handel allowed his concert-master a role in ensemble discipline, as is evidenced by his pride in Matthew Dubourg's leadership of the orchestra in Dublin: 'as for the Instruments they are really excellent, Mr. Dubourgh being at the head of them'.[21]

More germane to modern performances is the applicability of alternation of concertino and concerto grosso instrumentation as a routine practice in orchestral playing. While there is evidence of this alternation on his continuo lines (discussed below), Handel's scores show no sign that this division was used routinely in the upper strings. Even in the original Latin church music parts, and in the orchestral parts for *Messiah* left to the Foundling Hospital by Handel in his will, the part-books designated 'concertino' and 'concerto grosso' contain identical music. In orchestral parts from his Italian years this titling related to leadership, not concertino/concerto grosso string division; in England it related to part-copying procedures rather than to performance practice. Handel was familiar with the Corellian concerto grosso principle of contrasting concertino string players with the full strings, but he used it outside of purely instrumental movements and genres only on rare occasions, and in all cases the practice is clearly indicated in his score.[22]

He did enter markings for a somewhat different sort of division of the violins and violas into his oratorio scores for the 1749 oratorio season. These 'ripieno' markings appear to apply to a small group of added string players that Handel used for a single season only.[23] In his scores for the 1749 oratorios Handel therefore intended that his full regular string contingent should play throughout, with added power from the 'ripieno' players at various points. The use of 'ripieno' in these scores follows no predictable pattern, and may even be closely linked to the amount of rehearsal time available as the season progressed. This argues that his 'ripieno' directions reflect not a natural, established pattern in the orchestra pit, but rather an experiment in orchestral texture, using less experienced players. Handel's 1749 'ripieno' technique is quite different from that of the Corellian concertino/concerto grosso division, in which a very small group plays throughout, joined by the full ensemble from time to time.[24]

Handel was one of the most innovative orchestrators of all time. He always used unusual instruments when they were available: his scores include music for, or references to, the chalumeau (an ancestor of the clarinet), harp, trombones (surprisingly rare in England), carillon, serpent, piccolo, and recondite instruments like the 'violette marine' found in *Orlando*.[25] Furthermore, he employed standard instruments in colourful combinations. He possessed an amazing sensitivity to colour and balance in his orchestral writing.[26] Many studies of Handel's orchestration have dealt at length with these striking movements.[27] This is understandable, since in those movements where he used new orchestral effects Handel's scores are completely clear about the specifics of the instrumentation, while the vast majority of movements in his compositions use more routine orchestrations, ones that are often less well specified.

The extent to which Handel labelled his scores with details of the orchestration varied widely, with no clear progression or regression in the amount of detail over the course of his career. Two pairs of works composed successively serve to demonstrate this point. Handel's autograph score of *Radamisto* (HWV 12a and HWV 12b, 1720) is full of carefully marked detail (some of which has been lost through damage to the paper), while a clear majority of the concerted movements in his next full opera *Floridante* (HWV 14, 1721) have no instrumental specifications at their outset at all. Later in his career, a similar contrast can be seen between the scarcely marked score of *Messiah* (HWV 56) and the fairly detailed scoring of *Samson* (HWV 57), both of which were composed (at least in their initial forms) during August–October 1741.[28] The reasons behind these fluctuations in the clarity with which Handel marked his scores are largely unknown.

Problems in reading Handel's intentions about instrumentation arise in particular concerning the oboes and the continuo group. His scores usually have no indication of scoring for the continuo, and often he did not specify the instrumentation of the treble-clef accompaniment lines (for him this was hardly a difficulty, since any ambiguities could be cleared up at rehearsals, or by verbal directions to copyists), and the parts from his theatrical performances have not survived.[29] Oboes frequently double the violins on the top of Handel's orchestral texture. In some movements these doublings are indicated clearly throughout, and many of the later opera scores have clear markings. In other movements, however, Handel relied upon indirect indications for scoring, for example by simply writing 'tutti' at the start of the movement to indicate that oboes were to double the violins.[30] Even more common are individual 'violin' and 'tutti' annotations within a movement, indicating the exits and entrances of the doubling oboes. Markings such as these show that Handel's normal practice restricted the doubling oboes in solo vocal movements to the ritornellos:[31] Handel apparently felt that the weight of the oboe sound (perhaps involving three or four players) would otherwise compete with the solo voice. This convention is confirmed in contemporary orchestral part-books produced for Charles Jennens, Handel's friend and librettist in his later years,[32] which, although never used for performances, were produced by Handel's own music copyists. There are, of course, some arias in which Handel used one or more oboes in accompaniments or in contrasted solo obbligato passages, but these are exceptional and such uses of the oboe are almost always clearly marked.

Continuo instrumentation is a much murkier area. For some periods we know, from the orchestra lists discussed above, roughly what instruments Handel had in his continuo group, but the use of them was left almost entirely to convention and to performance practices which may have been flexible, and perhaps only reached precise definition during the preparation of performances. There are few markings in Handel's scores to indicate continuo instrumentation, and those that do exist mostly describe exceptional scorings. In London Handel seems to have used a single harpsichord in the continuo group of his opera orchestra until at least 1720, more probably until the late 1720s. Only a single movement written before 1728 (a duet written for the December 1720 revival of *Radamisto*) specifies two harpsichords, and the two-harpsichord markings in this movement cannot be definitively dated. We have Fougeroux's direct testimony that in 1728 Handel used two harpsichords in his orchestra, and some duet movements that Handel wrote after 1728 contain markings for two harpsichords to alternate, accompanying the two singers in turn. Once established, the use of two harpsichords in the pit possibly continued to the end of Handel's operatic career in 1741.[33]

In the oratorio orchestra more freedom was exercised, especially when oratorios supplemented Handel's opera programmes in the 1730s. In his first two public English theatre oratorios, *Esther* (HWV 50b, 1732), and *Deborah* (HWV 51, 1733), Handel's score calls for two harpsichords and two organs. After these works, the numbers appear to settle down to one harpsichord and one organ, with the exception of two organs in the oratorios written for 1739: the opulent *Saul* (HWV 53) and the polychoral *Israel in Egypt* (HWV 54). The theorbo, apparently a standard instrument in the opera pit after 1720, is not mentioned in Handel's scores after 1739. Although Handel calls for harp in *Esther*, *Alexander's Feast* (HWV 75, 1736), *Saul* and *Alexander Balus* (HWV 65, 1748), and for mandolin in *Alexander Balus*, these instruments were almost certainly confined to their written-out parts, not joining the general continuo group. In short, Handel experimented broadly with the continuo group in his oratorios until he departed the opera world in 1741. Thereafter, he seems normally to have relied on a single harpsichord for the principal continuo realisation: see Chapter 18 for further discussion of this period.

Pay-lists, part-books, copyist's lists and (most importantly) score markings all indicate that the instruments playing the continuo line in the score were divided into a small 'soli' group, and full 'tutti' group. The smaller group performed throughout, joined by the larger group for fuller passages. Unless otherwise indicated, Handel's full bass contingent – including all of the 'cellos, string basses, realising instruments and bassoons – played throughout instrumental movements, vocal ensembles with three or more singers, choruses, and the ritornellos in solo vocal movements. (Bassoons may sometimes not have participated in movements without oboes.) They may also have played during solo vocal passages when upper instrumental parts were also playing: Handel's markings are less clear on this point. The majority of this 'tutti' group rested at other times, leaving the small group to handle the continuo duties.

The small 'soli' group accompanied *semplice* recitatives (those with no upper instrumental parts), and all other solo singing. The precise membership of this 'soli' group is somewhat uncertain: according to scattered markings by Handel, it did not include bassoons, organ, or (normally) string basses.[34] Fougeroux tells us that one 'cello, the two harpsichords and theorbo accompanied recitatives in the 1728 operas (the harpsichords presumably alternated, each accompanying individual characters). This certainly appears the most likely instrumentation, but Handel's markings and documentary evidence allow for the interpretation that more than one 'cello played during the 'soli' passages in concerted movements. In Italy the 'soli' group was seated around the harpsichord (as in Plate 7, p. 187), but the situation suggested by the *Didone* part-book list is that by the late 1730s it may have been normal in London for the 'tutti' group to sit around the keyboards while the 'soli' group had a separate part-book.

The realising instruments were the most flexibly used portion of the continuo group. We have essentially no evidence, for instance, of exactly how Handel used the theorbo in the opera orchestra. Even the assertion that the two harpsichords alternated in recitatives is based more on musical instinct than solid evidence. The difficulty of interpretation arises (again) from Handel's close ties to the performances. He could alter the participation of the instruments by having part-books re-copied or by giving verbal directions in rehearsal. This is tellingly demonstrated in the surviving copies of an original organ part to *Alexander's Feast*, composed by Handel for an unknown player at his own performances, which in some places contradicts markings in his own scores.[35] In other words, while ostensibly composing an organ part, Handel re-thought the organ's role in the piece. The *Alexander's Feast* part shows that the organ might participate 'tasto solo' (playing the bass line only, sometimes in octaves, with no harmonies above) in movements for which the instrument was not named in the score, though the precise reasoning behind the inclusion of the organ in any particular movement is somewhat unclear; very few arias use the organ. In choruses, the organ played throughout, helping in all parts of the texture: using the organ in this way requires familiarity with the score and sympathy with the performers. The unfortunate conclusion must be that Handel's own markings in his scores may not represent his final thoughts on the work as presented in performance. Many practical decisions must have been worked out orally in rehearsal and perhaps even spontaneously in performance. This freedom, enchanting to Handel's contemporaries, sometimes poses maddening conundrums for us.

17 Production style in Handel's operas

Winton Dean

Handel's operas belong to a tradition, based on virtuoso singers (many of them castratos) and the almost exclusive dominance of the da capo aria, that has not only been totally lost but, since it differed radically from later developments in operatic genres, was for long universally condemned as naive, primitive and beyond hope of revival. Although the operas were acknowledged to be full of beautiful music, until very recently anyone who claimed that they qualified Handel as not merely an inventor of marvellous tunes but one of the greatest of dramatic composers would have been dismissed as a crank. To justify such a claim it is necessary to demonstrate the dramatic as well as the musical potency of the operas, and to show that the two components amount to something more than the sum of the parts. Great opera is great theatre, but recognisable as such only if both the musical and the stage performance attain the highest standard.

Although the tradition of performance was lost, it is not beyond recovery. On the musical side recent years have seen much progress, thanks to the movement for reviving early music in a form approximating as closely as possible to the manner of its original performance (the term 'authenticity' begs too many questions). It is the theatrical side that lags behind. From writers of the period and the research of modern scholars, backed up by the evidence of librettos and scores, we know a great deal about the theatres in which Handel's operas were performed and how they operated, about the scenery and costumes, about stage movement and the style of acting and singing.[1] The interpretation of this evidence requires a measure of historical imagination; slavish imitation of eighteenth-century accounts is not the only, or necessarily the best, approach to performance today. But there can be no excuse for ignorance of how the operas were done in Handel's day, or for failing to take this into consideration for revivals in the modern theatre.

Handel's stature as a dramatic composer can only be assessed in terms of the theatre for which he wrote. We used to be told – and sometimes still are – that *opera seria* was little more than a concert in costume. The singers, it was supposed, advanced in turn to address their arias to the audience without regard to anyone else who happened to be on stage. The recitative, devoid of musical content, then altered the situation, preparing

Plate 9 Anonymous drawing, 'Proscenium and Stage of the Queen's Theatre in the Haymarket'

the way for another character's similarly restricted utterance. Since there were very few duets or ensembles, in some operas none at all apart from the usually perfunctory *coro* at the end, there was no opportunity for the characters to strike sparks off one another in the manner of later opera. The implication is that *opera seria* had no backbone or dramatic thrust, especially as the individual arias, nearly all in da capo form, were generally confined to the expression of a single emotion or *Affekt*.

That is a superficial interpretation. It is true that stage actions were stylised and that, except in ritornellos which accompanied entrances and exits at each end of the aria (and perhaps a change of position in the middle), singers did not move about during arias. But they continued to act, and to give visual as well as vocal expression to the often intensely passionate arias they were required to sing. To this end they employed an elaborate system of gestures, which were often built into the music as well, for example in arias beginning with a single word like 'Barbaro!' or 'Impio!' ejaculated before the ritornello (if any), sometimes even without waiting for a recitative cadence. There is no reason to suppose that the singers took no notice of the other characters on stage: they are often directed to address two of them in alternate phrases, or one in the A section and another in the B section. In solo scenes they advanced to the apron and addressed the audience directly. It is also true that their movements and positions on stage were regulated by a hierarchy of rank. Pietro Metastasio, who had a great deal to say about matters of stage etiquette, once had occasion to remind Faustina Bordoni that the central position was determined by the rank of the character, not the reputation of the singer.[2]

Although the constitution of the scores, with their overwhelming dependence on recitative and da capo aria, reflects the primacy of the singers, they were not the only persons on the stage. Some operas made extensive use of dancing. Royal and other exalted persons such as generals were attended, escorted, guarded or arrested by supernumeraries, allotted to each according to his or her rank. A recently discovered printed libretto of *Radamisto*, used as a prompt copy at the opera's original production in April 1720, specifies these non-singing participants in detail. Large numbers were employed in ceremonial scenes, battles and sieges, which included a great deal of action. *Alessandro* begins with the storming of a city by scaling engine and battering ram, which creates a breach in the wall; *Scipione* begins with a victorious army, complete with prisoners of war, marching through a triumphal arch. In *Poro* an army crosses a river by a practicable bridge, which is later broken down at both ends by a troop of pioneers who then plunge into the river. Such episodes were accompanied by instrumental sinfonias, independent of the arias. They were staged realistically and involved a great deal of noise; according to *The Spectator*, battles on the Haymarket stage were audible as far afield as Charing Cross.[3]

Next to the singers, visual spectacle was the principal attraction of the Baroque theatre. This held good all over Europe, but was enhanced in London by the heritage of the semi-operas from Purcell's day, whose elaborate use of machines exercised a palpable influence, acknowledged in the libretto, on the design of Handel's first London opera *Rinaldo*. The London theatres where nearly all Handel's operas were produced, Vanbrugh's in the Haymarket (1705) and Rich's in Covent Garden (1732), were equipped with sophisticated apparatus for executing the transformation scenes, aerial manoeuvres and other sensational effects that were called for, particularly in the 'magic' operas. That Handel attached great importance to the visual impact of his operas can be deduced from the remarkable detail in which he copied (or amended) scenic descriptions and stage directions in his autographs; and pictorial imagery is a prominent feature of his musical style. Many of his operas were given with specifically designed sets, advertised in the press as major features of the production, whereas those of other composers were generally served from stock and contained far fewer special effects.[4]

One of the most important elements of the staging, because it radically affected the music, was the management of the scenery. The theatre's scenic equipment consisted of a series of movable wings set in grooves on either side of the stage, flying borders, ground-rows, and shutters that closed the prospect at different depths, so that new scenes could be set behind them and shallow and deep scenes played alternately. All these features, including the back-scenes, could be withdrawn and replaced simultaneously by a single movement of a set of pulleys, weights and barrels beneath the stage.[5] Such scene changes were executed in full view of the audience, and were regarded as a particular attraction. The front curtain did not fall between scenes or even between acts. It rose either after the overture or while it was still playing (Handel made striking and perhaps novel use of this opportunity in some operas, treating the last movement of the overture as the first of the action, giving the opera a strong initial boost); it fell at the end of the last act after the assembled company had sung the *coro*. What happened in the act intervals, or how long they lasted, is less clear, though dancing between acts was sometimes advertised.

At the back of the Haymarket stage an extra room could be taken in, so that the withdrawal of all shutters yielded an acting area of exceptional depth, considerably greater than that of the auditorium. It was used for spectacular scenes such as the battle in *Poro* or the arrival and departure of ships. In *Rinaldo* mermaids danced in the water, moving up and down presumably in traps, and the hero departed in a practicable boat. In *Deidamia* an entire wind band played on board ship as the leading characters disembarked. A simple but very effective device on rollers could depict the waves of the sea at various degrees of roughness. The theatre also boasted a live fountain, which in addition to performing a dramatic function in operas such as *Amadigi* was advertised as a means of cooling the building in hot weather.

The lighting was more flexible than might be supposed from its reliance on candles and oil lamps. Apart from chandeliers above the stage which ensured that it was never wholly dark (though they may have been raised to the flies for nocturnal scenes), gantries behind the wings on each side carrying eight lamp or candle brackets could be dipped or rotated slowly or rapidly to give varied intensities of light, and the footlight ramp lowered or raised. Coloured transparencies were sometimes used, and sulphur thrown on the candles to create a sudden blaze.

The crucial factor in these scenic operations is that, while making a strong appeal to the eye, they did not interrupt the action or the music. Their function was dynamic, not static; they transported the audience from scene to scene, almost in the manner of a modern film, and offered great scope to a composer able to exploit their potential. One of Handel's most memorable and least understood achievements is the skill with which he integrated scenic and musical conventions to enlarge the dramatic scale. By a flexible use of tonality – switches to unrelated keys at scene changes, the employment of certain keys to take up a point made earlier in the opera, recourse to the minor mode after a series of arias in the major (or the other way round) – by so placing the arias that they simultaneously advanced the plot and developed the characters, facet by facet, and by the variety and ingenuity of his treatment of da capo form, especially in the expansion, contraction or omission of orchestral ritornellos, Handel ensured that the opera, far from falling into detached segments, was in continuous fluid motion. This would have been of little avail without his ability to create an almost limitless range of memorable characters, dependent alike on rich musical invention, a profound insight into the intricacies of human nature, and the ability to express their emotions and sufferings in dramatic terms. The listener's interest is not only held but constantly drawn forward. In Handel's finest operas the unit is not the aria, or even the scene, but the whole act. The organisation is so taut, and the equilibrium between musical, dramatic and scenic components so nicely balanced, that almost any cut weakens the design. As a result the duration appears longer, not shorter, when cuts are made – a point demonstrated conclusively in a few modern productions.

The last performance of a Handel opera in the eighteenth century, *Admeto* at the Haymarket in 1754[6] while the composer was still living, was followed by a hiatus of more than 160 years. Chrysander's publication of the scores in the nineteenth century brought no response whatever from opera companies. The appearance of a single disarranged scene from Handel's first opera *Almira* in a triple bill at Hamburg in 1878, designed to commemorate the bicentenary of the Hamburg Opera (with later repetitions at Hamburg and Leipzig), scarcely constitutes an exception. The leading spirit in the first modern stage revivals was an art-historian, Oskar Hagen, who conducted his arrangement of *Rodelinda* at Göttingen in 1920 and followed it up with *Ottone*, *Giulio Cesare* and *Serse*. The operatic climate of the 1920s might be thought unpropitious to such an enterprise, though Hagen may have been sensitive to the neoclassical reaction, represented by Stravinsky, Hindemith and others, against the overblown post-romanticism of Wagner's successors and the sumptuously scored operas of Strauss and Schreker. He greatly admired Handel's music, but either failed to understand, or lacked confidence in, the dramatic structure of the operas. One sentence in his preface to the vocal scores published a little later reveals his attitude: 'All well-informed persons know that the unedited original form of Handel's operas does not meet the demands of the modern stage.'[7] To that end he drastically rewrote the scores and to some extent the plots as well, cutting much music, redistributing and sometimes rescoring the rest, and introducing pieces from elsewhere. The da capo aria and the high-voice male roles were felt to be major obstacles and were ruthlessly expunged by cuts and transposition. Scarcely an aria remained intact; they were chopped up, reduced to A sections (often abbreviated) or even to ritornellos, sometimes played more than once in order to break up the recitatives. The music of all high male roles was put down an octave. The staging, to judge from the copiously rewritten stage directions and contemporary photographs, seems to have been realistic to the point of expressionism.

No doubt compromise was inevitable at that date, but it had the unfortunate effect of clamping the operas in a new rigid performance tradition which persisted in Germany until very recently. Hagen's versions were immensely successful and were still being performed in the late 1960s. Ten more operas reached the German stage during the 1920s in productions which, though they restored more of Handel's music, consolidated some of the most constricting features of that tradition. In the period following 1945, when revivals of the operas became increasingly frequent, conductors and producers still felt free to play havoc with the scores, shifting arias indiscriminately out of context, sometimes from the first act to the third or vice versa. Heinz Rückert's version of *Radamisto*, performed almost 300 times in Germany after its premiere at Halle in 1955, and Joachim Herz's of *Serse*, produced at Leipzig in 1972 and toured all round Europe for several years, made complete nonsense not only of the design of the operas but of the characterisation (already undermined by octave transpositions), to which no thought seems to have been given. Productions at Halle, the city of Handel's birth and the seat of an annual festival of his music, in the 1970s and early 1980s affected a ponderous realism in the stage action and an almost total lack of sparkle in the music, with rumbling bass heroes, recitatives taken at snail's pace with frequent pauses, the curtain falling between each scene, and the opera losing all sense of direction or forward momentum. Perhaps in reaction against the deadly dullness of the current German tradition (typified on disc by Karl Richter's *Giulio Cesare*, sung complete, with no vocal decoration, by a cast containing a tenor and five basses in a score designed for no tenor and two basses, both in minor roles), the operas fell increasingly victim to the whims of producers loaded with concepts and bristling with ideas for gingering up the action and the audience by a species of shock-therapy. From the mid 1980s, as a result of pressure from Baroque scholars and influenced by British example, the German approach began to change. This coincided with the emergence of two or three first-rate countertenors, a type of voice previously regarded in Germany with suspicion, if not with ridicule. Unfortunately the production style did not evolve alongside the music.

Until the 1950s the staging of a Handel opera was an almost exclusively German phenomenon. Britain and the United States, much slower off the mark, saw only a handful of productions before 1939, confined to three or four performances and sometimes to only one, most of them in Hagen's editions and none in regular opera houses. In both countries the first post-war productions were given by universities and small-scale societies with limited facilities, in short runs of two or three performances. In Britain three such bodies extended their activities over a number of years: the Handel Opera Society in London (1955–1985), Unicorn Opera in Abingdon (1959–75), and the music department of Birmingham University (ten productions between 1959 and 1985). They were essentially amateur bodies, though they employed such professional assistance as they could afford, including singers who later attained great distinction.[8] For financial and practical reasons they concentrated on the music rather than the staging; very little was attempted on the visual side, even in spectacular magic operas like *Alcina* and *Orlando*, though Alan Kitching at Abingdon went some way towards recreating Baroque gesture. Theirs was a fresh start that owed nothing to German example. In spite of their defects, such as excessive or clumsy cuts, these revivals sought to improve the musical performance by introducing vocal decoration in da capos, and in particular (despite occasional backslidings) by getting rid of the incubus of octave transposition, long before this was attempted in Germany. Probably their most important – and lasting – achievement was to widen the audience for Handel's operas.

Although in Germany the operas had been performed in professional theatres, increasingly as repertory pieces, since the 1920s, it was a long time before major opera houses in the English-speaking countries tackled them at all. Some of the earliest ventures were far from happy. The New York City Opera *Giulio Cesare* in 1966 and the Houston Grand Opera *Rinaldo* in 1975 ruined the dramatic design by shamelessly rehashing the scores. In New York Cleopatra sang her tragic Act III aria 'Piangerò la sorte mia', a heart-broken lament over Caesar's reported death, at her first meeting with Caesar (played by a heavy baritone) in Act I, where she is putting on an act to engage his sympathy. In Houston Armida sang the A section of one of *Rinaldo*'s greatest arias in one scene and the B section in another. British productions have not always been free from topsy-turveydom (Scottish Opera's *Giulio Cesare* in 1992, among other absurdities, ended with part of the overture), but on the whole have been more faithful to the scores. The 'early music' movement, besides its influence on singing and vocal ornamentation, had by this time demonstrated the enormous gain in expressiveness obtainable from period instruments and Baroque performance practice, to the extent of persuading modern orchestras to modify their style accordingly. But there was no corresponding endeavour to apply this approach to the stage production. The major theatres made the same assumptions about the staging that had been made earlier (and disproved) about the music: that it would only be tolerable to a modern audience if subjected to drastic updating. They handed over the operas to producers who were not only ignorant of Baroque theatre practice but in some cases had worked only in the spoken theatre and had no experience of opera at all.

The dominant stage director is a modern phenomenon. In Handel's day regulation of the stage was the province of the librettist (in London, the theatre 'poet' who adapted the original libretto), though he may have had difficulty in controlling the singers. It would be interesting to know if Handel had any say in the matter. (Metastasio was so confident of his position in Vienna that he tried to keep composers as well as singers under his thumb.) In the nineteenth century the job passed to the composer, if he was still living; Wagner and Verdi in particular exercised a rigorous control over what happened on stage in their operas. After their time, when the repertory consisted more and more of works by composers no longer alive, the singers took the lead in stage movement, the production side being treated as of relatively minor importance. In any case the rapid dispersal of star singers from one theatre to another ensured that little time was available for stage rehearsal. Even in living memory it was common practice for some houses to mount operas without naming a producer other than a lowly stage manager. The consequent slackening of the dramatic component inspired a reaction, especially after the last war, in the work of Felsenstein and others in Germany. The independent producer who brought all the manifold centrifugal strands of an opera under single control, instead of allowing it to degenerate into a concert of nightingales, was a healthy development, provided the vision of its creators was respected, or at least not counteracted.

In Handel's operas, unless he (or she) has taken the time and trouble to study them in depth, the producer is confronted by what appears to be a *tabula rasa*, a genre with no long-standing tradition, and one in which the audience is unlikely to possess the knowledge to question anything he does. He may of course seek to discover and interpret what the composer was trying to convey. But in the late twentieth century self-indulgence and the urge to shock appear to have been endemic in opera producers, by no means only of Handel. A lunatic *Rigoletto* or *Carmen* does no lasting damage because the operas are familiar and will bounce back. That is not yet true of Handel or *opera seria*. The impact of the more self-willed producers, especially in Germany but also in Britain, the United States and elsewhere, has unquestionably obstructed the full appreciation of Handel's dramatic art. It is true that some of the more outrageous productions, encouraged perhaps by theatre managements hopeful that a nice little scandal will increase box-office returns, have been received with enthusiasm; but it is not difficult, and not very creditable, to excite a gullible public with no genuine *opera seria* experience and stir up controversy in the press by throwing the equivalent of a stink-bomb at a comparatively easy target. Whether the producers' antics have stemmed from ignorance, cynicism or the lust to exploit a hyperactive ego – all three motives have been in evidence – the result has been the same. The work of art is defaced by *graffiti*. The servant is exalted above the master. The client is sold damaged goods.

Of course there are many degrees. The productions of *Xerxes* (*Serse*) and *Ariodante* by the English National Opera in 1985 and 1993 were well received by the public and most of the critics, and the standard of musical performance was for the most part excellent; but for anyone familiar with the scores they put themselves out of court by altering the plots to accommodate conceptions that not only did not fit the operas but actively undermined them. Whatever we may think of these plots, they are what Handel confronted and enriched with his music, and both works are major masterpieces. The *Xerxes* production was permeated by a large chorus of sight-seers who wandered round the stage looking at exhibits in a museum and constantly broke into the action, not least when a character was expressing heart-felt emotion in an aria. The idea, presumably a dig at the opera as a museum piece, inevitably undercut a work whose masterly interplay of the comic and serious is rivalled perhaps only by Mozart's *Così fan tutte*. *Ariodante* has a straightforward story of love, jealousy and deception suited to any operatic convention, and is one of the few Handel operas in which the happy end, statutory in *opera seria*, is the natural outcome of the action. This was too simple for the producer, who decided to introduce a Freudian element. In the heroine's dream ballet he showed her being sexually abused by her father, and he devalued the happy end by stage actions designed to suggest the opposite. This was a cheap and pretentious attempt to cash in on fashionable preoccupations, for which there is no warrant whatever; the tender love between father and daughter is one of the most attractive features of the score and is clear in the libretto.

It would be easy to cite more extreme examples. *Giulio Cesare*, which presents a historical love story with a subtlety of characterisation worthy of Shakespeare, has been a particular target for gimmickry. A German production in 1972 portrayed Caesar as a mad bisexual dictator regularly acclaimed with Nazi salutes (pictures of Hitler and Mussolini in the programme) and treated the music as a necessary nuisance, cutting it by two-thirds.[9] The entire action was played on top of an outsize grand piano. In the version produced by Peter Sellars at Purchase, New York, Caesar became a silly-ass President of the United States, rushing around giving orders to very little purpose, and Cleopatra a gold-digging tart triumphantly brandishing dollar bills. This production was also a *locus classicus* for the scarcely less heinous sin of mounting irrelevant distractions during the arias. Caesar discharged a shower of missiles followed by a carafe of water at Ptolemy while singing the aria 'Va tacito e nascosto', whose text is concerned with a stealthy hunter stalking his prey. Since the producer is on record as discovering comic tendencies in at least a third of the arias,[10] it is perhaps not surprising that he seemed unable to resist the urge to send up much of the opera. A Paris production in 1987 turned *Giulio Cesare* into a Disneyland romp, with Cleopatra constantly opening bottles of champagne and Sextus chased up a pole by crocodiles. The Scottish Opera production (1992), with a German producer, likewise trivialised the characters, with Caesar a coarse buffoon, Cleopatra fondling everyone in sight, and Ptolemy a bisexual and incestuous transvestite. In 1994 Munich presented the opera beneath the shadow of a model Tyrannosaurus Rex, as if to brand the work itself as an operatic dinosaur. *Tamerlano* has undergone comparable maltreatment in productions at Cardiff, Halle and Karlsruhe, which (like two modern recordings) also mutilated the score. It may or may not be significant that the greatest operas have suffered the most. What these productions have in common is a desolating vulgarity and a contempt for the opera as a work of art.

Since 1920 the revival of Handel's operas has passed through several overlapping stages. The attitudes of management and performers, and to some extent of audiences, have fluctuated widely and continue to do so. The position today is paradoxical in at least two respects. Standards of musical performance in the commercial houses are high almost everywhere. We are no longer asked to tolerate outsize orchestras overflowing with Romantic vibrato or a barrage of vocal basses and baritones, with da capos either omitted or rendered tedious by literal repetition. There are still occasional solecisms such as the use of the organ, which has no business at all in a Handel opera,[11] and da capo ornamentation in the style of Rossini or Donizetti. The standard of singing, once considered an insuperable barrier to the revival of *opera seria*, has varied from the acceptable to the superlative. Several of the productions criticised above, including the Purchase *Giulio Cesare* and the English National Opera *Xerxes* and *Ariodante*, have given the operas without cuts. But the dislocation between musical and dramatic values persists unremedied. All too often the underlying consideration where the production is concerned seems to have been: how can we make this stuff palatable to the audience without boring them? The criterion becomes not what Handel is trying to say but what the public can be induced to swallow. This is a disappointingly modest advance on Hagen's apologetic attitude, and it shows little confidence in the perceptiveness of today's audiences.

The second paradox is that an increasing number of small-scale university and student productions, at any rate in Britain, have offered a clearer view of Handel's operatic achievement than those of most commercial houses. Technically less proficient, though often well sung, and generally rudimentary in their staging, these productions have not defaced the operas by interposing an alien conception between composer and audience. They have taken Handel seriously. The Birmingham *Giulio Cesare* in 1977, its first complete stage performance since the original run in 1724, demonstrated that even Handel's longest operas can grip a modern audience from beginning to end as coherent musical dramas without recourse to extraneous titivation. There have been other examples since.

The crucial question – are the operas viable in the modern professional theatre in their own terms? – has too often been allowed to go by default. Few major opera houses seem to have put it to the test. When this has been seriously attempted, the response of audiences has left no doubt of its effectiveness. The performances conducted by Nicholas McGegan, and sometimes directed by him, at Boston (1985) and Göttingen (1991 onwards), while open to criticism in some respects, have conveyed an overwhelming impression of the power of Handel's dramaturgy. Seated at the harpsichord in the middle of the orchestra, very close to the stage, he has been able to co-ordinate music and action in a manner that justified *opera seria* as practised by Handel (though perhaps by him alone) as an artistic solution fully as valid as that of opera in any other period. While wholly professional, employing first-rate period orchestras and distinguished singers, these productions – and there may have been others of comparable quality – have had limited runs of from three to five nights. The Göttingen performances were subsequently recorded – not, alas, on video – with the same casts, but none of them was taken up by a commercial opera house. To that extent their influence has been limited. Several other stylish opera recordings under various conductors have also confirmed that at least Handel's music is in good hands.

It has been claimed on behalf of the intrusive producer that he is adapting the operas to the tastes of a public that might otherwise find them tedious or incomprehensible.[12] The argument runs more or less as follows:

> We cannot replicate the performances of Handel's day. Apart from such impediments as the absence of castratos, we have different theatres and different audiences. A modern audience with its knowledge of all that has happened since the early eighteenth century in the realms of art, politics, society and psychology cannot be expected to leave its preferences and prejudices at home. It will receive the operas with them always at the back of its mind.

That is true enough as far as it goes. But it does not follow that a modern audience will find the operas obscure or simplistic, nor does it justify an attempt to stimulate those extra-mural associations by going outside the text. That would be to ignore the timeless quality of great art, which necessarily speaks in terms of its own period but also transcends them, dispensing universal truths to receptive listeners of any age. We might as well rewrite Shakespeare in the language of Hollywood. If the opera carries a coded moral or message, it will come across with far greater potency from within the dramatic framework, which is its source and support, than if the audience is nudged by more or less explicit references to Hitler, Freud, *apartheid* or the Vietnam War.

There may well be more than one way of producing Handel's operas. Anachronism is not necessarily an obstacle, though it is seldom an advantage. There was after all no attempt in Handel's day to recreate the environment of Ancient Rome, Persia, Armenia or wherever the action was supposed to take place. But if the letter permits a certain flexibility, it is essential to preserve the spirit. No producer will succeed in his job without studying in depth the musical and theatrical conventions of the period and recognising the way that Handel moulded them to his purpose. (The same applies to the set-designer and the dramaturge, or whoever is in charge of the enterprise.) This involves a measure of humility; he is the servant, not the master. He must accept the plots, not rewrite them, and refrain from scoring points at the expense of the opera or the convention. He must suppress the urge to introduce foreign matter incompatible with the text. What happens on stage must not only not conflict with what happens in the score; it should actively support and reinforce it.

And of course we should expect the producer to listen to the music; it is surprising how often he seems to ignore it. The first lesson to be taken to heart is that the substance of a Handel opera – the development of the drama, the exposition and interaction of the characters – is carried by the arias. This is obvious, but the consequence is not. It is the duty of the producer not to block the lines of communication with the audience by devising unnecessary business, introducing persons who have no right to be present, or playing ducks and drakes with the stage machinery while an aria is being sung. Anything that distracts attention from the singer and the emotions he or she is expressing weakens the impact of the aria.

At the same time he should retain his grasp of the opera as a closely wrought organism in continuous motion, despite the fissiparous tendencies created by the recitative–aria design. The opera should not be allowed to sag or come to a full stop after an aria; the next movement needs to be attacked as soon as possible. There is generally too much ritardando on the small and large scale. If the audience insists on breaking in with applause for the singer, well and good: to linger in the hope or expectation of applause is to break the thread. Handel helped here by generally placing the most vocally spectacular arias at the end of scenes, where the interruption is more tolerable.

In Handel's mind, it is safe to say, as in that of all great dramatic composers, music and drama were an indissoluble unity. The operas draw their strength from the skill with which he exploited the tension between a group of narrow conventions, whose very limitations are turned to advantage. That tension must somehow be recreated in the modern theatre. It can be done if the producer, honouring his obligations to the composer as well as to the audience (there is no necessary conflict between the two), submits himself without reserve to the work of art before him – not a naive but a highly sophisticated art, dependent on a perfect if precarious balance between all its parts. Only then can Handel's stature as one of the four or five supreme masters of opera be realised in the theatre.

18 Handel's oratorio performances

Donald Burrows

Handel's first oratorios *Il trionfo del Tempo* and *La Resurrezione* were produced at Rome in 1707 and 1708, respectively, under circumstances of private patronage, and the domestic records of his patrons Cardinal Pamphili and Marquis Ruspoli provide some clues about practical details of the performances. Pamphili's accounts include a payment for copying the performing material for *Il trionfo* – four part-books for the vocal soloists, and parts for a substantial chamber orchestra of strings and oboes.[1] The copying account, dated 14 May 1707, gives us our only documentary evidence for the period of the oratorio's composition, but it tells us neither the exact date nor the place of the performance, which had presumably taken place in Pamphili's Roman palace at some time during the preceding couple of months. For *La Resurrezione*, Ruspoli's accounts provide rather fuller information, including a complete list of the orchestral performers employed (which does not exactly match the resources required in Handel's score).[2] There were two performances, and the larger scale of the enterprise is indicated by the fact that 1500 copies of the libretto were printed: although the performance may have been a private one in Ruspoli's Bonelli Palace, it was hardly a chamber-scale event.

Two aspects of these Roman oratorio performances are not in doubt. First, there was no 'chorus' of singers. *Il trionfo* involved just four soloists: the score consists mostly of arias, with a couple of duets and an aria at the end of the first part in which all four characters participate, though not at the same time. The five soloists in *La Resurrezione* sing together in *coro* movements at the end of each part, but no additional singers were involved. While we do not know which singer took the role of Bellezza ('Beauty') in *Il trionfo,* Ruspoli's records show that the soprano Margherita Durastanti took the role of Mary Magdalene in the first performance of *La Resurrezione.* Ruspoli received a papal rebuke for allowing a woman to take part in the performance of a work on a sacred subject, and she was duly replaced by a castrato for the second performance: the role of Mary Cleophas was already taken by a castrato.

The second certainty about these two Roman oratorios is that they were not given fully staged presentations. Since the plot of *Il trionfo* mainly involves persuasive argument and influence rather than physical action, this was satisfactory enough. The content of *La Resurrezione* is more theatrical, and it was played in an elaborate concert setting involving a painted back-drop depicting scenes from the story: no expense seems to have been spared in an attempt to make a pleasing and striking visual setting in the great hall of Ruspoli's palace, and the carpenters even produced special music stands with desks and legs in the shape of fluted cornucopiae.

In their style of presentation, their musical construction and their scale, *Il trionfo del Tempo* and *La Resurrezione* might be regarded as typical products of Italian vernacular oratorio as practised at Rome in 1707–8. So it is perhaps rather surprising that Handel's first English oratorio, produced some ten years later, may have had much in common with these Italian oratorios. Although not a shred of contemporary documentary evidence has yet appeared to confirm the facts, it seems likely that Handel composed *Esther*[3] for the musicians employed by James Brydges, Earl of Carnarvon and subsequently Duke of Chandos, and that it was first performed at Brydges's mansion at Cannons in 1718.[4] While the Roman oratorios were two-part works, *Esther* is cast in six scenes with no obvious dividing-point, and may have been played as a continuous work without an interval. As with its Italian oratorio predecessors, the scoring of *Esther* seems to have been geared to the resources currently available from the patron. In 1718–20 Brydges was at the height of his fortune, was seriously engaged in completing and refurbishing his Cannons property and had built up a large domestic staff, including musicians. In his 'Concert' he is not known to have regularly employed more than about a dozen string players at any one time, so the orchestral forces for *Esther* may have been smaller than those for the Roman oratorios: however, extra players could have been engaged, and Handel's score required horns and harp as well as the normal basic orchestra of strings, oboes and bassoons.

The major roles of Esther, Ahasuerus and Haman were written for soprano, tenor and bass soloists respectively,[5] and the substantial chorus movements which are a feature of the score are laid out for five voices: soprano, alto, two tenors and a bass. A soprano was presumably brought in to play the part of Esther, but the male singers (alto, tenor and bass) could have been found from Brydges's own establishment. It would have been possible for the complete oratorio to have been covered by just five solo singers, taking the major solos in the arias, doubling up on roles as required[6] and joining together in the chorus movements. Something of the sort had almost certainly happened with *Acis and Galatea*, probably performed by just five singers at Cannons shortly before. But Brydges currently had quite a number of male singers (including boy trebles) on his establishment, and the music may have been spread around more than five singers. Perhaps some doubling of voices took place in the chorus lines, though this could easily have led to musical balance problems if the inner voices were not equally supported.

The flexibility with which singers could have doubled various solo roles in performance depended, of course, on whether *Esther* was given as a realistic stage presentation, and on this we have no information. It seems quite possible that, like the Roman oratorios, *Esther* was presented in a concert performance, though perhaps enlivened by a scenic setting and by occasional attempts towards a conversational style between the characters. The revivals of *Esther* for which Bernard Gates was responsible in 1732, using a cast from his Chapel Royal choristers, were certainly staged, but they took place in private venues and without Handel's direct involvement. According to Burney's account, written more than half a century later:[7]

> Mr. Handel himself was present at one of these representations, and having mentioned it to the Princess Royal, his illustrious scholar, her Royal Highness was pleased to express a desire to see it exhibited in action at the Opera-house in the Hay-market, by the same young performers; but Dr. Gibson then bishop of London, would not grant permission for its being represented on that stage, even with books in the children's hands. Mr. HANDEL, however, the next year, had it performed at that theatre, with additions to the Drama, by Humphreys; but in *still life*: that is, without action, in the same manner as Oratorios have been since constantly performed.

Whether Handel ever seriously considered transferring Gates's production as it stood to the public theatre is perhaps doubtful, but we need not doubt that he pondered the idea of putting on a staged version of *Esther* at the end of his opera season at the King's Theatre, probably using some of his regular opera cast along with the Chapel Royal tyros, and that the Bishop's intervention slanted this project towards the 'still life' manner in which the project was finally realised, thus setting the style for Handel's subsequent oratorio career in London.

Because Handel's Roman oratorios and his first version of *Esther* were undertaken in the context of private patronage, it is perhaps not surprising that we have only limited information about his performances, garnered from accidental information about the circumstances of performance rather than from descriptions of the events themselves. From 1732 onwards the performance of English oratorio in the London theatres became part of Handel's professional public activity, and from 1743 onwards it was the central element of his professional career; but it so happens that information about the way that Handel presented his theatre oratorios is hardly more plentiful than for the earlier works. The remainder of this chapter will be devoted to what is known about his London performances.

Between 2 May 1732, when he introduced *Esther* into his theatre programme at the Haymarket, and 6 April 1759, when he attended (and perhaps in some sense directed) his last performance of *Messiah* at Covent Garden, Handel presented more than 250 performances of English oratorios, odes, serenatas and similar works in regular seasons at the London theatres. In addition, between 1750 and his death he gave 11 performances of *Messiah* at the Foundling Hospital. While the musical scores for these works survive virtually intact, in Handel's autographs and his performance scores, and the dates and venues of the performances are well established, yet many questions remain about the circumstances of their performance. Some gaps in our knowledge are perhaps attributable to the fact that Handel established something of a regular performing tradition in these works, so that the practical arrangements from one year were simply followed again in the next season. Nevertheless it is perhaps surprising, in view of the important position that Handel's musical performances occupied in London, that no one tried to leave a pictorial record of one of his oratorio performances, that descriptions of the theatre performances are sparse and that our limited evidence is often of the most accidental kind.

Handel's career in London theatre oratorio may be conveniently considered in terms of three periods, more or less coinciding with numerical decades. In the 1730s the English-language works were not central to Handel's planning, but were brought in to diversify his Italian opera seasons. Since Handel was fundamentally engaged with Italian opera companies, his casts had a strong Italian bias, and there were many dual-language performances. It is only in 1738–9, with *Saul* and *Israel in Egypt*, that a significant change of balance occurs, but even this is not a simple fulcrum: in 1740–1 Handel returned to the Italian/English mix, giving his last Italian operas in London. A decisive change comes at the period of Handel's visit to Dublin in 1741–2: after he returned to London, he gave no more opera performances and no more music in Italian, save for some inserted arias in a revival of *Semele*. The shift towards English singers in his casts was significant but not absolute in the following years: against the English soloists Beard, Lowe and Mrs Cibber we must set the Italians Frasi, Galli and Guadagni. There were ebbs and flows in the success of Handel's oratorio performances in the 1740s, but by the turn of the decade we can talk of an oratorio 'tradition' in London as a result of his regular annual seasons, sufficiently established for both audiences and performers that it continued under its own weight throughout the period of Handel's blindness in his last years and, indeed, for more than a decade after his death.

Such descriptive material as we have about the theatre circumstances of Handel's performances comes from the first decade, when (as we must assume) new physical arrangements had to be made in the performing area of the theatres to accommodate non-acted oratorio performances. From the first *Esther* performances at the King's Theatre, Haymarket, in 1732 we have a contemporary note:[8]

> all ye Opera Singers in a sort [of] Gallery

and the famous satirical description in a contemporary pamphlet:[9]

> so away goes I to the *Oratorio*, where I saw indeed the finest Assembly of People I ever beheld in my life, but, to my great Surprize, found this Sacred *Drama* a mere Consort, no Scenary, Dress or Action, so necessary to a *Drama*; but H[ande]l, was plac'd in a Pulpit, (I suppose they call that their Oratory), by him sate *Senesino, Strada, Bertolli* and *Turner Robinson*, in their own Habits; before him stood sundry sweet Singers of this our *Israel*, and *Strada* gave us a *Hallelujah* of half an Hour long; *Senesino* and *Bertolli* made rare work with the *English* Tongue you would have sworn it had been *Welch*.

The 'gallery' or 'pulpit' was presumably at the centre front of the stage area, but where this stood in relation to the orchestra is not certain: possibly the orchestra remained in the pit, in front of the singers.

Here it is appropriate to pause and take account of the limited iconographical evidence that may be of some relevance. There are no contemporary pictures of Handel's oratorio performances, and for the earliest relevant material we have to move on sixty years from the first theatre presentation of *Esther*, and more than thirty years after Handel's death. There are two pictures of oratorio performances in Covent Garden Theatre which, thanks to the perpetual neurosis of theatre managements about changing the internal arrangements of the auditorium, can be dated fairly precisely.[10] The first shows Covent Garden Theatre after the reconstruction of the proscenium area by Henry Holland in 1792 (Plate 10), and the second shows it after the alterations by Creswell and Philips in 1803 (Plate 11). The proscenium height in the earlier picture is closer to that which Handel would have known. Both pictures seem to depict the same basic performing set-up. The singers are nearest the audience, with soloists at the very front. The performers appear to be directed by the central organist, who has the leading violinists and bass players within easy reach: the other players are ranged around the sides and on staging, probably in three tiers in Plate 10. In the earlier picture, lighting for stage

Plate 10   An oratorio performance at Covent Garden theatre in the 1790s. Drawing by
Benedictus Antonio Van Assen

and auditorium areas appears to be evenly distributed: the second picture
suggests that the stalls area was basically in shadow.

Whether these pictures reflect anything of Handel's own practice must
remain an open question: the arrangement certainly bears striking
resemblances to the Handel Commemoration of 1784 at Westminster
Abbey. The forward placing of the singers in relation to the orchestra is
practical, making for good communication between soloists and audience. It would be too hasty, however, to identify that front-of-stage space
(apparently overlooking a covered-in orchestra pit) with the 'gallery'
referred to in 1732. If Handel's set-up even remotely resembled the ones
depicted in the later pictures, then it was hardly practical for soloists to
adopt conversational stances towards each other in recitatives, let alone
for Belshazzar's knees to knock visibly when he saw the writing on the
wall. It must be doubted whether these pictures reflect any authentic
Handelian tradition. There are several practical snags. The dominating
organ in the centre surely reflects a post-Handelian performing tradition
in which the organ was regarded as the leading continuo instrument. As
will be noted later, the organ had a specific role in Handel's oratorio practice, but the main continuo instrument for Handel was almost certainly
the harpsichord. More to the point, it would have been difficult for

Plate 11   An oratorio performance at Covent Garden Theatre, as it appeared 1803–8. From Rudolph Ackermann, *The Microcosm of London* (1808–10), after A. C. Pugin and T. Rowlandson

Handel from a position at the organ (as shown in the pictures) to have exercised the control of the performance that one feels must have been a temperamental necessity for him. The soloists would have been too far away, and behind him.

There is, however, one piece of evidence that Handel did at one period direct his London oratorio performances from the organ, in a letter from Charles Jennens written in 1738:[11]

> [Handel's] second Maggot is an Organ of 400 £ price, which (because he is overstock'd with Money), he has bespoke of one Moss [Morse] of Barnet: this Organ, he says, is so contriv'd that as he sits at it, he has a better command of the Performers than he us'd to have: & he is highly delighted to think with what exactness his Oratorio will be perform'd by the help of this Organ; so that for the future, instead of beating time at his Oratorio's he is to sit at the Organ all the time with his back to the Audience.

The conclusion that Handel conducted his performances from the organ runs counter to the evidence from musical sources about the relative functions of the organ and harpsichord, but in 1738 Handel was still experimenting with performing layouts and the practical problems of directing theatre oratorio: it is also probably no coincidence that the new scores performed in the following season of 1739 (*Saul* and *Israel in Egypt*, at the King's Theatre) have unusually specific markings for the use of organ(s). Possibly a claviorganum was involved: if Morse's instrument was no more satisfactory than the one that he later built for the Foundling Hospital chapel, my guess is that his novel contraption gave trouble after a few performances and had probably collapsed entirely after a couple of seasons. The main feature of the instrument seems to have been the 'contrivance' which allowed Handel to sit at the front of the performers.

There is also a retrospective reference to Handel directing London oratorio performances from the organ, in the journal of the provincial musician John Marsh recording his attendance at a performance of a Handel oratorio at Drury Lane theatre in February 1774. This was the last season that John Christopher Smith junior was involved with presenting oratorios in London, though the musical direction was in the hands of John Stanley:[12]

> I adjourned in the evening to the oratorio of Sampson at Drury Lane, then conducted by Stanley, whose back as he sat at the organ was present as conspicuously to the audience as his predecessor Mr. Handel's used to be upon the same occasion, the space in front being not then filled as at present by a numerous group of chorus singers besides the principals.

Marsh was born in 1752 and cannot have attended Handel's own oratorio performances, so it seems very likely that he was mediating a comment made by an older member of the audience in 1774.[13] The statement that Handel did not place the singers behind his back is interesting, and I am disposed to take it seriously. Marsh is not clear as to whether he is referring to all of the singers in this connection. His statement might be read as suggesting that Handel's principal singers sat (or stood) apart from the chorus singers, though the evidence to be considered in a moment from the Foundling Hospital *Messiah* part-books indicates that Handel probably regarded his soloists as part of his 'chorus' resource, in which case there would have been good practical reasons for all the singers remaining together: in any case, some of the leading 'chorus' singers occasionally had brief roles as minor principals. It would be unwise to accept Marsh's journal entry uncritically as evidence that Handel conducted (and accompanied) his oratorios from the organ, but it may lend circumstantial support to the possibility that, perhaps from 1735 onwards, the organ usually formed the visual centrepiece of his arrangement of the forces for oratorio performances. Marsh's source of information may have been someone who attended oratorio performances during the composer's last years: in the years of his blindness from 1754 onwards Handel may have sat at the organ throughout while practical direction was in the hands of Smith junior at the harpsichord. There could have been a significant change of practice in the direction of the performance in the twenty years preceding 1774.

To return to the contemporary documentary record, a few snippets hint at various experiments with performing arrangements in the 1730s. For the performances of Handel's second theatre oratorio, *Deborah*, in 1733 there appears to have been some attempt to increase general auditorium lighting at the King's Theatre, and the newspaper announcement about this suggests that the audience 'house lights' were normally kept in place throughout.[14] When Handel moved to Covent Garden theatre, there are strong hints of teething troubles over performing arrangements. In 1736 *Alexander's Feast*[15]

> met with general Applause, tho' attended with the Inconvenience of having the Performers placed at too great a distance from the Audience, which we hear will be rectified the next Time of Performance.

And indeed, it was announced quickly that[16]

> For the better Reception of the Ladies, the Pit will be floor'd over, and laid into the Boxes; and the Orchestra plac'd in a Manner more commodious to the Audience.

Clearly Handel faced practical problems when he began to give concert performances in buildings that were fundamentally designed for staged dramatic productions. No doubt he solved the difficulties to everyone's satisfaction, for there are no further complaints of this sort from the 1740s and 1750s – but we do not know what his solutions were, or if he made changes to his performing layout from time to time. It is difficult to believe that he did not arrange some spatial separation between groups of singers in performances of those oratorios featuring double choruses (*Saul, Israel in Egypt* and *Solomon*). Perhaps 'double-choir' seating is even implied by the original theatre advertisements for *Esther* in 1732 – 'The musick to be disposed after the manner of the Coronation Service':[17] the choral establishments of the Church of England, from which Handel drew many of his oratorio chorus singers, normally sang their church services from choir stalls that were arranged in two facing 'sides'. On one occasion at least, Handel's benefit *Oratorio* on 28 March 1738, Handel even placed part of the audience on the stage at the Haymarket with his performers: the advertisement refers to 'Benches upon the Stage'.[18]

In consequence of the non-acted presentation of Handel's oratorios, there were no production rehearsals, and there was no need for the singers to perform the music from memory. Indeed, it seems very likely that Handel's oratorio performances took place after relatively few general rehearsals, and that their technical success relied heavily on the professional competence of the orchestral and choral performers, who were probably alert music-readers and were re-employed on a sufficiently regular basis to form a cohesive performing group. It may well have been the case that only the principal vocalists received extended rehearsal preparation, probably serviced by the attendance of basso continuo players.

For information about the size and composition of Handel's performing group for the oratorios we are driven first to the only surviving lists of performers, from the Foundling Hospital *Messiah* performances of 1754 and 1758.[19] It is no accident that the earliest surviving performers' list dates from 1754, the first year in which some control of the arrangements had to be devolved to other hands on account of Handel's blindness (Plate 12). The list names thirty-eight orchestral musicians and eighteen adult singers, plus an entry for 'Boys' that probably covers four trebles. Most of the other payments recorded in the list were to servants (who earned as much as the performers), though a small amount went to those essential musical functionaries, the organ blowers. From the list we have an accurate picture not only of the overall size of the performing force but also of the relative numerical balance between voices and instruments. The aural balance between the two groups was obviously affected by the nature of the orchestral instruments, the way that they were played, and the types of tone production favoured by the singers: and thanks to the present experimentation with 'authentic' instruments and styles of performance, this aural balance is to some extent recoverable in modern performances.

The question naturally arises as to whether the 1754 list can be taken as typical for Handel's previous performances. As the first list from the period of Handel's blindness, it seems reasonable to suppose that it repeats in general terms the managerial arrangements that had evolved in the immediately preceding years – that is, from the first Foundling Hospital *Messiah* performance of 1750 onwards. Obviously there would have been minor variations from year to year (and probably from performance to performance within years) according to the availability of performers. If the Foundling Hospital performances of the 1750s were fundamentally revivals of the last performances of Handel's theatre seasons, then the lists should also provide a general guide to his theatre oratorio forces in these years: furthermore, the lists may have relevance to Handel's practice in earlier years, if a regular annual pattern was followed. The following brief review of matters relating to Handel's singers, orchestra and continuo practice takes the 1754 Foundling Hospital list as its starting-point.

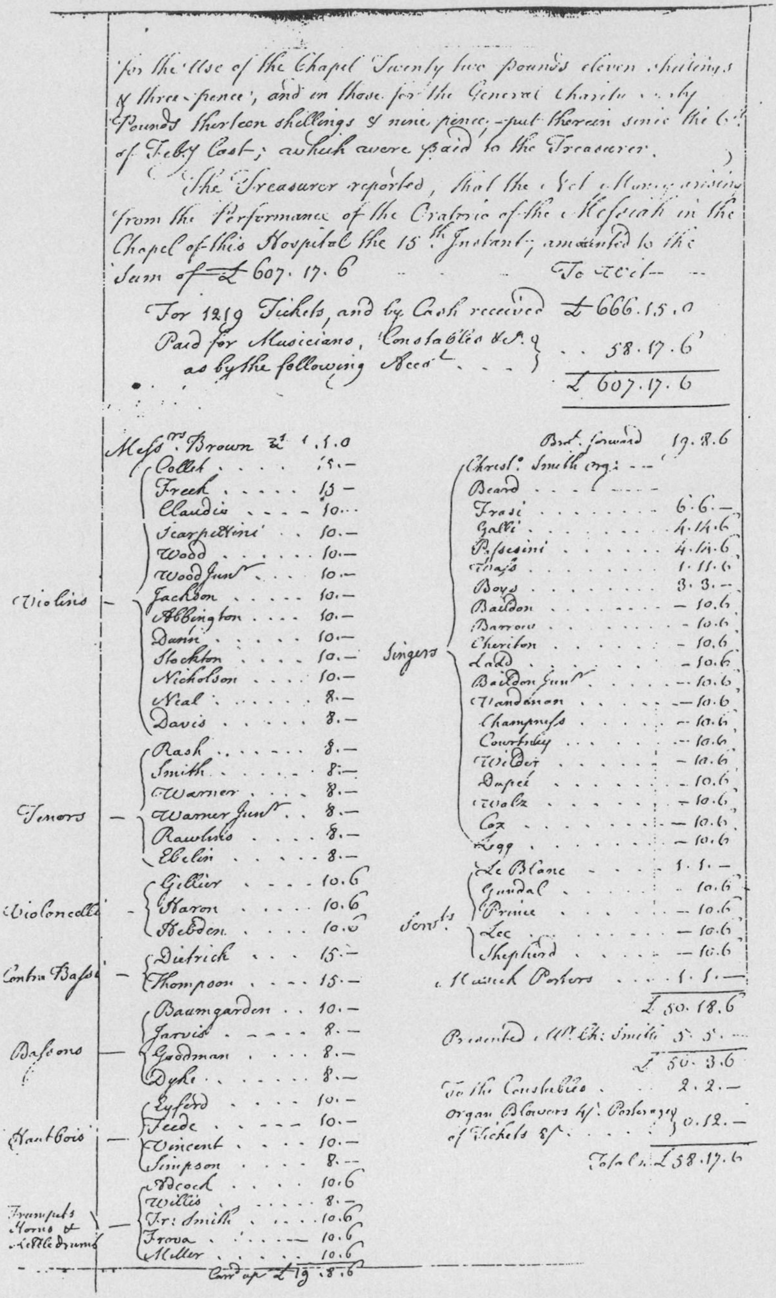
for the Use of the Chapel Twenty two pounds eleven shillings & three-pence; and in those for the General Charity ... by Pounds thirteen shillings & nine pence, -put therein since the 6th of Feby last; which were paid to the Treasurer.

The Treasurer reported, that the Net Money arising from the Performance of the Oratorio of the Messiah in the Chapel of this Hospital the 15th Instant, amounted to the Sum of £607. 17. 6 - - - To wit - -

For 1219 Tickets, and by Cash received	£666.15.0
Paid for Musicians, Constables &c. as by the following Accot.	58.17.6
	£607.17.6

	Messrs. Brown	1.1.0			Brot. forward	19.8.6
Violins	Collet	15.–		Singers	Christr. Smith Esq:	– –
	Freeke	15.–			Beard	– –
	Claudio	10.–			Frasi	6.6.–
	Scarpettini	10.–			Galli	4.14.6
	Wood	10.–			Passerini	4.14.6
	Wood Junr.	10.–			Wass	1.11.6
	Jackson	10.–			Boys	3.3.–
	Abbington	10.–			Baildon	–10.6
	Dunn	10.–			Barrow	–10.6
	Stockton	10.–			Cheriton	–10.6
	Nicholson	10.–			Ladd	–10.6
	Neal	8.–			Baildon Junr.	–10.6
	Davis	8.–			Vandenan	–10.6
Tenors	Rash	8.–			Champness	–10.6
	Smith	8.–			Courtney	–10.6
	Warner	8.–			Wilder	–10.6
	Warner Junr.	8.–			Dupeé	–10.6
	Rawlins	8.–			Walz	–10.6
	Ebelin	8.–			Cox	–10.6
Violoncelli	Gillier	10.6			Legg	–10.6
	Haron	10.6		Servts.	Le Blanc	1.1.–
	Hebden	10.6			Gundal	–10.6
Contra Basso	Dietrich	15.–			Prince	–10.6
	Thompson	15.–			Lee	–10.6
Bassoons	Baumgarden	10.–			Shepherd	–10.6
	Jarvis	8.–			Musick Porters	1.1.–
	Goodman	8.–				£50.18.6
	Dyke	8.–			Presented Mr. Ch: Smith	5.5.–
Hautbois	Eyferd	10.–				£50.3.6
	Teede	10.–			To the Constables	2.2.–
	Vincent	10.–			Organ Blowers 4/. Porterage of Tickets 8/.	0.12.–
	Simpson	8.–			Total Ch.	£58.17.6
Trumpets Horns & Kettle drums	Adcock	10.6				
	Willis	8.–				
	Tr: Smith	10.6				
	Frova	10.6				
	Miller	10.6				
	Carrd up	£19.8.6				

Plate 12 An account list for Handel's performance of *Messiah* on 15 May 1754 at the Foundling Hospital, from the minutes of the Hospital's General Committee, 29 May 1754

The first notable feature of the list of singers is that the vocalists are all grouped together, the only distinction for the soloists arising from their precedence at the top of the list and their greater emoluments. While most members of the orchestra were paid in round proportions of pounds, the singers worked for guineas: Frasi the first soprano received (no doubt demanded) 6 guineas, the second soprano and alto 4½ guineas: Beard, the tenor, evidently gave his services for the benefit of the charity, but was presumably paid regularly for the theatre performances. The chorus men received half a guinea each, the trebles 15s 9d (= ¾ guinea).[20] The listing of the soloists along with the chorus members, without the sort of 'section' distinction that is made in the orchestral lists, complements the musical situation revealed in the performing material for *Messiah* provided for the Foundling Hospital under Handel's will in 1759,[21] in which the chorus music is also written into the soloists' books. In modern terms, we would say that the soloists sang through the choruses: Handel's attitude might have been rather that the chorus movements were performed by the soloists with the support of other singers.[22] Either way, it seems that in 1754 the top chorus line was in the hands of four boy trebles and two 'theatre' soprano soloists, doubled by the oboes in the orchestra. The boys almost certainly came from the Chapel Royal: Bernard Gates, the Master of the Children, was thanked for supplying them in the Foundling Hospital minutes relating to several of the early performances. It also seems a reasonable presumption that, at least during the period of Gates's activity, the successive treble soloists used by Handel in various oratorio performances were taken from the best of the current Chapel Royal trebles.

This immediately suggests a link in Handel's oratorio performances stretching back to the first theatre version of *Esther* in 1732, which followed on Gates's own performances of the same work, and the list of chorus singers deserves further examination from this perspective. Of the thirteen chorus men named in 1754, about half were either Chapel Royal Gentlemen or were drawn from a related pool of professional singers in the circuits of London's major ecclesiastical choirs. One of the soloists, the bass Robert Wass, was also a Chapel Royal singer: he took solos both at the Foundling Hospital and in Handel's theatre performances. From this, one must presume that Chapel Royal singers were allowed to perform in Handel's oratorios, probably under some arrangement that had been negotiated with Bishop Gibson in 1732. Handel no doubt organised his rehearsals and performances so as to avoid any conflict with the Chapel singers' routine ecclesiastical duties. The only practical limitation to their participation seems to have been an obvious one: the Chapel Royal Gentlemen comprised priests and laymen, and none of the priests (some of whom were leading singers at the Chapel) appear in the Foundling Hospital list. Presumably the priests would not have been allowed to perform in the theatre, and the absence of their names from the Foundling Hospital lists increases the likelihood that Handel's charity performances were fundamentally revivals of his immediately preceding theatre productions, with the same performers. The list of chorus men in 1754 seems to be a mixture of 'Chapel' and freelance theatre singers, which is what we might have expected: in his oratorios Handel was making the best of both musical worlds. As to the balance of voices within the gentlemen of the chorus, it seems probable that the first three names in the 1754 list were altos, the next three were tenors and the remaining seven basses. This interpretation, which would produce a rather unexpected musical balance, is based on evidence from musical and documentary sources relating to the other known activities of individual singers: it must necessarily be tentative, not only because of the inequalities in our knowledge of individual musical biographies but also because of the chameleon-like abilities of chorus singers in changing voices in order to meet a shortage in any particular part.

The Foundling Hospital part-books for the solo singers include no written-in ornamentation to the arias. Since contemporary habits of ornamentation among theatre singers were improvisatory (if not necessarily improvised on the spot) and personal, it is not surprising that decorations were not normally committed to the formal music copy. The survival of near-contemporary ornamentation to some arias in the 'Goldschmidt' and 'Matthews' manuscripts (the latter derived from singers' performing parts) is of considerable illustrative value, though it need not be taken as immutably authoritative since none of it derives, as far as we know, from any of Handel's own performances.[23] The very fact that such ornamentation was written down in these copies might reflect the need to record a practice that was going out of fashion in oratorio performances, or an attempt to define the application of an opera-derived practice to the related but different genre of oratorio. Ornamentation was probably applied less copiously in English oratorio than in Italian opera: by the 1740s even opera-trained singers may have adopted a rather different style in Handel's oratorios, which could be regarded as a genre falling somewhere between Tosi's 'theatre' and 'chamber' styles.[24] As to the embellishment of the final bars of arias with vocal cadenzas, once again direct examples from sources deriving from Handel's own performances are lacking. The weight of probability is, however, in favour of the practice of including cadenzas of modest scope at appropriate points, and in some places Handel's scoring seems deliberately arranged to allow for this. To take a well-known example from *Messiah*, it is difficult to believe that the plain vocal ending to 'Every valley', accompanied by the tell-tale reduction of the orchestral accompaniment to bass line and continuo alone, was performed 'as written'. The training that John Beard had received in Handel's Italian opera company during the 1730s surely led his instinct to a cadenza here, and his formative musical experience as a Chapel Royal chorister no doubt influenced him to the effect that a suitable cadenza at this point ought to be dignified and fairly short. When Handel talked in a letter about having 'form'd' a tenor voice in Dublin,[25] he was perhaps referring to a crash course in stylistic training that was necessary in circumstances where the local singers could not have had comparable experience to Beard's.

The orchestral component of the 1754 performers' list suggests the probability of some continuity with the orchestras that had been associated with Handel in the London theatres during the previous four decades. The *Messiah* orchestra bears comparison in overall size with that of the opera house orchestra of the Haymarket theatre in the 1720s.[26] In the absence of intermediate lists it is difficult to know whether to attribute differences to conscious changes in musical practice and taste, or to the temporary warps associated with the availability of particular players and instruments. The 1754 string section of fourteen violins, six violas, three 'cellos and two double basses is just larger than the twenty-three players named in one authoritative London opera list in 1720, the numbers in the bass departments being identical. The 1754 orchestra looks marginally weaker on violins and stronger on violas, but the balance had shifted by the time of the next surviving Foundling Hospital list (1758) to twelve violins and three violas: in this sort of situation, it looks as if the populations of the back desks were affected primarily by the availability of players, and a difference of two or three players probably does not reflect a conscious change in musical policy. An equal division of violins into first and seconds may be assumed, though it is more difficult to guess how Handel managed his occasional tripartite division of the violins. The twenty-five-man string group comprised the basic ensemble to which Handel was able to add yet more string players in apparently lavish circumstances in 1749: the 'ripieno' marks that he added to the scores for his oratorio performances of that year refer to the addition of extra players and not to the reduction of the orchestra to a concertino group of soloists elsewhere. There is no evidence that Handel regularly employed the small-concertino principle in his oratorio performances, and his uses of a solo violin are few and specific. Handel's use of the 'tutti' and 'solo' indications in the orchestral bass, which can imply an occasional reduction in the scoring to a small continuo group, is also surprisingly restrained in the oratorio scores.

It is in the wind departments that we may suspect the greatest variations in Handel's orchestra through successive performances. Unfortunately nothing is known of the contractual arrangements that Handel
made with his players, though we may assume a principle of continuous
employment for oboes (some doubling flute) and bassoons. The multiplication of the instruments in 1754 (four oboes for two parts, four bassoons for one part) is noteworthy: it may reflect both Handel's general
preference for doubling the wind parts and the existence of a pool of
instrumental talent sufficient to make this possible. There were still four
each of oboes and bassoons in the next surviving Foundling Hospital list
(1758), which may reinforce the suggestion that such numbers were
regular in the oratorio orchestra. Trumpets and drums (of various sizes)
were routinely available for the oratorios. The biggest surprise and apparent anomaly about the 1754 list is the inclusion of two horn players, for
whom there is no music in the *Messiah* score. The most likely assumption
(unless these players performed only in some interval concerto) is that
the horns doubled the trumpet parts, sounding an octave lower, in the
final choruses of Parts 2 and 3. The general impression to be gained from
the 1754 list is that Handel took the complete riches of his theatre orchestra to the Foundling Hospital: if his priorities had been for economy
instead, he could have saved the cost of six players – two each of oboes,
bassoons and horns. Some instruments that appear only occasionally in
the oratorios may have been played by seasonal visitors, for example
trombones in 1739–41, and harp and mandolin in 1748. For the main
orchestra, however, Burney's statement that Handel 'always employed a
very numerous band'[27] – 'numerous', presumably in comparison with the
orchestra employed for English plays at the theatres – can be taken at its
face value.

It is appropriate to conclude with a brief consideration of Handel's
continuo practice in the oratorios, since it is intimately connected with
the part that the composer himself played in the performances. On this
subject the 1754 *Messiah* list is obscure, and understandably so because it
probably relates to the last occasion on which Handel, severely impaired
if not totally blind, may have attempted to take an active role in the performance.[28] The payment to the organ blowers and the entry for 'Christ?
Smith Org' indicates that it was at least expected that the organ would be
used. However, no payment is recorded against the entry for Smith as
organist. A payment of five guineas appears below, 'Presented Mr. Ch.
Smith', in an area of the account that may suggest a last-minute addition.

In view of possible ambiguity over the identity of 'Christopher Smith',
some uncertainty attaches to this entry. Three Smiths appear elsewhere in
the list. The organist must be John Christopher Smith junior; Frederick

Smith (no relation to the foregoing, as far as we know) played the timpani[29] and an undifferentiated 'Smith' the viola. Evidence from thirty years previously[30] strongly suggests that the viola-playing Smith may have been John Christopher Smith senior, whom in any case we would expect to have had some managerial association with the performance, presumably acting as music librarian and guardian of his precious copies of the music. One possibility is that the five-guinea entry to 'Ch. Smith' may cover the provision of the music and any related music-copying for the parts. However it seems more likely that this payment was made to Smith junior for taking over the direction of the performance because of Handel's incapacity. Since Handel seems previously to have given his own services freely, it is quite likely that he also arranged for the music copies to be used without charge to the Hospital, provided the same part-books from the theatre performances could be used without further major amendments involving copyists' charges.

Clearly the 1754 account seems to reflect an abnormal situation as far as the keyboard players are concerned: to gain some idea of 'normal practice' we have to look to other evidence relating to Handel's performances. It has to be admitted immediately that there is no firm evidence from the 1740s and 1750s, though some reasonable deductions can be made about that period: we have to begin with material from the preceding two decades, referring to Handel's performances of Italian operas and English oratorios and odes. The performers' lists and descriptions of performances from the 1720s suggest that the London operas of that period included two harpsichords (one played by Handel himself) and a theorbo or an archlute in their accompanying ensemble. Unfortunately no comparable descriptions from the 1730s have yet come to light, but this deficiency is more than compensated for by the existence of other valuable evidence. From the instrumental designations that Handel added to the bass lines of his scores, it is apparent that the organ entered his theatre orchestra with the oratorios in 1732. Although Handel used the organ occasionally in oratorio arias as a solo obbligato instrument, and the instrument of course fulfilled a stimulating solo role when Handel introduced organ concertos into the intervals of his oratorio performances, its main task was to support the voices in the choruses. In some years two organs were employed: this was particularly useful for the double-choir *Israel in Egypt*, first performed in 1739, where one organ accompanied each choir (as is clear from the markings in the score) and some separation of the performing groups thus created seems likely. The most practical assumption about the normal performance arrangements seems to be that Handel directed the performances from the harpsichord while subsidiary players took the organ (or organs), but changed places for the organ concertos.

Leaving aside for the moment the question of who played which instrument, the more musically significant question about the relative musical roles of the harpsichord and the organ is answered definitively by the very fortunate survival of harpsichord and organ parts from Handel's performances of *Alexander's Feast* (1736). The fully realised organ part,[31] perhaps written out in full for the instruction of a new player in Handel's team, confirms that the organ principally supported the voices in the chorus movements. Elsewhere it either remained silent or selectively assisted *tasto solo* in the continuo bass line: at no stage did it assume the principal chord-filling role in recitatives or arias. The surviving harpsichord part for *Alexander's Feast*,[32] which is demonstrably a practical document used in Handel's performances, contains (as we would expect from contemporary practice) the complete bass line, with rather sparse figuring, and the vocal lines of the arias; the first page is designated 'Harpsicord. Sig[r]. Pasqualini', suggesting that Handel directed the performance from another harpsichord, possibly reading from a score. Other plucked stringed instruments may also have contributed to the continuo accompaniment: the first performance of *Alexander's Feast* included the Harp Concerto Op. 4 No. 6, described in the libretto as a concerto for 'Harp, Lute, Lyricord, and other Instruments'.

Some attempt must now be made to bridge the tantalising gap between the 1730s and 1754. One fairly safe assumption is that, in Handel's later years, his continuo group rarely included a theorbo or archlute. The last mention of an instrument of this type in musical sources comes in the score of *Saul*, composed for performance in 1739. The employment of a lute may well have seemed anachronistic to Handel if he was attempting to give a new and modern look to his performances in the 1740s. There is one documentary reference to a lutenist being employed at the beginning of his 1744–5 season,[33] when Handel returned briefly to the King's Theatre and may have reverted to full-scale operatic practices in his accompaniment of the singers: otherwise there is no evidence for his use of a lute-type instrument in Dublin, or in London after his return. We can similarly dismiss for practical purposes the possibility that a harp took a regular part in Handel's London performances after 1742. The only season in which Handel used this instrument was 1748, when he gave it a solo in *Alexander Balus*. The single movement of *Esther* that required a harp was conspicuously absent from his later London revivals of that oratorio (1751, 1757). For the chord-playing continuo instruments, therefore, we return to the simple combination of organ and harpsichord, and we may begin from the assumption that at least one of each was used.

Handel's letter to Jennens of 29 December 1741, written just after the commencement of his first subscription concert (*L'Allegro*) in Dublin,

contains the tantalising phrase 'I exert myself on my Organ with more
than usual Success':[34] this might imply that Handel directed his performances from the organ, but it seems more likely to refer to the organ
concertos, in which Handel featured as the soloist and necessarily had to
'exert' himself, especially if some element of improvisation was included.
But a newspaper report of Handel's first Dublin performance of *Acis and
Galatea* with the *Song for St Cecilia's Day* seems unequivocal in describing
the occasion as 'conducted by that great Master Mr. Handel, and accompanied all along on the Organ by his own inimitable hand.'[35] Perhaps
Handel's practice in Dublin was different from that in London.

The original layout of the 1754 Foundling Hospital account clearly
suggests that Christopher Smith, as the only named chord-playing continuo player, was expected to perform the subsidiary role on the organ,
with the implication that Handel normally directed the performances
from the harpsichord. That seems the most plausible arrangement
throughout the period between 1742 and 1754 (though the organ-player
would not have been Smith in the earlier part of the period). The question
therefore arises as to how many organs and harpsichords may have been
employed in Handel's theatre performances. Two organs were clearly
available in the 1730s but circumstantial evidence is against Handel's use
of two for his performances after 1743. Thereafter his scores contain no
mention of 'organi', even for the double-choir choruses of *Solomon*, first
produced in 1749: by then Handel seems to have been more interested in
enriching the numbers of orchestral instruments than continuo players.
Handel's only mention of a chord-playing instrument in his autographs
and conducting score of *Messiah* is 'org' next to the bass line of the duet-
and-chorus setting 'How beautiful are the feet', composed in 1742 for
Dublin:[36] this may reinforce the possibility of a different, organ-led, continuo practice for his Dublin performances, or it may record an
unconventional specification for the bass line of this movement, empha-
sising a 'church' style appropriate to the cathedral alto soloists for whom
the movement was written. While special uses of the organ are noted in
Handel's scores, his continuo line is normally labelled (if at all) just 'Bassi'
or 'Tutti Bassi': the absence of regular references to the keyboard continuo presumably indicates that there were no serious divergences from
whatever 'normal' routine practices were in force at the time.

As far as Handel's London performances are concerned, retrospective
argument from the 1754 account seems the most fruitful way of pursuing this fugitive 'normal practice'. Not only does the 1754 account-list
seem to place Handel normally at the harpsichord and Smith junior normally at the organ, but it seems to cut out the possibility of a second
harpsichordist. While allowance must be made for the possibility that a

second harpsichordist might have played in the theatre oratorios but not in the Foundling Hospital performances of *Messiah*, the case for a single harpsichord and organ is convincing. *Messiah* may be a slightly special case, since the brevity of the continuo-accompanied recitatives reduced the load on the harpsichord player compared with operatic practice. But, given circumstances in which the composer/conductor was in close artistic collusion with soloists and the leaders of the orchestral sections (rendering only 'light' conducting necessary), and in which the organ supported (and if necessary to some extent led) the chorus, there is no reason why Handel should not have successfully combined the leading chord-playing function at the harpsichord with direction of the performance. There was no practical need for an array of further accompanying instruments. In the next surviving Foundling Hospital account after 1754, that for 1758, Smith is again paid a comparable fee but there is no mention of the organ blowers: it looks as if this performance was directed by Smith from the harpsichord with no support from an organist. If we read this situation back into the 1754 account, its most plausible interpretation is that in that year it had been intended that Handel should play/direct from the harpsichord, with Smith at the organ, but this proved impractical at the last minute through Handel's physical incapacity: Smith therefore took over at the harpsichord and Handel may have filled in as best he could from memory with the accompanying role on the organ, probably for the last time. While the use of one harpsichord and one organ is suggested as Handel's normal practice for his last active years (*c*. 1749–54), it is possible that a second harpsichord was used in the period 1742–8, when Handel may have been a little more lavish and opera-influenced in his approach to continuo practice. But this was perhaps no more than the fine shading to a change in Handel's attitude to continuo scoring, as he shifted decisively towards English-language works involving a regular chorus as the basis for his theatre seasons.

A few other matters about the treatment of the continuo also deserve notice. The musical sources do not give us much guidance on Handel's practice with regard to the string bass line. A 'cello may or may not have accompanied any of the *semplice* recitatives: probably not, since there was no differentiation of a leading player in the payments to 'cellists in the Foundling Hospital accounts. Some works, particularly from 1739–40, have 'cello solos, but there is nothing in the sources to suggest that the string bass section was regularly reduced to a single-cello continuo in the solo sections of arias (i.e. those sections without orchestral accompaniment above): directions are even sparse about the lightening of double-bass tone beyond those suggested by Handel's use of clefs – bass clef for all *bassi* strings, tenor clef for 'cellos without double basses, higher clefs for keyboard continuo leads.

Assuming that Handel delivered the principal chordal continuo accompaniment himself from the harpsichord, we are nevertheless left finally to our own imaginations about his tastes in the realisation of the bass part. His own basso continuo figurings, few and far between in the oratorios, seem to be mainly mnemonics to guide him with the harmony when he came to fill up the score,[37] and his scores give the harpsichord player very few opportunities for creative input. A virtuosic display in this area would in any case have been misplaced, for the continuo player's job was primarily to accompany: virtuosity enough could be saved for the organ concerto, and it is perhaps not being too cynical to suggest that an over-absorption in the continuo role would have left Handel with insufficient spare reserves of attention to forestall any potential break-downs or technical mishaps in the performances of those around him. In his performances Handel the performer-impresario surely did not put himself at odds with Handel the composer: indeed, it is the unity of these functions that made them in an unusually comprehensive sense 'his' performances.

Bibliographical note

The following frequently cited sources are referred to in abbreviated form in the notes.

Collected editions of Handel's music

HG
G. F. Händels Werke: Ausgabe der Deutschen Händelgesellschaft, ed. Friedrich W. Chrysander and Max Seiffert, Vols. 1–48, 50–96 (Leipzig and Bergedorf bei Hamburg, 1858–94, 1902); also 6 supplementary volumes of related music by other composers (1888–1902).

HHA
Hallische Händel-Ausgabe, im Auftrage der Georg-Friedrich-Händel Gesellschaft, Series I-V (Leipzig and Kassel, 1955–); also supplementary volume Aufzeichnungen zur Kompositionslehre (ed. Alfred Mann, 1978), referred to as HHA Supp.

Books, including reference works and eighteenth-century sources

Abraham, Handel
Gerald Abraham (ed.), Handel: A Symposium (London, 1954).

Biographical Dictionary
Philip H. Highfill jun., Kalman A. Burnim, and Edward A. Langhans, A Biographical Dictionary of Actors, Actresses, Musicians, Dancers, Managers, & other Stage Personnel in London, 1660–1800 (16 vols., Carbondale, Ill. and Edwardsville, Pa., 1973–93).

Burney, Commemoration
Charles Burney, An account of the Musical Performances . . . in Commemoration of Handel (London 1785; facsimile edition Amsterdam, 1964). This publication has a double sequence of paginations: references from the biographical section 'Sketch of the Life of Handel', are given as Burney, Commemoration, 'Sketch', and those from the later part of the book as Burney, Commemoration, 'Performances'.

Burney, History
Charles Burney, A General History of Music from the Earliest Ages to the Present Period (4 vols., London, 1776–89). References are to the edition in 2 vols., ed. Frank Mercer (London, 1935; repr. New York 1957).

Burrows, 'Chapel Royal'
Donald Burrows, 'Handel and the English Chapel Royal in the reigns of Queen Anne and King George I'

	(Ph.D. diss., The Open University, Milton Keynes, 1981).
Burrows, *Handel*	Donald Burrows, *Handel* (Oxford and New York, 1994).
Coxe, *Anecdotes*	[William Coxe], *Anecdotes of George Frederick Handel and John Christopher Smith* (London, 1799; facsimile repr. New York, 1979).
Dean, *Oratorios*	Winton Dean, *Handel's Dramatic Oratorios and Masques* (London, 1959; 2nd edn Oxford, 1990).
Dean & Knapp, *Operas*	Winton Dean and John Merrill Knapp, *Handel's Operas 1704–1726* (Oxford, 1987; 2nd edn Oxford, 1995).
Deutsch, Handel	Otto Erich Deutsch, *Handel: A Documentary Biography* (London, 1955; repr. New York, 1974). A revised and supplemented version is found at *HHB* vol. IV; where *HHB* repeats an entry from Deutsch, *Handel* without alteration, only the page reference from Deutsch is given.
Fortune, *Music & Theatre*	Nigel Fortune (ed.), *Music & Theatre: Essays in Honour of Winton Dean* (Cambridge, 1987).
Gibson, *Academy*	Elizabeth Gibson, *The Royal Academy of Music 1719–28: the Institution and its Directors* (New York and London, 1989).
Harris, *Librettos*	Ellen T. Harris (ed.), *The Librettos of Handel's Operas*, facsimile edition with introductions (13 vols., New York and London, 1989).
Hawkins, *History*	Sir John Hawkins, *A General History of the Science and Practice of Music* (5 vols., London, 1776). References are to the edition in 2 vols., published by J. Alfred Novello (London, 1853; repr. New York, 1963).
HHB	Walter Eisen and Margret Eisen, *Händel-Handbuch*, (4 vols., Leipzig, 1978, 1984–6). Vols. I-III contain the *Thematisch-Systematisches Verzeichnis* to Handel's works, the thematic catalogue prepared by Bernd Baselt which is the source for 'HWV' numbers. Vol. IV, *Dokumente zu Leben und Schaffen*, is a revised version of Deutsch, *Handel*.
Hogwood & Luckett, *18th Century*	Christopher Hogwood and Richard Luckett (eds.), *Music in Eighteenth-Century England: Essays in Memory of Charles Cudworth* (Cambridge, 1983).
LaRue, *Singers*	C. Steven LaRue, *Handel and his Singers: The Creation of the Royal Academy Operas, 1720–1728* (Oxford, 1995).
The London Stage	William van Lennep, Emmett L. Avery, Arthur H. Scouten, George Winchester Stone jr., Charles Beecher Hogan (eds.), *The London Stage 1660–1800, A*

	Calendar of Plays (5 parts, 9 vols., Carbondale, Ill., 1960–8)
Mainwaring, *Memoirs*	[John Mainwaring], *Memoirs of the life of the late George Frederic Handel* (London, 1760; facsimile reprint Buren, 1964, 1975).
Mattheson, *Grundlage*	Johann Mattheson, *Grundlage einer Ehren-Pforte* (Hamburg, 1740).
New Grove	Stanley Sadie (ed.), *The New Grove Dictionary of Music and Musicians* (20 vols., London, 1980).
New Grove Opera	Stanley Sadie (ed.), *The New Grove Dictionary of Opera* (4 vols., London, 1992).
Roberts, *Handel Sources*	John H. Roberts (ed.), *Handel Sources: Materials for the Study of Handel's Borrowings*, music facsimile edition with introductions (9 vols., New York and London, 1986).
Sadie & Hicks, *Tercentenary Collection*	Stanley Sadie and Anthony Hicks (eds.), *Handel Tercentenary Collection* (London, 1987).
R. Smith, *Oratorios*	Ruth Smith, *Handel's Oratorios and Eighteenth-Century Thought* (Cambridge, 1995).
Smith, *Handel*	William C. Smith, *Handel: A Descriptive Catalogue of the Early Editions* (London, 1960; 2nd edn Oxford, 1970).
Smith, *Walsh I*	William C. Smith, *A Bibliography of the Musical Works Published by John Walsh during the years 1695–1720* (London, 1948, 1968).
Smith, *Walsh II*	William Smith with Charles Humphreys, *A Bibliography of the Musical Works Published by the Firm of John Walsh during the years 1721–1766* (London, 1966).
Strohm, *Essays*	Reinhard Strohm, *Essays on Handel and Italian Opera* (Cambridge, 1985).
Vice Chamberlain Coke	Judith Milhous and Robert D. Hume (eds.), *Vice Chamberlain Coke's Theatrical Papers, 1706–15* (Carbondale, Ill., 1982).
Weber, *Classics*	William Weber, *The Rise of Musical Classics in Eighteenth-Century England: A Study in Canon, Ritual and Ideology* (Oxford, 1992).
Williams, *Bach, Handel, Scarlatti*	Peter Williams (ed.), *Bach, Handel, Scarlatti: Tercentenary Essays* (Cambridge, 1985).

Journals and periodicals

EM	*Early Music*
GHB	*Göttinger Händel-Beiträge*
HJb	*Händel-Jahrbuch*
JAMS	*Journal of the American Musicological Society*
JRMA	*Journal of the Royal Musical Association*

ML   *Music & Letters*
MT   *The Musical Times*
MQ   *The Musical Quarterly*
PRMA   *Proceedings of the Royal Musical Association*
SM   *Studi Musicali*
TJ   *Theatre Journal*
TN   *Theatre Notebook*

Editor's note

The books and music editions listed above constitute the core of the vast
literature relating to Handel and his music: many of the books cited carry further
extensive bibliographies, and a basic modern Handel bibliography may be found
in Mary Ann Parker-Hale, *G. F. Handel: A Guide to Research* (New York and
London, 1988). Substantial biographies of Handel include those by Friedrich
Chrysander (3 vols., uncompleted, 1858–67; repr. 1966); Victor Schoelcher
(London, 1857); Mrs. Julian Marshall (London, n.d.); W. S. Rockstro (London,
1883); R. A. Streatfeild (London, 1909; 2nd edn 1910, repr. 1964); Percy M. Young
(London, 1947 and subsequent edns); Paul Henry Lang (New York and London,
1966); Christopher Hogwood (London, 1984); Jonathan Keates (London, 1985)
and Donald Burrows (Oxford and New York, 1994); these are complemented by
Jacob Simon (ed.), *Handel: A Celebration of his Life and Times* (London, 1985).
Topics relating to individual chapters of the *Companion* can be followed up
through references given in the notes: for some chapters in Part I further
references are given under 'Additional Bibliography' at the end of the notes.

Notes

Introduction
1 Burrows, *Handel*.
2 Burney, *Commemoration*, 'Sketch', p. 26.
3 The original printed wordbooks have been re-published in facsimile in Harris, *Librettos*.

1 Germany – education and apprenticeship
1 Mainwaring, *Memoirs*.
2 Hawkins, *History*, vol. II, pp. 856–7.
3 Friedrich Chrysander, *Georg Friedrich Händel* (Leipzig, 1858–67); on Chrysander's attitude towards Zachow, see Günter Thomas, *Friedrich Wilhelm Zachow*, Kölner Beiträge zur Musikforschung 38 (Regensburg, 1966), pp. 21–3.
4 Significant contributions include Bernd Baselt, 'Handel and His Central German Background', in Sadie & Hicks, *Tercentenary Collection*, pp. 43–60, and various articles in *HJb* 36 (1990).
5 See Walter Serauky, *Musikgeschichte der Stadt Halle* [all references are to vol. II] (Halle and Berlin, 1939).
6 According to the Weissenfels concertmaster, Johann Beer: see Serauky, *Musikgeschichte*, p. 414.
7 *Ibid.*, pp. 412–13; see also Rolf Hünicken, in Richard Bräutigam, Rolf Hünicken and Walter Serauky, *Georg Friedrich Händel, Abstammung und Jugendwelt – Festschrift zur 250. Wiederkehr des Geburtstages Georg Friedrich Händels* (Halle, 1935), p. 56.
8 Guido Bimberg, 'Hallesche Anregungen zu einer Dramaturgie der frühdeutschen Oper', *HJb* 36 (1990), p. 35.
9 Mattheson, *Grundlage*, p. 93; Mattheson admittedly uses the term 'hohe Schule'. For Dreyhaupt 1749/50, see Bräutigam in *Händel, Abstammung und Jugendwelt*, p. ix.
10 Werner Piechocki, 'Die Familie Händel in der Stadt Halle. II. Der Wundarzt Georg Händel', *HJb* 36 (1990), p. 202; and Hünicken, in *Händel, Abstammung und Jugendwelt*, p. 51.
11 Hünicken, in *Händel, Abstammung und Jugendwelt*, pp. 53–5, summarising the chronicles of Dreyhaupt preserved in the Stadtarchiv, Halle.
12 Serauky, *Musikgeschichte*, pp. 381–4. Baselt notes the completion of a Halle dissertation by Johann Samuel Stryk in 1702, debating the usefulness of music in church, in 'Handel and His Central German Background', p. 49.
13 Serauky, *Musiksgeschichte*, pp. 436–42.
14 *Ibid.*, p. 442, and Hünicken, in *Händel, Abstammung und Jugendwelt*, pp. 71–2.

15   Serauky, *Musiksgeschichte*, pp. 400–1; see also the document recording
     Handel's appointment, *HHB* vol. IV, pp. 18–19.

16   Handel had deputised at the Cathedral before the time of his appointment.
     The previous organist, Johann Christoph Leporin, had been particularly
     negligent in his duties and apparently led a dissolute lifestyle. Thus, as
     Thomas suggests (*Zachow*, p. 14), Mainwaring's references to Handel's
     deputising for Zachow because of the latter's 'love of company and a chearful
     glass' (*Memoirs*, p. 15), might in fact relate rather to Handel's deputising for
     Leporin at the Cathedral.

17   Serauky, *Musikgeschichte*, p. 403.

18   Burney, *Commemoration*, 'Sketch', p. 3, note a; see pp. 182–3 above.

19   See Donald Burrows, 'Handel and Hanover', in Williams, *Bach, Handel,
     Scarlatti*, p. 37.

20   Mattheson, *Grundlage*, p. 358.

21   See Thomas, *Zachow*, pp. 113–15.

22   Kuhnau, organist of the Thomaskirche, Leipzig, was also a successful
     practising lawyer.

23   Mainwaring, *Memoirs*, pp. 9–13.

24   Piechocki, 'Die Familie Händel', p. 201.

25   Baselt, 'Handel and His Central German Background', p. 44.

26   *Ibid.*, p. 46.

27   Piechocki, 'Die Familie Händel', p. 206.

28   *Ibid.*, p. 213.

29   See Gerhard Poppe, 'Beobachtungen zu 'Georg Friderich Händels
     Lebensbeschreibung' von John Mainwaring and Johann Mattheson', *HJb* 36
     (1990), p. 179.

30   Bernd Baselt, 'Die Oper um 1700 in mitteldeutschen Raum', *HJb* 36 (1990),
     p. 20; Werner Felix, 'Johann Philipp Krieger und die Hofoper in Weissenfels',
     HJb 36 (1990), pp. 41–7.

31   Baselt, 'Handel and His Central German Background', p. 48.

32   Felix, 'Krieger', p. 41.

33   Krieger's son Johann Gotthilf was, like Handel, a pupil of Zachow; see
     Thomas, *Zachow*, pp. 115–16.

34   Hünicken, in *Händel, Abstammung und Jugendwelt*, pp. 52–4.

35   Mainwaring, *Memoirs*, p. 2.

36   Johann Gottfried Walther, *Musicalisches Lexicon* (Leipzig, 1732), p. 309.

37   See Bräutigam, in *Händel, Abstammung und Jugendwelt*, p. ix; Dreyhaupt
     perhaps derived the date from Walther's *Lexicon*.

38   Mainwaring, *Memoirs*, p. 5.

39   Serauky, *Musikgeschichte*, pp. 349–56, 412.

40   See *Aufzeichnungen zur Kompositionslehre, HHA Supp.*, pp. 57–9.

41   It is possible that Mylius was related to the wife of Johann Praetorius, the Rector
     of the Gymnasium, since she was the daughter of Samuel Mylius, cantor at
     nearby Merseburg. See Hünicken, in *Händel, Abstammung und Jugendwelt*, p. 55.

42   See John Butt, *Music Education and the Art of Performance in the German
     Baroque*, (Cambridge, 1994), particularly Chapter 5.

43   See *ibid.*, p. 173, for a reproduction of one of these pages.

44   G. Falck, *Idea boni cantoris* (1688); J. C. Lange, *Methodus nova et Perspicua* (1688); W. C. Printz, *Compendium musicae* (1689); J. C. Stierlein, *Trifolium musicale* (1691); M. Feyertag, *Syntaxis minor zur Sing-Kunst* (1695); J. S. Beyer, *Primae linae musicae vocalis*; and M. H. Fuhrmann, *Musicalischer-Trichter* (1706).

45   Thomas, *Zachow*, p. 114.

46   Mainwaring, *Memoirs*, pp. 14–15.

47   W. C. Printz, *Phrynis Mitilenaeus, oder Satyrischer Componist* (Quedlinburg, 1676–7, 1679; reprinted Dresden and Leipzig, 1696); F. E. Niedt, *Musicalische Handleitung* (vols. I–II Hamburg, 1700, 1706; vol. III published posthumously in 1717). See also David Schulenberg, 'Composition as Variation: Inquiries into the Compositional Procedures of the Bach Circle of Composers', *Current Musicology*, 33 (1982), pp. 57–87.

48   *Friederich Erhardt Niedt, The Musical Guide*, trans. Pamela L. Poulin and Irmgard C. Taylor (Oxford, 1989), p. 158.

49   *Ibid.*, p. 237.

50   Coxe, *Anecdotes*, p. 6. See also Robert Hill, '"Der Himmel weiss, wo diese Sachen hingekommen sind": Reconstructing the Lost Keyboard Notes of the Young Bach and Handel', in Williams, *Bach, Handel, Scarlatti*, pp. 161–72.

51   Mainwaring, *Memoirs*, pp. 17–26.

52   This second anomaly was noted by Johann Mattheson in *Georg Friedrich Händels Lebensbeschreibung* (Hamburg, 1761), his annotated translation of Mainwaring, *Memoirs*.

53   Piechocki, 'Die Familie Händel', p. 208.

54   Poppe, 'Beobachtungen', pp. 179–80.

55   Mattheson, *Grundlage*, p. 359. See also Burney, *Commemoration*, 'Sketch', p. 6: Burney's book incorporated at the last moment biographical material derived from Mattheson, *Grundlage*.

56   See Wolf Hobohm, 'Georg Philipp Telemann und die bürgerliche Oper in Leipzig', *HJb* 36 (1990), pp. 49–61.

57   Baselt, 'Handel and His Central German Background', p. 48.

58   Mattheson, *Grundlage*, p. 93.

59   In *ibid.*, p. 359.

60   *Ibid.*, pp. 93–5.

61   Hans-Joachim Marx, 'Die Hamburger Oper zur Zeit des jungen Händel', *HJb* 36 (1990), p. 117; Baselt, 'Handel and his Central German Background', p. 50.

62   Hünicken, in *Händel, Abstammung und Jugendwelt*, p. 74.

63   John H. Roberts, 'Keiser and Handel at the Hamburg Opera', *HJb* 36 (1990), pp. 64–5.

64   *Ibid.*, p. 64.

65   This is a habit that Handel might have acquired from Zachow, given the scale of his concerted works and the complaints voiced by the town council in 1695; see pp. 13–14 above.

66   Mattheson, *Grundlage*, p. 95.

67   Mainwaring, *Memoirs*, p. 40. But see p. 318 below.

2 Italy – Political, religious and musical contexts

1   Gilbert Burnet, *Burnet's Travels: or a Collection of Letters to the Hon. Robert Boyle, Esq., containing an account of what seem'd most remarkable in travelling thro' Switzerland, Italy, and some Parts of Germany etc. in the years 1685 and 1686* (London, 1737), p. 145. (1st edn: Rotterdam, 1686).

2   The number of workers employed at the Arsenal (state-owned shipyards) fell from 2,343 in 1645 to 1,393 half a century later; the shortfall of tonnage was made up by the purchase or hire of Dutch vessels. Silk production declined by 50 per cent between 1662 and 1712, and in the course of the seventeenth century the annual production of soap went down from 13 million to 3 million pounds weight.

3   Between 1661 and 1712 the number of clock-makers in Venice remained at the level of half a dozen, as against the 20–40 of Augsburg and the 100 or more of Geneva.

4   At the time of Handel's residence in Italy, the ducat (6.2 lire) was worth about 2s 9d in contemporary English coinage.

5   The *scudo* was worth just over a shilling in contemporary English coinage.

6   Sieur De Rogissart, *Les Délices de l'Italie* (Leiden, 1706).

7   The polemic, begun in 1703, broadened out to become, seven years later, the launching-pad for the periodical *Il giornale de' letterati d'Italia*, founded by Apostolo Zeno, Scipione Maffei and Antonio Vallisnieri, a professor of medicine at the University of Padua. In its pages they debated (in accordance with the broad contemporary understanding of the term 'letterato') historical, philosophical, technological and scientific matters as well as literature proper.

8   Among them were such illustrious names as the anatomist Malpighi, General Marsigli (founder of the Istituto delle Scienze of Bologna), the physicist Viviani (a pupil of Galileo and of Torricelli), Vallisnieri himself, Lancisi (botanist and personal physician to the Pope) and Count Magalotti, secretary of the Florentine Accademia del Cimento.

9   Half of the historical territory of the Duchy of Savoy lay in present-day France.

10   Reinhard Strohm, 'Händel in Italia: nuovi contributi' in *Rivista italiana di musicologia* 9 (1974), pp. 152–74, and 'Il viaggio italiano di Handel come esperienza europea' in G. Morelli (ed.), *III Festival Vivaldi: Händel in Italia* (Venice, 1981), pp. 60–71; Giovanni Morelli, 'Monsù Endel, servitore di due padroni (Per una nuova "giustificazione" dell'arte allegorica)', in Morelli (ed.), *III Festival Vivaldi*, pp. 72–82; Giovanni Morelli, 'Morire di prestazioni' in L. Bianconi and G. Morelli (eds.), *Antonio Vivaldi: Teatro musicale, cultura e società* (Florence, 1982), pp. 389–414.

11   Mainwaring, *Memoirs*, p. 43.

12   The Venetian sequin (22 Venetian lire, as compared with the ducat's 6.2 lire) was worth about 9s 2d in the middle of the eighteenth century, but slightly less at the beginning of the century.

13   Ludovico Antonio Muratori, *Della perfetta poesia italiana* (2 vols., Venice, 1724), vol. III, pp. 30–45 (1st edn: Modena, 1706); Carlo Vitali, 'I viaggi di

Faramondo', introduction to Apostolo Zeno and Carlo Francesco Pollarolo, *Il Faramondo* (facsimile edition), Drammaturgia musicale veneta IX (Milan, 1987), pp. ix–xxxv.

14   Mainwaring, *Memoirs*, p. 66; see Carlo Vitali and Antonello Furnari, 'Händels Italienreise – neue Dokumente, Hypothesen und Interpretationen', in *GHB* 4 (1991), pp. 41–66.

15   Mario Fabbri, *Alessandro Scarlatti e il Principe Ferdinando de' Medici* (Florence, 1961), p. 69.

16   Bologna, Biblioteca Universitaria, Zambeccari MS correspondence; also quoted by Lodovico Frati, 'Un impresario teatrale del Settecento e la sua biblioteca', *Rivista musicale italiana*, 18 (1911), pp. 6–26.

17   Charles Burney, *The Present State of Music in France and Italy* (London, 1771), pp. 189–90.

18   Mainwaring, *Memoirs*, pp. 43–69.

19   See Vitali and Furnari, 'Händels Italienreise''.

20   Mainwaring, *Memoirs*, pp. 39–41. It has been suggested that Handel's contact in Hamburg was not Grand Prince Ferdinando but his brother Gian Gastone: see, for example, Werner Braun, 'Georg Friedrich Händel und Gian Gastone von Toskana', *HJb* 34 (1988), pp. 109–21. However, there is no evidence from the Medici archives to support the presence of either man in Hamburg during 1705–6.

21   Original Italian text *HHB* vol. IV, p. 26.

22   Ursula Kirkendale, 'Nuovi documenti su Händel e il marchese Ruspoli nell'Archivio segreto vaticano: Cerveteri e Civitavecchia nel 1707': unpublished paper delivered at the conference 'La musica a Roma attraverso le fonti d'archivio', Rome, 5 June 1992. Thanks are extended to Ursula Kirkendale for communicating this discovery.

23   Mario Fabbri, 'Nuova luce sull'attività medicea di Giacomo Antonio Perti, Bartolomeo Cristofori e Giorgio F. Haendel: Valore storico e critico di una memoria di Francesco M. Mannucci', *Chigiana*, 21 (1964), p. 175.

24   Fabbri, 'Nuova luce', pp. 145–9; Juliane Riepe, Carlo Vitali and Antonello Furnari, 'Il Pianto di Maria (HWV 234): Rezeption, Überlieferung und musikwissenschaftliche Fiktion', *GHB* 5 (1993), pp. 270–307.

25   Letter of 9 March 1710 from Carl Philipp von Neuburg to Ferdinando de' Medici, *HHB* vol. IV, p. 45.

26   Mainwaring, *Memoirs*, pp. 65–6.

27   See Vitali and Furnari, 'Händel's Italienreise', pp. 63–4.

28   See Watkins Shaw and Graham Dixon, 'Handel's Vesper Music', *MT* 126 (1985), pp. 392–7.

29   The only clear evidence for Grimani's authorship of *Agrippina*, a printing licence published in Remo Giazotto, *Antonio Vivaldi* (Turin, 1973) is a manifest forgery.

Additional bibliography

R. Cremante and W. Tega (eds.), *Scienza e letteratura nella cultura italiana del Settecento* (Bologna, 1984); Frederic C. Lane, *Venice: A Maritime Republic* (Baltimore, 1973); Reinhard Strohm, 'Händel und Italien – ein intellektuelles

Abenteuer', GHB 5 (1993), pp. 5–43; Michael Talbot, 'An Italian Overview', in Julie
Anne Sadie (ed.), *Companion to Baroque Music* (London, 1990), pp. 3–17; also the
articles by Kirkendale and Hicks cited at Chapter 10, note 7 and Chapter 11, note 4
(pp. 311, 313 below).

3   Handel's London – social, political and intellectual contexts

1   For examples of this approach to British history, see Linda Colley,
    Britons: Forging the Nation, 1707–1837 (London, 1992); and John Brewer,
    Party Ideology and Popular Politics at the Accession of George III
    (Cambridge, 1985).

2   *The Devil to pay at St. James's*, quoted in Gibson, *Academy*, p. 428: see also
    The Miscellaneous Works of the Late Dr. Arbuthnot (2 vols., Glasgow, 1750),
    vol. I, pp. 213–23 (the attribution to Arbuthnot has been discounted).

3   See W. L. MacDonald, *Pope and his Critics: A Study in Eighteenth-Century
    Personalities* (London, 1951).

4   William Holmes, *The Trial of Doctor Sacheverell* (London, 1973), and Weber,
    Classics, pp. 96, 106–8.

5   Donald Burrows, 'Handel and Hanover' in Williams, *Bach, Handel, Scarlatti*,
    pp. 35–59.

6   It is important to remember that he came from a family of standing in Halle:
    his father was a respected physician and his brother became Valet de
    Chambre to the Duke of Saxe-Weissenfels. See Coxe, *Anecdotes*, p. 4, and
    Werner Piechocki, 'Die Familie Händel in der Stadt Halle', *HJb* 33 (1987),
    pp. 91–108 and *HJb* 36 (1990), pp. 200–21.

7   R. O. Bucholz, *The Augustan Court: Queen Anne and the Decline of Court
    Culture* (Stanford, 1993).

8   *The Weekly Journal: or, Saturday's Post*, 18 December 1725, quoted in Gibson,
    Academy, p. 388.

9   See John Brewer and Roy Porter, eds., *Consumption and the World of Goods*
    (London, 1993).

10 See David R. Ringrose, 'Capital Cities and Urban Networks in the Early
    Modern Period', in Bernard Lepetit and Peter Clark (eds.), *European Capital
    Cities* (Cambridge, forthcoming).

11 See Weber, *Classics*, Chapter 9.

12 Otto G. Schindler, *Das Burgtheater und sein Publikum* (2 vols., Vienna, 1976).
    Compare also the social separation inherent in the design of the Venetian
    theatres, described in Chapter 2.

13 See William Weber, 'The Myth of Mozart as Revolutionary', *MQ* 78 (1994),
    pp. 34–47.

14 Compare, for example, J. C. D. Clark in *English Society, 1688–1832: Ideology,
    Social Structure and Political Practice in the Ancien Régime* (Cambridge,
    1985) with Roy Porter in *English Society in the Eighteenth Century*
    (Harmondsworth, 1982); Linda Colley presents something of a middle
    ground in *Britons*.

15 See especially MacDonald, *Pope*; John Loftis, *The Politics of Drama in
    Augustan England* (Oxford, 1963); and Bernard A. Goldgar, *Walpole and the
    Wits: The Relations of Politics to Literature, 1722–42* (Lincoln, Nebr., 1976).

16   See Price, 'English Traditions in Handel's "Rinaldo"' in Sadie & Hicks, *Tercentenary Collection*, pp. 120–37; and Price, 'Political Allegory in Late-Seventeenth-Century English Opera', in Fortune, *Music & Theatre*, pp. 1–29.

17   For lists of the directors, and some of the subscribers, see Gibson, *Academy*. Carole Taylor offers lists of opera subscribers from the later period in 'From Losses to Lawsuit: Patronage of the Italian Opera in London by Lord Middlesex, 1739–45', *ML* 68 (1987), pp. 1–26.

18   Donald Burrows and Robert D. Hume, 'George I, the Haymarket Opera Company and Handel's Water Music', *EM* 19 (1991), pp. 323–41.

19   Ragnhild Hatton, *George I: Elector and King* (London, 1978) revealed the intelligence and political acumen of George I, in contrast to his received image as a rather boorish monarch.

20   Winton Dean tended to be sceptical of religious elements in Dean, *Oratorios*, but Ruth Smith began work in a new direction with 'Intellectual Contexts of Handel's English Oratorios', in Hogwood & Luckett, *18th Century*, pp. 115–34, and R. Smith, *Oratorios*. See also Alexander H. Shapiro, ''Drama of an Infinitely Superior Nature': Handel's Early English Oratorios and the Religious Sublime', *ML* 74 (1993), pp. 215–45.

21   Historians now take the impact of religious issues more seriously than their secular-minded colleagues tended to do a few decades ago. Conrad Russell has argued for religious division as the one long-term cause for the Civil War: see *Causes of the Civil War* (Oxford, 1990). Clark, in *English Society*, has likewise reviewed an extensive bibliography of sermons and early histories from the seventeenth and eighteenth centuries to show how integral religion was within English politics in that period, though his case may be somewhat exaggerated: Linda Colley presents a more balanced viewpoint in *Britons*, stressing the centrality of Protestantism to how the English perceived themselves.

22   John Bossy, *Christianity in the West, 1400–1700* (Oxford, 1985).

23   See Bennet Zon, 'Plain Chant in the Eighteenth-Century Roman Catholic Church in England 1737–1834', (D.Phil. diss., University of Oxford, 1993).

24   Colley, *Britons*, p. 25.

25   *The Devil to pay at St. James's*, quoted in Gibson, *Academy*, p. 429.

26   John Pocock, 'Clergy and Commerce: The Conservative Enlightenment in England', in *L'Età dei lumi: Studi storici sul settecento europeo in onore di Franco Venturi* (2 vols., Naples, 1985), vol. I, pp. 523–62; see also Roy Porter, 'The Enlightenment in England', in Roy Porter and Mikuláš Teich (eds.), *The Enlightenment in National Perspective* (Cambridge, 1981), pp. 1–18; and A. Guerrini, 'The Tory Newtonians: Gregory, Pitcairne and their Circle', *Journal of British Studies*, 25 (1986), pp. 301–21.

27   On Addison, Steele and Handel, see Henrik Knif, *Gentlemen and Spectators: Studies in Journals, Opera and the Social Scene in Late Stuart London* (Helsinki, Finnish Historical Society, 1995).

28   See Smith, 'Intellectual Contexts'.

29   This was noted by Dorothea Siegmund-Schultze in 'Some Remarks on the Interaction between G. F. Handel, his Librettists and the Conditions of his Time', *HJb* 34 (1988), p. 124.

30 See Ruth Smith, 'The Achievements of Charles Jennens (1700–1773)', *ML* 70 (1989), pp. 161–90.

31 Carole Taylor, 'Handel's Disengagement from the Italian Opera', in Sadie & Hicks, *Tercentenary Collection*, p. 174.

32 Weber, *Classics*, chapter 3.

33 This process is described in Colley, *Britons*, and Brewer, *Party Ideology and Popular Politics*. See specifically Colley's references to Handel on pp. 31–3.

Additional bibliography

For British history in this period, see also Tim Harris, *Politics under the later Stuarts: Party Conflict in a Divided Society, 1660–1715* (London, 1993); J. H. Plumb, *The Growth of Political Stability in England, 1675–1725* (Cambridge, 1975); William Speck, *Whig and Tory: The Struggle in the Constituencies, 1701–1715* (London, 1970); John Brewer, *Sinews of Power: War, Money and the English State, 1688–1783* (London, 1989), and Linda Colley, *In Defiance of Oligarchy: The Tory Party, 1714–60* (Cambridge, 1982). For contexts of Handel's career, see Paul Henry Lang, *George Frideric Handel* (New York, 1966); Robert Manson Myers, *Handel's 'Messiah': a Touchstone of Taste* (New York, 1948); Graydon Beeks, '"A Club of Composers": Handel, Pepusch and Arbuthnot at Cannons', in Sadie and Hicks, *Tercentenary Collection*, pp, 209–21; and Burrows, *Chapel Royal*.

4 Handel's London – the theatres

1 See Edward A. Langhans, 'The Theatres', in Robert D. Hume (ed.), *The London Theatre World, 1660–1800* (Carbondale, Ill., 1980); Richard Leacroft, *The Development of the English Playhouse* (London, 1973); Graham F. Barlow, 'Vanbrugh's Queen's Theatre in the Haymarket, 1703–9', *EM* 17 (1989), pp. 515–21.

2 See Richard Southern, *Changeable Scenery* (London, 1952).

3 Judith Milhous, 'The Capacity of Vanbrugh's Theatre in the Haymarket', *Theatre History Studies*, 4 (1984), pp. 38–46.

4 On the close parallels between Covent Garden and Lincoln's Inn Fields, see John Orrell, 'Covent Garden Theatre, 1732', *Theatre Survey*, 33 (1992), pp. 35–52.

5 See Hume, 'The Sponsorship of Opera in London, 1704–1720', *Modern Philology*, 85 (1988), pp. 420–32, and Milhous, 'Opera Finances in London, 1674–1738', *JAMS* 37 (1984), pp. 567–92.

6 Virtually complete daily performance records are available after 1705 for both opera and playhouses from newspaper advertisements: they are conveniently summarised in *The London Stage*.

7 See Milhous and Hume, 'The Haymarket Opera in 1711', *EM* 17 (1989), pp. 523–37, and 'Heidegger and the Management of the Haymarket Opera, 1713–1717', *EM*, forthcoming

8 See Donald Burrows and Robert D. Hume, 'George I, the Haymarket Opera Company and Handel's *Water Music*', *EM* 19 (1991), pp. 323–41.

9 See Milhous and Hume, 'The Charter for the Royal Academy of Music', *ML*

67 (1986), pp. 50–8; and 'New Light on Handel and The Royal Academy of Music in 1720', *TJ* 35 (1983), pp. 149–67.

10 On the Royal Academy's subscribers and patrons, see Gibson, *Academy*.

11 See Hume, 'Handel and Opera Management in London in the 1730s', *ML* 67 (1986), pp. 347–62.

12 See Milhous and Hume, 'Box Office Reports for Five Operas Mounted by Handel in London, 1732–1734', *Harvard Library Bulletin*, 26 (1978), pp. 245–66; and 'Handel's Opera Finances in 1732–3', *MT* 125 (1984), pp. 86–9.

13 See Milhous and Hume, 'Opera Salaries in Eighteenth-Century London', *JAMS* 46 (1993), pp. 26–83. For convenient biographical accounts of both major and minor operatic performers in Handel's time, see the relevant articles in *Biographical Dictionary* and *New Grove Opera*.

14 *Vice Chamberlain Coke*, document no. 123.

15 For example, the Privy Purse papers imply that George I attended Handel's *Admeto* 19 times between 30 January and 18 April 1727. See Burrows and Hume, 'George I'.

16 See, for example, *The Daily Courant*, 23 November 1720 and 22 January 1723.

17 Milhous and Hume, 'John Rich's Covent Garden Account Books for 1735–36', *Theatre Survey*, 31 (1990), pp. 200–41, esp. p. 218.

5 Handel's London – British musicians and London concert life

1 Hawkins, *History*, vol. II, p. 787.

2 See Stoddard Lincoln, 'A Congreve Masque', *MT* 113 (1972), pp. 1078–81. All three settings are discussed by Richard Platt in H. Diack Johnstone and Roger Fiske (eds.), *The Blackwell History of Music in Britain*, vol. IV: *The Eighteenth Century* (Oxford, 1990), pp. 97–103.

3 For a detailed comparison of both (and also the 1709 Croft setting), see Burrows, 'Chapel Royal', vol. I, pp. 106–39, and especially Table 1 (pp. 108–13).

4 Lbl Harleian MS 7342, fol. 12; for the context of this remark see Christopher Hogwood, 'Thomas Tudway's History of Music', in Hogwood & Luckett, *18th Century*, pp. 44–5.

5 See Curtis Price, 'Handel and The Alchemist: His First Contribution to the London Theatre', *MT* 116 (1975), pp. 787–8.

6 Mainwaring, *Memoirs*, p. 78.

7 Abel Boyer, *The History of the Reign of Queen Anne, digested into Annals* (11 vols., London, 1703–13), vol. IX, p. 335; also in Boyer, *The Political State of Great Britain*, vol. 1 (1711), p. 156 (see *HHB* vol. IV, pp. 47–8).

8 See Burrows, 'Chapel Royal', vol. I, pp. 140–51.

9 Deutsch, *Handel*, p. 299. Handel himself was one of the subscribers to *The Works of the late Aaron Hill*, published in four volumes in 1753.

10 See Deutsch, *Handel*, pp. 44–5. For Hughes's view on the combination of English words with Italian-style music, see Malcolm Boyd, 'John Hughes on Opera', *ML* 52 (1971), pp. 383–6.

11 See Brian Trowell, 'Acis, Galatea and Polyphemus: A "serenata a tre voci"?' in

Fortune, *Music & Theatre*, pp. 31–93, esp. pp. 82–93. *Venus and Adonis* (HWV 85) is included in Donald Burrows (ed.), *G. F. Handel: Songs and Cantatas for Soprano and Continuo* (Oxford, 1988): while Handel is known to have set Hughes's text, the identity of the composer of these two songs (the only surviving settings) is uncertain.

12   Gary C. Thomas, in 'Was George Frideric Handel Gay?: On Closet Questions and Cultural Politics', in Philip Brett, Elizabeth Wood and Gary C. Thomas (eds.), *Queering the Pitch: The New Gay and Lesbian Musicology* (New York and London, 1994), pp. 177–8, argues that this was also a 'homoerotic milieu'. However, it is difficult to interpret the significance of single-sex relationships from an age in which women were not expected to have an intellectual life of their own and, if they did, it was assumed that they would not wish (or be able) to share it with men: as a result, such intellectual groups were almost invariably single-sex.

13   Hawkins, *History*, vol. II, pp. 852n., 859. Hawkins's reference (p. 852n.) to Mattheson's recently published keyboard pieces being played on one such occasion would seem to place this in 1714, but the association clearly goes back at least to late 1712.

14   Burney, *Commemoration*, 'Sketch', p. 33 note 'a'.

15   Deutsch, *Handel*, p. 173.

16   Hawkins, *History*, vol. II., p. 879.

17   Burney, *History*, vol. II, p. 489.

18   Hawkins, *History*, vol. II, p. 879; see also p. 884. Cf. Burney, *Commemoration*, 'Sketch', p. 33.

19   Deutsch, *Handel*, p. 354; my italics. See also Mattheson, *Grundlage*, quoted in translation by Deutsch, p. 505. The pamphlet *Harmony in an Uproar*, from which this passage comes, is sometimes attributed – on no sound basis – to George Arbuthnot, in whose *Miscellaneous Works* (Glasgow, 1751) it was included. Whoever wrote it obviously had inside information.

20   See Robert Elkin, *The Old Concert Rooms of London* (London, 1955), pp. 29–49; also Bertha Harrison, 'A Forgotten Concert Room', *MT* 47 (1906), pp. 602–5, 669–72; and 'The Oldest Concert Room in London', *Monthly Musical Record*, 39 (1909), pp. 55–6.

21   Deutsch, *Handel*, p. 57.

22   See Deutsch, *Handel*, p. 363.

23   Hawkins, *History*, vol. II, p. 700; see also Curtis Price, 'The Small-Coal Cult', *MT* 119 (1978), pp. 1032–4.

24   See Deutsch, *Handel*, p. 65, and Hawkins, *History*, vol. II, p. 847.

25   See Deutsch, *Handel*, p. 459; also Pippa Drummond, 'The Royal Society of Musicians in the Eighteenth Century', *ML* 59 (1978), pp. 268–89, and Betty Matthews, *The Royal Society of Musicians of Great Britain* (London, 1985).

26   Burney, *History*, vol. II, p. 388; cf. Hawkins, *History*, vol. II, pp. 745–6.

27   *The Daily Journal*, 16 January 1731; the source given in *The London Stage*, Part 3, vol. I, p. 109, is wrong.

28   Lbl Add. MS 11732, fols. 11–12. The fullest and most accurate account of the Academy of Ancient Music so far published is to be found in Weber, *Classics*, pp. 56–74.

29   Lbl Add. MS 11732, fol. 16.

30   For further details, see Johnstone and Fiske (eds.), *The Blackwell History of Music in Britain*, vol. IV, pp. 36–8.

31   See Deutsch, *Handel*, pp. 498–9.

32   *Ibid.*, p. 217.

33   See Edmund Hobhouse (ed.), *The Diary of a West Country Physician* [Dr Claver Morris], *A.D. 1684–1726* (Rochester, 1934), p. 107.

34   See Deutsch, *Handel*, pp. 316–29.

35   See H. Diack Johnstone, 'The Chandos Anthems: The Authorship of no. 12', *MT* 117 (1976), pp. 601–3; also *MT* 129 (1988), p. 489. The anthem in question appears in *HHB* as HWV 257, and the music is to be found in *HG* vol. 36 (1872).

36   For details, see Warwick Wroth, *The London Pleasure Gardens of the Eighteenth Century* (London, 1896; facsimile reprint 1979); also Mollie Sands, *Invitation to Ranelagh, 1742–1803* (London, 1946) and *The Eighteenth-Century Pleasure Gardens of Marylebone* (London, 1987).

37   See Smith, *Walsh I*; Smith, *Walsh II*; and Smith, *Handel*.

38   Burney, *Commemoration*, 'Sketch', p. 33 (note carried over from p. 32).

39   Hawkins, *History*, vol. II, p. 884.

40   As recorded by Samuel Wesley in Lbl Add. MS 27593, fol. 35; wording slightly altered. See also William Linley, in the preface to his *Eight Glees* [1832].

41   Burney, *History*, vol. II, pp. 1010–11.

42   Burney, *Commemoration*, 'Sketch', p. 31.

43   Mantel (originally Johann Christian Scheidemantel) was born, the youngest of eleven children, near Erfurt in May 1706. He studied theology at Erfurt University but left when, in 1732, his parents died. It was evidently not long afterwards that he emigrated to Britain where, having shed the first half of his surname and exchanged Johann for John, he turns up – conceivably at Handel's suggestion – as organist of St Mary's Church, South Benfleet, Essex. In 1738, he subscribed to the publication of Handel's *Faramondo* (see Deutsch, *Handel*, p. 450); ten years later he moved to a better-paid organist's post at Great Yarmouth, where he died in 1761. This information is derived from the joint research of David Galbraith and Robert Hallmann, and I thank them for their ready willingness to share their results.

44   Westminster Public Library, MS C. 768: Vestry Minutes of St George's, Hanover Square, April 1741–June 1752, p. 93. Handel is named in the Vestry Minutes of 27 October 1725 (MS C. 766, p. 33) as one of five possible judges, but he evidently chose not to serve; see Deutsch, *Handel*, p. 188 and Vernon Butcher, 'Thomas Roseingrave', *ML* 19 (1938), pp. 280–94.

45   See Richard Platt, 'Plagiarism or Emulation: the Gerard Smith Organ Contract for St George's Church, Hanover Square'; *Journal of the British Institute of Organ Studies*, 17 (1993), pp. 32–46; also Deutsch, *Handel*, pp. 138, 259.

46   See Mark Argent (ed.), *Recollections of R. J. S. Stevens, An Organist in Georgian London* (London, 1992), p. 212.

47   Mary Nash, *The Provoked Wife: The Life and Times of Susannah Cibber* (London, 1977), p. 176.

48   Modern edn: *G. F. Handel: Songs and Cantatas for Soprano and Continuo* (see note 11 above).

49   See Deutsch, *Handel*, pp. 819–20.

50   For details, see Carl Morey, 'Alexander Gordon, Scholar and Singer', *ML* 46 (1965), pp. 332–5.

51   In Johnstone and Fiske (eds.), *Blackwell History of Music in Britain*, vol. IV (1990).

52   It is probably not entirely coincidental that Handel began work on *L'Allegro* on 19 January 1740, just seven weeks after the successful revival of Arne's *Comus* (first performed 4 March 1738). For more on the relationship of these two works, see Roger Fiske, *English Theatre Music in the Eighteenth Century* (London, 1973), pp. 181–3.

53   See Franklin B. Zimmerman, 'Purcellian Passages in the Compositions of G. F. Handel', in Hogwood & Luckett, *18th Century*, pp. 49–58; also 'Handel's Purcellian Borrowing in His Later Operas and Oratorios', in Walter Gerstenberg, Jan LaRue and Wolfgang Rehm (eds.), *Festschrift Otto Erich Deutsch zum 80. Geburtstag.* (Kassel, 1966), pp. 20–30. In neither case, however, is this particular example mentioned (though it is in Dean, *Oratorios*, p. 566).

Additional bibliography

Simon Heighes, *The Lives and Works of William and Philip Hayes* (New York and London, 1995); H. Diack Johnstone, 'The Life and Work of Maurice Greene', *(1696–1755)* (2 vols., D.Phil. diss., University of Oxford, 1967).

6   Handel's London – Italian music and musicians

1   Henry Purcell, *Sonnata's of III Parts* (London, 1683), Preface.

2   John Macky, *A Journey through England* (London, 1714), pp. 109–10.

3   'Notes of Comparison between Elder and Later Musick and Somewhat Historicall of both' [*c.* 1726], *Roger North on Music*, ed. John Wilson (London, 1959), pp. 307–11.

4   See Hans Joachim Marx, 'Some Unknown Embellishments of Corelli's Violin Sonatas', *MQ* 61 (1975), pp. 65–76; Owain Edwards, 'The Response to Corelli's Music in Eighteenth-Century England', *Studia Musicologica Norvegica*, 2 (1976), pp. 51–96; Denis Arnold, 'The Corellian Cult in England', *Nuovi Studi Corelliani: Atti del Secondo Congresso Internazionale, Fusignano, 5–8 Settembre 1974*, Quaderni della Rivista Italiana di Musicologia, 4 (1978), pp. 81–8; and Weber, *Classics*, pp. 74–89.

5   Johann Mattheson, *Das neu-eröffnete Orchestre* (Hamburg, 1713), p. 211: '*In Summa*: Wer bey diesen Zeiten etwas in der *Music* zu *praestiren* vermeinet, der begibt sich nach *Engelland*. In Italien und Franckreich ist was zu hören und zu lernen; in Engelland was zu verdienen; im Vaterlande aber am besten zu verzehren.'

6   The Italians employed by Charles II were forced to flee after the discovery of the Popish Plot of 1679; those in the Roman Catholic chapel of James II had to flee with him after the Glorious Revolution of 1688. See Margaret Mabbett, 'Italian Musicians in Restoration England (1660–90)', *ML* 67 (1986), pp. 237–47.

7   *The London Stage*, Part I, pp. 417, 428–9. A letter-writer's comments concerning the Italian lady are published in Curtis A. Price, 'The Critical Decade for English Music Drama, 1700–10', *Harvard Library Bulletin*, 26 (1978), p. 41, n.10, and partly published and discussed in Donald F. Cook, 'Françoise Marguérite de l'Epine: The Italian Lady?', *TN* 35 (1981), pp. 58–60.

8   'Il paradiso terrestre', according to a letter from Luigi Mancia to Cosimi, written in Düsseldorf on 15 January 1702 [possibly 1702/3], and carried to London by the alto Carlo Luigi Pietra Grua: see Lowell Lindgren, 'Nicola Cosimi in London, 1701–5', *SM* 11 (1982), p. 237, and Lindgren, 'The Accomplishments of the Learned and Ingenious Nicola Francesco Haym (1678–1729)', *SM* 16 (1987), pp. 252–5.

9   Eight rosters are printed in *Vice Chamberlain Coke*, pp. 30–4, 118–19, 127–8, 151–2, 158–61, 179–80, and three are in Milhous and Hume, 'New Light on Handel and The Royal Academy of Music in 1720', *TJ* 35 (1983), pp. 157–61.

10 They are the main source for the information concerning concerts given in *The London Stage*, *Biographical Dictionary* and Michael Tilmouth, 'A Calendar of References to Music in Newspapers Published in London and the Provinces, 1660–1719', in *Royal Musical Association Research Chronicle*, 1 (1961), entire issue, and 2 (1962), pp. 1–15.

11 See the summary given in Elizabeth Gibson, 'Italian Opera in London, 1750–75: Management and Finances', *EM* 18 (1990), p. 48. Gibson does not mention Ricciarelli, but he and Giardini are listed as 'Associates' for 1756–7 in Mingotti, *A Second Appeal to the Publick* (London [1756]), p. 9. Gibson lists Paradisi and Vanneschi only for an unused licence of 17 January 1752, while they are listed together for 1753–6 in *New Grove Opera*, under 'Paradies, (Pietro) Domenico'.

12 See Enrico Careri, *Francesco Geminiani (1687–1762)* (Oxford, 1993); Geminiani's directorship is discussed on p. 16, and eight of his illustrious students are named on pp. 19–20.

13 See Roberts, *Handel Sources*; John H. Roberts, 'Handel and Vinci's "Didone Abbandonata": Revisions and Borrowings', *ML* 68 (1987), pp. 141–50; and John H. Roberts, 'Handel and Charles Jennens's Italian Opera Manuscripts', in Fortune, *Music & Theatre*, pp. 159–202. Borrowing occurred at all points in Handel's career, as noted in Stanley Sadie, review of Roberts, *Handel Sources*, *EM* 17 (1989), pp. 103–6. Handel's contemporaries accused him of plagiarism, but they were unsure of his sources, and thus questioned the accusations, according to Antoine-François Prévost, *Le pour et contre* (1733); see Deutsch, *Handel*, pp. 333–4.

14 See George Dorris, *Paolo Rolli and the Italian Circle in London, 1715–44* (The

Hague, 1967), and Paolo Rolli, *Libretti per musica*, ed. Carlo Caruso (Milan, 1993).

15 See *New Grove Opera*, 'Cori, Angelo' and 'Vanneschi, Francesco'. Vanneschi was excoriated in Giuseppe Baretti, *The Voice of Discord* (London, 1753), and in Mingotti, *An Appeal to the Publick* and *A Second Appeal to the Publick* (London [1755, 1756]).

16 See the poem by Lord Halifax, printed in *Biographical Dictionary*, vol. IV, p. 294. She was also identified as 'Tuscan' in a poem in *The Diverting Post*, 20 January 1705.

17 George Farquhar, *The Beaux Stratagem*, Act III, Scene 2 (London, 1707), p. 25.

18 *Heraclitus Ridens*, 12 February 1704. Tofts subsequently disclaimed all responsibility for the actions of her 'late' servant, whom she asked Rich to prosecute, 'that she may be punish'd as she deserves'. Tofts's letter, printed in *The Daily Courant*, 8 February 1704, has been reprinted in Mollie Sands, 'Mrs. Tofts, 1685?-1756', *TN* 20 (1966–7), p. 103, and partly in *The London Stage*, Part II, p. 56.

19 John Downes, *Roscius Anglicanus* (1708), ed. Judith Milhous and Robert D. Hume (London, 1987), p. 99. *Arsinoe* and *Ergasto* were respectively composed by Thomas Clayton and Jakob Greber, each of whom had been in Italy.

20 Evidence for L'Epine's performance in April 1706 is in *Vice Chamberlain Coke*, p. 3; that for Valentino's performance in December 1706 is in the preface to Mary de la Rivière Manley, *Almyna: or, the Arabian Vow* (London, 1707), fol. 2r–v. The performance on 6 December 1707 with L'Epine as Prenesto (partly in Italian), Valentino (in Italian) and Joanna Maria (mostly in Italian) is listed in *The London Stage*, Part II, p. 160. For a facsimile of the only extant score in English, see Giovanni Bononcini, *Camilla: Royal College of Music, MS 779*, with introduction by Lowell Lindgren, Music for London Entertainment, 1660–1800, E/1 (London, 1990).

21 *Vice Chamberlain Coke*, p. 99.

22 Without him the opera floundered badly in 1714–15; see the letter of 18 March 1715 from Giuseppe Como to Cosimi, printed in Lindgren, 'Nicola Cosimi in London', p. 246, and that of 8 June 1715 from Giovanni Battista Primoli to Giuseppe Riva, in Modena, Biblioteca Estense e Universitaria, Campori Z.4.3: 'Già mi è nota l'impazienza con cui costi si stava aspettando il Cav.r Nicolino, mentre si spera ch'egli rimetterà in piedi l'opere già caduto con tanto pregiudizio degl'Impresarij.'

23 *Vice Chamberlain Coke*, p. 120: Swiney, the manager, proposed to 'pay him £150 for a fair Score with the words & parts of an Opera to be by him fitted for the English stage every Season, if such Opera's shall be approved of'. Troupes of comic singers typically managed their own productions; for the first five seasons of 'burlettas' in London (1748–50 and 1753–6) see Sybil Rosenfeld, *Foreign Theatrical Companies in Great Britain in the 17th and 18th Centuries*, Society for Theatre Research, Pamphlet Series no. 4 (London, 1955), pp. 32–7, and the article cited in note 45 below.

24   See Richard Steele in *The Tatler*, 3 January 1710, and Joseph Addison in *The Spectator*, 15 March 1711; they are reprinted in *Biographical Dictionary*, vol. XI, pp. 25–30.

25   Gay's letter and the anonymous poem are reprinted in Deutsch, *Handel*, pp. 149, 163–70.

26   Letter of 25 September 1722 from Lord Perceval to Alexander Pope, printed in Pope, *Correspondence*, ed. George Sherburn (5 vols., Oxford, 1956), vol. II, p. 136. Most evidence for teaching by Italians is found in such incidental remarks and in expense diaries. Published mentions are rare: two examples are in *The Daily Post*, 23 December 1730, where Bononcini is named as the teacher of a singer and her brother, the violinist John Clegg, and in *The Daily Advertiser*, 10 May 1745, where Bononcini is named as the teacher of Mrs Davis, a singer, who may well be the unnamed sister of Clegg.

27   See Owain Edwards, 'Espionage, a Collection of Violins and *Le Bizzarie Universali*: A Fresh Look at William Corbett', *MQ* 73 (1989), pp. 331–2.

28   See 'Rochetti, (Gaetano) Filippo', in *New Grove Opera*. Rochetti sang in London until 1744, then in Edinburgh in the 1750s. The other six Italian tenors who portrayed serious roles in Handel's London stayed no more than one or two seasons.

29   According to Burney, *History*, vol. II, p. 876, Guadagni's 'ideas of acting were taken ... from [David] Garrick, who, when he performed in an English opera called the *Fairies*, took as much pleasure in forming him as an actor, as Gizziello [Gioacchino Conti] did afterwards in polishing his style of singing'. His role of Lysander was originally intended for another Italian, Rosa Curioni, who later created Ferdinand in Smith's *The Tempest* (Drury Lane, February 1756); see *New Grove Opera*, 'Curioni, Rosa'.

30   *Biographical Dictionary*, vol. VI, pp. 104–12.

31   Rosenfeld, *Foreign Theatrical Companies*, pp. 14–17.

32   See *Biographical Dictionary*, 'Fausan' and 'Rinaldi, Antonio'.

33   *Ibid.*, vol. V, pp. 187–8.

34   They are listed in Smith, *Walsh II*, pp. 176–80. According to the titles of vols. II–VIII, their contents are 'opera dances as perform'd ... at the King's Theatre in the Hay Market'.

35   Judith Milhous, 'Hasse's "Comic Tunes": Some Dancers and Dance Music on the London Stage, 1740–59', *Dance Research*, 2/2 (1984), pp. 41–55.

36   Deutsch, *Handel*, pp. 35–8, reprints passages from *The Spectator*, 6 and 16 March 1711.

37   *The Spectator*, 18 April 1711, cited in Lowell Lindgren, 'The Staging of Handel's Operas in London', in Sadie & Hicks, *Tercentenary Collection*, p. 113.

38   Lindgren, 'The Staging of Handel's Operas', pp. 94–5, 98.

39   They are discussed and reproduced in Lindgren, 'The Accomplishments of Nicola Francesco Haym', pp. 268–9 and Plates 1–2.

40   Lindgren, 'The Staging of Handel's Operas', p. 95 and n. 16.

41   *Ibid.*, n. 27, cites the report of Servandoni's activities in London from the *Mercure de France* for October 1726.

42   *Ibid.*, p. 105. For conjectures about Devoto's country of birth, see Edward

Croft-Murray, *John Devoto: A Baroque Scene Painter*, Society for Theatre Research, Pamphlet Series, no. 2 (London, 1953), pp. 5–6.

43 Edward Croft-Murray, *Decorative Painting in England, 1537–1837* (2 vols., London, 1962–70), vol. II, p. 164. He was reportedly in England in 1729–39 and 1741–2; see *New Grove Opera*, 'Amiconi, Jacopo'.

44 See Lowell Lindgren, 'Musicians and Librettists in the Correspondence of Gio. Giacomo Zamboni (Oxford, Bodleian Library, MSS Rawlinson Letters 116–138)', *Royal Musical Association Research Chronicle*, 24 (1991).

45 See Richard G. King and Saskia Willaert, 'Giovanni Francesco Crosa and the First Italian Comic Operas in London, Brussels and Amsterdam, 1748–50', *JRMA* 118 (1993), pp. 246–75.

46 *The Post Boy*, 20 November 1697, cited in *New Grove*, 'Kremberg, Jacob'.

47 [Francis Fleming,] *The Life and Extraordinary Adventures, the Perils and Critical Escapes, of Timothy Ginnadrake, that Child of Chequer'd Fortune* (3 vols., Bath [1771]), vol. II, pp. 91–2.

48 John Evelyn, *Diary*, ed. E. S. de Beer (6 vols., Oxford, 1955), vol. IV, p. 270. Evelyn also recorded when he heard of others who had 'lately been roming in *Italy*': Mrs. Knight on 1 December 1674 (vol. IV, p. 49), Mr. Pordage on 27 January 1685 (vol. IV, p. 403), and Mr. Pate on 30 May 1698 (vol. V, p. 289).

49 *Biographical Dictionary*, vol. I, pp. 6–9, doubts the 1715 billing of 'lately return'd from Italy', but Abell advertised his return 'to his Native Country, after having had the Honour of Singing in most Parts of Europe to the greatest Princes and the Nobility', in *The Daily Courant*, 26 and 30 May 1715. I am grateful to Judith Milhous and Robert D. Hume for informing me of Abell's advertisement.

50 *The Daily Post*, 2–5 December 1719. The same billing is utilised in the advertisement for his next concert; see *ibid.*, 18 January 1720.

51 *New Grove Opera*, 'Gordon, Alexander'.

52 *New Grove*, 'Roseingrave, Thomas'.

53 Burney, *History*, vol. II, p. 704.

54 See Martin Medforth, 'The Valentines of Leicester: A Reappraisal of an 18th-Century Musical Family', *MT* 122 (1981), pp. 812–5.

55 See Henry Foley, *Records of the English Province of the Society of Jesus* (7 vols. in 8, London, 1875–83), vol. VI, nos. 1205, 1230, which concern two of their sons, Joseph and Josiah, born at Rome in 1713 and 1719, respectively.

56 *The Daily Courant*, 18 March 1724. While in London, Corbett advertised items for sale in *The Daily Journal*, 16 and 18 May 1724: 'a Series of the finest Instruments' by named makers, 'several hundred of original Manuscripts' in named musical genres, and 'a small Collection of Pictures, Medals and some Drawings, with Valuable Books of the Theory of Musick, and others of different Languages'.

57 *Do you know what you are about, or, A Protestant Alarm to Great Britain* (London, 1733), p. 15: 'He must be ignorant indeed who knows not that *C-rb-t*, under the disguise of a Fiddler, has for many Years past acted the Spy and shamm'd the Madman, to hide the Cunning Fellow, for he is no Fool I assure you. Upon what Motive could he quit a very considerable Business,

leave a Place, where he was in Eminence and Respect, to go a Strolling into a
Country where he was sure of finding so many superiors in his Profession: It
may be objected, he did it for Improvement; to which I Answer, he is so far
from being improv'd, that he has almost forgot what he was then Master of;
besides, how could he support himself? not by his Fiddle, 'tis very well
known, he gets nothing by that in *Italy*. In short my Conjecture is so
probable, there is no need for any body to draw other Conclusions, the Thing
explains itself.' Only the first sentence of this passage is cited in William C.
Smith, 'Do you know what you are about?: A Rare Handelian Pamphlet', *The
Music Review*, 25 (1964), p. 117. This passage was unknown to Edwards, who
discussed the possibility that Corbett was a spy in 'Espionage' (see note 27,
above), pp. 335–7.

58   *Do you know what you are about*, pp. 16–22, names G[eminia]ni,
     S[en]esi[n]o, Porta, Attilio (Ariosti), Catsoni (= Cuzzoni), and
     'G[a]mb[a]r[i]ni, the Picture-monger' (conjecturally the father of the
     composer Elisabetta Gambarini). All but Gambarini are named in the
     abbreviated version given in Smith, 'Do you know', pp. 117–18.

59   See Gibson, *Academy*, pp. 166–72, for a summary of Bononcini's familiarity
     with notorious Jacobites; his ties forestalled further operatic commissions
     for him during the year following the Jacobite plot of spring 1722. Similar
     ties may have been largely responsible for the termination of Rolli's
     appointment to the Royal Academy of Music in spring 1722.

60   Evelyn, *Diary*, vol. V, p. 531 (28 February 1703). This singer may have been
     Joanna Maria, Baroness Linchenham, but may instead have been Anna, the
     wife of Francesco Lodi, or Maria Margherita Gallia, the wife of Giuseppe
     Fedeli detto Saggione.

61   *Roscius Anglicanus* (see note 19 above), p. 97.

62   Judith Milhous and Robert D. Hume, 'Opera Salaries in Eighteenth-Century
     London', *JAMS* 46 (1993), pp. 26–83.

63   *Vice Chamberlain Coke*, pp. 116, 120–1, 139–42.

64   See, for example, Judith Milhous, 'Opera Finances in London, 1674–1738',
     JAMS 37 (1984), pp. 567–92; Sybil Rosenfeld, 'An Opera House Account
     Book [for 1716–17]', *TN* 16 (1964–5), pp. 83–8; Gibson, *Academy*, pp. 121–7,
     311–33; Judith Milhous and Robert D. Hume, 'Box Office Reports for Five
     Operas Mounted by Handel in London, 1732–4', *Harvard Library Bulletin*, 26
     (1978), pp. 245–66; Milhous and Hume, 'Handel's Opera Finances in
     1732–3', *MT* 125 (1984), pp. 86–9; Carole Taylor, 'From Losses to Lawsuit:
     Patronage of the Italian Opera in London by Lord Middlesex, 1739–45',
     ML 68 (1987), pp. 1–25; and Gibson, 'Italian Opera in London, 1750–75',
     pp. 47–59.

65   Lowell Lindgren, 'Ariosti's London Years, 1716–29', *ML* 62 (1981), pp. 346–7.

66   Gildon, *The Life of Mr. Thomas Betterton* (London, 1710), pp. 143–4.

67   For a list and summary of such attacks, see Lowell Lindgren, 'Critiques of
     Opera in London, 1705–19', in Alberto Colzani, Norbert Dubowy, Andrea
     Luppi and Maurizio Padoan (eds.), *Il melodramma italiano in Italia e in
     Germania nell'età barocca* (Como, 1995), pp. 145–65.

68 A fine survey of the masques of 1715–18 is given in Dean, *Oratorios*, pp. 155–9.

69 See Lowell Lindgren '"Camilla" and "The Beggar's Opera"', *Philological Quarterly*, 59 (1980), pp. 44–61.

70 See Phillip Lord, 'The English–Italian Opera Companies, 1732–3', *ML* 45 (1964), pp. 239–51.

7 Handel's English librettists

1 For fuller discussion of Handel's English librettists see R. Smith, *Oratorios*. On Jennens, see further Ruth Smith, 'The Achievements of Charles Jennens (1700–1773)', *ML* 70 (1989), pp. 161–90. One indication of the librettists' relative financial situations is suggested by the first codicil of Handel's will (Deutsch, *Handel,* p. 776). He left bequests to Hamilton and Morell; Humphreys and Miller predeceased him. Jennens, to whom he left two portraits by Balthasar Denner (Deutsch, *Handel,* p. 789), was immensely rich and owned one of the largest picture collections in England.

2 *Historic Manuscripts Commission*, 15th Report, App., Pt. II, Hodgkin MSS, p. 92; cited in Deutsch, *Handel,* p. 851.

3 Deutsch, *Handel,* p. 590–6.

4 John Nichols, *Literary Anecdotes of the Eighteenth Century* (2nd edn: 9 vols., London, 1812–15), vol. I, pp. 651–6; vol. III, pp. 89–91; vol. IV, pp. 599–603; vol. V, pp. 251–2, 711–12; vol. IX, p. 789. Nichols is not always a reliable source.

5 The best account is Paula O'Brien, 'The Life and Works of James Miller' (Ph.D. diss., University of London, 1979).

6 See further R. Smith, *Oratorios,* Chapter 6.

7 *Bibliotheca Historico-Sacra: or, an Historical Library of the Principal Matters relating to Religion Antient and Modern* (London, 1737; re-issued 1742, 1756),

8 The leaf in Morell's hand, dated 1735, 'I was preparing these for the Cave [the Queen's grotto] by Order' is apparently inserted opposite the title page of his *Notes and Annotations on Locke on the Human Understanding, written by order of the Queen*, which was finally published in 1794 to elucidate an edition of Locke brought out the previous year. The copies in Lbl (information from Leslie Robarts) and Cambridge University Library both have this page.

9 On Hamilton see further Ruth Loewenthal [= Smith], 'Handel and Newburgh Hamilton: New References in the Strafford Papers', *MT* 112 (1971), pp. 1063–6, and R. Smith, *Oratorios,* Chapters 8, 12.

10 See Ruth Smith, 'The Argument and Contexts of Dryden's "Alexander's Feast"', *Studies in English Literature*, 18 (1978), pp. 465–90.

11 See O'Brien, 'Miller'; *Are These Things So?* and *The Great Man's Answer*, ed. I. Gordon, Augustan Reprint Society no. 153 (Los Angeles, 1972).

12 This volume (pages numbered 1–155, with no pp. 14–15, 96–7, 100–3, 128–33, 146–7) of poems in Morell's hand, many signed with his monogram, and with annotations addressed to his wife (of which one is dated 1779, five years before his death), is now in the Osborn Collection, Yale University

Library, shelf mark Osborn Shelves c.395: see Stephen Parks, 'The Osborn Collection: a 4th Biennial Report', *Yale University Library Gazette*, 50 (1975–6), p. 182.

13   Robert Halsband, *Lord Hervey: Eighteenth Century Courtier* (Oxford, 1974), pp. 107–20.

14   Thirty lines of pentameter couplets; Osborn MS fols. 26–7.

15   MS fols. 22–3.

16   For a full account of the Excise and its reception see Paul Langford, *The Excise Crisis: Society and Politics in the Age of Walpole* (Oxford, 1975).

17   Averyl Edwards, *Frederick Louis, Prince of Wales 1707–1751* (London, 1947).

18   Undated, Osborn MS fols. 135–9, praising Frederick at fol. 137.

19   MS fols. 63–5.

20   Christine Gerrard, '*The Castle of Indolence* and the Opposition to Walpole', *Review of English Studies*, New Series no. 41 (1990), pp. 44–64.

21   See *Historical Manuscripts Commission*, 15th Report, App., Pt. II, Hodgkin MSS, p. 91; cited in Deutsch, *Handel*, p. 851.

22   See Dean, *Oratorios*, p. 87.

23   Discussed in R. Smith, *Oratorios*, Introduction.

24   The development of the libretto of *L'Allegro* can be traced through documents in the Harris papers, Hampshire Record Office, 9M73/G500/1–2, 9M73/G980/18, 9M73/G887: I am grateful to the County Archivist, Rosemary Dunhill, for bringing them to my attention. See also the letter from Jennens to his friend Edward Holdsworth, 4 February 1742, *HHB* vol. IV, p. 344.

25   For Mrs Delany as potential Handel librettist see Deutsch, *Handel*, pp. 587–8; for Upton, see Clive T. Probyn, *The Sociable Humanist: The Life and Works of James Harris 1709–1780* (Oxford, 1991), pp. 72–3. Synge's plan is transcribed in *HHB* vol. IV, pp. 353–4, and discussed in R. Smith, *Oratorios*, Introduction.

26   See Smith, 'Achievements of Charles Jennens'.

27   For discussion of Jennens's possible authorship of *Israel in Egypt* as well as *Messiah*, see R. Smith, *Oratorios*, Chapter 12.

28   On Hamilton as the possible librettist of Handel's *Semele* see Brian Trowell, 'Congreve and the 1744 Semele Libretto', *MT* 111 (1970), pp. 993–4.

29   For Italian and German precursors of English oratorio see further e.g. Dean, *Oratorios*, pp. 7, 11, 12; Howard E. Smither, *A History of the Oratorio*, vols. I and II, *The Oratorio in the Baroque Era* (Chapel Hill, N.C., 1977); Denis and Elsie Arnold, *The Oratorio in Venice*, Royal Musical Association Monographs no. 2 (London, 1986); Carolyn Gianturco, '"Cantate spirituali e morali", with a Description of the Papal Sacred Cantata Tradition for Christmas 1676–1740', *ML* 73 (1992), pp. 1–31. For drolls see Sybil Rosenfeld, *The Theatre of the London Fairs in the Eighteenth Century* (London, 1960). For mentions in poems to Handel of later oratorio subjects see e.g. Deutsch, *Handel*, pp. 139–43, 306–7, 322, 533. See also John Lockman, *Rosalinda: A Musical Drama . . . to which is prefixed, An Enquiry into the Rise and Progress of Operas and Oratorios. With some Reflections on Lyric Poetry and Music* (London, 1740), pp. xx–xxi.

30   Letter to Holdsworth, 3 March 1746, *HHB* vol. IV, p. 401. 'Sternhold and Hopkins' was *The Whole Booke of Psalmes, Collected into the Englishe Meter*, a publication more notable for its antiquity and popularity than for its literary quality: a '19th edition' was published in 1738, about 180 years after the first edition.

31   Henry Fielding, *Amelia* (London, 1751), Book IV, Chapter 9.

32   Dean, *Oratorios*, p. 392; see also *ibid.*, pp. 349, 471 and Appendix I.

33   On the printing of the librettos, see Dean, *Oratorios*, pp. 95–101.

34   John Dryden, preface to *Albion and Albanius* (1685).

35   Deutsch, *Handel*, pp. 851–3.

36   See Merlin Channon, 'Handel's Early Performances of *Judas Maccabaeus*: Some New Evidence and Interpretations', *ML* 77(1996), pp. 504–5.

37   Letter to Holdsworth, 21 February 1743, *HHB* vol. IV, p. 357.

38   Dean, *Oratorios*, p. 549.

39   King's College, Cambridge, Modern Archives, Coll. 34.11, consulted with the kind assistance of the archivist, Jacky Cox.

40   See further R. Smith, *Oratorios*.

41   Letters to Holdsworth, 10 July 1741, 2 December 1741: *HHB* vol. IV, pp. 334, 339.

42   Joseph Warton, *An Essay on the Genius and Writings of Pope* (London, 1756), quoted in Deutsch, *Handel*, p. 780.

43   Letters to Holdsworth, 7 May 1744, 26 September 1744, partly transcribed *HHB* vol. IV, pp. 376, 379: see Smith, 'The Achievements of Charles Jennens'.

44   John Loftis, *The Politics of Drama in Augustan England* (Oxford, 1963).

8   Handel and the aria

1   See, for example, the letter of the Modenese diplomat Giuseppe Riva to Ludovico Antonio Muratori, 7 September 1725: 'If your friend wishes to send some [librettos], he must know that in England they want few recitatives, but thirty arias . . .' (Deutsch, *Handel*, p. 186). The first editions of music from Handel's operas, published by Walsh and Cluer, generally contain no recitatives but all of the arias: see Smith, *Handel*.

2   So prevalent was the form of the da capo aria in eighteenth-century opera seria that in 1720 the Italian composer Benedetto Marcello, in his satirical *Il teatro alla moda*, could confine his sarcastic remarks to musical style in the aria without reference to the form at all: for Marcello, 'aria' was synonymous with the da capo form. For Marcello's text, trans. Reinhard G. Pauly, see *MQ* 34 (1948), pp. 371–404; 35 (1949), pp. 85–105.

3   The most famous eighteenth-century condemnation of the da capo aria is that found in the preface to the first edition of Gluck's *Alceste*:

> I did not think it my duty to pass quickly over the second section of an aria [the B section] in which the words are perhaps the most impassioned and important, in order to repeat regularly four times over those of the first part [the A section], and to finish the aria where its sense may perhaps not end for the convenience of the singer who wishes to show that he can capriciously vary a passage in a number of guises.

See Alfred Einstein, *Gluck*, trans. Eric Blom (London, 1936), pp. 98–100; the passage quoted is reprinted in Oliver Strunk, *Source Readings in Music History: The Classic Era* (New York, 1965), p. 100.

4   Mattheson, *Grundlage*, p. 93, trans. Deutsch, *Handel*, p. 502.

5   The scores for *Nero, Daphne* and *Florindo,* Handel's other German operas, are lost, apart from some fragments from *Florindo.*

6   The aria 'Schönste Rosen und Narcissen' follows the da capo form through the A1, A2 and B sections (the B section is even in a contrasting metre), but the return to A1 is almost immediately altered in order to bring the piece to a close only ten bars later.

7   One of the principal distinctions between German and Italian opera librettos at that time is the placement of arias within scenes: while Italian librettos are characterised by scene-ending exit arias, German librettos contain numerous scene-opening arias and medial arias. See Harris, *Librettos*, vol. I, pp. xxxiii–xxxv.

8   *Ibid.*; see also Robin F. C. Fenton, 'Almira (Hamburg, 1705): The Birth of G. F. Handel's Genius for Characterization', *HJb* 33 (1987), pp. 109–30.

9   The exact date of the premiere of *Agrippina* is not known, although it is clear that it was performed early in the Carnival season of 1709 (that is, sometime shortly after the beginning of Carnival on 26 December).

10 Bars 25–27.

11 As, for example, in the arias 'Ach wiltu die Herzen' and 'So ben che regnante'.

12 Burney, *History*, vol. II, p. 701.

13 Translated in Paul Nettl, *Forgotten Musicians* (New York, 1951; repr. New York, 1969), p. 312.

14 See LaRue, *Singers*, Chapter 4.

15 Burney, *History*, vol. II, p. 722.

16 Translated in Nettl, *Forgotten Musicians*, pp. 312–13.

17 See Strohm, *Essays*, p. 53.

18 See LaRue, *Singers*, chapter 7.

19 An examination of the parts sung by the alto castrato Francesco Bernardi (Senesino) during the Royal Academy years makes it clear that he, too, was a singer of considerable versatility as well as virtuosity, and that the roles Handel composed for him were of the 'versatile virtuoso' type; see LaRue, *Singers*, chapter 5.

20 Another comparable case is Alceste's aria 'Luci care' in *Admeto* (1727), sung before she sacrifices herself for Admeto, which follows a similar pattern, except that the abbreviated return to the A section is somewhat altered.

21 Harris, *Librettos*, vol. VII, p. xiii.

22 David Ross Hurley, 'Handel's Compositional Process: A Study of Selected Oratorios' (Ph.D. diss., University of Chicago, 1991), pp. 318–63.

23 Ultimately, the aria was rejected due to a change of cast in which the originally intended singer for the part of Bajazet was replaced by the well-known tenor Francesco Borosini: for details of this cast change and its significance to Handel's composition of *Tamerlano*, see LaRue, *Singers*, Chapter 3.

24   Handel considerably shortened the aria; see Dean, *Oratorios*, pp. 614–15.
25   See Donald Burrows, *Handel: Messiah* (Cambridge, 1991), pp. 69–70.

9   Handel's compositional process

1   The themes of this chapter are to be explored more fully in David Ross Hurley, *Handel's Compositional Choices: the Genesis of the Oratorios, 1743–1748* (Oxford, forthcoming).

2   In this chapter I use the term 'fragment' solely in reference to a piece that Handel did not complete, as distinct from pieces that Handel completed but which survive only in part.

3   There are four versions of 'The leafy honours': 1. 3/8 fragment, in the autograph of *Belshazzar*, Lbl RM 20.d.10, fols. 61v, 66r–v; 2. Complete 3/8 setting (published in *HG* vol. 19, pp. 83–91), also in RM 20.d.10; 3. Complete 12/8 setting in RM 20.f. 12, fols. 39r–42v; 4. Common-time fragment, RM 20.f.12, fol. 43r (published in *HG* vol. 46B, pp. 86–7). The first (and earliest) is the fragment under discussion; the second is the complete version of the aria as used in the first performance of the work in 1745. Recent paper studies have suggested that the third setting of 'The leafy honours' was one of the numbers for Nitocris that Handel reset *c.* 1748, probably for a revival of *Belshazzar* that never came to pass: this version was probably used in the 1751 performance. The fourth version is a fragment based on the music of 'Gentle Morpheus' in *Alceste* (HWV 45/7a).

4   We know from Handel's letters to Charles Jennens that the composition of the first two Acts (or Parts) of *Belshazzar* took place before Handel received the text of Act III. Handel began work on the score on 23 August 1745; he finished the skeleton draft of Act I on September 3 and Act II on 10 September; he returned to Act I and completed it (after much revision) on 15 September. See Dean, *Oratorios*, pp. 434–5, 452.

5   LaRue, *Singers*, Chapter 2.

6   Gerald Abraham, 'Some Points of Style', in Abraham, *Handel*, p. 266.

7   Cfm MU MSS 251–264. A description of this material is included in the Preamble to Donald Burrows and Martha Ronish, *A Catalogue of Handel's Musical Autographs* (Oxford, 1994), pp. xx-xxii.

8   See Dean, *Oratorios*, p. 87.

9   Robert Marshall, 'The Sketches', in *The Music of Johann Sebastian Bach* (New York, 1989), p. 111.

10   There are, of course, times when Handel's sketches are more extensive. See the discussion of 'As the Sun' from *Solomon* in Hurley, *Handel's Compositional Choices*, Chapter 3.

11   These include a number identified by John Roberts: see in particular Roberts, *Sources*; John H. Roberts, 'Handel's Borrowings from Telemann: An Inventory', *GHB* 1 (1984), pp. 51–76, and John H. Roberts, 'Handel's Borrowings from Keiser', *GHB* 2 (1986), pp. 147–71.

12   If the act of creating thematic material was not a completely spontaneous task for Handel, then he resides in the company of many. Haydn is said to have claimed that composition was quite easy after you found the

appropriate theme. And much later Richard Strauss claimed that 'the
melodic ideas which provide the substance of a composition seldom consist
of more than two to four bars, the remainder is elaboration, working out,
compositional technique': see Carl Dahlhaus, *Between Romanticism and
Modernism*, trans. Mary Whittall (London, 1980), p. 40.

13   See Robert Marshall, *The Compositional Process of J. S. Bach* (Princeton,
1972), p. 239.

14   The terminological confusion surrounding the word 'form' is discussed in
Mark Evan Bonds, *Wordless Rhetoric: Musical Form and the Metaphor of the
Oration* (Cambridge, Mass., 1991). As Bonds points out, two of the meanings
of the word 'form' are diametrically opposed: '"form" is commonly used to
denote those features a given work shares with a large number of others, yet
it is also often understood as the unique structure of a particular work'
(Introduction, p. 1). This terminological confusion is sometimes avoided by
using 'outer form' to denote the former and 'inner form' to denote the latter;
although 'outer form' is generally understood, 'inner form' is more
mysterious, sometimes bearing meanings that are most compatible with
nineteenth-century music. I have adopted the term 'outer form' in its most
common meaning and I use 'inner structure' to refer to smaller-scale aspects
of form, such as phrase structure, key areas, and so forth – all of which play a
role in the creation of outer form, but which can be distinguished from it.

15   This model is obviously related to Abraham's, quoted above, but it differs
in certain ways. First, the 'data' with which Handel worked was not limited
to borrowings; as I have pointed out here, sketches are similarly pre-
compositional. Second, Abraham restricts his discussion to pre-existent
matter that was used at the beginning of a piece as a way of getting started:
research by John Roberts has shown that borrowings also feature in later
parts of movements. I have argued elsewhere that these internal borrowings
are often pre-compositional, although a certain number of them may have
emerged as Handel composed (see *Handel's Compositional Choices*, Chapter
3). I am suggesting a broadening of Abraham's model, but Abraham did not
take into account the fact that large-scale form was also often a pre-
compositional decision.

16   I am grateful to John Roberts, the discoverer of this borrowing, for drawing it
to my attention.

17   Ellen Harris has identified Handel's typical harmonic patterns in 'Harmonic
Patterns in Handel's Operas', in Mary Ann Parker (ed.), *Eighteenth-Century
Music in Theory and Practice* (Stuyvesant, N.Y., 1994), pp. 77–118.

18   For this form, see Chapter 8, p. 111.

19   These attempts can be outlined as follows. In the original autograph version
(Lbl RM 20.e.8) fol. 89r followed fol. 86v, the intervening folios in the
autograph being a later insertion. In other words, the first version of the duet
follows Chrysander's edition up to bar 111 (*HG* vol. 4, p. 180 bar 8): thereafter
comes Example 9.3. Handel did not complete this version of the duet. The
second version of 'Joys of Freedom' exists, crossed out, on fol. 87r-v. (See
Example 9.4.) This version, too, was not completed. The third version,

beginning on the bottom system of fol. 87v and continuing on fol. 88r, is like
HG to bar 141 (p. 181 bar 14), followed by Example 9.5. Again, Handel
abandoned this version before completing it. The fourth version on fol. 88v is
the first performance version as we have it in *HG*. (See Example 9.6.)

20 See especially bars 56–64 and 68–72 (*HG* vol. 32, pp. 139–40).

21 See bars 131–7 and 143–8 (*HG* vol. 32, pp. 141–2).

22 These revisions focus on the idea that appears six bars before the end of the
fragment; in the second setting (bars 62–3) Handel repeats one bar which
prolongs the secondary dominant, making the resolution to the dominant
key more emphatic, and decorates the bass with triplets, allowing it to share
in the motivic make-up of the aria. The resulting two-bar passage is also
added (in a less elaborate form) to the opening ritornello in the second
setting (bars 25–6), as discussed in the course of this chapter.

23 For first complete printed edition of *Clori, Tirsi e Fileno*, see *HHA* series V,
vol. 3 (1994), where the aria is printed on pp. 161–8: Chrysander printed
only a fragment of the cantata in *HG* vol. 52B. Roberts has pointed out that
the second setting of 'The leafy honours' draws heavily upon 'Và col canto',
and has identified certain borrowings from 'Và col canto' within A1 of the
new setting, some of which are also found in the first setting; these will be
pointed out as they arise. The most substantial borrowings noted by Roberts
occur in the second setting beyond the point where the fragment ends, which
raises the possibility that the new borrowings in A1 plant seeds for a
continuation that relies more extensively on the cantata aria, but this is
difficult to prove. It is not entirely clear that the borrowings in the later parts
of the new setting would not have been included in the old version, if Handel
had continued; for the most part they do not rely on new material within A1
of the second setting that was not also present in the fragment. In any case,
the new version is audibly different from the old, which Handel surely
intended. I thank John Roberts for privately communicating his discovery of
the borrowings, and his interpretation of their significance, while this
chapter was being prepared.

24 Paul Brainard, 'Aria and Ritornello: New Aspects of the Comparison
Handel/Bach', in Williams, *Bach, Handel, Scarlatti*, pp. 24–30. The idea added
in bars 19–20 of the second setting of the ritornello, for instance, serves to
preview the return of this material in bars 62–3, 87, 89, and 101–2: the
passage appeared near the end of the fragment (bar 54), but it was not
featured in the ritornello of the first setting. This example illustrates what
Brainard calls the 'retroactive' effect of the body of the aria upon the
ritornello. A more subtle long-range connection might have influenced
Handel's revision of the triplet/dotted crotchet pattern at bars 11–16. The
original ritornello had featured the two-bar idea that later appeared in the
vocal A section of the second setting at bars 114–23. Although Handel did
not reach this point before abandoning the fragment, the presence of this
material in the ritornello might indicate that he had planned to use this
passage in A2 even in the first version, although this is impossible to
demonstrate. In any case, the new version makes the relationship between

the two passages even closer, for the transposition up a third in bars 13–16 recurs in bars 120–3.

25 Roberts notes that bars 41–4 of the new setting bear a closer resemblance to bars 24–30 of 'Và col canto' than did the corresponding bars in the first setting. In my view, the middle of this passage (bars 42–3) resembles bars 35–7 of the fragment more closely than the cantata aria. The descending line from C to E♮ in bars 43–4 might represent a simplification of 'Và col canto' bars 29–30. However, the treatment of the tail-motif which follows (described above) is by no means controlled by the source.

26 Handel's revision also provides a different approach to the passage in the dominant (a setting of the text 'in giddy dissipation'). In the old version, the second half of the passage begins in the dominant (C major), and the use of B♮ creates a tonicisation of C before the 'giddy dissipation' passage. In the second version of the aria, on the other hand, the use of B♭ suggests the dominant seventh chord of F major: we expect to return to F until the tonality is diverted when the C major 'giddy dissipation' passage appears.

27 Gerald Abraham ('Some Points of Style', p. 270) discusses this phenomenon in the harpsichord Sonata HWV 580 and the opening of the Trio Sonata Op. 2 No. 1 (HWV 386b). Composing a new melody over a pre-existent bass-line was, of course, an extremely common technique in Baroque music.

28 See Dean, *Oratorios*, pp. 531–2.

29 J. Robert Oppenheimer, *Atom and Void: Essays on Science and Community* (Princeton, 1989), pp. 31–2.

10 Handel and the idea of an oratorio

1 For detailed accounts of the origins of oratorio in Italy and Germany, see Howard E. Smither, *A History of the Oratorio,* vols. I and I (Chapel Hill, N.C., 1977).

2 'Oratorium' is the more common German form, being the equivalent in ecclesiastical Latin of the Italian *oratorio*, in its older meaning of a place of prayer.

3 A setting of the Passion of St John, based on the Gospel text with interpolated texts by C. H. Postel, has long been attributed to Handel and has been published as his in *HG* (vol. 9) and in *HHA* (series I, vol. 2). The attribution is almost certainly false, but the true composer has yet to be convincingly identified.

4 The longer title appears on the title page of the working copy used for the first performance (D-MÜs MSS 1896, 1914a), prepared by Antonio Giuseppe Angelini, Handel's chief Roman copyist, and in Angelini's bill of 14 May 1707 for making the copy (*HHB* vol. IV, p. 27). On the first page of Handel's autograph of the opening Sonata (Lbl RM 19.d.9, fol. 69r) Angelini added the heading 'Sonata dell'Overtura del Oratorio à 4. con Stromenti Il Trionfo del Tempo e del Disinganno', justifying the shorter version of the title. These documents all describe the work as an 'oratorio'. Carolyn Gianturco, '*Il trionfo del Tempo e del Disinganno*: Four Case-Studies in Determining Italian Poetic-Musical Gestures', *JRMA* 119 (1994), pp. 43–59, attempts to define the

work more precisely as a 'moral cantata', which indeed it is; but the references to it as an 'oratorio' remain perfectly valid in the broad use of that term, and suggest more clearly a work of substantial length divided into two parts.

5 The original wordbook gives the full title as *Oratorio per La Risurrettione di Nostro Signor Giesù Cristo.*

6 The title of this work is given in the original wordbook as *La Passione del nostro signore Gesù Cristo*, though a CD was issued in 1992 under the title *La Colpa, il Pentimento, la Grazia*, the names of the three principal characters.

7 Details derived from the original accounts are given by Ursula Kirkendale, 'The Ruspoli Documents on Handel', *JAMS* 20 (1967), pp. 222–73. The arrangement of the musicians is likely to have resembled that for B. Pasquini's serenata *Applauso musicale* (Rome, 1687), illustrated in Hans Joachim Marx, 'The Instrumentation of Handel's Early Italian Works', *EM* 16 (1988), pp. 496–505. For a detailed discussion of *La Resurrezione*, see Ellen Rosand, 'Handel paints the Resurrection', in Thomas J. Mathiesen and Benito V. Rivera, *Festa Musicologica: Essays in Honor of George J. Buelow* (Stuyvesant, N.Y., 1995), pp. 7–52.

8 J. C. Pepusch, musical director at Cannons, was the composer of four of these English theatre masques.

9 Score in the Earl of Malmesbury's collection, originally copied for Elizabeth Legh (d. 1734): this is referred to as Source B in *Esther (1. Fassung), HHA* series I, vol. 8, ed. Howard Serwer.

10 In 1732 the text was attributed to Alexander Pope (Lord Perceval's Diary, 23 February, and *The Daily Journal*, 19 April; Deutsch, *Handel*, pp. 286, 288) and to John Arbuthnot in Dublin wordbooks of 1741 and 1742.

11 The chorus 'Mourn all ye Muses' is based on the trio 'O Donnerwort! O schrecklich Schreien' in the Passion, but the additional unaccompanied choral passages echoing the words 'No more' – especially the closing sequence with its 'English' false relation – impart greater emotional depth to the chorus.

12 Handel's indications for shortening the final chorus are discussed in the commentary to the *HHA* edition(see note 9), pp. 205–6.

13 See Edmund Hobhouse (ed.), *The Diary of a West Country Physician* [Dr Claver Morris], *A. D. 1684–1726* (Rochester, 1934), pp. 64 and 107.

14 Diary, 23 February 1732: Deutsch, *Handel*, p. 286.

15 In Britain the public staging of sacred drama was effectively forbidden by King James I's statute of 1605 against blasphemy. By then biblical drama had already become distasteful in Protestant eyes because of its potential to distort scriptural truth, and, by extension, to subvert the authority of church and state. The publication of the Authorised Version of the Bible in 1611 increased the reverence accorded to the exact words of the Scriptures. On this topic, see Murray Royston, *Biblical Drama in England* (London, 1968), especially pp. 109–120.

16 Burney, *Commemoration*, 'Performances', pp. 100–1.

17 This phrase presumably refers to the physical arrangement of the band of musicians ('the Musick'), but its precise implications are regrettably unclear.

18   Anon., *See and Seem Blind* (London, [1732]), pp. 15–16, 19–20; Deutsch, *Handel*, p. 301.

19   All subsequent similar dates are of first performances.

20   Less than would appear from the table of borrowings in Dean, *Oratorios*, p. 643: the movements in the Trio Sonatas Op. 5 Nos. 4 and 5 are derivatives of *Athalia* movements, not sources for them; the 'Hallelujah' chorus was not taken from any anthem but is an original movement that was later added by Handel to one of the Chapel Royal versions of his anthem *As pants the Hart*.

21   Not *Il Parnasso in Festa*, a form of the title which seems to have been invented by Friedrich Chrysander.

22   On readings of the poem, see Ruth Smith, 'The Argument and Contexts of Dryden's "Alexander's Feast"', *Studies in English Literature 1500–1900*, 18 (1978), pp. 465–90.

23   See Ruth Smith, 'The Achievements of Charles Jennens (1700–1773)', *ML* 70 (1989), pp. 161–90.

24   Jennens's attempts to revise Handel's score are discussed in Anthony Hicks, 'Handel, Jennens and *Saul*: Aspects of a Collaboration', in Fortune, *Music and Theatre*, pp. 203–27.

25   Handel added Italian arias for the second performance. There was one further performance in 1739 and one more in 1740. The oratorio was not subsequently revived until 1756, and then with a new (pastiche) Part I and damaging alterations to the rest of the work.

26   The recently discovered information on Harris's connection with *L'Allegro* is taken from Rosemary Dunhill, *Handel and the Harris Circle* (Hampshire Papers 8; Winchester, 1995), pp. 6–7.

27   Handel's programme even included an Italian opera, *Imeneo*, presented as a serenata.

28   Jennens's concern with the validity of biblical prophecy, prompted by a desire to refute Deist arguments against irrationality, is also apparent in his other original oratorio texts. In *Saul* the King's death is foretold by the ghost of Samuel as a consequence of earlier disobedience. In *Belshazzar* Daniel interprets the fall of Babylon and the coming of Cyrus as the fulfilment of the prophecies of Jeremiah and Isaiah.

29   For the controversy see the texts in Deutsch, *Handel*, pp. 563–6; *HHB* vol. IV, pp. 359–61.

30   Dunhill, *Handel and the Harris Circle*, p. 6 (corrected from the original document, Hampshire Record Office, 9M73/G349/29).

31   Deutsch, *Handel*, pp. 533. Tollett's poem *To Mr. Handell* was published after her death in 1755, but its content suggests that it was written in 1740 or 1741.

32   Preface to the original wordbook of *Samson*, reprinted in full in Robert Manson Myers, *Handel, Dryden and Milton* (London, 1956), pp. 63-4.

33   Letter of 28 July 1743, *HHB* vol. IV, p. 364.

34   Winton Dean, 'Charles Jennens's Marginalia to Mainwaring's Life of Handel', *ML* 53 (1972), pp. 160–4; slightly revised in Winton Dean, *Essays on Opera* (Oxford, 1990), pp. 74–7.

35   Letter of 21 February 1744, Deutsch, *Handel*, p. 584.

36 For the problems, articulated through press announcements, see Deutsch, *Handel*, pp. 602–6.

37 Letter of 21 February 1745, *HHB* vol. IV, pp. 386.

38 The interlude *The Choice of Hercules* (HWV 69; 1 March 1751, presented with a revival of *Alexander's Feast*) was a re-working of music written in the winter of 1749–50 for Tobias Smollett's play *Alceste* (HWV 45) which never reached performance. The high quality of the music, inspired by a classical tale, suggests that Handel's decision to avoid treating secular subjects in oratorio form was made with regret.

39 *The Triumph of Time and Truth* (HWV 71; 11 March 1757) was not a new composition, but a version with English text of *Il trionfo del Tempo e della Verità* (HWV 46b; 23 March 1737), Handel's own substantial revision of his 1707 Roman oratorio. The amount of new music in the English version, other than recitative, is slight (most of the numbers not from the 1737 *Trionfo* are taken from other works) and the arrangement may well have been made under Handel's supervision by the younger John Christopher Smith.

40 Lord Malmesbury (ed.), *A Series of Letters of the First Earl of Malmesbury* (London, 1870), vol. I, p. 74. The phrase 'it will not insinuate itself' is quoted correctly in R. A. Streatfeild, *Handel* (London, 1910), p. 199; but the further quotations in Deutsch, *Handel*, p. 657, and *HHB* vol. IV, p. 419, omit the word 'not'.

41 In a letter of Thomas Morell, *c.* 1770, Deutsch, *Handel*, p. 852.

42 Hawkins, *History*, vol. II, p. 890.

11 Handel's sacred music

1 Various sacred works with German texts have been attributed to Handel, but none convincingly. Eight works are ascribed to Handel in a catalogue of the library of St Ulrich's Church in Halle from November 1718, but none are known to survive. See *HHB* vol. IV, p. 77.

2 The numbering of Psalms in the Roman Catholic usage derives from the Vulgate Bible and differs (from Psalm 42 onwards) from the numbering which is found in Protestant Bibles and *The Book of Common Prayer*; the latter numbering is used here.

3 See *HHB* vol. II, p. 659–60; also Burrows, *Handel*, p. 42.

4 Mattheson, *Grundlage*, p. 93; see also Anthony Hicks, 'Handel's Early Musical Development', *PRMA* 103 (1976–77), pp. 80–9.

5 The Marian motet *Giunta l'ora fatal* (HWV 234), known as *Il Pianto di Maria*, has now been identified as a composition by G. Ferrandini (1710–91): see Chapter 2, note 24 (p. 290 above).

6 See James S. Hall, 'Handel among the Carmelites', *The Dublin Review*, 223 (1959), pp. 121–31, and 'The Problem of Handel's Latin Church Music', *MT* 100 (1959), pp. 197–200.

7 See Watkins Shaw, 'Handel's Vesper Music – Some MS Sources Rediscovered', *MT* 126 (1985), pp. 392–3; Graham Dixon, 'Handel's Vesper Music – Towards a Liturgical Reconstruction', *MT* 126 (1985), pp. 393–7; Anthony Hicks,

'Handel's Vespers', *MT* 126 (1985), p. 201; and Watkins Shaw, 'Some Original Performing Material for Handel's Latin Church Music', *GHB* 2 (1986), pp. 226–33.

8   The term 'canticle' generally refers to scriptural hymns apart from the psalms, although it is also loosely applied to the Te Deum (or Hymn of St Ambrose) and other non-scriptural texts as well as to certain psalms. In the Roman rite canticles were used as regular elements of the Office: the Magnificat, for example, was proper for Vespers. *The Book of Common Prayer* specified that two canticles should be sung at Morning and Evening Prayer: by the eighteenth century the most common morning canticles were the Te Deum and Jubilate, while those generally used for Evening Prayer were the Magnificat and Nunc dimittis. The Venite (Psalm 95, sometimes preceded by a seasonal antiphon), which serves as the Invitatory or opening chant for Morning Prayer, is also referred to as a canticle. See *New Grove*, 'Canticle'.

9   This and much of the remaining discussion of Handel's music for the Chapel Royal is derived from Burrows, 'Chapel Royal'.

10   Burrows, 'Chapel Royal', vol. I, p. 92.

11   See Donald Burrows, 'Handel's "As pants the Hart"', *MT* 126 (1985), pp. 113–16.

12   The undertaking of this commission resulted in Handel's temporary dismissal from the service of the Elector in Hanover, the future King George I, whose best interests the Peace of Utrecht did not serve. See Donald Burrows, 'Handel and Hanover', in Williams, *Bach, Handel, Scarlatti*, pp. 35–59.

13   The date of completion is missing from the Jubilate autograph. Burrows has suggested that work on this project was interrupted by the need to compose the Ode for Queen Anne's Birthday (HWV 74); the birthday was celebrated on 6 February, although the Ode itself was almost certainly not performed in 1713. See Burrows, 'Chapel Royal', vol. I, pp. 140–6.

14   See Burrows, 'Chapel Royal', vol. II, p. 94.

15   *The Post Boy*, 28 September 1714.

16   *Hamburger Relations-Courier*, 9 November 1714; original in German, translation by Donald Burrows in 'Chapel Royal', vol. I, p. 156.

17   For a discussion of the original organ, and of the new organ installed at St Lawrence's in 1995, see Dominic Gwynn, 'An Organ for St Lawrence, Whitchurch', *Choir & Organ*, 3/1 (February 1995), pp. 30–4.

18   Handel's music for his two tenors, James Blackley and Francis Rowe, requires light, flexible voices capable of negotiating a high tessitura. Although Handel always writes for them in the tenor clef, Pepusch wrote for Blackley in the alto clef. This suggests that they may have been examples of the Purcellian low counter-tenor, with perhaps some additional usable notes at the bottom of the range.

19   See Graydon Beeks, 'Handel and Music for the Earl of Carnarvon', in Williams, *Bach, Handel, Scarlatti*, pp. 1–20. Donald Burrows has argued convincingly that *As pants the Hart* most likely preceded *O sing unto the Lord*. See Burrows, 'Chapel Royal', vol. I, pp. 71–7.

20   Music from many of these sonatas was later published as contributory movements to the Concerti Grossi Op. 3 (1734) and *Select Harmony* (London, 1740), and to the Trio Sonatas Op. 5 (1739): see Hans Joachim Marx, 'The Origins of Handel's Opus 3: A Historical Review', in Sadie & Hicks, *Tercentenary Collection*, pp. 254–70.

21   In the Anglican tradition such texts, which also occasionally drew on other Books of the Bible, were generally restricted to celebrations of political and dynastic events. See John Morehen, 'The English Anthem Text, 1549–1660', *JRMA* 115 (1992), pp. 62–85. A recent example which Handel might have heard was Croft's *O Sing unto the Lord a New Song*, performed on 7 November 1710 'upon the great successes of that Year in Spain and Flanders', which combined verses from Psalms 89, 28 and 29. In Handel's later Cannons Anthems he drew from as many as eight different Psalms in a single work. This pattern also holds true for the anthems written for Cannons by Pepusch, whose work overlapped with Handel's. See Graydon Beeks, 'The Chandos Anthems of Haym, Handel and Pepusch', *GHB* 5 (1993), pp. 161–93.

22   Brydges's library copy is now Lbl Add. MS 62561. The dedication makes it clear that the anthems were designed to be performed by the entire complement of the Cannons Concert, and one should probably assume that the same goal was sought by Handel and Pepusch in their anthems for Cannons. The forces available to Haym in 1716 were smaller than those used by Handel, including only treble and bass singers, two violins, 'cello and organ, supplemented occasionally by oboe and transverse flute.

23   It was published in full score by Birchall & Beardmore in 1783 as 'a favourite anthem'; by Wright & Wilkinson in 1784 as one of 'Ten Anthems composed chiefly for the Chapel of his Grace the late James Duke of Chandos', and by Harrison in 1785 in piano/vocal score. It was also arranged (with some alterations) for voices and continuo for use in the Chapel Royal by William Boyce some time in the 1750s or 1760s: see Graydon Beeks, 'Boyce's Arrangements of Handel for the Chapel Royal', *HJb* 39 (1983), pp. 42–59.

24   The earliest sources, including the Cannons Music Library Catalogue (Huntington Library, San Marino, California, Stowe MS 66) and the 'Malmesbury' copy of the score, refer to this work as 'The Oratorium'. The name *Esther*, by which the work is generally known, seems first to have been attached to it in the 1730s. Handel's theatre version of *Esther* in 1732 incorporated music from English anthems that he had written in the intervening period. The name 'Haman and Mordecai', which was used by Chrysander to designate the Cannons version of the work, derives from a single manuscript copy (D-Hs MB/1667) and has no claim to authenticity.

25   See Graydon Beeks, '"A Club of Composers": Handel, Pepusch and Arbuthnot at Cannons', in Sadie & Hicks, *Tercentenary Collection*, pp. 209–21.

26   Dominic Gwynn, *St Lawrence Whitchurch, Little Stanmore, Middlesex. Organ by Gerard Smith c. 1716*, The Harley Foundation Technical Report No. 17 (1995), p. [22].

27   The revised version of 'Vouchsafe, O Lord' (HWV 280/5B) almost certainly
     dates from a performance in the 1720s, see Burrows, 'Chapel Royal', vol. I,
     pp. 168–74, 322–4.

28   Burrows, 'Handel's "As pants the Hart"'. The situation is confused by Boyce's
     arrangement of HWV 251b: see note 23, above.

29   See Donald Burrows, 'Handel's 1738 "Oratorio": A Benefit Pasticcio', in
     Konstanze Musketa and Klaus Hortschansky (eds.), *Georg Friedrich Händel –
     ein Lebensinhalt: Gedenkschrift für Bernd Baselt* (Halle, 1995), pp. 11–38. The
     music for HWV 251e is printed in full in *HHA* series III, vol. 9, and is clearly
     distinguished in *G. F. Handel, As pants the Hart*, ed. Burrows (Novello
     Handel Edition, London, 1988).

30   Details of the coronation and its preparation are taken from Donald
     Burrows, 'Handel and the 1727 Coronation', *MT* 118 (June 1977),
     pp. 469–73.

31   Burrows, 'Chapel Royal', vol. II, pp. 120–3.

32   See Carole Taylor, 'Handel's Disengagement from the Italian Opera', in Sadie
     & Hicks, *Tercentenary Collection*, pp. 165–81.

33   He had previously considered a plan to use some of the music in *Saul* (HWV
     53), as the 'Elegy on the Death of Saul and Jonathan': see Dean, *Oratorios*,
     pp. 309–10, 312.

34   Burrows, 'Chapel Royal', vol. II, pp. 108–9.

35   David Hurley, '"The Summer of 1743": Some Handelian Self-Borrowings',
     GHB 4 (1991), pp. 174–93.

36   For a detailed account, see Donald Burrows, 'Handel's "Peace Anthem"', *MT*
     114 (1973), pp. 1230–2.

37   See Donald Burrows, 'Handel and the Foundling Hospital', *ML* 58 (1977),
     pp. 269–84.

12   Handel's chamber music

1   It is true that instrumental pieces were not, as a rule, published in the same
     volumes, or copied into the same manuscripts, as vocal works. The reason for
     this, of course, is that such publications or collections were designed for a
     particular kind of performer, not for a particular milieu.

2   Burney, *Commemoration*, 'Sketch', p. 3. The nobleman referred to was
     probably Hugh Hume-Campbell (1708–94), styled Lord Polwarth from 1724
     and Earl of Marchmont from 1740; or possibly his father Alexander
     (1675–1740), Lord Polwarth from 1709 and Earl of Marchmont from 1724.

3   See especially Terence Best, 'Handel's Chamber Music: Sources, Chronology
     and Authenticity', *EM* 13 (1985), pp. 476–99.

4   The rhythmically inactive bass of the first movement of HWV 393 has been
     put forward as one reason for questioning Handel's authorship; but a similar
     bass (and, incidentally, a similar thematic opening) is found in the
     corresponding movement of the trio sonata HWV 386.

5   Bernd Baselt listed them as doubtful and dated them 1700–5. See the entry
     for HWV 380–5 in *HHB* vol. III, pp. 161–6.

6   The structural uniformity of HWV 380–5 is, however, one feature which

counts against Handel's possible authorship. Rarely do we find a run of works by him as conformist as this.

7   Henry Watson Music Library, Newman Flower Collection, MS 130 Hd4, vol. 312, p. 154.

8   E. Hanley, 'Alessandro Scarlatti's Cantate da camera: A Bibliographical Study' (Ph.D. diss., Yale University, 1963). These totals include some works of doubtful authenticity.

9   The cantata texts often provided for the expressive dualism of the R–A–R–A scheme. In Handel's *Mentre il tutto è in furore* (HWV 130), for example, the singer first urges her lover to join battle in a recitative and aria replete with phrases imitating trumpet-calls; in the second recitative and aria she entreats him to return to the pleasures of love when the battle is over.

10   Michael Talbot: *Tomaso Albinoni: the Venetian Composer and his World* (Oxford, 1990), p. 135.

11   Library of the Conservatoire Royale de Musique, Brussels, MS Litt. XY.15.115. David Lasocki and Terence Best ('A New Flute Sonata by Handel', *EM* 9 (1981), pp. 307–11) compare the movement to the brief central Adagio of the Sonata in G major HWV 358, in which, however, the solo part displays neither the rhythmic flexibility nor the melodic contours of vocal recitative.

12   On Handel's cantatas, see John Mayo, 'Handel's Italian Cantatas', (Ph.D. diss., University of Toronto, 1977) and John Mayo, 'Einige Kantatenrevisionen Händels', *HJb* 27 (1981), pp. 63–77.

13   These figures do not include later versions of cantatas that Handel revised, except in those cases where the revision affected the actual make-up of the work. One example is *Nell'africane selve*, which in its first version from *c.* 1708 (HWV 136a) consisted of R–A–R–A; in a second (?later) version (HWV 136b) the second recitative was replaced by a new, shorter recitative and an aria.

14   'Dominant' in this context includes the diminished seventh on the leading-note, a chord often used for an abrupt, dramatic opening to a cantata; the few examples in Handel's cantatas, however, are deployed over a tonic pedal.

15   For example, in Beethoven's Piano Sonata in B♭ Op. 106 ('Hammerklavier'); in violin concertos by Saint-Saëns (No. 3, Op. 61) and Elgar (Op. 61); and in Britten's opera *Billy Budd*.

16   Dean & Knapp, *Operas*, p. 15.

17   See *New Grove*, 'Cantata', section I, 7, p. 699.

18   On the cantatas for Ruspoli, see especially Ursula Kirkendale: 'The Ruspoli Documents on Handel', *JAMS* 20 (1967), pp. 222–73; on those for Pamphili, see L. Montalto, *Un Mecenate in Roma barocca* (Florence, 1955) and H. J. Marx, 'Die "Giustificazioni della Casa Pamphilj" als musikgeschichtliche Quelle', *SM* 12 (1983), pp. 121–87.

19   On Handel's ownership of Lbl Add. MS 37779, a manuscript copy of Steffani duets dated 'Roma 1706', see Colin Timms, 'Handel and Steffani: A New Handel Signature', *MT* 114 (1973), pp. 374–7; on the dating of Handel's chamber duets, see Donald Burrows, 'Handel and Hanover', in Williams, *Bach, Handel, Scarlatti*, pp. 35–59; and on Steffani's influence on Handel, see

Colin Timms, 'Steffani's Influence on Handel's Chamber Duets', in Sadie & Hicks, *Handel Tercentenary Collection*, pp. 222–45.

20   No tempo indications for these two sections are given in the source, but a slow–fast interpretation is obvious from the music itself.

21   Chamber duets could, of course, have been performed instrumentally without any arrangement, in the same way that solo cantatas were frequently played, in England at least, as flute pieces.

22   On the complexities of Handel's sonata publications, see especially Donald Burrows: 'Walsh's Editions of Handel's Opera 1–5: The Texts and their Sources', in Hogwood & Luckett, *18th Century*, pp. 79–102, and Best, 'Handel's Chamber Music'.

13   Handel as a concerto composer

1   From the fifth letter of 'Voiage d'Angleterre' by Pierre-Jacques Fougeroux: see Winton Dean, 'A French Traveller's View of Handel's Operas', *ML* 55 (1974), pp. 172–8. Original (in French) in the Gerald Coke Handel Collection; translation by Donald Burrows and Terence Best. Hickford, a dancing master, first promoted his large room in Panton Street as a concert-room in the 1690s: in 1739 he moved to a new room in Brewer Street.

2   Burney, *History*, vol. II, p. 825n.

3   See Neal Zaslaw, 'When is an Orchestra not an Orchestra?', *EM* 16 (1988), pp. 483–95; John Spitzer, 'The Birth of the Orchestra in Rome – An Iconographic Study' *EM* 19 (1991), pp. 9–27. The November 1988 issue of *EM* also includes articles by Hans Joachim Marx and Eleanor Selfridge Field relevant to orchestral practice in Italy during Handel's time there.

4   The two sections (which originated as a succession of two different dances) were not usually linked thematically, and might be regarded as separate 'movements' in the sense that they had contrasted tempi and moods: however, the binary-scheme tonal linkage has resulted in the two-section overture being generally regarded as a single piece or movement.

5   In this Handel may have been influenced by Ouvertures from French composers which followed the same procedure. A similar plan is found also at the opening of the second section of *Agrippina*, and may be a stylistic feature of Handel's earlier works, which he quickly discarded after *Rinaldo*.

6   See Gerhard Poppe, 'Eine bisher unbekannte Quelle zum Oboenkonzert HWV 287', *HJb* 39 (1993), pp. 225–35. Another possible orchestral work from Handel's Hamburg years is the three-movement Sinfonia HWV 339.

7   See Chapter 12, reference at note 2 (p. 315 above).

8   *Select Harmony, Fourth Collection. Six concertos in Seven Parts For Violins and other Instruments Composed by M^r. Handel, Tartini and Veracini*, published by Walsh in 1740. The Handel concertos were Nos. 2 and 3 of the set.

9   The oboes are specified at the beginning of the first movement in Handel's autograph: in the last movement he took the orchestral violin parts down to low B♭, below the oboe range.

10   This passage is printed correctly in *HHA* series IV, vol. 12 and in the Sonata
      as published by Edition Peters (ed. Burrows), but wrongly in Chrysander's
      edition, *HG* vol. 21.

11   In the adaptation, Handel added trumpets: the trumpet parts printed in
      Chrysander's edition of *Il trionfo del Tempo* (*HG* vol. 24, pp. 7–8) are
      incorrect for that oratorio.

12   There are only occasional appearances of this style in Handel's later works,
      but one example is in the second movement (sometimes called 'The Cuckoo
      and the Nightingale') of the 'Second Set' organ concerto HWV 295 (1739). It
      is interesting that, when Handel rearranged the music of the movement for
      use in one of his Op. 6 concertos, he departed from the formal clarity of the
      previous ritornello scheme.

13   Mainwaring, *Memoirs*, p. 57.

14   HWV 336 is in the wrong key for use in the oratorio. The overture to *The
      Triumph of Time and Truth* (1757), which contains a borrowing from Keiser,
      may reflect the original overture to *Il trionfo*.

15   It looks as if Walsh printed Op. 3 in a hurry, perhaps in order to capitalise on
      the current popularity of concertos in London, following Geminiani's
      concert series at Hickford's Room in 1731–2 and Walsh's publication of
      Geminiani's Op. 2 and Op. 3 concertos in 1732: see Enrico Careri, *Francesco
      Geminiani* (Oxford, 1993), pp. 68–9. The pattern of the elder Walsh's
      dealings with Geminiani over his Concertos (Hawkins, *History*, vol. II,
      p. 850) may have been repeated with Handel over the latter's Op. 3, but it
      seems more likely that Walsh printed Handel's concertos from
      'surreptitiously obtained' copies, without any reference to the composer.

16   This is one reason for doubting that the multi-movement overture to
      Rodrigo, as found today in Handel's autograph, was the version performed
      with the opera.

17   Movements 1 and 3 are associated with the Brockes Passion in some sources.

18   There are also some other detached orchestral movements (e.g. HWV 302b,
      HWV 337) which are undoubtedly genuine but whose context has yet to be
      established.

19   See the various versions printed in *HHA* series IV, vol. 1, *Die acht grossen
      Suiten*, revised edn. (ed. Terence Best, 1993), Anhang 5–7. Anhang 5 probably
      gives the earliest version, perhaps with the addition of some spurious
      passage-work in bars 79–111.

20   The organ was not usually present in the orchestra for Handel's opera
      performances but, exceptionally, it was specified by Handel for use in
      Terpsicore, the prologue to *Il pastor fido* at the Covent Garden revival in
      November 1734.

21   Hawkins, *History*, vol. II, p. 881; Burney, *Commemoration*, 'Sketch', p. 23.

22   *The London Daily Post*, 1 March 1735.

23   The title page of Op. 4 reads *Six Concertos for Harpsicord or Organ*, but the
      solo instrument in Handel's performances was always the organ, except for
      the special case of the original version of the concerto for harp, Op. 4 No. 6.

24   Handel drew on several musical ideas from two recent collections of

harpsichord music: Domenico Scarlatti's *Essercizi* (i.e. sonatas), which had been published in London in 1738, and Gottlieb Muffat's *Componimenti Musicali*, published in Augsburg *c.* 1739.

25 This is proved by the figurings that Handel added to the autograph of Op. 6 No. 9 (HWV 327), movement 4: the music was written in G major, originally as part of the overture to *Imeneo*, but Handel's figurings are written with accidentals applicable to F major, the key of the concerto.

26 HWV 295, HWV 296a. These were published by Walsh in 1740, as the first items in *A Second Set of Six Concertos For the Harpsicord or Organ Compos'd by Mr. Handel*. The set, which bore no opus number, was made up to six concertos with four keyboard arrangements from Handel's *Concerti Grossi* Op. 6; these arrangements, so far as is known, were not made by the composer.

27 To *Imeneo* (HWV 41, composed 1738) and the *Song (Ode) for St Cecilia's Day* (HWV 76, composed in September 1739, immediately before Handel embarked on the concertos).

28 The organ was no doubt Handel's own. Following his 'new large Organ' of 1735, Handel seems to have experimented further with new instruments – or adaptations of existing ones – in 1737–40: see the letter quoted in Chapter 18, p. 268.

14 Handel and the keyboard

1 Mainwaring, *Memoirs*, p. 5.
2 Two are in 3/8, one in 6/8.
3 It is described in Coxe, *Anecdotes*, p. 6n.
4 Quoted in Donald Burrows and Martha J. Ronish, *A Catalogue of Handel's Musical Autographs* (Oxford, 1994), p. 267.
5 Mainwaring, *Memoirs*, p. 14.
6 See Terence Best, 'Handel's Harpsichord Music: A Checklist' in Hogwood & Luckett, *18th Century*, pp. 171–87.
7 Principally Lbl RM 18.b.4, RM 18.b.8, RM 19.a.3, RM 19.a.4, Add. MS 31577, and a few in other collections (Malmesbury, Coke, Flower).
8 HWV 435, 437, 439 without its Sarabande, HWV 440, 441 and 442/2 in the Second Collection of 1727/1733–4, and the Sarabande from HWV 439 in the First Collection of 1720.
9 J. W. Lustig, in F. W. Marpurg, *Kritische Briefe über die Tonkunst* (3 vols. in 2, Berlin, 1759–63), vol. II, p. 467.
10 Original Italian text *HHB* vol. IV, p. 26.
11 Werner Braun, 'Händel und der römische "Zauberhut"', *GHB* 3 (1987), pp. 75–6.
12 Mainwaring, *Memoirs*, pp. 51–2.
13 Mainwaring, *Memoirs*, pp. 60–62. See also Graham Pont, 'Handel versus Domenico Scarlatti: Music of an Historic Encounter', *GHB* 4 (1991), pp. 232–47.
14 The Electress's quaint French spelling has been modernised: for a transcription see Donald Burrows, 'Handel and Hanover' in Williams, *Bach, Handel, Scarlatti*, p. 39.

15   Lady Llanover (ed.), *Autobiography and Correspondence of Mary Granville, Mrs Delaney* (London, 1861), pp. 5–6.

16   Printed in *HG* vol. 48 (1894), pp. 206–9, and *HHA* series II, vol. 4/1, *Rinaldo* (1993), pp. 134–41.

17   It might have been the Prelude and Sonata in B♭, HWV 434 Anhang; there is a sketch for this in Handel's autograph, on a single leaf in the Coke Collection, and 1713 is one of the possible dates for it.

18   See Winton Dean, 'The Malmesbury Collection', in Terence Best (ed.), *Handel Collections and their History* (Oxford, 1993), pp. 29–38.

19   MS 1977/85.

20   The title page has the plate-number 490. F. Lesure, in *Bibliographie des Editions musicales publiées par Etienne Roger et Michel Charles le Cène* (Paris, 1969), dates the edition to 1721, but it could be as early as 1719, and the sense of Handel's preface implies that it had already appeared by November 1720.

21   David Fuller, in *New Grove*, 'Suite', suggests that it might be more logical not to assume that there ever was a concept of the 'traditional' suite.

22   On the history of these, see *G. F. Handel, Twenty Overtures in Authentic Keyboard Arrangements*, ed. Terence Best (3 vols., Novello, London and Sevenoaks, 1985–6). Some of the authentic versions were published in Walsh's series of keyboard arrangements of Handel's overtures.

23   See Donald Burrows, 'Walsh's Editions of Handel's Opera 1–5', in Hogwood & Luckett, *18th Century*, pp. 79–102.

24   In *The Lady's Banquet*, Book 5. Reference from Lustig in Marpurg, *Kritische Briefe*, vol. II, p. 467.

25   The fugues were published as *Troisieme Ovarage* [sic], which was confusing, since the previous year Walsh had issued a set of concerti grossi as Op. 3 (*Opera terza*).

26   Handel was so described in a press notice on 29 August 1724; see *Deutsch, Handel*, p. 173. Princess Anne was Handel's student by June 1723: see Richard G. King, 'On Princess Anne's lessons with Handel', *Newsletter of the American Handel Society*, 7/2 (1992), p. 1.

27   Autograph in Cfm MU MS 260, pp. 27–39, 42. Published in facsimile in *HHA Supp.*, and with realisations and commentary in David Ledbetter, *Continuo Playing according to Handel* (Oxford, 1990).

28   Hawkins, *History*, vol. II, p. 912.

29   See Deutsch, *Handel*, pp. 675–6.

30   Raymond Russell, *The Harpsichord and Clavichord* (London, 1959; rev. 1973), pp. 75–6; *HHB* vol. IV, p. 91 (where the J. Ruckers instrument is incorrectly listed as having three manuals).

31   Now in the Victoria and Albert Museum, London. See *New Grove*, 'Harpsichord', illus. 9 and accompanying text.

32   Russell, *The Harpsichord and Clavichord*, pp. 165–8.

33   See *EM* 21 (1993), p. 335.

34   Hawkins, *History*, vol. II, p. 412.

35   See Michael Cole, 'A Handel Harpsichord', *EM* 21 (1993), pp. 99–109.

15   Handel and the Italian language

1   Letter to Charles Burney from Dr Quin, 16 July 1788, quoted in Burney, *History*, vol. II, p. 1007.

2   9 November 1709, *HHB* vol. IV, p. 43.

3   Of the seven surviving letters to his brother-in-law, Michael Dietrich Michaelsen, five are in French and two are in German, though with the French form of address. The texts of all seven are printed in Deutsch, *Handel*, though the letter of 17/28 August 1731 is mis-dated to 1736.

4   Mainwaring, *Memoirs*, p. 110n.

5   For instance the one to Jennens from Dublin, describing the success of *Messiah*, 9 September 1742.

6   Mainwaring (*Memoirs*, p. 14) says that Zachow, Handel's first teacher, 'had a large collection of Italian as well as German music: he shewed him the different styles of different nations'.

7   There were in fact fourteen, but no music by Handel survives for one of them, 'Ingrato, spietato' at the end of Act I.

8   D-Hs M/A 1056.

9   Chrysander occasionally misread the Italian in the autographs, even when Handel's writing is perfectly clear. In the cantata *Dunque sarà pur vero* ('Agrippina condotta a morire', HWV 110) the recitative following aria no. 4 begins as follows in the autograph (Lbl RM 20.e.1, fol. 48v): 'Prema l'ingrato figlio di plaustro trionfal gemmate sponde' – 'Let my ungrateful son lean on the bejewelled sides of his triumphal chariot'. Chrysander printed 'Trema' for 'Prema' and 'plauso' for 'plaustro', rendering the passage meaningless; in the Preface to the volume containing the cantata (*HG* vol. 52A) he specifically comments on the obscurity of this line, and tells us that a certain Signor Rizzelli, who had often helped him, had not been able to find any acceptable sense in it. In the same Preface there is another complaint about an 'unintelligible Italian text' in the cantata *Figlio d'alte speranze* (HWV 113), where Handel's clearly written 'rimirava' is printed as 'riandava' (RM 20.e.1, fol. 54v). The first comment reveals that Chrysander had an Italian colleague to whom he referred problems with Handel's Italian texts, but it is clear that his rendering of them in print is not to be relied on. In the Preface to *Rodrigo* (*HG* vol. 56), he acknowledges the assistance of B. von Gugler in the preparation of the Italian text.

10   Proof of this is that Handel wrote 'lo portate' instead of 'la portate' in the fourth line from the end of Bajazet's death scene. Gasparini's score has 'la', which makes better sense, but the 1719 wordbook reads 'lo', which is probably a misprint; the 1724 wordbook also has 'lo'.

11   A copy of Gasparini's 1719 score, now in the Staatliche Museen, Meiningen, was presented by Borosini in 1727 to Duke Anton Ulrich of Sachsen-Meiningen. The title-page reads 'La Poesia è del Nobile Venetiano Pioveni Toltone l'ultima Scena che fù Composta dal Zanella secondo L'Idea del Sig[re] Borosini . . .'. See Strohm, *Essays*, p. 50.

12   I am grateful to John Roberts for this suggestion.

16 Handel and the orchestra

1 Johann Mattheson, *Exemplarische Organisten-probe* (Hamburg, 1717), vol. I, p. 85.

2 Hans Joachim Marx, 'Die "Giustificazioni della Casa Pamphilj" als musikgeschichtliche Quelle', *SM* 12 (1983), p. 179.

3 A bassoon is mentioned in 'Risorga il mondo' in this oratorio: a player of another instrument may have doubled for that movement, which would explain the lack of a bassoon player in the orchestra list. Hans Joachim Marx, in 'The Instrumentation of Handel's Early Italian Works', *EM* 16 (1988), p. 502, argues against the presence of bassoons in Italy during the period that Handel was there, suggesting that the bassoon reference in this movement was not realised in performance. The violin count given here is the maximum number of violinists listed: some of these players did not play in all three performances, but it is presumed here that the full complement played for the initial performance, since all of these players are listed as attending all rehearsals.

4 Described in Watkins Shaw, 'Some Original Performing Material for Handel's Latin Church Music', *GHB* 2 (1986), pp. 226–33; see also Watkins Shaw, 'Handel: Some Contemporary Performance Parts Considered' in Mary Ann Parker (ed.), *Eighteenth-Century Music in Theory and Practice* (Stuyvesant, N.Y., 1994), pp. 59–75.

5 This presumes that the 'concertino' part was read by two players: see note 17, below.

6 For *Laudate pueri* two organ parts were copied, but for *Haec est regina* and *Te decus virgineum* only one survives. No organ part survives for *Saeviat tellus*.

7 It was also found in London: the lists of instrumentalists at Cannons in Graydon Beeks, 'Handel and Music for the Earl of Carnarvon', in Williams, *Bach, Handel, Scarlatti*, pp. 8, 17–18, include some who doubled on unrelated instruments.

8 Data from *Vice Chamberlain Coke*, pp. 127, 151, 159–61. There is no indication in any of Handel's early London scores for a 'ripieno' group of violins: we do not know whether the two 'ripieno' players briefly listed were substitute or supplementary musicians, but they were not a 'concerto grosso' in the Corellian fashion.

9 See Beeks, 'Handel and Carnarvon', p. 8. Information in this paragraph includes conclusions from Graydon Beeks's subsequent work on the Cannons lists, and I thank him for making the information available.

10 *Ibid.*, pp. 17–18. This list shows two keyboard players, not including Handel. One, Johann Christoph Pepusch, was also a composer and violinist: the other, George Munro, is listed only as a keyboard player. There are no score markings or other indications in *Esther* to indicate that more than one harpsichord was used in performance, and it was Handel's practice to cover this duty himself. The other players may have assisted in rehearsals, and possibly directed performances of non-Handel works. The Cannons musical establishment was at its largest in 1720, after the main period of Handel's association.

11   Milhous and Hume, 'New Light on Handel and the Royal Academy of Music in 1720', *TJ* 35 (1983), pp. 158–61: as in the earlier London opera lists, the successive documents have variations in details.

12   Winton Dean, 'A French Traveller's View of Handel's Operas', *ML* 55 (1974), pp. 177-8.

13   Jacob Simon (ed.), *Handel: A Celebration of his Life and Times* (London, 1985), p. 145. This list, like those for the 1709–11 theatre orchestras, mentions just two oboes: further sources suggest that Handel's practice at other times was to double at least Oboe I.

14   Hans Dieter Clausen, who first brought this source to light in *Händels Direktionspartituren ('Handexemplare')* (Hamburg, 1972), p. 61, insists that it is an incomplete list of orchestral parts. However, if we allow for 'cello, bass and theorbo players reading over the harpsichordists' shoulders, the list could provide for the entire orchestra. To account for the five or six 'concerto grosso' 'cellos and string basses and the theorbo (as mentioned by Fougeroux and Clerk) in this fashion would require three players around each harpsichord, but the composition of the orchestra may have changed by 1737. It is possible that an additional continuo bass part had been copied earlier for rehearsals, and that this list covers only the remaining orchestral parts. Arguing against this is the fact that the single 'cello part in the *Didone* list is for the lead 'cellist, who would presumably have been needed for the earlier rehearsals: in this case, he must have read from the keyboard score in rehearsals with soloists, as shown in Plate 7.

15   Printed in Deutsch, *Handel,* pp. 751, 800–1.

16   Even as late as the 1770s, Charles Burney reported that the orchestra at the San Carlo opera in Naples was led by the concert-master: see Percy A. Scholes, *Dr. Burney's Musical Tours of Europe* (2 vols., London, 1959), vol. I, pp. 283–4.

17   It is also possible that this 'concertino' part was shared by two violinists, one playing Violin I and one Violin II, so that both sections were led from the front, a practice apparently confirmed by paintings and drawings of the time. The parts to Handel's Latin church music contain equal numbers of first and second violin parts, in addition to the concertino part (which contains both), suggesting that the first and second violin sections for the church music would have been equal in numbers.

18   Parts of this sort appear also in sets for Antonio Caldara's oratorios performed in Vienna after his arrival from Rome in 1716: see Ursula Kirkendale, *Antonio Caldara: Sein Leben und seine venezianisch-römischen Oratorien*, Wiener Musikwissenschaftliche Beiträge 6 (Graz, 1966), pp. 122–7. Caldara imported this orchestral practice to Vienna from Italy; in Rome he had been in service for eight years to Marquis Ruspoli, the same patron that employed Handel for nearly two years.

19   Shaw, 'Some Original Performing Material'. The scores to these works likewise contain no indications of concertino/concerto grosso practice.

20   Burney, *History*, vol. II, p. 1010; Burney, *Commemoration*, 'Sketch', p. 27.

21   Letter to Jennens, 29 December 1741, Deutsch, *Handel,* p. 530.

22 It is used, for instance, in the 'Sonata' (Overture) to the Roman version of *Il trionfo*, where the 'concertino' violins are on separate staves in Handel's autograph score. Three arias from early in his career – 'Per me gia' and 'Se impassibile' from *La Resurrezione*, and 'Venti, turbini' from *Rinaldo* – imitate concerto grosso scoring, but these carefully written features cannot support the supposedly routine practice of a concertino/concerto grosso convention.

23 See Clausen, *Händels Direktionspartituren*, pp. 58–9.

24 This issue is somewhat contentious at present: for the argument against the older view that Handel used concertino/concerto grosso divisions throughout his works, see Mark W. Stahura, 'Hidden Scoring in Handel's Theater Works' (Ph.D. diss., University of Chicago, 1992), pp. 65–96.

25 The chalumeau aria in *Riccardo Primo* may not have been performed, but Handel clearly intended to use the instrument. Similarly, while the serpent listing is deleted in the autograph of the *Fireworks Music* (Handel's only score to include the instrument), it is named in an undated part-copying list for *Samson* and *Solomon* (Cfm MU MS 259, p. 79). An interesting case with demonstrable performance implications is that of Carlo Arrigoni, a singer and lutenist whose presence in London inspired Handel to use both of his talents in 1736: see Winton Dean, 'An Unrecognized Handel Singer: Carlo Arrigoni', *MT* 118 (1977), pp. 556–8. On the rarity of trombones, see Donald Burrows, 'Handel, the Dead March, and a Newly Identified Trombone Movement', *EM* 18 (1990), pp. 408–16, and Trevor Herbert, 'The Sackbut in England in the 17th and 18th Centuries', *EM* 18 (1990), pp. 609–16, esp. p. 612.

26 In the score to *Poro* Handel divided the violins into three sections, but fussed with this balance further in 'Vil trofeo', moving some ('qualche') second violins down to the Violin III line.

27 Bernd Baselt, 'Instrumentarium und Besetzung bei Georg Friedrich Händel, dargestellt an ausgewählten Beispielen aus seinen Opern', in Eitelfriedrich Thom (ed.), *Zu Fragen des Instrumentariums, der Besetzung und der Improvisation in der ersten Hälfte des 18. Jahrhunderts*, Studien zur Aufführungspraxis und Interpretation von Instrumentalmusik des 18. Jahrhunderts (Part 1, Magdeburg, 1976), pp. 26–32; Dean, *Oratorios*, pp. 72–80; Winton Dean, *Handel and the Opera Seria* (Berkeley, 1969), Chapter 10; and Dean & Knapp, *Operas*, pp. 33–5. Even Dirk Möller's *Besetzung und Instrumentarium in den Opern Georg Friedrich Händels* (Frankfurt, 1989) dwells on ranges and exceptional uses, not standard practices.

28 It is impossible to know for certain when Handel completed the orchestration of *Samson*, but he probably filled in at least some of the orchestral parts when he expanded the work in 1742, after his return from Dublin.

29 Of his London theatre works (operas, oratorios, odes, etc.), no complete original orchestral string, wind or brass parts survive. Only a single harpsichord part survives that was certainly used in performance: a figured bass part to *Alexander's Feast* (HWV 75, 1736), copied even before the

conducting score was produced, and used through several revivals (see Chapter 18). See also note 33, below, concerning 'harpsichord scores'. Some of Handel's original orchestral parts may have perished in the fires that destroyed the King's Theatre in 1789 and Covent Garden in 1808.

30   When there are two treble-clef lines, 'tutti' in some cases implies the use of oboes on both lines; this use of 'tutti' needs to be carefully distinguished from Handel's use of 'Tutti unis[oni]', indicating all Violin I and Violin II playing together. Oboe cues need to be considered carefully for each score: see for example Terence Best's preface to *Tamerlano*, *HHA* series I, vol. 15, pp. xxiv–xxv.

31   An absolute definition of 'ritornello' for this context is impossible, since there are examples in Handel's scores of oboes added to the violins for only two notes between vocal phrases, as well as examples of oboes being restricted to the longest of orchestral passages. In ensembles and choruses the oboes could play throughout.

32   This collection is now known as the 'Aylesford Collection', after the titled family who inherited Jennens's library on his death. The majority of the Aylesford Collection is now in the Henry Watson Music Library, Manchester Public Library. For a fuller account of the origins and peregrinations of the Aylesford Collection, see John Roberts, 'The Aylesford Collection: History and Reconstruction', in Terence Best (ed.), *Handel Collections and their History* (Oxford, 1993), pp. 38–85.

33   Second copies of performance scores, designated 'harpsichord scores' by Clausen in *Händels Direktionspartituren*, survive for some of Handel's operas performed between 1729 and 1741: see Hans Dieter Clausen, 'The Hamburg Collection', in Best (ed.), *Handel Collections*, pp. 17–21. There is some doubt as to whether these functioned as performing parts, though their contents accurately reflect Handel's performing version from these years, and they might have been used by the second harpsichordist.

34   The bassoons, as part of the 'tutti' group, played with the full continuo even in some movements without oboes. Handel's markings in *Alexander's Feast* and *Saul* (and occasional markings elsewhere) show that the organ could be used in the oratorio 'soli' group for extraordinary reasons, but these instances are normally clearly and explicitly marked in the scores. On Handel's general use of the organ in oratorios, see Chapter 18.

35   Barry Cooper, 'The Organ Parts to Handel's "Alexander's Feast"', *ML* 59 (1978), pp. 159–79. The surviving sources are copies of the original organ part: for further details of the organ parts, and the performance history of *Alexander's Feast*, see Donald Burrows 'Handel and "Alexander's Feast"', *MT* 123 (1982), pp. 252–5; Burrows, 'The Composition and First Performance of Handel's "Alexander's Feast"', *ML* 64 (1983), pp. 206–11, esp. pp. 210–11; and the correspondence in *ML* 65 (1984), p. 324; *ML* 66 (1985), pp. 87–8.

17   Production style in Handel's operas

1   The fullest account, covering the whole subject, is Joachim Eisenschmidt, *Die szenische Darstellung der Opern Händels auf der Londoner Bühne seiner*

Zeit (2 vols., Wolfenbüttel and Berlin, 1940–1). See also Dene Barnett, 'The Performance Practice of Acting: The Eighteenth Century', a series of articles in *Theatre Research International*, 2–3 (1977–8); Lowell Lindgren, 'The Staging of Handel's Operas in London', in Sadie & Hicks, *Tercentenary Collection*; Edward A. Langhans, 'The Theatres', in Robert D. Hume (ed.), *The London Theatre World, 1660–1800* (Carbondale, Ill., 1980); Richard Leacroft, *The Development of the English Playhouse* (London, 1973); Graham F. Barlow, 'Vanbrugh's Queen's Theatre in the Haymarket, 1703–9', *EM* 17 (1989), pp. 515–21; and Richard Southern, *Changeable Scenery* (London, 1952).

2   Eisenschmidt, *Szenische Darstellung*, vol. II, p. 26.

3   *The Spectator*, no. 42, cited by Eisenschmidt, *Szenische Darstellung*, vol. II, p. 87.

4   Lindgren, 'The Staging of Handel's Operas'.

5   W. R. Chetwood, *A General History of the Stage* (London, 1749) mentions 'a Machine to move the Scenes regularly all together' as a common feature in English and French theatres. It may have been employed by Davenant as early as 1661. Chetwood was the prompter at Drury Lane.

6   Handel was not personally involved, though he may have lent material; this could account for the disappearance of both his autograph and his performing score. The *Giulio Cesare* staged at the Haymarket Theatre in 1787 was not the opera but a pasticcio put on at the request of King George III.

7   Preface to the vocal scores of *Rodelinda* and *Julius Caesar*, English edition (Peters, n.d, [*c.* 1927]).

8   Among them Joan Sutherland, Janet Baker, James Bowman, Philip Langridge and Felicity Lott.

9   *Opera*, April 1972, pp. 351–3.

10 *Opera*, August 1988, p. 944.

11 Handel wrote for it in *Terpsicore*, performed as a prologue to *Il Pastor Fido* in 1734, but this is a French-style *opéra-ballet*, a genre in which the organ is appropriate.

12 Sellars's reported claim, in connection with his production of *Giulio Cesare*, that his only intention was to render the motives of the characters meaningful for a historically uneducated public has been stigmatised by Terence Best as both patronising and arrogant: see 'Die Händel-Szene unserer Zeit', in Hans Joachim Marx (ed.), *Zur Dramaturgie der Barockoper* (Karlsruhe, 1994), pp. 128–9.

18   Handel's oratorio performances

1   *HHB* vol IV, p. 27; see also Chapter 16.

2   See Ursula Kirkendale, 'The Ruspoli Documents on Handel', *JAMS* 20 (1967), pp. 222–73, 517–18.

3   The first page of Handel's autograph is lost, but he almost certainly headed it 'Oratorium', with no further title: see chapter 11, note 24. The work was always referred to as *Esther* in the revivals of 1732: see Deutsch, *Handel*, pp. 286–8.

4 See Graydon Beeks, 'Handel and Music for the Earl of Carnarvon' in Williams, *Bach, Handel, Scarlatti*, pp. 1–20.

5 There was also a substantial role for an Israelite, with music in the alto clef.

6 This would have involved one of the tenors taking the upper voice in the duet for two bass-clef voices in the final chorus.

7 Burney, *Commemoration*, 'Performances', pp. 100–1. All but one name from the cast-list that Burney gives on p.100 are identifiable as boys who were discharged from the Chapel Royal with broken voices between June 1733 and June 1737, so it seems likely that Gates's production had entirely treble-voice soloists, though it is possible that Gentlemen from the Chapel provided lower voices in the choruses.

8 'Colman's Opera Register', 29 May 1732: Deutsch, *Handel*, p. 292.

9 Anon., *See and Seem Blind: or, a Critical Dissertation on the Publick Diversions, &c* (London, [1732]): extracts in Deutsch, *Handel*, pp. 300–1.

10 See F. H. W. Sheppard (general ed.), *Survey of London*, vol. 35 (London, 1970), Chapter 6. Plate 10 was published as an etching and coloured aquatint: two of Pugin's sketches for the picture survive (at The Art Institute of Chicago), but they do not supply further details of practical relevance. I thank David Hurley for examining the sketches and confirming this.

11 Letter, Jennens to Lord Guernsey, 19 September 1738: printed, with minor errors, Deutsch, *Handel*, pp. 465–6.

12 Journal of John Marsh, vol. IV, p. 134, entry for 22 February 1774, Huntington Library, San Marino, California, Ms. 544757. The entry is mis-dated: Handel's *Samson* was performed at Drury Lane under the direction of Smith and Stanley on 23 February. Although this entry is dated 1774, Marsh wrote up his Journal in its final form in the 1790s, drawing presumably on an entry in an earlier diary. I thank Brian Robins for drawing this reference from Marsh's Journal to my attention.

13 Marsh wrote up the items in his Journal as if they were contemporary diary entries, but he included material from later sources as part of his narrative. In the entry dated 22 February 1774, the sentences following that quoted here include references to the 1784 Handel Commemoration, and an unacknowledged quotation from Burney, *Commemoration*, 'Sketch', p. 29.

14 *The Daily Journal*, 12 March 1733, Deutsch, *Handel*, p. 308.

15 *The London Daily Post*, 10 February 1736, Deutsch, *Handel*, p. 440.

16 *The London Daily Post*, 25 February 1736, Deutsch, *Handel*, p. 400: see also *The Dublin Journal*, 14 February 1744, Deutsch, *Handel*, p. 583.

17 *The Daily Journal*, 19 April 1732.

18 *The London Daily Post*, 28 March 1738: Deutsch, *Handel*, p. 455: see Donald Burrows, 'Handel's 1738 "Oratorio": A Benefit Pasticcio', in Konstanze Musketa and Klaus Hortschansky (eds.), *Georg Friedrich Händel – ein Lebensinhalt: Gedenkschrift für Bernd Baselt* (Halle, 1995), pp. 11–38.

19 The lists are printed in Deutsch, *Handel* and *HHB* vol. IV: there (and elsewhere) an error in transcription from the 1754 list puts the viola player Rash into the violin section.

20   Beard was paid, but returned, 2 guineas for his first Foundling Hospital
      performance in 1751: one would expect his regular fee to have been larger.
      Similarly, the payment of only 1½ guineas to Wass, the bass soloist, in
      1754 looks unrealistically modest when compared with the payments to
      the ladies. The choristers' rate is revealed by an entry in the Foundling
      Hospital *Messiah* account for 1759 (Deutsch, *Handel*, p. 825): '6 Boys –
      £4 14s 6d'.

21   See Watkins Shaw, *A Textual and Historical Companion to Handel's 'Messiah'*
      (London, 1965), Chapter 4.

22   Handel's chorus voices were always provided by professional singers in
      London: the first Foundling Hospital *Messiah* performance to break with this
      practice was in 1771, twelve years after Handel's death, when thirty
      professional singers were supplemented with '26 Chorus singers Volunteers
      not paid'.

23   See Shaw, *Textual Companion*, pp. 79, 82–3, 205–10: the ornamentation from
      these sources is printed in the vocal scores of *Messiah* edited by Shaw
      (London, 1992) and Burrows (London, 1987).

24   Pier Francesco Tosi, trans. J. Galliard, *Observations on the Florid Song*
      (London, 1743): Tosi makes the distinction between church, theatre and
      chamber styles in the context of his chapter on the performance of recitative
      (Chapter 5), but the implications of different manners of performance seem
      to have wider application.

25   Letter, Handel to Jennens, 29 December 1741, Deutsch, *Handel*, p. 530.

26   See Donald Burrows, 'Handel's London Theatre Orchestra', *EM* 13 (1985),
      pp. 349–57.

27   Burney, *Commemoration*, 'Sketch', p. 29.

28   His organ voluntary at the Foundling Hospital *Messiah* performance on
      1 May 1753 is the last reference in the London newspapers to Handel
      playing the organ in public: however, he seems to have continued playing
      concertos at theatre oratorio performances, at least occasionally: see the
      reference from 1756 in Rosemary Dunhill, *Handel and the Harris Circle*,
      Hampshire Papers 8 (Winchester, 1995), p. 16. Nevertheless, it is unlikely
      that he attempted to direct any other aspect of the oratorio performances
      after 1754.

29   He was also responsible for collecting the artillery drums from the Tower of
      London in 1750 for use in Handel's Covent Garden performances: see
      Deutsch, *Handel* p. 681.

30   In payments to additional players for services at the Chapel Royal.

31   The original copy is lost but there are authoritative secondary copies: two of
      them (deriving from the 'Aylesford' Collection) are now with the Royal
      Music Library collection at the British Library (RM 19.a.1 and RM 19.a.10).

32   London, Royal College of Music MS 900.

33   Letter to James Harris, describing the performance of *Deborah* on 14
      November 1744, Hampshire Record Office, 9M73/G308/20.

34   Letter from Handel to Jennens; see note 25 above.

35   *The Dublin News-Letter*, 23 January 1742 (Deutsch, *Handel*, p. 535). It is

possible that the 'Organ' referred to is Handel's specially constructed instrument from 1738 which, as noted above, may have been a claviorganum.

36 Autograph, Lbl RM 20.f.2, fol. 133r.

37 As a result, his figurings sometimes conflict with the completed harmony above. In the 1720s, however, Handel did add more copious 'practical' figuring to some instrumental sonatas and to at least one opera, the latter apparently in connection with the preparation of a printed edition.

Handel's works

The following summary list follows the order and categories of the standard catalogue of Handel's works, *Verzeichnis der Werke Georg Friedrich Händels*, prepared by Bernd Baselt. The full version of this catalogue, which is the source of the 'HWV' identifying numbers, is published in vols. I–III of the *Händel-Handbuch* (ed. Walter Eisen and Margret Eisen, Leipzig and Kassel, 1978–86). Other useful catalogues are to be found in the work-list to the 'Handel' article in *New Grove* (published separately as Winton Dean and Anthony Hicks, *The New Grove Handel*, London, 1982) and in Appendix 2 to Donald Burrows, *Handel* (Oxford, 1994).

Titles of major works are given in the short forms by which they are generally known. Dates for major works are shown only as a guide. '1748/1749' indicates that the work was composed in 1748 and first performed in 1749: '1731–2/1732' indicates that the composition straddled 1731–2, and the first performance took place in 1732. Many works were revived by Handel in years subsequent to the year of first performance, usually with significant changes to the musical content. (Dates given to works in the chapters of the *Companion* may be those of composition or performance, as seems most appropriate.) In the sections for theatre works, places of first performance apply to all subsequent entries until superseded. Queen's Theatre, King's Theatre, Covent Garden and Lincoln's Inn Fields are all London theatres: the Queen's Theatre (Haymarket) was re-named as the King's Theatre on the death of Queen Anne and the accession of King George I in 1714.

Vocal music

Operas

HWV	Title	
1	*Almira*	?1704–5/1705 (Hamburg)
2	*Nero*	1704–5/1705
3	*Florindo*	?1706/1708
4	*Daphne*	?1706/1708
5	*Rodrigo*	1707 (Florence)
6	*Agrippina*	1709 (Venice)
7	*Rinaldo*	1711 (Queen's Theatre, London)
8	*Il pastor fido*	1712
8b	*Terpsicore* (Prologue to revival of *Il pastor fido*)	1734 (Covent Garden)
9	*Teseo*	1712/1713 (Queen's Theatre)
10	*Silla*	1713
11	*Amadigi*	1715 (King's Theatre)
12	*Radamisto*	1720

HWV	Title	
13	*Muzio Scevola* (only Act III by Handel)	1721
14	*Floridante*	1721
15	*Ottone*	1722/1723
16	*Flavio*	1723
17	*Giulio Cesare*	?1723–4/1724
18	*Tamerlano*	1724
19	*Rodelinda*	1725
20	*Scipione*	1726
21	*Alessandro*	1726
22	*Admeto*	1726/1727
23	*Riccardo Primo*	1727
24	*Siroe*	1728
25	*Tolomeo*	1728
26	*Lotario*	1729
27	*Partenope*	1730
28	*Poro*	1731
29	*Ezio*	?1731–2/1732
30	*Sosarme*	1732
31	*Orlando*	1732/1733
32	*Arianna*	1734 (Covent Garden)
33	*Ariodante*	1734/1735
34	*Alcina*	1735
36	*Arminio*	1736/1737
37	*Giustino*	1736/1737
38	*Berenice*	1736–7/1737
39	*Faramondo*	1737/1738 (King's Theatre)
40	*Serse*	1737–8/1738
41	*Imeneo*	1738,1740/1740 (Lincoln's Inn Fields)
42	*Deidamia*	1740/1741

Uncompleted operas

A[2]	*Genserico*	1728
A[5]	*Titus l'Empereur*	1731

'Pasticcio' Italian operas

These were performing versions by Handel from pre-existing scores. In most cases Handel adapted music by other composers, adding newly composed recitatives, but the three operas marked * drew on Handel's own previous music.

A[1]	*L'Elpidia*	1725 (King's Theatre)
A[3]	*Ormisda*	1730
A[4]	*Venceslao*	1731
A[6]	*Lucio Papirio*	1732
A[7]	*Catone*	1732

HWV	Title	
A[8]	*Semiramide*	1733
A[9]	*Cajo Fabbricio*	1733
A[10]	*Arbace*	1734
A[11]*	*Oreste*	1734 (Covent Garden)
A[12]	*Didone abbandonata*	1737
A[13]*	*Alessandro Severo*	1738 (King's Theatre)
A[14]*	*Jupiter in Argos*	1739

Music for English plays

43	*The Alchemist*	Incidental music for a version of Ben Johnson's play, London 1710; music drawn from the overture to *Rodrigo* and probably pirated
44	*There in blissful shade and bow'rs* (Music for *Comus*)	Three arias and chorus as additions for a private performance of *Comus*, 1745 (Exton)
45	*Alceste*	Music for a lost play by Tobias Smollett, Covent Garden, 1749–50, rehearsed but never performed

Oratorios (including secular English works of similar type)

46a	*Il trionfo del Tempo e del Disinganno*	1707 (Rome)
46b	*Il trionfo del Tempo e della Verità*	1737 (Covent Garden)
47	*La Resurrezione*	1708 (Bonelli Palace, Rome)
48	*Brockes Passion*	*c.* 1716; date and place of first performance unknown
49	*Acis and Galatea*	1718 (HWV 49a, ?Cannons) 1732 (HWV 49b, King's Theatre)
50	*Esther*	*c.* 1718 (HWV 50a, ?Cannons) 1732 (HWV 50b, King's Theatre)
51	*Deborah*	1733 (King's Theatre)
52	*Athalia*	1733 (Sheldonian Theatre, Oxford)
–	*An Oratorio*	1738 (King's Theatre); English/Italian, pasticcio from Handel's works
53	*Saul*	1738/1739
54	*Israel in Egypt*	1738/1739
55	*L'Allegro, il Penseroso ed il Moderato*	1740 (Lincoln's Inn Fields)
56	*Messiah*	1741/1742 (Dublin)
57	*Samson*	1741–2/1743 (Covent Garden)
58	*Semele*	1743/1744

HWV	Title	
59	Joseph and his Brethren	1743/1744
60	Hercules	1744/1745 (King's Theatre)
61	Belshazzar	1744/1745
62	Occasional Oratorio	1746 (Covent Garden)
63	Judas Maccabaeus	1746/1747
64	Joshua	1747/1748
65	Alexander Balus	1747/1748
66	Susanna	1748/1749
67	Solomon	1748/1749
68	Theodora	1749/1750
69	The Choice of Hercules	1750/1751
70	Jephtha	1751/1752
71	The Triumph of Time and Truth (extended English version of HWV 46b)	1757

Italian serenatas

72	Aci, Galatea e Polifemo	1708 (Naples). Two-part extended dramatic cantata
73	[Il] Parnasso in Festa	1734 (King's Theatre). An opera-length London theatre work

English odes

74	Eternal Source of Light Divine [Ode for the Birthday of Queen Anne]	?1713; ?not performed
75	Alexander's Feast	1736 (Covent Garden)
76	Song [Ode] for St Cecilia's Day	1739 (Lincoln's Inn Fields)

(HWV 55, *L'Allegro, il Penseroso ed il Moderato,* may also be regarded as an ode.)

Secular cantatas

HWV 77–177 include thirty Italian cantatas with obbligato instruments or orchestral accompaniment: some of these are extensive dramatic cantatas involving more than one solo singer. Rather confusingly, several of the larger cantatas are known by alternative names – the first line of text and a title (sometimes Handel's own). Examples of the larger cantatas are *Ah! crudel, nel mio pianto* (HWV 78), *Amarilli vezzosa* ('Il Duello d'Amore', or 'Daliso ed Amarilli' HWV 82), *Arresta il passo* ('Aminta e Fillide' HWV 83), *Cor fedele in vano speri* ('Clori, Tirsi e Fileno' HWV 96), *Da quel giorno fatale* ('Il delirio amoroso' HWV 99), *Dunque sarà pur vero* ('Agrippina condotta a morire' HWV 110), *Figlio d'alte speranze* (HWV 113), *La terra e liberata* ('Apollo e Dafne' HWV 122), *Oh come chiare e belle* ('Olinto pastore, Tebro fiume, Gloria' HWV 143), and *Qual ti riveggio, oh Dio* ('Ero e Leandro' HWV 150). The serenata *Sorge il di* ('Aci, Galatea e Polifemo' HWV 72) is also arguably an extended dramatic cantata. Most of these cantatas were composed during Handel's years in Italy, but an important exception is *Cecilia, volgi un sguardo* (HWV 89, with its variant component section *Carco sempre di gloria* HWV 87), which was composed to accompany *Alexander's Feast* in 1736; the related English work *Look down, harmonious Saint* (HWV 124) comes from the same period. Another English cantata, *Behold where weeping Venus stands* ('Venus and Adonis' HWV 85), to a text by John Hughes, was composed more than twenty-five years previously, but the authenticity of the music in the form it has come down to us is uncertain. Handel's music for *Comus* (HWV 44, see above under 'Music for English Plays') may also be performed as a cantata.

The remaining Italian cantatas are for single solo voice with basso continuo accompaniment; there are more than sixty-five titles, several of the cantatas having complete variant versions. The continuo-accompanied cantatas include *Del bel idolo mio* (Bass voice, HWV 104), *Ditemi, o piante, o fiori* (Soprano, HWV 107), *E partirai, mia vita?* (Soprano, HWV 111), *Filli adorata e cara* (Soprano, HWV 114), *Lungi dal mio bel nume* (Soprano, HWV 127), *Mentre il tutto è in furore* (Soprano, HWV 130), *Nell'Africane selve* (Bass, HWV 136) and *O numi eterni* ('La Lucretia', Soprano, HWV 145). Many of the 'soprano' cantatas may have been composed for castrati. Most of the cantatas (of both types) were composed in Italy, and they include one setting of text in praise of Handel himself (*Hendel, non può mia musa* HWV 117). However, Handel continued to compose Italian cantatas in London: his latest is *Quel fior, che all'alba ride* (HWV 154, *c.* 1740).

Italian chamber duets and trios

HWV 178–99 are for two voices with continuo accompaniment: they include *Beato in ver che può* (HWV 181), *Giù nei Tartarei regni* (HWV 187), *No, di voi non vuo fidarmi* (two settings, HWV 189, 190), *Se tu non lasci amore* (HWV 193) and *Troppo cruda, troppo fiera* (HWV 198). The composition of duets was spread throughout Handel's life, in Italy, Hanover and London (the latest *c.* 1745). Handel's trio with continuo *Se tu non lasci amore* (HWV 201) was written in Naples in 1708, and its companion *Quel fior, che all'alba ride* (HWV 200) probably also dates from Handel's Italian period.

Arias and songs

HWV 202–10 constitute a set of nine German Arias with obbligato instrument(s), to religious texts by B. H. Brockes. HWV 211–27 are individual arias, most of them Italian and some of them perhaps intended for operatic contexts. However, there are also English songs: these include a hunting song, *The Morning is Charming* (HWV 226, *c.* 1751) and *Love's but the frailty of the mind* (HWV 218, written for an English play in 1740), both of which survive in Handel's autograph. A number of original English songs (HWV 228[1–24]) were also published during the composer's lifetime: they include two patriotic songs from the period of the 1745 Jacobite rebellion.

Church music

From Handel's Italian period come two Italian sacred cantatas, *Ah! che troppo ineguali* (HWV 230), and *Donna, che in Ciel* (HWV 233); and a substantial repertory of Latin church music, including the motets *Coelestis dum spirat aura* (HWV 231) and *Saeviat tellus inter rigores* (HWV 240), the antiphons *Haec est regina vir-*

ginum (HWV 235), *Salve Regina* (HWV 241) and *Te decus virgineum* (HWV 243), and the psalms *Dixit Dominus* (HWV 232), *Laudate pueri* (HWV 237) and *Nisi Dominus* (HWV 238). All of these are accompanied by instrumental or orchestral ensemble. A further motet, *Silete venti* (HWV 242), was composed *c.* 1724 in London.

In England, Handel composed two continuo-accompanied settings of the anthem *As pants the Hart* (HWV 251a, d) for the Chapel Royal. For James Brydges's singers and players he wrote eleven Cannons ('Chandos') Anthems (HWV 246–56) and a Te Deum (HWV 281). Some of the Cannons Anthems were recomposed in variant versions for the Chapel Royal, for whom Handel also reworked some of the music from HWV 281 in the Te Deums in D major ('Caroline' Te Deum, HWV 280) and A major (HWV 282). But Handel's best known English church music consists of larger-scale works for special occasions: the four Coronation Anthems for King George II and Queen Caroline (*Zadok the Priest, Let thy Hand be strengthened, The King shall rejoice* and *My Heart is inditing* (HWV 258–61), the wedding anthems *This is the Day* and *Sing unto God* (HWV 262, 263), the Funeral Anthem for Queen Caroline (*The Ways of Zion do mourn* HWV 264), the Foundling Hospital Anthem (*Blessed are they that considereth the Poor and Needy* HWV 268), the 'Utrecht' Te Deum and Jubilate (HWV 278, 279) and the 'Dettingen' Te Deum and Anthem (HWV 283, 265).

During the period *c.* 1734–47 Handel also composed cantata-style settings of 'Amen' and 'Hallelujah, amen' texts for soprano and continuo (HWV 269–77) and also, at the end of that period, settings of three hymns by Charles Wesley (HWV 284–6), including 'Rejoice, the Lord is King'.

Instrumental music

Concertos for solo instrument with orchestra
Early works include the Concerto for Oboe and Orchestra (HWV 287) and the *Sonata a 5* (HWV 288): two further oboe concertos (HWV 301, 302), published in London in 1740, have an uncertain history. The Organ Concertos were published in two major sets of six works: Op. 4 (HWV 289–94, of which the solo part in HWV 294 was composed for harp) in 1738 and Op. 7 (HWV 306–11) in 1761, after Handel's death. A 'Second Set' of Organ Concertos was published in 1740 (HWV 295–300), of which the first two are original works and the others are arrangements.

Concerti grossi and orchestral concerti
Two sets of orchestral concertos were published during Handel's lifetime: six Concertos Op. 3 (HWV 312–17, published 1734 but composed earlier) and 12 Concerti Grossi Op. 6 (HWV 319–30, composed 1739 and published 1740). Other major orchestral works include the *Water Music* (three suites, HWV 348–50, *c.* 1717), the *Music for the Royal Fireworks* (HWV 351, 1749) and two related concertos (HWV 335a, 335b), and three *Concerti a due Cori* (HWV 332–4, 1747–8). Many orchestral works and movements remained unpublished during Handel's

lifetime: these include a concerto in F major (HWV 331, *c.* 1723), a concerto in D major (one movement in HWV 317, two others detached as HWV 338, *c.* 1722), the 'Alexander's Feast' Concerto Grosso (HWV 318, 1736) an early Sinfonia in B♭ major (HWV 339) and an Ouverture in the same key (HWV 336). There is also a repertory of authentic music for ensembles of oboes, bassoons and horns (HWV 346, 410–11, 414–18, 422–4), and a five-movement Ouverture for clarinets and horn (HWV 424).

Chamber music

HWV 357–79 are 'solo' sonatas for a melody instrument accompanied by basso continuo. Much confusion about the history of these sonatas (and the intended solo instruments for individual works) has been caused by editions published in the 1730s (and subsequently) and by retrospective numberings of the sonatas as 'Op. 1'. Works referred to in this book are HWV 358 (violin or recorder, *c.* 1707–10), HWV 378 (flute, *c.* 1707), HWV 363, 366 (oboe, *c.* 1711–16), HWV 360, 362, 365, 369 (recorder, *c.* 1725–6 and HWV 371 (violin, *c.* 1750).

Most of Handel's trio sonatas for two treble instruments (principally two violins) and continuo were published in two sets: six sonatas as Op. 2 (HWV 386–91) in 1733 and seven sonatas as Op. 5 (HWV 396–402) in 1739. A number of trio sonatas (HWV 392–5, 403–5) did not appear in these collections. A further set of six sonatas for violin, oboe and continuo (HWV 380–5) are presented as early works of Handel's in a manuscript source, but their authenticity is doubtful.

Music for keyboard instruments (principally harpsichord)

There were three substantial published collections of Handel's keyboard music during his lifetime: eight *Suites de Pièces* (HWV 426–433) 'printed for the Author' in 1720, nine further suites (HWV 434–42) in a 'Second Volume' published by Walsh *c.* 1733–4, and *Six Fugues* from Walsh in 1735. Many authentic suites did not appear in the published collections: these include the Partita in G major HWV 450 (*c.* 1700–5) and the Suites in C major (HWV 443, *c.* 1700–3), D minor (HWV 449, *c.* 1705), G minor (HWV 453, *c.* 1705–6), B♭ major (HWV 455, *c.* 1706), D minor and G minor (HWV 447, 452, *c.* 1738–9).

There are some authentic keyboard versions of Handel's ouvertures, including HWV 456[1–5]. HWV 457–586 are individual pieces for keyboard, including two *Airs for a two-rowed harpsichord* (HWV 466, 470, *c.* 1710–20) and many early works composed *c.* 1703–9: the latter include a *Capriccio* in F major (HWV 481), two *Chaconnes* (HWV 485, 486), *Fantasie pour le Clavecin* in C major (HWV 490), *Prélude e Capriccio* in G major (HWV 571), *Prelude ed Allegro* in G minor (HWV 574), *Sonata (Fantasia) pour le Clavecin* in C major (HWV 577) and a *Sonata (Fantasia) for a Harpsichord with double keys* (HWV 579). ('Double keys' or 'two rows' denote a two-manual harpsichord). Handel also composed sets of pieces for mechanical organs in clocks (HWV 587–604).

Index